MONEY! HAPPINESS! SUCCESS!

WITH THIS BOOK,
IT'S ALL WITHIN YOUR REACH.

"If you sincerely want freedom, 'being your own boss' is it in the real sense of the word. To most folks who own their own business, the hard work of developing their enterprise becomes a pleasure because they directly receive all the benefits of their labor.

"Much to most people's dismay, the old cliche, 'You'll never get rich working for a living' generally proves true. If you choose to be a seeker of opportunity, and are willing to take a calculated risk, then it is possible to see your dreams turn into reality with a proud estate to pass on to your sons and daughters."

—*Chase Revel*

AFTER READING THIS BOOK,
THE ONLY PERSON TO BLAME FOR A DULL,
LOW-PAYING JOB IS YOURSELF.

184 BUSINESSES
ANYONE CAN START AND MAKE
A LOT OF MONEY

D0967760

184
BUSINESSES
ANYONE
CAN START AND
MAKE A
LOT OF MONEY

CHASE REVEL

BANTAM BOOKS
TORONTO · NEW YORK · LONDON · SYDNEY · AUCKLAND

184 BUSINESSESS ANYONE CAN START AND
MAKE A LOT OF MONEY

A Bantam Book / March 1981

*Sections of this book originally appeared in
Entrepreneur magazine in a different form.*

Back cover photo by Steve Smith

Book design by Kathleen Ferguson

ISBN 0-553-01298-3

Library of Congress Catalog Card No.: 80-70656

Published simultaneously in the United States and Canada

---

*Bantam Books are published by Bantam Books, Inc. Its trade-
mark, consisting of the words "Bantam Books" and the por-
trayal of a bantam, is Registered in U.S. Patent and Trademark
Office and in other countries. Marca Registrada. Bantam
Books, Inc., 666 Fifth Avenue, New York, New York 10103.*

PRINTED IN THE UNITED STATES OF AMERICA

FG   0

CONTENTS

Introduction   xi

SERVICE

1. Car-Pooling Service   3
2. Tool and Equipment Rental Service   3
3. Dry-Cleaning Shop   5
4. Pet Talent Agency   7
5. Copy Shop   8
6. Trade School   9
7. Retail Travel Agency   12
8. Chimney Sweep Service   14
9. Checking Employment Applications   16
10. Maid Service   17
11. Tutorial Service   19
12. Mobile Surface Cleaning   20
13. Computer-Trading Center   22
14. Liquidated-Goods Broker   23
15. Home Historian   25
16. Coin-Op TV   26
17. Singing Telegrams   27
18. Plastics-Recycling Center   28
19. Roomate-Finding Service   30
20. Movie-of-the-Month Club   32
21. Handicraft Co-op   33
22. Discount Painter   35
23. Lawyer's Aide   36
24. Digital Watch-Repairing Service   36
25. Insulation Contracting Business   38
26. Gift-Wrapping Service   40
27. Coin Laundry   41

28. Letter Writing 43
29. Security Patrol Service 44
30. Closet Design 46
31. Pay-TV Service 47
32. Pet Portraits 49
33. Financial Broker 50
34. Family Hair Salon 52
35. Furniture Rental Service 54
36. Consulting Business 56
37. Really Help the Handicapped 58
38. Flat-Fee Real Estate Company 59
39. Telephone-Answering Service 60
40. Secretarial Service 62
41. Teachers Agency 64
42. Rent a Best-Seller 66
43. Vinyl-Repairing Service 67
44. Seminar Promoting 69
45. Day-Care Center 71
46. Furniture-Stripping Service 73
47. You Call, We Haul 74
48. Carpet-Cleaning Service 75
49. Bike Surgeon 78
50. Employment Agency 79
51. Janitorial Service 81
52. Pet Hotel and Grooming Service 83
53. Parking Lot Stripping Service 85
54. Statue Repair 87
55. Rent-a-Plant 88
56. Instant Print Shop 91
57. Window-Washing Service 94
58. Cross-Country Trucking 95

FOOD

1. Breakfast in Bed 98
2. Mushrooming Business 98
3. Mobile Restaurant 99
4. Low-Cal Bakery 100
5. Chip Shop 102
6. Cookie Shop 103
7. Frystick Snack Shop 105
8. Shrimp Peddling 107
9. Ice Cream Parlor 110
10. Convenience Food Store 112
11. Submarine Sandwich Shop 114

12. Soup Kitchen   116
13. Pub/Nightclub/Disco   118
14. Health Food Store   120
15. Salad Bar Restaurant   122
16. Homemade Cake Shop   124
17. Yogurt Bar   126
18. Hotdog Stand   128
19. Homemade-Candy Stand   130
20. Doughnut Shop   131
21. Grandma's Bread Shop   133
22. Cash In on Corn   135
23. No-Alcohol Bar   136
24. Coffee Shop   139
25. Hot Dog Goes French   141
26. Fried-Chicken Takeout Restaurant   142
27. Popcorn Vending   143
28. Gourmet Cheese and Wine Shop   146
29. Hamburger Stand   147
30. Pizzeria   149

RETAIL

1. Plant Shop   153
2. Moped Shop   155
3. T-Shirt Shop   157
4. Women's Apparel Shop   159
5. Gift Shop   161
6. Do-It-Yourself Framing Shop   162
7. Antique Store   164
8. Wedding Store   166
9. Vitamin-Nutrition Store   168
10. Children's Apparel Store   170
11. Liquor Store   173
12. Lingerie Shop   175
13. Bicycle Shop   177
14. Flower Shop   179
15. Tropical Fish Store   181
16. Gourmet Cookware   183
17. Selling Old Barn Siding   185
18. Christmas Tree Lot   186
19. Christmas Ornament Store   187
20. Furniture Store   188
21. Hobby Shop   190
22. Discount Fabric Shop   192
23. Record Peddler   194

24. Paint and Wall Covering Store 195
25. Do-It-Yourself Cosmetic Shop 197
26. Pipe Shop 199
27. Used-Book Store 201
28. Mattress Shop 203
29. Pet Shop 204
30. Cat Paraphernalia 206
31. Shell Shop 207
32. Video Store 209
33. Retail Phone Store 211

RECREATIONAL SPORTS

1. Soccer Specialty Store 217
2. Roller-Skate Rental Shop 217
3. Hot-Tub Spa Facility 219
4. Athletic-Shoe Store 222
5. Wind-Surfing School 224
6. Archery—Right on Target 226
7. Physical Fitness Center 227
8. Sailboat Leasing 229
9. Tennis & Racquetball Club 231
10. Female Sports Market 233
11. Amusement Game Center 234
12. Roller-Skating Rink 236

AUTOMOTIVE

1. Muffler Shop 241
2. Consignment Used-Car Lot 243
3. Do-It-Yourself Auto Repair Shop 245
4. Parking Lot Car Wash 247
5. Tune-up Shop 247
6. Auto-Parking Service 249
7. Car-Care Co-op 251
8. Auto-Painting Shop 252
9. Automobile Dealing 253
10. Car Wash 256
11. Ten-Minute Oil-Change Shop 259

MANUFACTURING

1. Handicraft Manufacturing 265
2. Miniature Furniture 267
3. Sculptured-Candle Making 267

  4. Name That Scarf   269
  5. Custom Rugmaking   270
  6. Stained-Glass-Window Manufacturing   272
  7. Hot-Tub Manufacturing   274
  8. Burglar Alarm Manufacturing   277

TOURISM

  1. Stuffed-Toy Animal Vending   281
  2. Balloon Vending   282
  3. Multi-Theaters   283
  4. Antique Photo Shop   284
  5. Handwriting Analysis by Computer   286
  6. Flower Vending   288
  7. Dive-for-a-Pearl Shop   291
  8. Book Balloon Tours   293

PUBLISHING

  1. *Who's Who* Publishing   297
  2. Rental List Publishing   299
  3. The Novel About You   301
  4. Free Classified Newspaper Publishing   302
  5. Newsletter Publishing   305

FRANCHISES

  1. Franchising: Ready for the Eighties   310
  2. The Pros and Cons of Buying a Franchise   319
  3. Where to Find the Money for your Franchise   326

THE UNUSUAL

  1. Import and Export   347
  2. Jojoba Plantation   349
  3. Rent a Picket   351
  4. Book Your Valuables   352
  5. Paper Recycling   353
  6. Your Own Stock Market   355
  7. Swap-Meet Promoting   356
  8. Antler Recovery   359
  9. Bonsai Collecting   359
 10. Cardboard Caskets   362
 11. Contest Promoting   363
 12. Art-Show Promoting   364

13. Flea Markets—Finding Products   366
14. Making Class Reunions Pay   368
15. Mail-Order Business   369
16. Off to the Hunt   371
17. Candid Keychain Photos   372
18. Hold Fashionable Parties   374
19. Robots Are a Reality   375
20. Gold Prospecting and the Gold-
    Prospecting Store   375

INTRODUCTION

If you sincerely want freedom, "being your own boss" is it in the real sense of the word—the freedom the pioneers sought when they came to the new world.

If you choose to be uncommon, a seeker of opportunity, willing to take a calculated risk, then it is possible to see your dreams turn into reality with a proud estate to pass on to your sons and daughters.

To most folks who own their own business, the hard work of developing their enterprise becomes a pleasure because they directly receive all the benefits of their labor. And even though there's no one to pass the buck to, making those hard decisions alone through sleepless nights, entrepreneurs rarely return to working for others once they've had a successful taste of "being their own boss."

Much to most people's dismay, the old cliche, "You'll never get rich working for a living" generally proves true. An overwhelming majority of the millionaires in the United States and Canada became wealthy through their own enterprise. Rare is the individual who makes it working for someone else.

Also, seldom do we see one of these millionaires revealing the extent of his wealth except when his company's stock is offered on the public market.

Their secretiveness is not ill-founded. Money, like honey, attracts flies, and disclosure is a sure way to bring competition from all sides.

Over my 20-year business career, I became a millionaire many times over with the 18 different businesses I founded. And you can believe I never revealed my profits and trade secrets to anyone. A fool and his money are soon parted.

I spotted a lot of new, lucrative businesses during that time and developed a research staff and techniques for finding out all about the moneymakers—including exactly how much profit they were making and what their trade secrets were. *There's no business operating about which my team and I can't find out everything we need to know.*

In the following chapters you'll read about some amazing businesses with incredible profits and about many that were started with virtual shoestrings.

We do not recommend that anyone start with the low-end capital we found in these case histories, nor do we expect you to earn the high-end profits that a few achieved. But even the average earnings are very enticing for most of these businesses.

We also chose to include several *popular* businesses that are not very profitable to give you a comparison, and some first-timer businesses with low capital requirements for the mass of people who are eager to be their own boss but haven't a lot of cash to invest.

And we won't leave you hanging. When I read something in magazines or newspapers that interests me, I usually feel there's much more I want to know. Well, if any of the one hundred and eighty-four businesses covered herein intrigue you, a complete startup manual is available from American Entrepreneurs Association Research Department on each of them. Ordering details are on pages three hundred and seventy-eight through three hundred and eighty-one.

Chase Revel

184
BUSINESSES
ANYONE
CAN START AND
MAKE A
LOT OF MONEY

SERVICE

CAR-POOLING SERVICE

With the gas situation getting critical, more and more people are looking to car pooling as a way to cut their gas bills in half or better. But finding a reliable person to pool with is something akin to finding a good mate in life.

Car-pooling services are beginning to surface and as the situation becomes worse, they may become the business of the future. Matching riders' destinations to home base is a simple matter.

You should distribute cards in large office buildings. Ask for home addresses and business addresses. Also ask which days of the week they would like to drive and which days they want to ride.

From there it's just a question of sorting it all out. You can charge a flat fee of $10. If something happens and one of the pool members pulls out, you can make another match for a lower fee— say $5. You'll always have repeats because people are constantly switching jobs.

We can even see offering such a service on longer trips. Why stick with business shuttles? Arrange to match people and drivers on interstate and cross-country rides. Drivers will welcome the company of passengers and the savings of splitting the gas.

Make sure you check out both driver and passenger, though. Call his or her employer and get a few details. Safety is what you're promising, so some background checking is important.

TOOL AND EQUIPMENT RENTAL SERVICE

High net profit B/T (before taxes):	$70,000
Average net profit B/T:	33,000
Minimum investment:	22,000
Average investment:	54,000

Twenty years ago a tool and small equipment rental business was almost unheard of. Today there are over 10,000 rental outlets throughout the nation and they gross over $2 billion annually.

The industry has enjoyed an average growth rate of 15 percent and predicts no slowdown within the next five years. Many operators who got into tool renting during its infancy believe that the business has just begun to show its real potential. They think the predicted future growth rate is very conservative. Many are enjoying a 20 percent annual increase in business and expect it to continue.

Consumers—and businesses even more so—are demanding to rent items never rented before. Some industry spokesmen envision giant rental supermarkets with every imaginable reusable item for rent. Delivery will become very important, as most of the business will be conducted by phone (today it is done in person).

Government-subsidized health-care programs, longer life spans, and the high cost of hospitalizing geriatrics have made the rental of medical equipment a lucrative and fast-growing activity.

Homeowners have always tried to avoid the high cost of outside labor for their home projects; today they are also concerned about conserving leisure time. They are no longer willing to give up a couple of weekends, breaking their back to put in a new lawn or build a patio by hand. They want to rent modern professional equipment to get the job done quickly and efficiently.

A NEW ERA—RENTING INSTEAD OF OWNING

Businesspeople and consumers have acquired a new attitude toward the use of their money. The pride of ownership is rapidly being replaced by the more realistic idea of getting the most value from each dollar.

Tax-laden business people consider write-off rental and leasing a boon to freeing their capital, thereby enabling them to expand their businesses more rapidly. Consumers, looking for more variety during frequent vacations and weekend trips, can now enjoy skiing, camping, and boating without tying up all their cash in one item and restricting their activities as a result.

This kind of trend can only grow. We tend to agree with some of the old-timers. The renting phenomenon has just begun.

The concept is simple: Buy some tools and rent them out. Of course, operating the business is more involved than that. But following certain guidelines, anyone can put together a rental store and operate it successfully.

Start-up Manual #28 is available on this business. See page 378.

DRY-CLEANING SHOP

High net profit B/T:	$210,000
Average net profit B/T:	30,000
Minimum investment:	30,000
Average investment:	100,000

Would you believe that the owner of your local dry-cleaning shop may be making from $40,000 to $100,000 per year?

Well, perhaps not—but over 20 percent of the shops in the country do net in that range, plus a salary for the owner if he operates the shop himself.

Your first thought might be, But I don't know anything about the dry-cleaning process.

First you should know that there are over 26,000 dry-cleaning shops in the United States. Over 200,000 people are employed in these shops. Specialty schools and local trade schools turn out thousands of people each year educated in all phases of the dry-cleaning business. Therefore, it is usually not difficult to obtain experienced managers and personnel.

Second, a dry-cleaning machine operates almost like a regular washer and dryer. The main difference is that instead of using soap and water, the dry-cleaning machine uses a solvent called "perc" or a similar solvent sold under different names. A special detergent and sizing are mixed with the perc, and the clothes go through a washing cycle and then a drying cycle, similar to that of a washer and dryer.

ANYONE CAN OPERATE PRESSING EQUIPMENT

Pressing is the simplest part of the process. We are sure that everyone has used an iron, or has observed someone else using one. Pressing equipment is nothing more than a large, specially shaped iron designed to press 20 to 30 times the amount of clothes that can be done with a hand iron. The special irons are simple to operate.

Schools in some states will prepare you to take the state exam for a dry-cleaner's license in as little as 45 hours.

TRAINED PERSONNEL ARE PLENTIFUL

The point we are trying to emphasize is: This is not a complex business, or one that you should shy away from because you do not have any knowledge of the technical end.

Naturally, we have simplified our description of the various processes. Just as a homemaker must know how to wash different fabrics, the dry-cleaner must also make variations in the system to treat each fabric properly. But there are thousands of trained and experienced cleaners available.

NET $100,000+

As in many service businesses, the more volume you do, the higher your margin of profit. For example, the small dry-cleaner doing only $50,000 per year in volume will have difficulty netting 10 percent of the gross before taxes.

But the dry-cleaner who is grossing $200,000 per year will probably net close to 30 percent.

We discovered a two-store operation grossing $456,000 and netting almost $210,000 before taxes, depreciation, and owner's salary.

ONE KEY FACTOR TO SUCCESS!

Our main concern in investigating businesses is to discover why a few make a great deal of money compared to others in the same business. (This seems to be true in every business.)

Fewer than 15 percent of the dry-cleaners in this country gross over $150,000 each year; the average is around the $100,000 mark. We found stores spending $5,000 to $7,000 annually on promotion and advertising; but a few blocks away, a competitor with no advertising budget was grossing three times as much—and sometimes charging more than his advertising competitor. Often, too, the appearance of the store, quality of service, and other factors seemed equal.

The distributors of dry-cleaning supplies were most helpful in pointing out the stores that purchased the most supplies—and which consequently were doing the greatest business. Discussions with suppliers, equipment dealers, and several successful shop owners gave us a consensus of opinion on what makes a dry-cleaning business a success.

THE DETERMINANT: LOCATION

The consensus could be summed up in a single word: location! This was the primary factor behind a high-grossing store.

The owner of two stores netting over $200,000 is a prime example of this. Before obtaining his current locations, he owned three stores in various locations. None grossed over $60,000; all were sold.

The first year in one of his new locations, however, he enjoyed a gross of $196,000.

Start-up Manual #37 is available on this business. See page 378.

_____New Idea_____

PET TALENT AGENCY

It may be a dog's life, but if you happen to own the latest Lassie, it's not too bad. An enterprising pet-shop owner in Dallas, has found that he can get more from his pets by renting them out!

Mike Stower and his partner, Deena the Chimp, attended a child's birthday party. Word about Rent-a-Chimp spread, and now they charge $65 an hour to break the monotony of children jaded by too much cake and ice cream.

Noticing that advertising media rely heavily on animals to get messages across, Mike began a pet talent agency. Using newspaper ads, The Stower Group contacts owners and lines up animal talent, charging a $20 listing fee. If a photo layout for a catalog nets $75, the talent gets $40. The beauty of this system is that Stower doesn't have to feed and care for the animals, but he still profits from them. Since he doesn't represent people, no special licenses or contracts are required.

Television commercials, films, newspaper and magazine ads, promotional events, fashion shows, and catalogs use animals. Dogs and cats are popular, but birds, frogs, and chickens are also used. Whether a pet is ugly or cute, big or small, there's an ad for him.

Once ad agencies, businessmen, and the like know that you have pets for hire, the phones will start ringing. Call and write these people to let them know you're in business.

Interview prospective models and take pictures to show clients. Make sure the animal is reasonably well behaved and can stand crowds and flashing lights, or rampaging pets will hurt your reputation.

COPY SHOP

High net profit B/T:	$40,000
Average net profit B/T:	24,000
Minimum investment:	2,500
Average investment:	5,000

Thirty years ago very few people would have predicted that Xerox would become a household word. Rarely do you hear someone say "Copy this." Rather they say "Xerox it," even if they have a different brand of copier.

It goes without saying that Xerox has sold or leased hundreds of thousands of machines over the past two decades. But did it ever occur to you that you could make a lot of money by using their machines—making Xerox copies for others?

On every business street you see signs advertising "Photocopies, 10¢"; "Xerox Copies, 4¢"; "Xerox—3¢ a copy." Every instant print shop promotes the sale of photocopies. Drugstores, discount stores, supermarkets, even post offices have photocopy machines which enable you to make a copy for ten cents or less.

This certainly appears to be a competitive field. Nevertheless, we know of a copy shop in our area that makes over 500,000 Xerox copies a month. That is a monthly gross of over $20,000.

A chemical salesman opened a copy shop with one Xerox machine a short time ago, with his wife and daughter running the business. His "copy spot" did almost 150,000 copies per month the first year.

Initial cash outlay was about $2,500. This shop nets over $3,000 per month before income taxes, and the higher the volume, the higher the percentage of profit on each copy. (Company salaries of $800 per month are paid to his wife and daughter and were deducted before the net figure was ascertained. If family members were not operating the shop, labor costs would probably increase about $200 per month.)

This operator could increase his profit by $500 per month by buying the Xerox machine on the installment plan rather than leasing it; this is in his future plans. Also, by offering sorting, collating, and folding services, he could increase his volume.

According to the Xerox representative for our area, his company can point to success stories like this in nearly every major city.

Start-up Manual #38 is available on this business. See page 378.

TRADE SCHOOL

High net profit B/T:	$50,000+
Average net profit B/T:	26,000
Minimum investment:	11,000
Average investment:	22,000

Back in the '30s, the '40s—and even into the '50s—it was common to hear a father telling his son to prepare for the future: "Learn a trade, my son, and you won't have to worry."

Through the '50s and '60s, fathers urged: "Go to college and get a degree, my son, and you won't have to worry."

Well, the decade of the '70s has brought some disillusionment to the young men and women graduating from college. They are finding that a bachelor's degree doesn't guarantee them a thing, except possibly qualification for the low-paying jobs that a few years ago required only a high-school diploma.

"We get several in here every day," states one trade-school representative, "college diploma in hand and they can't find a job." Seeing uneducated bartenders, carpenters, and plumbers earning $15,000 to $30,000 a year is frustrating to the college grad who is lucky to find a job paying $10,000 to start. The typical reaction is to take grandfather's advice and "learn a trade."

"Today you must have a master's degree to get anywhere." So claims one educator we talked to. "But by 1990, with our constant technology growth, most people won't be qualified for jobs in commerce and industry unless they hold doctoral degrees."

BUT TRADES WILL GROW

Regardless of technological growth, there will always be a need for people who perform services—bartenders, plumbers, truck drivers, barbers, real estate salespeople, cashiers, and repair people. In fact, sociologists claim that the demand for service personnel will increase in direct proportion to the level of industrialization, automation, and technological advancement. This has been well documented through the last three decades.

In addition to this, the increasing strength of trade unions will keep wages for service workers growing at a much faster rate than for white-collar workers. No more striking evidence of this can be found than in the building trades, where workers receive from $10 to $15 an hour.

NO COMPARISON!

How do you compare a one-week bartender's course that will qualify a young man or woman to earn $10,000 to $20,000 a year with a six-year college prerequisite for a job paying in a similar range?

The argument might be that the earnings potential is much greater for the degree holder. But there are many young people whose experience is different. One of our staff is an example. A few years ago, after a long struggle supporting a family and going to school, he finally obtained a master's degree in art and a teaching credential. He soon found, however, that because of cutbacks in school funds and a growing surplus of art teachers, he couldn't land a job.

Because his training was in fine art, he couldn't qualify for commercial artists' positions—which were few in number anyway. Discouraged, he became a photocopier salesman.

TRADE SCHOOLS BOOMING

Because of these realities, the number of graduates from trade schools has tripled the figures of ten years ago. In the same period, the number of trade schools has doubled.

In the past 20 years some billion-dollar giants like LaSalle Extension University have grown from small mail-order houses that offered training through correspondence courses. On the local level in-class training schools are proliferating, and it is not unusual to see a school with a dozen branches in a single large city.

The variety of trades taught is almost endless—secretary, medical technician, court reporter, contractor's license preparer, hotel-motel manager, insurance salesperson, securities salesperson, building tradesperson, barber, beautician, manicurist, computer programmer, keypuncher, PBX switchboard operator, bookkeeper, draftsperson, TV technician, auto mechanic, printer, auto body repairperson, welder, typesetter, upholsterer, real estate worker, pilot, detective, insurance investigator, model, credit collector, auctioneer, fashion buyer, actor, dog groomer, passenger ticket agent, travel agent, photographer, radio announcer, disk jockey, machinist, TV cameraperson, horticulturist, dry cleaner, truck driver, office machine repairperson, landscapist, interior decorator, veterinary assistant, makeup artist, massager, bartender, waitress, electrologist, floral designer, watch repairperson, locksmith, polygraph operator, jewelry designer, candy maker, chef, and milinery tradesperson. We even found a school that taught horseshoeing!

YOUR OWN SCHOOL

Start your own school? Easy! But what will you teach? Do you have a trade or profession from which the average person can earn a steady living or a decent wage? If so, why not promote it? You already have the instructor—yourself!

If this won't work for you, that's no problem. In fact, it may be better if you don't have a trade you can teach—you might end up teaching instead of promoting or running the business, which is much more rewarding.

So pick any trade or profession that is currently being offered—or maybe one that is not being offered. Hire someone successful at that trade as your instructor and you are in business. As simple as that.

COMPANION COURSES

The needs of the marketplace change daily. Trends create demands for new services.

For example, due to the high cost of living, and divorce, many women with children are forced to look for higher-paying jobs. Many have only high-school educations and no marketable skills. Until a few years ago a woman could get a job as a cocktail or food waitress fairly easily even if she had no experience. Now, though, because there are so many women swamping the market for these jobs, the inexperienced are usually turned down. So why not start a school for waitresses?

A second area of current interest is antiques. Furniture refinishers are doing fantastic business today because most antiques must be refinished to be salable or presentable. When we were preparing a report detailing the furniture refinishing business, one of the biggest problems shop owners mentioned was finding qualified workers to restore antiques. One of our staff attempted to research antiques in the local library. The catalog listed 18 books on the subject, but not one was on the shelves. A very popular field, you might say. Take advantage of it. Hire an experienced refinisher at a higher-than-normal wage and start a course.

We investigated the profit and gross figures for many different trade schools and found them identical in one respect: There was a direct correlation between advertising dollars spent and gross sales. Slight variations appeared, but in every case we found close to a one-to-three ratio; $1 of advertising returned $3 in gross sales. And the net before taxes appeared to be a fairly uniform 30 percent.

Start-up Manual #47 is available on this business. See page 379.

RETAIL TRAVEL AGENCY

High net profit B/T:	$300,000+
Average net profit B/T:	12,000
Minimum investment:	42,000
Average investment:	60,000

For most Americans, there's nothing more exciting and glamorous than travel to "faraway places with strange-sounding names." Almost everyone travels these days, from businessmen heading out of town to students touring Europe or groups of retired couples on a dream vacation in Hawaii. Travel is a multibillion-dollar business that has mushroomed in size since the first commercial jet took off in 1957.

In 1978 North American travel spending amounted to $149 billion, and worldwide spending reached a record $448 billion, according to the American Society of Travel Agents.

Within this framework, the nation's 14,000 retail travel agencies had a total gross sales volume of nearly $15 billion. Seventy-five percent, or $11 billion, was in airline tickets alone. These impressive numbers and the overall boom in travel have led to a steady increase of 12 percent per year in the number of retail travel agencies, which are opening at the rate of three or four per day nationwide.

GLAMOUR: BIG ATTRACTION

Many would-be travel agents are drawn by a love of travel and believe that the business offers a glamorous career, adventure, and excitement as well as the opportunity to help other people achieve their lifelong dreams.

In fact, an important benefit of operating a travel agency and selling travel to others is the opportunity to take trips all over the world by ship, plane, or train to places most of us can only dream about. For free. Or at bargain basement costs. Most major airlines, cruise-ship operators, and tour promoters offer what are called "familiarization" trips to groups of travel agents. The object of these excursions is to introduce agents and to promote tourism to a certain area, new route, or new resort hotel that's opened up. These trips are normally paid in full by the promoters.

Agents who package tours often go along for the ride with the rest of the group, and there are other opportunities for travel as well. Several agents told us that if they took advantage of every "freebie," they'd never get any work done!

PROFITS CAN BE HIGH

We found one agency in San Francisco with gross sales of nearly $20 million from a single office location. And over 25 percent of established agencies gross $1 million or more a year. But the average agency has sales of $500,000 to $700,000, a far lower amount. Commissions (which are paid by the transport company, not the traveler) vary depending on the type of travel, but range from 7 to 11 percent of ticket price, room rate, or rental fee. Tour operators pay the highest commissions—up to 17 percent for large group tour bookings including overrides or bonuses. But tours and other high margin sales are a small part of the overall picture for typical new agencies.

Combining commissions for all sources results in an average nationwide of 8 to 8.5 percent of gross sales for most agencies. Those who specialize in a high volume of tour business can reach a mix of 10 percent or higher, but normally on a lower overall sales volume.

So a $1 million agency with an 8.5 percent mix will have a gross profit of $85,000.

WHERE THE BIG MONEY IS

The bread-and-butter business for most retail travel agencies comes not from the occasional vacationer, but from the frequent business traveler. Most successful agencies start by building a base of large commercial accounts with businesses requiring travel services regularly. Locate near as many large companies and small businesses as possible.

LOCATION IMPORTANT

We have found successful, well-managed travel agencies, which provide a good living for owner/operators, in communities with as few as 20,000 people. However, they were the "only game in town."

For highest volume and profit potential you should plan to locate in or near a major metropolitan area. While competition will be more intense, there will be a larger pool of potential travelers from which to draw.

A street-front location in a high-rise office building filled with commercial account prospects is ideal, according to successful agents we contacted. Especially if the surrounding area is middle to upper-middle income in nature—or the area attracts such people during the workday.

This type of location allows you to tap both major markets at the same time—the businessman and vacationer with discretionary dollars to spend. Your best prospects will be business travelers or vacationers between the ages of 30 and 45. Families are likely to have an income of $20,000 or more a year. Concentrate on this primary market.

Start-up Manual #154 is available on this business. See page 378.

CHIMNEY SWEEP SERVICE

High net profit B/T:	$55,000
Average net profit B/T:	28,000
Minimum investment:	600
Average investment:	3,500

Chimney sweeps are back and dancing on rooftops all over the country. This flair for the dramatic draws crowds—and profits to the tune of $300 a day. Capitalizing on the revival of this 19th-century trade can easily net you profits of $30,000 a year before taxes. Even on a part-time basis we found it possible to clear up to $10,000 annually.

UNBELIEVABLE PROFITS

Our researchers found sweeps grossing over $40,000 for only 10 months work each year with incredible net profits of 55 to 60 percent before taxes, including the owner's salary. One chimney sweep, who only works weekends, grossed $16,000 last year.

Profit potential of a chimney sweep depends on the number of chimneys he is able to complete each day, and the number of customers he can maintain during the year. The average charge across the country is $40 with a range of $25 to $75.

Pricing depends on the market, the height of the chimney, and the complexity of the job. Some sweeps charge per flue—old-fashioned chimneys can have 20 flues! It is better to set a flat fee for the first chimney and a reduced rate for each additional one.

A cleaning job will take a skilled sweep a maximum of an hour and a half. This represents five to six jobs a day. The very best sweeps with efficient equipment can handle eight a day. One experienced sweep in Florida claims he can whip through most jobs in 45 minutes.

A sweep working on his own should be able to gross over $40,000 annually. With several sweeps, this figure jumps to $100,000 or more. As investment costs and expenses are minimal, a lot of money winds up in the owner's pocket.

SLICK GIMMICK

Of course, there's more to being a chimney sweep than meets the eye. It takes showmanship, hard work, and determination to establish a profitable sweep business. But the rewards are well worth the effort.

The modern chimney sweep looks as if he stepped out of a scene from *Mary Poppins*. Dressed like English sweeping boys who scurried down chimneys a century ago, today's sweeps arrive at the job in top hat and tails. They realize the entertainment value they provide a customer is as important as the service they perform.

The most profitable sweeps play on the familiar lore and magical traditions that surround their profession. The superstition that a chimney sweep brings good luck to anyone who touches him draws crowds of people who flock to see and touch this character as he performs his attention-getting act.

And an act it is. For the best sweeps are hams as well as servicemen. In spite of modern equipment, they recreate the feel of old-time tradesmen. They create such a sensation in the neighborhood that friends are often invited to watch the rooftop performance. Before getting down to the business of cleaning, a sweep will climb to the roof and with a great flourish do a sort of jig, all the time explaining that without his trusty top hat, good luck would desert him and he would fall off the roof!

People laugh at the antics and are genuinely delighted. The sweep has successfully grabbed the attention of the public so that he can begin educating them about the real benefits of chimney cleaning—avoiding chimney fires. With all the dramatics, this is a serious business.

MARKET IS EVERYWHERE

We have seen the profession grow by leaps and bounds. With over 25 million fireplaces in the nation and only about 2,000 established chimney sweeps to clean them, the market is wide open. As one sweep from Connecticut told us, "If 3,000 sweeps got busy in the next five years, it would still take another 10 years to clean all the chimneys that need it!"

You might think that chimney sweeping is a regional business for cold climates only, but this is not so. There are millions of homes in the country without central heating, where fireplaces and wood-burning stoves ward off the cold. Of course, in northern states where wood is burned for at least half the year, the need is greater. Several sweeps can exist happily together in these regions.

START FOR A SONG

One of the biggest attractions of becoming a chimney sweep is the very low initial investment. Many chimney sweeps have started for as little as $600 which covers the cost of basic equipment such as a small variety of brushes with extension rods, tarpaulins to protect homeowners' floors, and, of course, the traditional top hat for good luck. That's all the equipment it takes to clean a chimney the old-fashioned way.

In order to achieve a higher volume of business and minimize labor, most sweeps have adopted modern technology. They use a high pressure dust collector to speed up and mechanize the cleaning process. Adding this equipment and an initial advertising campaign brings start-up costs to $3,000 to $4,000.

Regardless of the investment amount, it should be fully recouped within the first month or two of opening.

Start-up Manual #155 is available on this business. See page 378.

New Idea

CHECKING EMPLOYMENT APPLICATIONS

Employment application forms are a standard tool of personnel departments. Their value, however, only lies in the extent to which they are honestly filled out by prospective employees. Hiring an employee who has fudged on his application can be disastrous. A Massachusetts company has devised reference auditing as an effective means of checking information on applications.

Most employers or personnel department heads will do some elementary checking of applications before making a hiring decision. This checking usually consists of a phone call or two to former employers. With higher-level employees it may mean digging a bit deeper into the candidates' backgrounds.

Bartholdi & Company penetrates far beneath the surface of the application. In addition to contacting old employers, they conduct their own 30-minute interviews with the applicant, speak with his former co-workers and subordinates as well as his superiors, and get a full picture of the potential employee.

With thousands of people changing jobs and looking for work, and women rushing into the job market as well, this seems a particularly good time for such a business, since company personnel departments must be flooded with work. You might even go directly to corporate managers and suggest that your reference auditing service take the place of their personnel department, cutting their cost on the basis of service when needed.

This type of service would also appeal to smaller companies who can't afford a full-time personnel department.

You'll need a good nose for sniffing out facts about employees. A good phone manner is important, since you'll be talking with former bosses. Most bosses are willing to talk, though, if you make them feel they're doing you a favor.

Charge a flat fee—around $50—for checking an applicant. It's a small price for a boss to pay to have the peace of mind that comes with hiring the right employee.

MAID SERVICE

High net profit B/T:	$350,000
Average net profit B/T:	32,000
Minimum investment:	1,900
Average investment:	4,400

The cliché "It's impossible to find good help" has never been truer than it is today. You can supply the solution to this age-old problem and pull in $40,000 to $70,000 your first year in business.

With the low overhead of this service business, you can realize net profit before taxes in the 23 to 30 percent range. Why? Look at some case histories:

In New York the shortage of maids has become so severe that friends have been sharing their maids. One Florida couple secured a reliable maid only after the husband (a lawyer) received a client's domestic as part of his fee for handling a divorce case!

Low start-up costs are another plus of the maid service business. One service, started by an Atlanta housewife, began for literally next to nothing—a mere $5 in supplies. Yet in her first year of operation she established a neighborhood service that grossed $45,000. Today she's taking in over a million dollars a year.

INSIDE SECRETS OF THE SERVICE INDUSTRY

Two words say it all: "team concept." Two to four maids descend upon a house or apartment. Each maid cleans a different room in the residence. With this technique, cleaning time is cut so much that up to ten apartments or homes can be covered in a single day. Stated in business terms, work time is at a minimum; profits are at maximum.

It is best to begin small—with a couple of maids. You run the telephones and the office, since soliciting business for your cleaning teams is going to be the nitty-gritty of your operation.

ORGANIZE, ORGANIZE, ORGANIZE!

Arm your maid staff with practical uniforms and cleaning tools from top to toe so that they won't waste any time or effort planning how to do a cleanup job. They'll be prepared to get busy and do it.

Work out a system of cleanup operations that can be applied anywhere, then work on speeding up the system. One of the most successful maid services in the country runs drills up to 50 times for its team; only then can the maids go on a solo mission!

MAKE YOUR LOCATION WORK FOR YOU

A maid service is one of the few businesses that can be run from a desk in the corner of a room at home. Location is not the most vital consideration. However, it's obvious that the nearer a service is to the homes or apartments it serves, the lower overhead will be.

Clients of a maid service have to be kept happy. They want fast and dependable service, and it's important to maintain a good public image even with affluent clients who may try to fake a breakage claim now and then.

MINIMAL EQUIPMENT NEEDS

In this business the tools of the trade are the ones that have worked for thousands of years. Your equipment needs are simple—mops, buckets and brooms, and soap.

The equipment needs of a maid service are going to vary in cost if not in style. As the business grows, you will be able to buy in large volume on every item used on the job.

This is where good PR comes in. Volume buying on a regular basis—especially as your clientele becomes more established and predictable—will mean that you can take advantage of wholesale price breaks, seasonal buying, and special orders.

MAKE YOUR CUSTOMERS DO THE WORK FOR YOU!

How's *that* for a revolutionary business concept? But in a service business—especially this one—that's exactly what happens.

Customer satisfaction on the smallest scale is all you need to generate more and more business for your maid service. The byword is, of course, referrals. You'll be building your reputation every time a satisfied customer looks at the snappy job your team of professionals has done on a home.

Team-cleaning operations are what make the difference. A two-person maid team can finish a ten-room mansion in less than six hours. By cutting client costs in half you can double business volume and make your maid service a long-term profit maker.

Systematic teamwork, dependable service, and satisfied customers will all work toward the only goal worth having in any business—high profits. With low investment, low overhead, and that bonus of no experience required, the growth curve of the maid service industry is accelerating at an unprecedented rate. The burgeoning market in this business means excellent profit potential for the future.

Start-up Manual #160 is available on this business. See page 378.

New Idea

TUTORIAL SERVICE

"Why can't Johnny read?" is a common question these days. We don't know the answer, but we do know a way you can turn dissatisfaction with the school system into a profitable business. Run a tutorial service.

You don't need to teach anything; just organize the service. There are several makets. Grade-school and high-school students may need help in arithmetic, reading, languages, and other subjects. Someone with a teaching credential at the appropriate levels makes the best tutor, but an outstanding student at a higher level may be acceptable.

Standardized exams are of tremendous importance to students today. High-school students must take them to get into college, and college students take them to get into graduate or professional school. Preparatory courses are available for these exams, but many students would prefer private instruction in their homes.

Professional qualifying exams exist in law, medicine, accounting, and a host of federal and state civil service occupations. Foreign language study, the study of English by speakers of other languages, and studies relating to career advancement are all areas where tutors are in demand.

Setting up a tutorial service is simple. A typewriter, telephone, and other office equipment are all you need. A continuing small ad in the local and university papers, supplemented by a Yellow Pages listing and fliers distributed near schools will provide adequate promotion. Many teachers are looking for extra income, and word-of-mouth referrals will bring them to you.

Be certain to check the tutors' credentials and qualifications closely. Students should have the option to change tutors at any time; consistently unpopular tutors should be dropped. Consider offering a money-back guarantee that students will improve.

Payment should be made to you. Keep 25 percent and forward the rest to the tutor.

MOBILE SURFACE CLEANING

High net profit B/T	$200,000
Average net profit B/T	30,000
Mimimum investment:	8,000
Average investment:	14,500

Cities and towns across the nation are plagued by visual pollution—a polite term for good old-fashioned dirt. Office buildings, historical monuments, houses, and other structures from bridges to billboards are discolored by layers of soot, smoke, and sulfur compounds that accumulate over the years. On the highways there are thousands of vehicles with oil and grease deposits, rust, and road grime.

HOT NEW SERVICE BUSINESS

A new service business is sweeping the country. Mobile surface cleaning is a phenomenal concept that is operated out of a self-contained van unit. The vehicle is outfitted with all the necessary equipment and supplies to tackle the toughest job. The unit is driven to the job site for on-the-spot cleaning of anything from boats, cars, planes, or farm equipment to swimming pools, oil refinery tanks, and sports arenas. The secret is spray and rinse: a biodegradable chemical is sprayed on to lift the dirt, then it is rinsed off with water.

OWNERS REALLY CLEANING UP

It is the owners of vans who are really cleaning up, to the tune of $70,000 gross profits a year before taxes with one van! They realize incredible net profits of 40 to 45 percent pretax. We found one owner of eight van units grossing an unbelievable $500,000 annually after only three years in business. Because his cost for chemicals and supplies is lowered through large purchases, he nets 50 percent pretax.

Many people we spoke with went into the business originally on a part-time basis and did so well they soon decided to go full-time. It is possible for one person to operate a unit 15 to 20 hours per week, easily gross $30,000 a year, and net up to 65 percent before taxes and owner's salary. Not bad for part-time work!

The profit potential in this business is limitless because almost every exposed outdoor surface is attacked by atmospheric grime and man-made pollutants, called "carbons" in the surface-cleaning industry. Owners of buildings, truck fleets, and houses are anxious to preserve their investment, and to do their share to keep America clean.

EASY TO GET STARTED

It is possible to work around the dealership programs. You can get into mobile surface cleaning for as little as $8,000 and begin realizing a profit within the first few months. This kind of capital provides you with basic equipment, chemicals, and supplies. The only limitation is that you will be doing all the work yourself at the beginning, without the assistance of an additional employee.

It is best to figure on spending $14,000 to $16,000 to position yourself for long-term growth and maximum profits. This gives you the option of buying top-quality equipment and hiring a part-timer to help you set up and clean up. The time you save will turn into extra jobs, and it won't be long before you can buy your second unit.

One major advantage to this business is that you can run it from your home. There is no need for a fancy office with a secretary because your customers only see your van. It is a good idea, however, to have an answering service handle calls or at least to install an answering machine. The cost is minimal when you consider the number of sales you may miss by being away from home. Many answering services will even schedule appointments and job dates for you, but until you have the experience to predict exactly how long it will take to complete a cleaning assignment, it is best to simply have the service take messages.

LOTS OF REPEAT BUSINESS

The best part—and the secret of long-term success—is that after you have done a cleaning job, the structure will get dirty again. Once people have seen how a spick-and-span exterior improves their local image, they will want to maintain the new standards. In many cases, such as the gas station where oil and grease stains are a constant problem, it shouldn't be difficult to set up a contract for regular service.

MANY MORE PROFITABLE MARKETS

Another profitable market for many operators is car lots. It is hard enough for salesmen to sell cars, especially used ones, under the best of circumstances. If every vehicle on the lot is covered with a layer of dust, it is almost impossible. Lot owners often hire someone full-time to keep cars clean and shiny or they use a local car wash. However, this is more expensive and time consuming than having you stop by every few days for a quick wash-and-rinse job.

Owners of truck or car fleets will also be interested in contracting you for periodic cleaning. This prolongs the life of a paint job, ensures that their vehicles are presenting a good image, and in snowy regions, protects undercarriages from corrosion caused by road salt.

Real estate brokers will also provide you with a substantial amount of business because, like car dealers, they find it much easier to sell a clean house. Painters and architects can save a great deal of time by hiring you to prepare a surface. With the addition of a special compound to the chemical base, you can actually strip off a peeling layer of paint.

More unusual customers include cemetery managers, who realize the benefit of having stone monuments cleaned. Insurance brokers will contract you to work on their claims: for example, smoke- and fire-damaged exteriors and interiors.

You will quickly discover that the potential for new customers is endless. One owner we spoke to cleaned a friend's trailer as a birthday present and left the mobile park that afternoon with 14 new customers who had wandered by while he was doing the job.

Start-up Manual #150 is available on this business. See page 378.

New Idea

COMPUTER-TRADING CENTER

The computer age is here and a Georgia entrepreneur is taking advantage. Irene Erlenwein runs a computer-matching service for buyers, sellers and swappers.

Irene operates the Apple Pie Trading Post, Inc. She runs the business out of her home with two basic pieces of equipment: A telephone and a home computer unit.

The system works fairly simply. Someone with something to sell calls Irene; their item is entered into the data bank. With luck, the computer comes up with a match. Irene then gets buyer and seller together and everyone's satisfied.

The fee structure varies. Sellers are charged according to the item they're selling. Buyers can receive free information unless they're seeking a specific product. Then they are listed on the computer for two weeks for a $5 fee.

Apple Pie also offers a $10 three-month membership program. For this fee, members are given names and numbers of other members; then they travel from one home to another swapping merchandise.

LIQUIDATED-GOODS BROKER

High net profit B/T:	Unlimited
Average net profit B/T:	$40,000
Minimum investment:	1,000
Average investment:	20,000

If you are a gambler at heart, confident in your negotiation and sales technique, imaginative, curious, and if you enjoy day-to-day challenges, you could join the ranks of the men who call themselves liquidators and make as much as $250,000 per year. Even the average fellow in this business nets close to $40,000 before taxes.

The personality characteristics we described are essential to even average success, but start-up costs are minimal, overhead is light, and you can start part-time, operating from your home. The only real problems you might have are lack of capital and contacts, but these obstacles can be overcome with patience and hard work.

You can start tomorrow, outbid the old-timers by maybe only a penny per item, and turn the inventory over to the same source they would have used as an outlet. The business couldn't be simpler in structure—all you do is find sellers and buyers of distressed merchandise.

Your markup percentage can be astounding. We heard stories from the old pros of 600, 700, even 1,000 and 2,000 percent markups, though most deals fall in the 50 to 100 percent range. On the other hand, high-quantity deals in a very competitive market may bring only 1 cent of profit on a 10-cent item, but volume will make it worthwhile.

Liquidators are a tight-lipped group; the fewer there are, the greater their individual profits.

HOW THEY OPERATE

A fire races through the basement of a local clothing store. It is extinguished before it reaches the main floor, but not before much of the merchandise has been ruined by smoke. The next morning a liquidator, Mr. X, pays a visit to the store's owner, asking about the extent of damage to merchandise. The owner, after a thorough inventory check, informs Mr. X that $20,000 of his uninsured stock has been smoke-damaged and he must liquidate it.

Mr. X offers $2,000 cash (or 10 cents on the dollar) for the ruined goods. The store owner initially rejects Mr. X's offer as too low, only to find himself calling back a week later to accept it after a fruitless effort to obtain a better offer.

Mr. X has not been sitting idle waiting for this call; he's been preparing for it. Immediately after making his offer to the store owner, he placed a number of calls to sources within the clothing industry. Within two days he located the owner of a large second-hand shop willing to pay $3,500 for the goods, delivered. As soon as Mr. X's offer was accepted, a truck was hired and the goods reached their new owner within 48 hours.

Transporting the goods cost $200, leaving Mr. X with a profit of $1,300 for his efforts, which consisted of his initial visit to the store and eight or nine phone calls!

This scenario is an example of a liquidator at work. Circumstances may vary but the basic ingredients are always the same: somebody, for whatever reason, is forced to convert tangible property into cash. Someone else (the liquidator) steps in and purchases the goods at a fraction of their original cost. The liquidator then turns around and, using his resources and contacts, converts the goods back into cash as quickly as possible.

The liquidator must know the value of goods in today's market—his profit is at stake. A high bid may get him the goods, but not at a price that allows profitable resale. The liquidator is not in the business of owning goods—just buying and selling them. The longer it takes him to sell goods, the less his real profit—time is money!

Liquidators deal strictly in cash. There is no such thing as installment or time payments for them. You need only enough starting capital to conclude your first deal. This may be $1,000 or $10,000 or $50,000.

AN EXAMPLE OF UNUSUAL OUTLETS

We discussed the variety of distribution contacts with a liquidator who had just purchased 3,600 framed, low-priced, mass-produced paintings from a defunct art distributor. Using a small classified ad in the *Wall Street Journal* he had sold every painting within 24 days.

A motel operator purchased 1,000 with plans to lease them to new motel owners. A bank bought 800 as gifts for new depositors. A supermarket chain bought 1,200 to promote as a special. And a small furniture store chain purchased the other 600 simply to sell in its stores.

The liquidator told us: "I could have sold another 4,000 if I'd had them."

Start-up Manual #98 is available on this business. See page 379.

_____ **New Idea** _____

HOME HISTORIAN

Over 2 million new homes are built in the United States each year. What proud owner wouldn't want a photo history of his home being built? Bob Sprock is a Connecticut entrepreneur who caters to proud homeowners by offering to do just that.

Sprock will make a photo story of the house's development through various stages of construction. Sprock first takes a picture of the empty lot. He makes periodic visits to the work site and takes pictures to chronicle the progress. Interesting shots include the arrival of the bricks, wood, and raw materials, the grading of the site, and the frame of the house as it goes up.

His fee depends on the number of shots taken, but prices are taken with slide film in order to keep prices low. Prints are 50 cents each and 8 by 10 color shots are $7.

Sprock also offers to take pictures of the house to show changes after it has been completed, such as room additions, new colors, or how the house looks through the change of seasons.

With the popularity of videocassette recorders, we can also see offering a film record of construction on the house. One could produce a movie of the house going up, condensing months of building into an hour-long tape.

Another possibility is to offer the film or photo records to companies constructing large buildings or apartments. They'd enjoy having "building stage" photos to frame and place in the offices of the building when it's completed.

COIN-OP TV

High net profit B/T:	$80,000
Average net profit B/T:	40,000
Minimum investment:	20,000
Average investment:	36,000

(These figures are based on full-time operation of 100 or more coin-operated units.)

You can still find small coffee shops or "hamburger joints" with coin-operated record selectors in the booths. Remember those? You'd turn the wheel and select your favorite "platters" on the corner jukebox by remote control. And feed dime after dime into them. If you were on a date and out to impress, you might drop a quarter in the slot for a whole album of hits.

Now you can gross $70,000 or more annually, and net a fantastic $40,000 with a terrific reprise of this idea: tiny coin-operated TV sets, in booths at pizza parlors, quick-steak houses, or almost anyplace where there's a built-in waiting period for service. We've even seen them at bus terminals, airports, and railroad stations!

TV-ADDICTED

On any evening, millions of Americans wind up a long day "glued to the tube." Television is pervasive in our society—it even may be addictive! In a recent study homeowners were offered cash—no strings attached—to allow their TVs to be removed for a week. The consequences were scientifically examined. The result: normally peaceful families fought like tigers, stress levels skyrocketed, and there were reports of one or two nervous breakdowns among viewers denied their evening "pacifier."

Tie this in with the fact that more and more wives are working outside the home, the steady increase in food costs, and the resulting increase in "eating out," and you can see why pay TVs in family restaurants returned thousands of dollars a year to vending operations we researched.

Restaurant proprietors have noted an increase in business after TVs are installed. And they like it. It is a service to customers that gets very favorable response. Large groups of adults and children will often come in and ask for a TV booth!

Although you might expect these TVs to be used mainly by kids, adults view just as much, especially during the World Series and Monday night football games. People will even wait for a TV booth. Others will sit at a small table where they can view—on the other person's quarter!

Two southern California aerospace engineers grossed $45,000 last year, part-time, on 100 machines located in restaurants around Los Angeles. Five years ago they started with eight small Sony sets costing $340 apiece to build. After using their profits to obtain more sets, they now serve 24 restaurants, each with four to six machines—some with as many as ten. Their initial investment was $3,000.

Most vending operations start small; but ultimately, gross profits depend on the number of machines you have installed and the daily take from each of them. This has ranged from a low of $1 per day per TV to a high of $3 for the operations we investigated.

It is the small change that customers carry in their pockets that makes the machines work. A quarter gets you 15 minutes of viewing. Viewers also get hooked on a story line and want to see the end of the show.

The business owners' locations you are using will want a percentage of the daily take ranging from 20 to 50 percent. An average daily take of $2 on 100 machines, after 40 percent to the proprietor, will yield an annual gross profit of $44,000! On the same basis a $3 average take will generate $65,000.

Net profit margins are substantially higher than in most other vending-type businesses, because there's no inventory expense or cost of sales—expenses that amount to as much as 55 percent on a cigarette or candy vending route, for example.

Assuming about $2,000 per month in ongoing expenses including repair costs, a 100-machine operation worked full-time will return almost $3,500 per month before tax and owner's salary.

Start-up Manual #121 is available on this business. See page 379.

New Idea

SINGING TELEGRAMS

Remember when Western Union messengers would burst into song on your doorstep during the holidays or on your birthday?

Ever since Western Union discontinued the service years back, no one has offered melodic messages guaranteed to surprise, excite, fluster, and bring a smile to the face of the grouchiest recipient.

Until now. We've found a super update on their data called Live Wires. Costumed messengers for Live Wires will sing standard or specially composed ditties that congratulate, say hello or goodbye, or happy anything.

Normally closed doors of stuffy bank presidents, harassed producers, stone-faced judges, advertising executives, and purchasing agents have opened for the singing telegram people from Live Wires.

For these occasions, custom lyrics will plug a product, a script, or even a resume. An actual wire with printed message is also given to the surprised and usually delighted recipient, along with a sample of whatever you want him to see.

Prices start at $27 for an in-person telegram, depending on what you want to do and where. Messengers have gotten on planes and flown to remote places to do doorstep theater. For $12 a telegram will be delivered by phone anywhere in the world. Custom lyrics composed for special situations cost extra.

This is a great gimmick that can work in nearly any major city in the country. Live Wires is in southern California, and there are similar services in San Francisco. But plenty of other cities could support such a service.

Operation is simple, using college students, out-of-work theater folk, and adventuresome secretaries looking for an out-of-the-ordinary job. Messengers have delivered ten or more a day in their own cars or on bicycles.

Publicity for a service like this should be easy to obtain; the service is unknown in most major cities.

PLASTICS-RECYCLING CENTER

High net profit B/T:	$200,000+
Average net profit B/T:	40,000
Minimum investment:	18,000
Average investment:	32,000

Plastics are everywhere! In any household or business in America, a quick check will reveal that they have replaced glass, metal, and wood in everyday items from milk bottles to trash bags, from furniture that "looks like" wood to major components of the family car.

Annual consumption of plastics was 30 billion pounds in 1976 and by 1985 it is expected to grow to 60 billion pounds! Most of this will become trash and be picked up—or worse, littered across the landscape. The latest figures show that about 11 billion pounds of scrap plastics will be thrown out by "use it up and throw it away" Americans this year.

Environmentalists are concerned, because many plastics don't decompose. They lie in fields and streams for years and years because they are not biodegradable like other discarded stuff. Instead of breaking down into common elements and reentering the environment, they just lie there in their original form.

Municipalities are looking for ways to reduce the amount of garbage they have to collect and dispose of. Plastics are a never-ending problem for them. Because they are not biodegradable, they must be buried in sanitary landfills or burned in incinerators.

Landfills are becoming scarce and plastics must be mixed carefully with other waste for burning because of high combustibility. Most municipal incinerators are outdated and can't handle today's volume of garbage, so about 80 percent of trash, including plastics waste, winds up in open dumps where it is supposed to rot and burn. But because of the low heat in an open fire, the plastics just melt.

There's a way you can help solve the ecological nightmares that plastics create, serve your community, and make a handsome profit at the same time.

BE A RECYCLER!

Paper, glass, aluminum, and other metals have been recycled for years. Plastics manufacturers have recycled their in-house virgin scrap for a long time. But little attention has been paid to "postconsumer" recovery of waste plastics, because of the historic low cost of new plastics. This is changing, because plastics are made from petrochemicals which are getting scarce. Recycling this resource presents a fantastic opportunity for high profit.

We've located existing plastics recyclers who collect up to 500,000 pounds of scrap plastics per month. The scrap is then sold to reprocessors or manufacturers for an average of 15 to 35 cents per pound. The average small recycling operation can collect as much as 500,000 pounds of scrap the first year and at an average of 20 cents a pound can gross $100,000 from sales! Operating expenses for a small recycling plant will range from a monthly low of $1,900 to a high of $3,500; net profits before tax and owner's salary range from $2,400 to $5,200 per month!

HUGE MARKET

Every day more and more industries switch to plastics because of low cost, light weight, and easier processing and fabrication.

There is a wide variety of plastics manufacturers all over the country. Extruders make sheets, films, or forms like pipe. Injection molders make toys, model airplane kits, caps and lids for bottles, even telephones. Blow molders make bottles and other types of containers.

Most of these manufacturers find it more economical to blend reprocessed plastics with their own virgin material to extend their supply of costly resins, and produce more for the same or lower cost.

PLASTICS POWER!

A remarkable down-the-road use of plastics is based on the fact that it has a high energy content and that pure hydrocarbon plastics have a heat value equal to the best fuel oils! In Chicago and St. Louis, waste plastics are burned with other garbage right now to generate steam and electric power.

We predict that the usefulness of recycled, granulated plastics as an energy source will become even greater than its value to manufacturers! The method here is to provide "regrind," as it is called in the trade, to local power plants that use coal.

The regrind is mixed with powdered coal and blown into the furnace to generate more BTUs from the same amount of coal. This is because 150 pounds of plastics is roughly equivalent to 75 pounds of coal in energy value. So mixing two to one will stretch coal resources and provide a cheap source of fuels at the same time.

The potential for visionary marketers who get into this business now has got to be phenomenal!

Start-up Manual #122 is available on this business. See page 379.

ROOMMATE-FINDING SERVICE

High net profit B/T:	(variable)
Average net profit B/T:	$20,000
Minimum investment:	2,000
Average investment:	4,200

One of the most successful shows in ABC's roster of hits is "Three's Company," a lighthearted look at two girls and a guy sharing an apartment. The young main characters, all single, share quarters due to economic necessity. They simply cannot make ends meet by living alone on their modest incomes. The "arrangements" they've made and their life-style become high comedy.

But underneath the humor is a very real problem, and at the same time an exciting business opportunity. High rents, taxes, the cost of living, and skyrocketing inflation are no laughing matter. And millions of Americans—a giant growing market—are finding roommates as one way to solve the problem. You can get in on the ground floor of this important trend by setting up a roommate-finding service.

GROWING NEED ACROSS THE COUNTRY

Elderly people suffer from many problems aside from their health. Climbing inflation nibbles away at their Social Security and pension payments. Those who own a home aren't excluded from the inflationary spiral in housing costs, because insurance and property taxes are at the head of the inflationary list all over the country.

Men typically die younger than their wives and many widows live in almost continual loneliness. The answer is to find a friend to share the rent, and end the loneliness.

Divorce rates continue to increase at an accelerated pace. Not just in California, where last year there was almost one divorce for every two new marriages, but in the rest of the nation as well. The "ex's" find immediate financial problems. The ex-husband may have the cost of alimony, child support, and higher food and entertainment expenses. The ex-wife must attempt to survive on meager or nonexistent divorce payments while trying to establish her self-worth and value in the job market, in which she may never have worked.

Both ex-spouses will find it more expensive to live as singles. In addition, both are accustomed to steady companionship and, regardless of the quality of the relationship, miss having someone around. Loneliness is a pronounced problem for divorced people. The answer is to find a roommate to satisfy financial and solitude problems at the same time.

Single folks with newly acquired roommates told us, "I never realized how much more I enjoy going home when I know someone is there."

Others claimed, "No matter whether I see my roommate often or my roommate is busy with various activities, I feel more secure and happy knowing there's someone living there with me."

Young singles are amenable to the roommate system for the same reasons as the elderly and divorced, but from a different point of view. Young singles like to live in more glamorous areas. Due to increased housing costs in these regions and the fact that these young people have just begun their careers, financial obstacles loom large in their path; a comfortable life-style is tough to achieve.

For years, single women just out of college have grouped together in apartments to alleviate the financial problem. Young men and women, after living at home or in a dormitory at college, where they've always had people around, respond dramatically when forced out on the street to fend for themselves. Loneliness and financial problems set in, and become a new and scary experience.

17 MILLION ARE SHARING NOW!

In 1976 the Department of Commerce estimated that 17 million people shared households with individuals not related to them (and the figure has increased since). The market is even bigger when you consider that people living alone—who could use a roommate service right away—are your prime prospects!

Most newspaper classified sections have an Apartment to Share column under the apartments to rent. Advertisers using this approach can find roommates after a tedious month or two of advertising, if they are at all particular. Our surveys show, however, that the people using this approach do so as a desperation move, with many fears and reservations.

A roommate service provides clearance, screening, reference verification, and introduction service for potential roommates. It is an ideal business for a man or woman who is sensitive to people's needs and wants. The desire to help, direct, and mesh the complex natures of your fellowman is paramount. Those who approach with an impersonal "supermarket" attitude are destined for failure. It is a professional, personal services business.

Start-up Manual #130 is available on this business. See page 378.

_____ **New Idea** _____

MOVIE-OF-THE-MONTH CLUB

We have learned that Time-Life is about to start a video Movie-of-the-Month Club. The club will be run along the lines of the Book-of-the-Month Club, offering a movie to members each month along with a number of alternatives.

There's no reason other entrepreneurs shouldn't capitalize on this idea. We'd recommend going Time-Life one better. Why not specialize? Offer a Western Movie-of-the-Month Club, or even a Porno Movie-of-the-Month Club.

With the large number of videocassette movies available to retailers, there should be a large selection for you to choose from when you start these specialized video clubs. We'll be seeing more movies on cassette in the future.

You could also hop the nostalgia bandwagon and offer a

Classics-of-the-Month Club, featuring such films as *Citizen Kane* or *Casablanca*. The possibilities are endless: a Bogart Video Club, a John Wayne Video Club.

Because you'll have steady subscribers, you'll be able to offer the tapes at lower-than-retail prices. Also you won't have the rent overhead of video stores. Offer a special incentive—maybe four tapes for the price of one—to new subscribers.

You can obtain mailing lists by contacting video stores and buying theirs. Just don't tell them what you want them for!

HANDICRAFT CO-OP

High net profit B/T:	$100,000+
Average net profit B/T:	65,000
Minimum investment:	15,000
Average investment:	35,000

Here's a business that violates all the rules! No inventory. Minimum overhead. And an incredible 20 to 50 percent net profit margin!

We've uncovered a few smart marketers who have adapted the flea market concept and organized artisans into craft co-ops indoors. In high-volume shopping mall locations!

Couple this innovation with the resurgence of interest in quality handcrafted items taking place all over the country and you have the potential for net profits that exceed $130,000 a year.

For years artisans have had to make their own products and sell them on consignment—or in person in rented booths—on the flea market gift and art show circuit, to eke out a living.

But most flea markets are seasonal or weekend-only operations held in out-of-the-way places. They attract bargain hunters in droves but are less attractive to the affluent market needed if you sell gift or jewelry items.

NEW CONCEPT

The handicraft co-op offers advantages to both buyer and seller. The buyer enjoys the convenience of a well-located store where he can buy unique, reasonably priced handiwork without paying the admission required at fairs and flea markets. The seller has monthly sales of $30,000 to $50,000; grosses this high are common and attest to the popularity of the co-op approach. The accessibility and year-round high traffic and sales of an enclosed mall lure the artisan as well. The craft co-ops we have investigated have long waiting lists of craftspeople eager to pay for such excellent exposure. Often the total cost to them is less than that of a good booth space at a desirable weekend flea market; best of all, they don't need to spend their time selling, and are free to do what they do best, and like to do most—creating more handsome handicrafts to sell.

EXCELLENT PROFITS

All the stores we've seen are located in high-traffic enclosed shopping malls. We investigated several operations and found one store that nets its young owner $135,000 before taxes! This store charges about $60 per month to displaying crafters and takes 30 percent of gross sales as well.

The store is located in an "artsy-craftsy" part of Los Angeles and has 6,500 square feet filled with the wares of over 120 artisans.

Each artisan grosses $500 to $700 per month from displays. Booth rental revenue of $7,200 is sufficient to cover all lease costs and most other overheads.

PHENOMENAL GROSS

The whole store grosses over $50,000 sales in an average month, taking into account the peak holiday period. The Christmas season amounts to over 25 percent of annual volume, and displays are usually picked clean by Christmas Eve.

The store has been established in an ideal spot for over four years. A more representative gross for a typical store is $38,000 to $42,000 per month. Expenses, including the 70 percent returned to exhibitors, amount to an average of $32,000 to $34,000 per month, leaving average net profit in the $6,000 to $8,000 range monthly before tax and owner's salary.

A mall or shopping-center site can be expected to yield such amounts, given good management. A carefully selected high-traffic location attractive to affluent browsers can also generate excellent margins, though grosses will be lower.

Even a smaller store, a 2,000-square-foot setup in a good "arty" or high-traffic tourist area, can yield $8,300 to $16,500 gross per month. This results in $1,600 to $3,300 monthly net before taxes to an owner/operator if a 30 percent commission is charged to approximately 60 or 70 artisans. This assumes full utilization and break-even pricing on display space.

HOW YOU OPERATE

First you must lease a location, whether in a mall, cluster shopping complex, group of browsing shops, or other high-traffic area. An area of 3,000 to 4,000 square feet should be ample. Then you rent all the display space to artisans anxious for a ready market for their wares.

Rental fees to craftspeople, ranging from $25 to $70 a month depending on the store location, amount of space, and owner's overhead, recover most or all of the cost of store rental and may even offset other costs. The artisans must build and light their displays at their own cost and along guidelines provided to keep decor consistent. Occasionally, owners build displays for craftspeople at an extra charge. Also, all lessees must stock their displays, set prices, and provide their own insurance coverage.

In addition to the rental fee, you charge a percentage of the gross sales from each display, usually ranging between 24 and 30 percent at most locations we checked out.

Start-up Manual #118 is available on this business. See page 379.

__New Idea__

DISCOUNT PAINTER

Here's an idea any organized entrepreneur should be able to copy with success. A Toronto, Canada, college student, Greig Clark, has put together a network of 19 college students who each run their own painting business.

The student-run businesses appeal to homeowners because students paint houses for 25 to 30 percent less than conventional firms. The 19 young businessmen will employ over 250 students during the summer school break. Before they return to classes this fall, they'll have painted over 2,000 homes from contracts Clark has lined up. That's over $1 million of business.

Clark provides each manager with between $500 and $1,000 worth of painting equipment to get them started. He also helps rent a van and because he buys in volume, they can establish a line of credit with paint stores.

Clark gives the managers a training manual and on-the-job training. Part of the training program consists of a film on professional painting techniques.

One of the best things he offers is the contracts. Because of the low cost to homeowners, Clark has no trouble lining up enthusiastic clients.

Entrepreneurs living in major urban areas should be able to duplicate this idea by pulling from the large pool of college students who will be looking for summer work. You may want to work with an experienced painter in developing a manual for your budding Rembrandts.

Advertising in local papers in the real estate and home sections should pull a healthy response from bargain hunters.

New Idea
LAWYER'S AIDE

Anyone who has dealt with an attorney knows that time costs plenty. No one knows this better than the attorney himself, and it takes plenty of that expensive time to research and prepare briefs for cases he's working on. An Ohio company, Johnson Legal Research, offers to perform any of a number of mundane, time-consuming tasks for lawyers who are too busy with more important matters.

These services include library work, research, actual compilation, typing, photocopying, and computer research. Johnson Legal Research prepares motion, trial, posttrial, and appellate briefs as well as pleadings and memoranda. All work is done by law students and is reviewed and edited by Alan Johnson himself.

This idea should appeal to small as well as large law firms. There is no reason for a competent attorney to spend valuable time doing chores that were learned in the first year of law school. This service should appeal particularly to lawyers who have more than one case coming to a head at the same time.

Johnson charges $20 per hour for research, plus costs. This is an idea that would work well in any city that has a large legal community. One needn't be a lawyer, although having one on your staff would be a definite plus. Local law colleges should be happy to supply you with students looking for work.

DIGITAL WATCH-REPAIRING SERVICE

High net profit B/T:	Unknown
Average net profit B/T:	$28,000
Minimum investment:	2,500
Average investment:	4,000

Over 12 million digital watches were sold in the United States in 1977. This cut Swiss watch production as much as 70 percent! In fact, after the United States, Switzerland was the largest importer of electronic digitals from Hong Kong in 1976 — a true "coals to tle" event. All over the world, consumers are buying digital from $9.95 kits to $2,500 14-karat-gold future heirlooms. T̲ ̲ ̲ ̲ ̲ ̲ big business, and the repair of these watches is wide open—regular watch repairmen can't handle them.

Make no mistake, the digital watch is a far cry from the conventional wristwatch. There are no visible moving parts to go wrong or wear out, but to paraphrase Murphy's law, "If it is made by man, it can go wrong, and probably will." And it does.

Of the watches sold, 30 percent will be in for service within six months. And therein lies the opportunity. Traditional watchmakers don't understand and are generally afraid even to look at a digital watch. Those who provide digital watch repair are really cashing in!

When the idea of the digital watch caught on with the public about five years ago, it seemed every company with the capability of turning out a diode or semi-conductor jumped into the field. When some of the larger electronic companies moved in, like Fairchild and Harris Intertype, the smaller producers found themselves in trouble. They couldn't compete with these giants in the field of low-cost assembly. The small companies' products might be equal to or better than those of their "big brothers," but the pricing was killing them. Many pulled out, and those who did not, now find themselves in a financial bind. We know of at least two such firms now in bankruptcy courts. We found that 17 of these assembly companies had folded and there are probably more. The secondary market is people who bought watches from now defunct companies and can't send them back for repair to the manufacturer.

Those who bought from the larger American companies are experiencing long delays in factory service—in most cases one to two months. The jeweler or department store manager is anxious to please his customer. Therefore, if he knows that local service can be obtained within a few days he will forgo the factory warranty to satisfy his customer.

Even though hundreds of different brands of digital watches are offered, the modules come from just five or six suppliers. The representative of one such company told us it had almost 100 assembling companies buying their modules. So replacement parts are no problem.

REPAIR IS NOTHING MORE THAN POPPING PARTS IN OR OUT

The digital watch is amazingly simple in operation compared to the conventional watch. A quartz crystal replaces the balance wheel; a battery, the mainspring; and light-emitting or crystal diodes on the face, the hands. Moving parts that wear out have been replaced by printed circuits. The watch doesn't tick or hum, but the basic theory of timekeeping is the same as that of the antique pendulum clock. You can isolate problems with a simple tester and repair is mostly a matter of replacing defective parts.

GETTING ESTABLISHED

We foresee one problem in establishing your business: the old-fashioned jewelers! In our interviews with jewelers, we found many of them wanted to turn their heads away from the electronic phenomenon! Many felt it was a fad which would turn away their best customers. Others would replace batteries, but if battery replacement didn't solve the problem, they would try to sell the customer a new mechanical watch.

The watch industry estimates that over half of watches are sold as gifts. Even though repair costs on a cheap watch may exceed its original value, people will pay the price because of the sentimental value of the gift.

Many jewelers are ignorant of these facts and refuse to change their habits because their business has never had a major change, at least in their lifetime. Consequently, you must subtly inform your potential clients that they are missing some profitable business.

Start-up Manual #95 is available on this business. See page 378.

INSULATION CONTRACTING BUSINESS

High net profit B/T:	$500,000
Average net profit B/T:	$30,000
Minimum investment:	9,000
Average investment:	15,000

While you are reading this article, most of your neighbors are wasting precious energy and hard-earned dollars. How? By heating or cooling poorly insulated homes.

Already, millions have been made by bright entrepreneurs who have capitalized on the energy crisis with perfect timing. One contractor we spoke to left a dead-end corporate job six years ago and now nets over $500,000 a year on gross sales of more than $2 million. Two years ago he bought out his supplier and now manufactures insulation material, but $600,000 or more of his current revenue still comes from residential and commercial contracting jobs.

We found many contractors working just the residential market who were grossing between $300,000 and $500,000 a year with two or more crews working full-time. Most had more business than they could handle. The average small operator with one crew is making $125,000 to $150,000 yearly—and netting from 21 to 35 percent pretax!

MAKE BIG MONEY BY SAVING CUSTOMERS BIG MONEY

These contractors "retrofit" existing homes and other buildings with insulation to improve energy efficiency in winter and summer as well as help consumers save plenty of money. In millions of older homes, especially those built before 1950, as much as half of the heat escapes through the roof, walls, and windows.

EASY TO DO

Improving insulation in an existing building can be done without tearing the house apart. In fact, a trained crew can do the whole job in about a day, and the only way to tell they have been there is to check the heating bill. Just adding blown-in insulation to the attic can cut heat loss by 40 percent.

Loss of heat through the walls will still be a severe problem, which is where modern technology takes over. Most contractors drill holes in the exterior walls and pump in cellulose fiber or a type of plastic foam that looks like shaving cream. This insulation hardens quickly, fills the entire space, and does an excellent job of keeping a house warm in winter and cool in summer.

MILLIONS OF HOMES NEED HELP

While 8 to 9 million houses have been fitted with additional insulation since the 1973-74 energy shortage, most of these were retrofitted with attic insulation only.

There's no question that in most parts of the country the market is immense and virtually untouched in the residential sector. There is another virgin market for retrofitting on the commercial side. Older stores, garages, heated warehouses, office buildings, and commercial structures are other markets to tap. Public buildings like schools and courthouses can also be considered a wide-open market.

LEADS TO ADDITIONAL LUCRATIVE JOBS

Many insulation contractors are using their reputation and experience in the retrofit residential market as a springboard into more difficult commercial/industrial retrofit work. And they are getting into new construction projects too.

EASY TO GET STARTED

One advantage of the insulation contracting business is that you needn't spend a fortune on a fancy office in a prime location. It is rare that a customer will want to visit your shop; sales and installation activity take place on the site.

You will need about 1,200 square feet of storage space for supplies and a small, strictly functional office where you can do paperwork. Many contractors begin working out of their homes, if they have enough space to store bulky insulation materials.

The price range for new equipment is $3,800 to $12,000 for high-quality hardware. Used equipment can be obtained at even lower prices, but availability is difficult to predict.

We recommend that you finance or lease equipment to minimize start-up expenses. Manufacturers may offer lease options, and there are many equipment-leasing firms and banks that finance purchases. Usually an equipment-leasing firm or bank will buy the equipment you specify and lease it to you for a five- to seven-year period (depending on the depreciable life of the asset). Equipment leasing usually costs $20 to $30 monthly per $1,000 of purchase price.

Start-up Manual #145 is available on this business. See page 378.

Start-up Manual #145 is available on this business. See page 378.

New Idea

GIFT-WRAPPING SERVICE

A nicely wrapped gift that looks "too pretty to open" is always appreciated, and says something extra about the giver. But most of us are all thumbs at fancy gift wrapping, or don't have the time it takes to do the job right.

Not too many stores offer gift wrapping for free anymore—and in some it's a chore just to get a box that fits the items purchased. Even larger stores that gift-wrap use inexpensive, look-alike commercial wrapping.

We've found a few gift-wrapping services that operate out of the home, stressing luxury wrappings and personalized work. Why not take the idea a step further and set up a kiosk in a large regional shopping mall?

Anyone with some artistic ability can offer fancy gift wrapping paper and those nifty custom bows (hand-made) as a clear step up from the stick-on kind we usually have to settle for. Personalizing the wrapping to the occasion—and the recipient—is vital.

Custom packaging and wrapping of oddly shaped items should be a specialty. Ever try to wrap a record album or bicycle in a way that made the gift a surprise? Of course, you charge extra for this type of service.

A service like this, perhaps called "The Wrapper" and stressing custom work with creativity, should get plenty of business in a high traffic mall, especially around the holidays. The "We Wrap Anything" angle should be worth some free publicity from the media. Send them good photos of your most unusual creations.

A spin-off idea is to tie the service with a drop-off service for mall shoppers, who tire of lugging purchases and packages around with them during a day's browsing. A simple "hat-check" system is sufficient, and a reasonable charge will minimize abuses. Of course, it offers salespeople the chance to ask if any of the items checked need wrapping as gifts.

COIN LAUNDRY

High net profit B/T:	$100,000
Average net profit B/T:	15,000
Minimum investment:	45,000
Average investment:	77,000

Coins can be turned into folding money, and fast, in the new concept of coin laundries. Coin laundromats have come a long way since the '30s. The days of the dimly lit, somewhat seedy neighborhood coin laundromat are gone. And the days of incredible profits are at hand, *if you know what you are doing.* There's a lot more to opening and running a coin laundry than installing the machines and collecting the coins.

We found neighborhood coin laundries returning as much as 40 percent pretax net profit—with sound management. They were packed at all hours with people plunging coins into washers and dryers as if they were slot machines. There are over 42,000 coin laundromats in the country, with over 1,000 opening every year.

NEW HOME-STYLE CONCEPT

The old laundromats have been upgraded or replaced by exciting concept stores like Maytag's Home Style Laundry and similar packages offered by Norge, Westinghouse, Speed Queen, and other equipment manufacturers.

These bright and cheerful operations take as much of the drudgery of washday away as possible and attract customers like never before. Believe it or not (it's true), laundromats have become the newest gathering place for singles. One aspiring California entrepreneur is planning to install a bar in his laundromat! Far-fetched? Not all all, although you might want to settle for a nonalcohol bar serving soft drinks and juices.

Wall coverings, plants, even Tiffany lamps are part of the decor of these new laundromats. Some owners add handsomely to profits by considering themselves vending retailers and adding a wide variety of vending machines. Besides detergents and additives, which are a must, many operators add hot and cold drinks, snacks, packaged goods, cigarettes, coin-operated TVs, and electronic games. These are not just gimmicks adding to the image of the laundromat, but add profits by drawing more patrons to the store!

INCREDIBLE RESULTS

Owners are achieving incredible results with these new laundries. We found one operator grossing $7,800 a month after just a few months. Another, whose first store will return its initial capital investment in 36 months, has opened four other operations in his city—each is grossing over $5,000 monthly. With skillful operation the average store will generate from $4,000 to $6,000 per month in gross sales from washers and dryers alone! Net profits at a well-run laundry will range from 25 to 35 percent pretax. This does not include investment tax credits or depreciation write-offs.

SITE IS EVERYTHING

Nothing you do will overcome a poor location. Without question, the most important decision you will face is where to locate your coin laundry.

The most profitable location is one surrounded by as many people as possible. Densely populated urban apartment areas, college campuses, resort areas, and suburban locations with lots of children have good potential. Our research shows that the ideal place to locate for highest profit potential is in a neighborhood shopping center. We have also concluded that you can save substantial start-up costs by taking over an existing old-fashioned coin-op laundry that's going out of business. The new look you will achieve should overcome mistakes made by the previous operator and beat competition to a pulp.

Some locations, such as those surrounded by a high concentration of busy working wives and singles, can add up to 50 percent to gross sales by including a fluff-and-fold or drop-off service.

THE CLEAN IMAGE

It is essential that your coin laundry be spotless. The entire image you are trying to create with a modern design and equipment will be ruined if spilled detergent accumulates on the carpeting or the machines are dirty. Maintenance is vital, and obviously affects profitability. Not only will a well-run laundromat prevent customer dissatisfaction, it will keep costs low.

SELLING CONVENIENCE

Many coin laundromats are open 24 hours a day. Our researchers have found, however, that this is no longer cost-effective, for many reasons. The most profitable stores operate from 7:00 a.m. until 11:00 p.m. And, of course, an attendant should always be on hand.

There are several factors that have contributed to the resurgence of the coin laundromat. There are a vast number of singles living alone, working mothers, single-parent families, and highly mobile apartment dwellers who would rather invest in a stereo set than a washer and dryer.

The days of the old open-it-and-forget-it coin laundromat are clearly over. But with sound management and promotion, you can be cleaning up in an exciting business.

Start-up Manual #162 is available on this business. See page 378.

New Idea

LETTER WRITING

Debbie Solomon is pulling in over a grand a month writing letters to people she doesn't know. She writes love letters, and letters ending affairs. In fact she writes over a hundred letters a month.

The Chicago entrepreneur writes for people who hate to write letters. She charges a modest $10 for 250 words. After she placed a small ad in a Chicago free paper, the phone started ringing off the hook. "I was surprised and a little shocked that there were so many people who could not express themselves."

She says that writing is apparently a lost art. If you've got a literary streak in you, this may be just the right business.

Millions of people have been putting off writing letters, either to friends or enemies, because they don't have the time, energy, or the ability. You can fill that void.

Place an ad in local papers offering your service. Offer to write all kinds of correspondence. Most people will want someone who can convey the personal touch, so a little sensitivity in your ad will go a long way in getting clients.

SECURITY PATROL SERVICE

High net profit B/T:	$250,000+
Average net profit B/T:	87,500
Minimum investment:	6,000
Average investment:	17,000

Crime does pay, and we've found the business that makes it legal! A security patrol service has extremely high profit potential, and it's a growing concern in an age of diminishing expectations. The low overhead and fast return on investment in this business make it easy to enter and secure in prospects.

Next time you see a cop ask him how long it takes the neighborhood police to arrive on the scene of a burglary or other residential emergency. Chances are he'll tell you it takes from 30 to 45 minutes. In major cities all around the country that's how long it takes to get police protection when you need it most.

Overworked and understaffed police departments in cities all over the country are unable to cope with runaway crime. Burglary has risen at an average of 38 percent a year for the past five years, by some estimates. This has led to an exciting new business opportunity—private security patrols for home and business protection.

LOCK UP THE MARKET

Your security patrol service is the answer to the horrendous increase in city police calls. It will provide many services that local police can never offer. The very presence of a security patrol car in a neighborhood has been shown to reduce crime rates. Why? Because burglars don't want to risk operating in neighborhoods where private police are constantly patrolling.

Cruising the neighborhood is only one aspect of your service. When your customers are away on vacation you'll check on doors and windows or pick up the newspaper every day. If burglars know there's a cop—private or city—on the beat, they'll go elsewhere for their activities. You're selling crime prevention, and security-conscious clients will demand the opportunity to pay for it.

SOLID PROFITS IN SECURITY HARDWARE

In conjunction with a patrol service, the simplest form of alarm

44

equipment should give customers that added feeling of security. But don't go overboard on gadgets right away. You're selling the *idea* of protection and peace of mind.

Emphasize your professionalism and your eagerness to fill the void of inefficient police departments. Contact people concentrated in an area you want to patrol, and sell them on your ability to save their lives before there's trouble.

WHAT IF YOU HAVE TO HANDLE EMERGENCIES?

Communications are the heart of the security patrol industry. Set up a precise phone system and office-client code numbers. Your relationship with the police will be of vital importance when you call in an emergency.

Judgment is important in your patrol staff. They will have to know when to call the cops in on a job—and when to alert the police that the danger has passed. Run a smooth, professional organization for client safety as well as confidence.

FEES VARY ACCORDING TO SERVICE

Contracts will vary. Will your service include drive-bys, or walking through the front gates? Across the country our researchers found big differences in client charges. Emergency responses, though, commonly run about $15 per response. False alarms are a hazard a good security service will have to cope with.

Residential and business clients should be on your list of sales prospects. Typically, homes of $150,000 and more in the exclusive neighborhoods will want more individualized attention to protect expensive property. That doesn't mean you should ignore the $85,000 to $125,000 homes. Smaller property owners need peace of mind for their property too: they will be in a worse position if somebody robs their home.

EXCITING AND LUCRATIVE, TOO!

The market is booming in security patrol services. A neighborhood patrol in your city can gross between $90,000 and $100,000 in the first year. This is because you are getting paid by your neighbors to do the police department's job—making people feel safe in their homes at night.

The field is wide open because only a handful of established security patrols are in operation around the country. Once established, the security patrol business has a long range factor of stability. Because of low overhead (no need for a high-rent office in this nuts-and-bolts operation), many three-man patrols have turned high gross sales into 25 to 31 percent net profits pretax.

Selling a broad range of services in a trustworthy fashion—then delivering on promises in emergency situations—is the main idea here. Established patrols rack up contracts in the $300,000 to $500,000 range. One operation we investigated has 4,000 homes on its patrol route.

Security patrol services see the needs of their community, and they fill them. And it pays off in big figures. After just two years in the patrol business, the operation we covered grosses a whopping $1.5 million a year!

Start-up Manual #159 is available on this business. See page 378.

New Idea

CLOSET DESIGN

If you're like most people, chances are your closets are a mess, filled with flotsam and jetsam collected over several years that don't seem to fit anywhere else in home or office.

An innovative Florida company called The Closet People has made a business out of this mess! They specialize in distinctive and functional closet interiors, custom-designed for individual needs.

Storage space is often doubled using shelving, drawers, baskets, and boxes as part of the designs. They transform an unkempt, poorly utilized closet into an organized system—where everything is easy to locate!

The Closet People also market a modular system consisting of separate components that a do-it-yourselfer can use to get organized. Their patented Closet Organizer can be put together piece by piece or all at once, in designs that will fit even the oddest size of closet or crawl space.

Here's a business idea that has plenty of room for expansion. All you need is premade closet components made of wood, clear acrylics or colorful plastics, in standard sizes. They can nest together, lock together like Tinkertoys, or be fastened with nuts and bolts.

Drawers, boxes, or even hanging baskets can be used in various sizes to organize everything from tiny closets to large office storerooms. And you can offer this service to homeowners, apartment dwellers or business offices, together with sorely needed help in getting organized.

Designed components similar to those available from The Closet People should sell well in hardware stores, do-it-yourself outlets, decorating shops, and department stores. For additional details write

to The Closet People, Dept. IEA, 2800 S.W. 28th Lane, Miami,
Florida 33133.

PAY-TV SERVICE

High net profit B/T:	$950,000
Average net profit B/T:	70,000
Minimum investment:	60,500
Average investment:	104,500

Now you can be a big wheel in show business with your own pay-
television system. You don't have to live in Hollywood or rub elbows
with the stars. We have found a way you can get into the business for
less than you'd spend to open a hardware store!

One established company grosses more than $3,600,000 per
month. Another landed 17,000 customers at $20 monthly in its first
two months. Typical net incomes pretax are in the 25 to 35 percent
range!

The video revolution is exploding with profit potential. Television pictures are bouncing off satellites, major movie companies are
creating new films just to be shown on pay TV, and even the singing
cowboy, Gene Autry, is producing a wide range of programs—from
sports events to adult entertainment.

The average American watches 18 hours of television a week.
The three major networks cash in on this addiction by selling prime-
time commercial spots for fees of up to $500,000 a minute. This
leads to lots of commercials and a lot of turned-off customers who
are willing to pay for first-rate commercial-free entertainment in their
homes. We found subscription fees ranging from $15 to $25 a
month; some companies even charge on a per-movie basis.

CASH IN WITHOUT DELAY

Of all the pay-television systems we investigated, the least costly
to set up, the most practical, and the most immediately profitable is
called Multi-Point Distribution Service or MDS. With MDS, you send
movies over a special microwave frequency to anyone living within a
25-mile radius. The trick is, only those who have rented a special
antenna from you can pick up the signal. With 1,000 subscribers at a
$25 monthly fee, your projected monthly gross is $25,000! Two
thousand subscribers at $25 a month will give you a yearly gross of
$600,000 from residential customers alone!

HOW THE SYSTEM WORKS

An MDS system has three components: transmitting antenna, program equipment, and home receiving antennas. Avoiding the technical jargon, this is what happens: You lease a videotape of a movie like *Jaws*. The tape runs through a series of amplifiers which convert the electronic impulses into superhigh frequency. The antennas at your customers' homes convert the signal to their home television sets—without commercials, and with fantastic broadcast quality.

Your programming company will make your role similar to that of a movie theater owner. But instead of being in a high-rent building with lots of seats, your theater is in everyone's living room.

The best programming features some of each of these: situation comedies, news/current events, family shows, movies, sports, children's programs, and educational shows. The key is a good programming mixture.

GET SUBSCRIBERS QUICKLY

You need to build a base of subscribers as quickly as possible to make this business profitable. Operators we talked to spent time developing a sales strategy combining direct mail with telephone follow-up.

To copy their approach you'll need a salesroom and a good system of solicitation. A good telephone salesperson can make 50 calls daily, or 300 a week.

LOCATION: FIRST YOU NEED A TOWER

Success in the pay-TV business depends on the right location in your market area. You'll have two sites: a tower and a control room-office.

We found leasing fees from $150 to $800 per month for a tower. This is negotiable, so drive the best bargain. Keep in mind that if you don't lease a tower you'll have to build one and go through more red tape with the FCC. So don't be afraid to pay for a good location: you'll make up for it in more business.

HOW TO ESTIMATE YOUR PROFITS

You will have to set monthly gross based on the number of subscribers you have, whether you run this business as a landlord and lease your system to other programming companies, or do your own programming.

If you rent programming for $120,000 per year and charge $200,000 for that programming, the $200,000 is deducted from the $500,000 you collect from 2,000 residential customers. On the other hand, if you simply lease your MDS system to outsiders, you have money coming in not only from your subscribers but from th. programming companies.

Along with entertainment programming, MDS operators are bringing in money from special sources. A department store chain recently leased time on an MDS system to meet once a week on the air with its employees, and paid $2,000 for the hour. It cost the MDS operator $200 in operating costs.

A TV repairman whose job was installing decoder boxes for other MDS companies built himself an MDS system and began running programs over it in 1974. Today he's a millionaire several times over. Now his eyes are on making more millions with satellite pictures. With an MDS system you can be tomorrow's self-made millionaire.

Start-up Manual #175 is available on this business. See page 378.

_____ **New Idea** _____

PET PORTRAITS

We've found an easy way to turn Americans' fondness for their pets into dollars for your pocket! Start a pet portrait service. One company is doing so much business it takes weeks for clients to get an appointment.

With this business you can start small and expand your operation as the money pours in. At the beginning, if you are handy with a camera, you can take the pictures yourself. If not, it's best to get an experienced photographer and/or salesperson.

The photographer can be paid a commission based on how many pictures the clients purchase. Find an experienced photographer willing to work at lower rates at local high schools and colleges.

One of the major selling points of this business is that the pictures are taken in the client's home. The pet is generally better behaved there, so it's easier to get quality photographs. (It also eliminates a major overhead expense for you.)

When you set rates, make sure you take film developing and processing costs into account. For instance, it costs about $9 to get an 8-by-10 inch color photograph developed. You can charge the customer $15. Throw in a frame and you can raise the fee to $25. Set a minimum order per sitting; $15 would be a fair amount.

FINANCIAL BROKER

High net profit B/T:	$100,000
Average net profit B/T:	40,000
Minimum investment:	3,000
Average investment:	6,500

If you enjoy day-to-day challenges for high stakes, have patience, and can work with an air of confidence that inspires others, you may be able to become a member of one of the most prestigious groups of entrepreneurs in the country—the financial brokers.

These powerful people average $65,000 annually in salary and net profit before taxes. Moreover, they operate by themselves, usually in professional office suites, without having to supervise employees and with very little overhead. They are able to keep almost every dollar they make.

Becoming a financial broker is an ideal way for an entrepreneur to break into the high-profit arena with very little invested capital. There are no barriers limiting your earnings. Assisting others in finding big money can bring you a large brokerage fee. There is hardly any business that requires less initial start-up capital or has a lower monthly overhead. Brokers our researchers interviewed had recently earned commissions of $2,000, $8,250, and up to $167,000 for a single loan arrangement!

A CASE STUDY

While our researchers were talking to one successful broker in his office, they listened when he received a call. He was being contacted by a client who was seeking a $9 million financial package to convert an apartment house complex into condominiums.

The broker knew of a local savings and loan that was interested in financing new projects but not interested in new construction. It had currently begun specializing in condominium conversions, and the broker told the prospective client to come to his office the next day to discuss the details.

A few days later, the broker revealed to us that the client had come by, laid out his plans and financial projections, and signed a full disclosure contract agreeing to pay the broker a ½ percent fee when the money was out of escrow and all conditions of the loan were met.

Only ½ percent? That figures out to $45,000! With some patience and hard work, later this year he will receive a bottle of Scotch from his client—and a check for the full $45,000 from the escrow officer at the local savings and loan office!

COMPLETE SERVICE IS THE KEY

Brokers provide complete financing services by working with their clients every step of the way. The broker prepares a detailed loan package and then tries to market the package to every appropriate funding source, helping the client determine what kind of financing he needs, how much, and when he will need the money.

Brokers can earn big fees by offering consulting services after the loan has been approved and the initial commission fee has been received. We interviewed more than one broker who cleared over $500 weekly by consulting with clients on a high hourly fee basis. Top-rank brokers can ask as much as $100 for one hour's worth of advice!

YOU DON'T HAVE TO BE AN EXPERT

You don't have to have both sales ability and financial knowledge to become a financial broker. You only need one or the other. Experience really counts in this business—once you get started preparing loan applications you begin to get a feel for the proper way to present a package to the lender.

By using the techniques used by experienced people in this field, you can screen out the unpromising borrowers and concentrate on the high-payoff applicants. Successful brokers claim they do very little "pitching" to develop clients. Most of their business comes from a referral system which they have developed during their practice.

HUGE LOAN MARKET

There are several million business loans made every year—by the 15,000 banks in the U.S. A random survey revealed that 340 banks made more than 230,000 loans during one week! By helping borrowers find the right lending source for their business you can hook up with this fantastic market and make huge commissions. Even the smallest loan earns a commission of 10 percent and most brokers demand a minimum flat fee of $750 for their services. As the size of the loan increases, so does the amount of the fee!

Start-up Manual #168 is available on this business. See page 378.

FAMILY HAIR SALON

High net profit B/T:	$273,000
Average net profit B/T:	126,000
Minimum investment:	31,000
Average investment:	57,000

Trends of the '70s—toward health, fitness, a more' informal life-style—sparked new consumer needs. One of the hottest business trends to emerge from these new directions in living is family hair centers. This newest concept in haircutting is raking in fantastic profits by making haircutting convenient, economical, and enjoyable. These centers let mom, dad, and the kids all get clipped at once without an appointment, and turn a handsome profit for the owners.

Women may be as style-conscious as they were in the '60s when teasing and beehives were the hair fashion fads, but they now want an easy-to-care-for style, and a more expedient way of getting it. Men too have become more style-conscious. Old-style barber-shops and beauty salons have made changes to adjust to these new trends, but they still don't meet the needs of a nation on the go. While unisex beauty salons are growing in popularity, they are expensive, and for the most part don't want to accommodate the kids.

A NEW MONEY MARKET

The most fantastic aspect of this new business is that *you don't have to be a barber or professional hairdresser* to cash in. The secret to high profits is good management coupled with a flair for promotion.

We discovered centers grossing from $500,000 to $600,000 annually. One outlet in Texas did $100,000 gross in just two months! Weekly grosses of $10,000 to $15,000 are the norm. All these centers reported pretax nets of 25 percent, with some operators netting 35 percent.

There are two major franchisors—Fantastic Sam's and Command Performance—opening outlets at the rate of one every five days. Even at this rate we predict the market won't be saturated until the late '90s.

THE MARKET FOR STYLE

The hairstyling industry is a $5 billion market with a steady 10

52

percent annual growth. Some 200 million Americans need haircuts, so the market is healthy. Most of today's hairdressing establishments have turned into full-service salons offering everything from hair coloring to manicures, foot massage, waxing, and makeup. Such salons charge higher prices for just haircutting ($30 compared to $14 at family hair salons), and it's hard to get an appointment. Add the cost of a baby-sitter.

Nationwide figures show that roughly 60 percent of customers at the all-purpose family centers are women between the ages of 18 and 44; about half of them are married and have children. These women are attracted to the concept because they can get their kids' hair cut while they are shampooed, cut, and blown-dry or set.

Most of these centers appeal to the middle-class suburban family with an income of $20,000 and up, who need to look good on a budget. In inflationary times everyone is looking for the best deal. With an average family bill of $35 (based on shampoos and styling for a family of four), it's a real bargain for the family, and a real source of profit for you.

LOCATE IN YOUR MARKET

Choosing a location will be one of the two most critical decisions you make. (The other will be deciding whom to hire.) It is absolutely necessary to locate in an area that has a large population of families in the $20,000 economic bracket. A mall or strip shopping center is your best bet. And be sure there is superhigh vehicle and foot traffic, high visibility, and good shopping boutiques.

Since the successful operations have a no-appointment policy so the whole family can come in, you must locate where there are stores that promote family shopping. You must also stay open longer hours than a regular barbershop or beauty salon.

LAYOUT AND DECOR

Since this is the barbering concept of the future, the choice of decor is crucial. Bold, bright colors that suggest contemporary moods are important. When planning your family haircutting salon, you will have to divide the space into four main areas: reception area, shampoo station, cutting stations, and employee areas and storage.

SHORTCUTS TO START-UPS

New equipment can cost you $10,000 to $30,000. Alternatives include leasing, used equipment, and auctions. Fortunately, because most of the stylists you hire will bring their own working implements, you will not need to equip them. Also, most successful operators are hiring sharp young stylists right out of professional barber and beauty schools. Not only do they work for less than more experienced operators, they can be more easily trained in the newer hairstyling techniques.

PRICING IS CRITICAL

The majority of your sales volume will come from your styling operations, so pricing is critical. We discovered styling prices ranging from $10 to $12 for men, $11 to $17 for women, and $4 to $7 for children. Although your prices may be lower than those at the high-priced salons, it's the volume which will make the difference. And don't overlook sales from hair-care products.

Going into this business can be the handle you've been looking for to achieve a business opportunity with shear profits.

Start-up Manual #170 is available on this business. See page 378.

FURNITURE RENTAL SERVICE

High net profit B/T:	$78,000+
Average net profit B/T:	45,000
Minimum investment:	45,000
Average investment:	65,000

The nation has gone crazy about renting! Everything from roller skates to jumbo jets, from bartenders to football fields, can be rented for an hour, a day, or a month.

In one month over 350,000 Americans furnished their apartments or homes with rented furniture. Owners of furniture rental stores are making chests full of money meeting the needs of today's mobile society. We found several established stores making $90,000 to $350,000 a year. One store owner started out in the '60s, when the furniture rental business was virtually nonexistent, with an investment of $40,000. Ten years later he sold his business for over $2 million! Now the stores are each grossing $550,000 annually, and the business is just beginning to finds its legs.

Over $300 million was spent on renting furniture in 1978, triple the amount spent in 1970. Figures are expected to exceed $1 billion by the mid-'80s. A phenomenal 20 percent growth rate per year is projected for the next five years. And with only 200 furniture rental companies operating in the U.S. this service business can be an open-and-shut case for profitability!

The reason is that more and more Americans are opting for easy living. This means having the flexibility to get up and go when changing jobs or locations without the hassle and responsibility of moving cumbersome furniture. Young professionals, students, and the increasing "singles" population can inexpensively rent furniture that reflects their life-style. And when they move—they can change their environment by starting all over.

WIDESPREAD MARKET

There is no typical renter of furniture. This is one of the attractions of the business—the market is so varied. Of course, there are certain characteristics common to rental customers. They are responsible persons who simply want freedom from being tied down by possessions. Or they may be forced to move often in order to satisfy job obligations. Corporate employees, athletes, and recently divorced people fit into these categories. Newlyweds, college students, and military and airline personnel are potential renters. They usually do not want to invest heavily in permanent furnishings until they get settled.

There is a prime market in apartment dwellers. National figures show that the annual turnover rate for apartments is 30 percent. And don't forget building owners and managers! Their profits are higher when they rent furnished units.

As many men as women rent furniture, and ages range from 20 to 75. Widowed people often rent after liquidating an estate. Annual income ranges from $15,000 to $35,000, with some exceptions.

Your profitability depends on factors that include location, inventory utilization, competition, capacity for growth, and initial investment. An investment of $55,000 to $75,000 will put you in the driver's seat of a furniture rental store in a good location with excellent profit potential. But you can shoestring it, as most of the industry biggies did when they began, for as little as $45,000. This would mean a minimum opening inventory—no more than 20 rental packages—and an inexpensive building of about 2,000 square feet. With careful management, you could turn this into a very profitable situation over the long term.

One advantage of this business is that there is no big rent requirement for a fancy mall or major storefront location. When people decide to rent furniture, they go right to the source—even if it's out of the way. Volume doesn't depend on heavy-foot-traffic or being able to attract impulse shoppers.

Start-up Manual #137 is available on this business. See page 379.

CONSULTING BUSINESS

High net profit B/T:	$115,000
Average net profit B/T:	45,000
Minimum investment:	600
Average investment:	3,500

Imagine making $600 per day giving advice to corporation presidents, small business owners or individuals. Sounds too good to be true? Well, thousands of people are paid as much as $100 an hour for their knowledge alone.

Although consulting has long been considered the business of retired diplomats or top corporate executives, the number of consultants in a wide variety of areas has mushroomed in recent years, making independent consulting one of the fastest-growing businesses nationwide.

GREAT NEED FOR THIS SERVICE

The need to call in an expert has never been greater than in the fast-paced business world today. Major corporations value an outsider's objectivity and fresh viewpoint when faced with complex problems. Medium-sized companies are turning to consultants paid by monthly retainer to provide help "as needed" instead of hiring costly staff. And smart small businessmen hire consultants for both reasons.

EASY TO CAPITALIZE ON THIS TREND

You don't have to be a business whiz kid to capitalize on this trend. The first step is a candid look at your experience and analysis of the salable features. You may have a background in business systems design, economics, marketing, personal finance, or party planning. We found successful consultants in all these areas.

Many people claim that they could never be consultants because they don't have enough experience, but almost everyone has some specialty that can be cashed in on. In fact, most people don't realize how much they really know, or don't understand how to sell knowledge as a product.

Our investigators found professional garage sale consultants who went into business after having their own successful sales. Two women in New York City run a thriving $50-an-hour consulting business rearranging furniture for clients' homes or offices to achieve a new look. Their experience? Rearranging furniture in their own homes over the years. These are classic examples of how you can turn an unusual skill or specialty into a thriving consulting business without an impressive string of degrees or years of training.

HIGH-PAYING BUSINESS

The effort is well worth the rewards. Research shows that most full-time consultants are grossing $300 to $600 per day. On the average 14 working days per month are billed to clients, so monthly gross revenue ranges from $4,000 to 8,400 for established, independent consultants.

Most of these consultants have been working hard for three or four more years. But a beginning consultant should be able to earn from $20,000 to $40,000 before tax and salary in the first year.

Experts predict that you can leave your regular job on a Friday, start a consulting business on Monday, and earn 70 percent of your current annual salary within five months working full time. It is possible to do even better than that.

START PART-TIME

We found many successful consultants who started on a part-time basis, and had one or more regular clients before taking the step to full-time practice. This approach gives you the opportunity to maintain a regular income while getting the business going. One marketing consultant we interviewed for this report serves only two clients and earns $300 per week working only 12 hours on evenings and weekends!

WORK AT HOME FIRST

You don't need a fancy office with high-class rent to get your consulting business off the ground, especially if you are starting out on a part-time basis. A spare bedroom, a basement, or a garage will do nicely. Because you are self-employed, there are certain tax advantages you can claim when you work at home. Rules have been toughened by the Internal Revenue Service, so ask a good accountant about deductions.

Start-up Manual #151 is available on this business. See page 378.

REALLY HELP THE HANDICAPPED

Dennis Cannon pulls in $250 a day plus expenses for his consulting fees—big bucks. But what's more impressive is that he's confined to a wheelchair. Cannon is the classic example of a man who has turned an adversity into an advantage. He is a design consultant for architects and he specializes in problems of the handicapped.

The federal government has passed a plethora of regulations that directly affect the building industry: long-needed laws that demand equal access to public buildings and transportation for the handicapped also created a business for Cannon.

Confined to a wheelchair all his life, Cannon is familiar with the problems of handicapped people. Often the answers are incredibly simple—a ramp, a hydraulic lift, a wider doorway.

But they're not simple to architectural and construction firms that wrestle with the problem. That's why they're willing to pay him $1,250 a week to work on their problems. He recently worked for two regional transport authorities, redesigning a fleet of over 200 buses.

If you're handicapped, there's no reason why that should stand in the way of your entrepreneurship. Draw on your own experience and make yourself available to your city's construction and architectural firms. You're likely to discover that they've been crying for someone like you.

If you're fortunate enough to be physically sound, find someone who isn't and offer to form a partnership; they can provide the knowhow and you can supply the leg power and "sell."

Breaking down barriers can be more than just satisfying; it can be profitable too!

FLAT-FEE REAL ESTATE COMPANY

High net profit B/T:	$108,000
Average net profit B/T:	40,000
Minimum investment:	12,000
Average investment:	25,000

There's a revolutionary new concept rocking the real estate world! The rug has been pulled out from under traditional realtors by a handful of real estate companies who accept a flat fee to help homeowners sell their own homes!

This form of do-it-yourself realty is the answer for millions of Americans who would like to sell their own homes, but shy away from the hassle of attempting it alone.

Now homeowners need no longer pay 6 percent or more in commission fees to a broker. They can turn instead to flat-fee real estate companies for assistance. By opening a flat-fee real estate company, you can tap into the red-hot $250 billion real estate market. You'll be solving a major consumer problem while making a pile of money.

Sellers are able to save on the commission fee, and thus are able to price their homes below the going rate.

BIG PROFITS

We have found a company in Houston with only three salespeople which is netting $108,000 a year before taxes, or from 30 to 35 percent, by pulling customers away from realtors who have been selling houses for years. Another Arizona firm nets $72,000. There are a handful of other successful companies throughout the country, but the market is still wide open.

We found a flat-fee office in Memphis, Tennessee with two people and a yearly gross income of $150,000! The owner told us that his gross profit margin is 54 percent after subtracting sales commissions and advertising. With careful organization, he manages a $50,000 to $55,000 net income, or about 35 percent pre-tax.

One beginning salesperson we interviewed works for a large Arizona firm. She brought in *20 listings* during her first few weeks in the field. At $400, the fee for each listing, she earned $8,000 for the company. With salespeople like this, the company is realizing gross annual figures of $240,000 for a five-person office. At over 30 per-cent net profit the firm was quickly in the black after only a few months.

GREAT NEW IDEA

These companies simply provide advice and paperwork services to homeowners selling their homes. For flat fees ranging from $175 to $1,000, several services are provided.

Basically, all the companies do is carry out the detail work of writing appraisals (telling the seller how much he should ask for his home), helping with negotiations, financing and closing details. Some of the companies provide the homeowner with "For Sale" signs and an effective advertisement to place in the newspapers.

The flat-fee real estate companies don't waste time driving pros-pects around or sitting at an open house. It's the homeowners who save commission money by carrying out the time-consuming job of showing off their own homes. This frees the salesmen's time so they can concentrate on what they do best—getting "listings," formal authorizations to sell a house.

LOTS OF REFERRAL BUSINESS

The ultimate goal of your operation is to have repeat customers and other prospects come to you by referral. This comes with good service and getting your name known as a respected professional.

You are there to help instruct a homeowner and make it easier for him to sell his own home. When homes sell quickly, eco-nomically, and efficiently, your flat-fee company's phones will keep ringing!

Start-up Manual #153 is available on this business. See page 378.

TELEPHONE-ANSWERING SERVICE

High net profit B/T:	$78,000
Average net profit B/T:	35,000
Minimum investment:	9,000
Average investment:	24,000

Imagine making $2.8 million a year just answering someone else's phone! Well, we found some people in Michigan doing just that. They opened a small two-person telephone answering service with $4,000 in cash and now have 14 offices serving about 6,000 cus-tomers!

Today's come-and-go life-styles coupled with the fast pace of personal and business decision making have made millions for several owners of the answering services we investigated to prepare this report. Services nationwide now take in over $400 million a year with no end in sight.

HUGE DEMAND

There are several reasons for this growth. One is increasing dependence on the telephone as a communication device. More and more important decisions are being made over the phone every minute of the day and night by corporations, small businesses, doctors, and others. Many businesses would be literally helpless without a telephone; staying in touch by phone can even mean the difference between life and death. The alternatives—lengthy meetings, letters, memoranda, and the like—are just too slow.

Even the recent development of electronic answering devices that hook up to a user's phone hasn't measurably slowed the growth of answering services. The most expensive of these machines can't guarantee that an important message will be left at the sound of the tone. Many people are so put off by these devices that they hang up immediately. And one lost call can mean thousands of dollars to an entrepreneur.

To many individuals, nothing replaces the personal touch of a friendly, professional telephone operator. And by signing up with an answering service, a customer's business or home phone is tied into a switchboard manned by such a person 24 hours a day!

The operator can pick up any home or office phone, answer as the customer wants, and take messages, so there's little possibility that crucial calls are missed. Messages are held until the customer calls to collect them—all done over the magic box we can't seem to do without. At many services the operators develop relationships with customers they may never meet personally, acting as distant "secretary."

BIG PROFITS TOO

Of course, not all answering service operations gross $2 million annually. It takes a chain of locations to do that. But the typical one-office operation, once established, will gross from $150,000 to $200,000 annually depending upon the number of switchboards in operation and the number of calls taken. Net profits reach 35 percent in well-run shops. The national average is 15 to 20 percent.

EASY TO GET STARTED

You can start out small as most answering services do and build volume to this level—or even higher—over a period of time. The largest one-office operation we found grossed $450,000 yearly. And two that were started at home in a garage and a spare room now gross over $150,000 yearly. Each of these was opened by one person using a ten-position, call director phone system and is now housed in fancy offices with four switchboards each.

Our research shows, however, that it is best to plan for this kind of expansion from the beginning. It is too expensive and time-consuming to have equipment moved once it is in place and operating. Some utility companies charge a penalty fee if an answering service relocates, so it is better to find a permanent location from the start.

By opening on a shoestring, you can start in a 200- or 300-square-foot location for about $7,500. This covers the cost of installing one switchboard and the trunk-line cable from the telephone company, as well as "bare bones" office furniture and supplies. But with this amount of start-up capital, you limit expansion and long-term profitability.

PROSPECTS BY THE THOUSANDS

Anyone with a telephone and a busy schedule is a good prospect, from busy families to busy businessmen who are always out of their offices. Your best prospects are doctors, salesmen, and other professionals, as well as repair service business owners like plumbers, electricians, and anyone else who relies heavily on the telephone to conduct his business. Focus on those who need 24-hour help because of "on call" status.

Start-up Manual #148 is available on this business. See page 378.

SECRETARIAL SERVICE

High net profit B/T:	$100,000
Average net profit B/T:	20,000
Minimum investment:	2,000
Average investment:	6,500

American businesses are drowning in a sea of paperwork. The cost of getting a letter out recently rose 16 percent in nine months. It's not surprising that many secretarial service firms are netting as much as $100,000 from the overflow work available.

Secretarial services reduce costly overhead. It costs the average business $7 for a one-page typed letter mailed by its own employees.

An outside service can do the job for only $2.50—half of that can be gross profit.

Big corporations, municipalities, and hospitals have enormous monthly dictation and transcription needs. They can cut payroll costs by contracting for this work with outside services on a regular or "as needed" basis.

One bright operator now has eight branch offices with more than 200 employees, and grosses more than $1.2 million per year. The firm has contracts with large hospitals for all their transcription work, and the owner nets more than $300,000 from his automated setup.

YOU CAN START SMALL

Most secretarial services start out small with a one-person office offering a variety of typing and bookkeeping services to general business clients. We found many individuals netting as much as $30,000 per year with a simple one-room office, desk, typewriter, and file space. A service sometimes operates out of a spare room, garage, or basement in private homes or apartments, but we have found that this limits profit potential.

THE MARKET NEEDS PERSONAL SERVICE LIKE THIS

Large corporations can afford typing pools and private secretaries, but most smaller businesses can't keep a full-time secretary busy enough to justify the added payroll costs. That's the market for a service like this. Customers typically pay from $7 and $15 per hour for that occasional letter or mailing. And a good location coupled with personal service is what will "erase" your competition.

Our research shows that most one-person secretarial firms will net a minimum of $12,000 their first year with little more than a Yellow Pages ad to attract customers. However, aggressive personal promotion, a speedy word processor, and two or three part-timers can build gross revenue up to $100,000!

Profits in this business depend on location, efficiency, and hustle. Some of the most profitable services we've seen offer dictation pickup and delivery, using part-time help.

SERVICES YOU SHOULD OFFER

Small operators begin by offering a variety of typing services: correspondence, manuscripts, editing, proofreading, reports, financial statements, dictation, transcription, file organization, and statistical typing. Some services offer to do research or special services for clients as well, but this time must be priced carefully so that it is profitable. Many smart owners offer résumé typing and preparation services.

If you or one of your employees has a special skill, like ability to do medical or legal typing, you can charge more for it. Be sure potential clients know the variety of services you offer. Some successful extras are translation services, bookkeeping and record keeping, file organizing and preparation, and engineering or scientific typing. Another excellent service is notary public work.

By stressing personal service, quality work, and fast response you can build a clientele that will come to depend upon you for very profitable secretarial services.

Start-up Manual #136 is available on this business. See page 378.

TEACHERS AGENCY

High net profit B/T:	$135,000
Average net profit B/T:	41,000
Minimum investment:	18,000
Average investment:	30,000

Less than a decade ago, the San Francisco Bay Area gave birth to an innovative educational concept—the free university. The prototype of a free university (or teachers agency) offered courses in exciting areas of education that are rarely included in university curricula: several hundred courses such as "Making Your Own Shoes," "Volkswagen Repair," and "Belly Dancing" appeared in the initial tabloid catalog of Heliotrope University.

David Marmon, the school's founder, established Heliotrope in a low-rent district, and provided the Bay Area with some of the most unusual, multidimensional education it had experienced.

Heliotrope grossed over $500,000 in one year, with close to 30 percent left over after all expenses (before executive salaries).

By strict definition, a free university is a place where people are learning without grades. Typically, no degrees are granted.

Originally free universities were run by students who were discouraged by the more traditional methods of learning. No tuition was charged; rather, students and faculty exchanged ideas—hence the term "free university."

Today free universities may be college-affiliated, or rural models, or independent universities in metropolitan areas. They are all supported by some form of tuition structure, and they show good profit potential: 25 to 30 percent net profit is common after a couple of years.

Since they are no longer free to the students, free universities are probably more aptly called teachers agencies.

HOW IT WORKS

Teachers work for preestablished salaries in the university system. They don't get a percentage of the school's take, no matter how popular their courses or overcrowded their classrooms may be.

The typical teachers agency presents a better idea! A student desiring a course such as "Astrology and Tarot Reading," for example, purchases a ticket from the agency. The ticket has the tuition price and the meeting location of the class. Instead of a fixed salary, the agency pays the professor half of the price of each ticket. Some teachers make more money moonlighting education from their homes than they do working for the university.

The classes are held wherever the teacher chooses, at his own expense—in his home, garage, or basement, or in a rented room.

THE FIRST STEP

Finding the right city for your teachers agency is the first step. It should have a population base of at least 100,000. A city with an existing university can be a good bet, since you have a solid source for teaching staff. However, if the university sponsors its own adult education program, locate in another part of town. Most of your faculty will be nonacademic experts in their fields anyway.

THE TEACHER PAYS YOU TOO!

You should have no trouble recruiting teachers. Many agencies report that they have an excess of teachers on their books. Experts, from marketing executives to plumbers, find the agencies an excellent means of supplementing regular income.

Aside from initiating a university, you are providing an employment service for out-of-work professors, part-time teachers, innovative instructors, and qualified experts and others with the urge and ability to educate and train.

Usually the instructor pays you $25 to $50 for his initial listing in your monthly catalog. The catalog will list the class with a 50-to-100-word description by the instructor.

Fees from 35 to 50 teachers should cover the printing cost of your first monthly catalog.

The fee also makes the instructor feel that he has an investment to recover. Besides writing a description, the professor is also charged with arranging the times and location of the class meetings. At all the teachers agencies we contacted, the professors make their own arrangements for classrooms. Many use their own homes; some rent utside space for their classes. One San Francisco teacher of disco dancing charges $20 for four classes, and has 80 to 105 students per class. Her cut—after the agency divides the profits—is between $800 and $1,050, which isn't bad money for teaching four one-hour classes a month.

MOST POPULAR CLASSES

After the first catalog printing, you will soon find out which classes pull high attendance. Ballet, Chinese cooking, group therapy, photography, film production, tennis, hiking, chess, sex therapy, yoga, guitar, and witchcraft have been among the winners.

Start-up Manual #89 is available on this business. See page 379.

New Idea
RENT A BEST-SELLER

With the price of hardcover books ranging from $10 to $15, one bookseller may have come up with a wise alternative for customers. Best-Seller is the name of the shop, and it rents popular books at 25 percent of the cover price.

This idea makes a great deal of sense, since most new books aren't out in paperback for at least a year after hardcover publication, and public libraries only get a few copies of each book.

Best-Seller carries 1,700 volumes directly from the *New York Times* best-seller list. By leasing the books, he is selling the same item over and over without having to replenish his inventory.

Of course, the product has a limited life span, but he only has to lease a book twice to cover his initial product cost and everything after that is gravy. When the book finally comes out in paperback, he can sell the hardcover at a low discount price and buy new best-sellers to rent again!

This idea will work in almost any city. Locating near a college campus or in a downtown area is best. We think a great idea is to locate next to a major bookstore chain. You may just blow them right out of the water and emerge as a real literary lion with this idea.

VINYL-REPAIRING SERVICE

High net profit B/T:	$60,000
Average net profit B/T:	25,000
Minimum investment:	800
Average investment:	4,000

We live in a plastic, vinyl, and naugahyde world, from the seats of our cars to the sofas in our living rooms. The restaurant seats you sit on and the bar stool you may be leaning against are vinyl. And until something better comes along, the automakers and the furniture industry will continue to churn out several million yards of plastic covering that sooner or later will be nicked, burned, cracked, or torn.

The vinyl repairman is there to color, mend, and patch up the damage. Several manufacturers sell vinyl repair kits and offer training. They show testimonials in their ads such as "I made $440 in just nine hours." We decided to see if there was any truth in their claims.

A call to a local car dealer led us to a vinyl repairman who had left a successful job in aerospace. He decided his degree in electrical engineering wasn't worth the parchment it was written on when he compared his beat-up Nash Rambler and three aerospace recessions to his neighbor's new Cadillac and job security. The neighbor, of course, was an experienced vinyl repairman. So our former engineer went to work for him and nine years later has parlayed his old Rambler into four specially equipped trucks that gross him an amazing $200,000 a year with a net before taxes of about $60,000.

We found several like this man across the nation, so his is not an isolated case. Note, though, that the majority of those who enter this business know how to do vinyl repair well enough, but have little if any basic business sense or training. That is why more business-minded people can enter the field and become whopping successes while most repairmen make meager livings or drop out altogether.

Vinyl repair is a service industry. If you can't approach and discuss a customer's problem intelligently and gain his confidence, you won't be very successful.

WHERE'S THE MARKET?

The majority of your business will come from three sources: auto dealers; restaurants, hotels, motels, and cocktail lounges; and furniture dealers. There's a lot of business to be obtained from homes and offices, but people in these markets do not know about vinyl repair. They are unaware that cuts and tears in their plastic upholstery can be mended to look like new, so they are likely to make do with adhesive tape until they can replace the upholstery entirely.

But vinyl can be undetectably repaired. To the average eye there remains no visual indication that a cut ever existed—provided the mending is done properly.

Auto dealers selling used cars are a lucrative source of income for the vinyl repairman. Not only do cuts and nicks in the seats and upholstery need repair, but vinyl landau tops are prone to weather damage and must be recolored as well as repaired.

It is not uncommon for a vinyl repair artist to walk into a car lot and come away with a thousand dollars' worth of business. Once you have established a good working relationship with a car dealer, he will be a steady customer who needs your services from once to four times per month.

Restaurants, hotels, motels, and cocktail lounges also need regular servicing. Along with the regular wear and tear their upholstery receives from constant hard use, in some areas outright vandalism occurs, creating more business for you.

Used office furniture dealers are another good source of business, though there aren't many dealers in most cities. These dealers buy up offices full of furniture from bankrupt, relocating, or redecorating companies and know that the smallest nick in a secretarial chair can reduce its resale value by 50 percent.

Furniture stores are a good source of retail customer business. Occasionally they have a piece damaged in their warehouse or showroom, and their customers call regularly for referrals to repairmen.

Municipal bus lines, taxi companies, school-bus companies, airlines, car rental agencies, bowling alleys, theaters, schools, colleges, auditoriums, landlords of furnished apartments, boat owners, and beauty shops are other prime prospects.

Start-up Manual #77 is available on this business. See page 379.

SEMINAR PROMOTING

High net profit B/T:	$100,000
Average net profit B/T:	20,000
Minimum investment:	1,100
Average investment:	13,200

The simple process of putting on seminars has become, in the last few years, one of the most profitable methods of selling information.

It is possible for the promoter of a two-day seminar to earn $20,000 net profit on an investment as low as $2,000. Some promoters put on only three or four seminars each year and take home net profits before taxes of $50,000 to $100,000.

THE REASON THEY ARE SUCCESSFUL

People want to get their information from the horse's mouth; and in addition, the seminar format offers a chance to ask questions afterward. This explains the popularity of the field. Although many of the experts who speak at seminars have already written all of their information in books, the public feels that to hear the words firsthand is more valuable.

For this privilege, attendees pay as little as $40 for a one-day or evening seminar to as much as $2,500 for a weeklong conference—plus their travel expenses. Fees vary with the market.

The rate for most one-day seminars ranges from $50 to $150. The majority of seminars are held for two days—to justify a higher fee and therefore generate more profit. We discovered $500 to $600 as average for two- to four-day seminars. We might point out that the words "workshop," "conference," "course," and "meeting" are synonymous with "seminar"; however, there are variations in the way the material is presented.

SUBJECT MATTER—UNLIMITED

The range of subjects covered in the seminars is extensive, from "Selling to Nigeria" to "How to Play the Stock Market." The subject matter is oriented toward those who wish to increase their education, technical skills, or ability to invest wisely.

Large corporations are the biggest subscribers to workshops. The well educated seem to be the most attuned to this service;

because of their earnings or positions, they are more able to pay the price or pass it on to their employees.

There are exceptions to the rule, of course. The famous mail-order salesman Joseph P. Cossman (author of *How I Made a Million Dollars in Mail Order*) has been holding seminars on "Mail-Order Ideas" a few times each year for the last decade or so and draws a wide cross-section of the public.

THE BIG ANGLE—FREE EXPERT SPEAKERS

The amazing thing is, you don't need to know anything about the subject! Suppose, for example, your subject is "Make a Million Dollars Weaving Baskets." Obviously there are many people who could be cited as experts at weaving baskets, from executives of basket-manufacturing companies to authors of books on the subject.

Such people will probably speak at your seminar absolutely free if they live nearby. And even if they must travel a great distance, they will still speak if you pay their expenses.

WHY WILL THEY SPEAK GRATIS?

The key to that statement lies in the ego. Most successful people have healthy self-images, and speaking at a public gathering gives them a giant boost. Many, too, such as authors and people with new ideas to push, are looking for publicity. And everyone likes the idea of his name appearing in your literature, in ads, and in publicity releases.

"The Conference on Conferences" in New York City (actually a "seminar on seminars") featured eight promoters who spoke about their experiences in staging seminars. A few were netting over $200,000 every year for their efforts. All claimed that they never paid their speakers—except expenses.

A recently built suburban hotel/motel can provide you with a meeting room capable of holding 100 people (your maximum expected audience), and will usually have a public-address system already installed.

The workbook that you present to each attendee at the beginning of the show is a simple loose-leaf affair with little detail. Only brief outlines of each speaker's presentation, and some extra pages for notes, are provided.

Expenditure of $12,000 is average for a low-investment seminar, but many preopening expenses have not been included. There are some successful promoters who begin planning five to six months in advance.

PROFIT PROJECTION AND BREAK-EVEN

If you charge $295 a head and fill the house with 100 attendees, you will gross $29,500 (less any discounts for cash and advance reservations). At these rates and with average expenses, your break-even point is 22 or 23 attendees.

Direct mail methods will be your most efficient marketing tool and choosing a direct mailing list is of prime importance. If you choose the names on your mailing list very carefully, have a salable subject, and the price is right, an educated guess is that you can expect much more than 1/10 of 1 percent return on your list alone. A few promoters with small lists have gotten returns as high as 5 percent, but 1 percent is generally considered a high return. It is realistic if the names on the list have been prequalified as highly interested in the subject and if the price is right. Experienced promoters, however, usually make more than one mailing to their list. Saturation-type marketing pays high dividends.

POTENTIAL UNLIMITED

On the other hand, if you've chosen a hot topic with speakers everyone is eager to hear and promoted it the best possible way at the right time, you may draw 400 to 500 people—for a profit of over $100,000. And it has happened!

If you keep advertising expenses down, have a free speaker, and generally cut corners, you can make a profit of $20,000 to $23,000.

Start-up Manual #71 is available on this business. See page 379.

DAY-CARE CENTER

High net profit B/T:	$112,000
Average net profit B/T:	60,000
Minimum investment:	35,000
Average investment:	65,000

There are 6.5 million working mothers with 9 million children under the age of six in the United States today, according to Census Bureau figures. Yet only 1.2 million spaces are available in day-care centers.

The crying need for more centers has been brought to the attention of legislators in practically every state. Many states and the federal government have allotted funds to subsidize low-income families who need baby-sitting services.

Middle-income mothers don't qualify for such subsidies, but they recognize the advantage of having their children in a center where structured learning and activity will help their offspring develop and serve to replace the individual attention the kids would receive if the mother was at home. They realize that the neighborhood lady who baby-sits is not qualified to give such attention.

Consequently, day-care centers in average neighborhoods usually operate at full capacity. But we are at the beginning of a capacity crunch.

In 1973, only 3.14 million babies were born—the lowest number since the early 1940s. In 1975, however, 4.3 million were born, exceeding even the postwar baby boom of the late forties.

Between 1980 and 1990 over 1 million women with children will enter the labor market. By 1990 only 25 percent of two-parent families will have one parent in the home. These factors will push the demand for day-care centers higher than ever.

DIVORCE RATE CLIMBING AT ASTOUNDING PACE

The number of divorces has been doubling every ten years nationwide. California has always headed the list of divorce statistics, running about 40 percent above the national average. But recently California broke all records with a 148 percent increase over the previous year. The national trend has always followed the Golden State's lead, which indicates we can expect a big jump in the national figures.

What this means in practical terms is that more mothers will be forced to work, or to move from part-time to full-time employment, generating a substantial increase in the need for preschool centers.

PRESCHOOL EDUCATION IS VERY IMPORTANT

Social researchers have learned that the most important years affecting the development of a child's intelligence are from age one to six. With structured teaching during this period, it is theorized, IQ can be increased; the ability to learn during the formal school years later may also increase.

In light of this research the concepts originally pioneered by the Montessori schools many years ago are now being applied to the larger, more modern day-care centers. Educated, aware young middle-income mothers groups are demanding this type of care for their children, even when the mothers are not forced to work. They simply realize that qualified teachers have the training necessary to provide maximum stimulation to the child's developing intelligence.

A FANTASTIC MARKET FOR DAY-CARE CENTERS?

Our conclusion is that an enormous market is opening for child-care centers which meet the criteria discussed. Yet few new ones are opening! The reason is economics—day-care centers don't

seem to be very profitable. And yet that statement should be q
ified.

The average-sized school with a capacity for 50 youngsters is a
typical low-profit enterprise, with the owner/operator usually netting
around $10,000 before taxes. But favorable economies of scale
come into play if you enlarge the operation. A school for 200 kids
can be expected to net over $100,000 before taxes. That is the kind
of figure we consider profitable, although the cash investment for
such a large school can exceed $100,000—depending on whether
you can find the right building and land in the right location.

Start-up Manual #58 is available on this business. See page 378.

FURNITURE-STRIPPING SERVICE

High net profit B/T:	$57,000
Average net profit B/T:	22,000
Minimum investment:	3,600
Average investment:	18,000

Buying, selling, and collecting antiques, always a popular hobby
among select groups, is now spreading to practically every corner of
the American scene. Antique dealers, ranging from small shops in
private homes to large commercial enterprises, enjoy an endless flow
of interested, well-heeled buyers as well as Johnny-come-lately collectors with limited budgets, seeking their first "piece."

Whenever a business is booming, a related service business is
usually born to feed from it. And so it is with the business of furniture
stripping. Furniture stripping is not new; people have been doing it
for years whenever they wanted to prepare an old piece of furniture
for refinishing. There have always been commercial furniture-
refinishing shops. But specialty houses that strip furniture as a consumer service, are relatively new.

Strippers specialize in removing the old, many-layered finishes
from old furniture. The general public seeks out this service because
it:

1. Saves hours, sometimes days, of hard, sweat-inducing work;
2. Allows do-it-yourselfers to tackle the pleasanter aspects of refinishing jobs while avoiding the hard part; and
3. Eliminates the possibility of ruining a precious piece of old furniture by employing improper stripping methods.

Antique shop owners and others in similar businesses employ the services of furniture stripping outfits so they won't have to maintain refinishing facilities on their own premises.

People are willing to pay $7 and up to have a straight chair stripped (a task which will take a professional about 15 minutes), or from $150 to $200 for an entire dining set of table and six chairs. These fancy fees are charged for stripping jobs which require a minimum of time for the professional.

HOW IS THE PROFIT PICTURE?

Besides lush profits, another factor makes this business interesting to the person with little cash to invest. You can start in your own home, if you have a garage or basement in which to work. But note this limits your profit potential and should be very temporary.

One-person operations, using occasional part-time help for pickup and delivery, are doing amazingly well. A volume of 25 to 30 jobs a month is common after the first few months of promotion and operation, and grosses range from $1,500 to $3,000 per month! Older shops, with one or two full-time employees, quoted gross figures of $5,000 to $7,000 monthly—and they'd all been in business less than two years.

Net profits vary, but most strippers have estimated that 50 percent is adequate to cover overhead, materials, and all operating costs. The profit margin is related to volume because overhead is virtually fixed. Owner/operators are selling a service, and have low materials costs. Thus a successful shop grossing $7,000 a month will net about $3,000 for an owner/operator with two employees.

Start-up Manual #52 is available on this business. See page 378.

New Idea

YOU CALL, WE HAUL

What do a corporate executive, a busy housewife, and a nursing home have in common? They all use the services of We Drive, Inc. an unusual business run by Linda Wise of Houston.

We Drive provides chauffeurs who drive the client's car. An oil company uses the service to chauffeur executives to and from work; a housewife needed someone to drive her underage son on a date; a nursing home uses drivers to take patients to church. Half the business comes from businesses, 25 percent of which use the service for airport trips.

The charge for in-town driving is $6 an hour with a two-hour minimum. There's a flat rate for out-of-town trips and airport runs— an average of $15 one way, depending on the distance.

Wise uses a city map to keep track of the whereabouts of 75 to 100 drivers who take their own cars to a client's location and then drive the customer's car from there. Since the business is run from Wise's home, the only expenses are for advertising, salaries, and insurance.

This is a business that can work in any area with a good-sized population, particularly if there's a busy airport. Clients have to pay the expense of gas and depreciation. Overhead stays low because there's no fleet to buy, insure, and fuel. Hire accident-free drivers and test them in your own vehicle before turning them loose in someone else's. Check local regulations to see if a chauffeur's license is necessary, and be sure to consult an insurance agent.

CARPET-CLEANING SERVICE

High net profit B/T:	$100,000
Average net profit B/T:	32,000
Minimum investment:	7,000
Average investment:	22,000

One of the hottest small-investment businesses today is carpet and upholstery cleaning on location. A Department of Commerce bulletin indicates that in the last 20 years these cleaning services jumped from $10 million to $90 million in annual sales. The predictions are that they will grow to $150 million within a few years!

Your first reaction may be to pick up the telephone directory and check the Yellow Pages to see what kind of local competition you will have to deal with. Fine—do it! That's a good place to start when considering any new business venture.

But if you do, you may find yourself reeling back in disbelief. If you live in a metropolitan area you will, no doubt, find many pages of carpet cleaners listed. Even a small city may have more than a page.

Does this mean the field is overcrowded? Yes and no! The carpet-cleaning business is large, but a high percentage of the crowd consists of jackleg operators who run around on a part-time basis picking up whatever business they can, giving little thought to repeat business or to the quality of service they provide. Remember, any-one can get a listing and buy ad space in the Yellow Pages if he can pay the going rate for a business phone. Anyone can contract for rug-cleaning jobs. Then, once he has a few lined up, he can go out and buy an over-the-counter rug-cleaning detergent and run a few doors down the street to rent a shampoo machine. This is a businessman?

The difference between this type of operation and your professional rug-cleaning business is, of course, that you will enter the field in a businesslike manner, knowing what you are doing, with your own equipment and cleaning solutions that have been manufactured for the professional! And friends, that makes all the difference in the world to your clients!

"QUALITY OF SERVICE IS LOUSY," SAY MOST CUSTOMERS

We interviewed ten housewives who had recent experiences with rug-cleaning services in their homes. Here are a few of their comments:

"They told me we could walk on our carpets in three hours. It took four days for them to dry out enough not to feel wet to the bare foot."

"When our carpeting dried out, I could pick dirt out of it with my fingers."

"I hired my carpet cleaner this time, although I have cleaned the carpet myself in the past. I wanted to get a better, more professional job. Now that it's done, it doesn't look any better than when I did it myself!"

"The man who sold me the service was very businesslike in his talk, appearance, and dress. But when the guy who did the work came, he acted like he didn't have a brain in his head. He caused more mess than he did good."

Comments like these indicate that there is a crying need for *good* carpet cleaning on location. If you can meet the needs and desires of your customers, you'll get as much business as you can handle!

GROSS $12 TO $15 PER HOUR!

If netting $7 to $10 an hour on an employee's time (at $5 per hour) sounds attractive to you, and you have some time to spend setting the thing up and getting your work force trained to do the job on their own, carpet cleaning can be the ideal business for you. There is money to be made here—lots of it, for the enthusiastic, customer service-conscious small businessperson.

WHY THIS BUSINESS IS ON THE RISE

Twenty-five to 30 years back, decorating emphasis was on hardwood floors for homes, and tile flooring at commercial locations.

Today, however, you're likely to find wall-to-wall carpeting in every room in the house, even the bath and kitchen. Business establishments carpet everything but the walls—and a few way-out decorators have even tried that!

To remove wall-to-wall carpeting for cleaning is impractical. Even if you could do it economically, it wouldn't be the same size and fit when you went to lay it down again. So a new industry has been born—the in-home carpet-cleaning business. In the industry it is called on-location cleaning. Manufacturers have been quick to recognize the market for machinery that can do the job, and they are available to help the beginner get into this lucrative business.

CAN MONEY BE MADE?

The going rate for cleaning a square foot of carpet varies from city to city, depending on population density and whether you are serving the upper crust or just average families. But some of the big franchisors suggest 15 cents per square foot. Cleaning 300 square feet of carpet properly takes one person about one hour, and you can charge $45. The cost of materials is about $2, and you will pay your worker about $5 an hour—including travel and set-up time between jobs. Thus, when the 300-square-foot job is completed, you will have netted $28! And remember, with properly trained personnel you don't even have to spend time supervising the job!

If every serviceperson you hire can be kept busy, and could complete a minimum of one hour work for every three hours of pay (allowing for travel and setup time between jobs), you can make at least $84 per worker every day! The on-location cleaner who is sharp enough to keep ten people busy can, in a short time, show a gross profit of $840 per day!

THE KEY TO SUCCESS

We found the average operator in this field was doing 5.4 jobs per week, and grossing an average of $563. We did not find any who were absentee owners, although there probably are some. This is the kind of business that is difficult to operate on a small scale with a hired manager. Most of those we surveyed operated from their homes, and spent less than $100 per week on advertising.

By choice, we surveyed only those who had been in business from six months to two years. Most seemed to understand little about promoting their business. This leads us to believe that anyone with a strong promotional sense can build a very profitable business in carpet cleaning. The successful operators were averaging 10 to 15 jobs per week.

We found several people who had been in the business for less than one year and were grossing an average of $750 to $900 and as much as $1,500 to $2,000 per week! The difference between these successes and more average operators lies in two things: (1) the quality of their workmanship and technique in handling customers brought a higher number of referrals per job; (2) none of these successful operators had been afraid to plow profits back into advertising from the beginning. All those in the successful group were spending between 20 and 30 percent of their gross on advertising and promotion.

Obviously this lowered their percentage of net profit. But the tremendous growth rate clearly compensated for this. Some owners had reached the point where they were executives only, supervising their business from a desk and handling only estimating and scheduling of jobs.

Start-up Manual #53 is available on this business. See page 378.

_____New Idea_____

BIKE SURGEON

Remember when doctors made house calls? One in Toronto still does. He's a bike doctor, and he's making the kind of dough that could put him in the same tax bracket as regular M.D.s.

John Calladine is the "chief of staff" who supervises eight bike doctors who make house calls. With the gas shortage and the emphasis on healthy sports, Calladine finds he has more patients than he can handle. He offers a $10 preventive overhaul for bicyclists who are interested in stopping problems before they start.

Calladine says his main expense is a dispatcher. This enables him to charge clients about half the going rate for bicycle repairs, plus saving customers the trouble of taking the bike into a shop.

This 21-year-old entrepreneur is pulling in about $1,500 a week. His staff keeps $6.75 from a $10 overhaul. Members, Calladine says, make about $100 a week for 12 hours work.

This is an easy idea to copy in any major urban area. Getting staffers should be no problem. Try advertising in college newspapers for students who want to pick up extra bucks. Advertise in local newspapers and put up notices on grocery store bulletin boards. You might just become a bike tycoon!

EMPLOYMENT AGENCY

High net profit B/T:	$50,000
Average net profit B/T:	30,000
Minimum investment:	20,000
Average investment:	33,000

How would you like to go into a business that can reach the six-figure income level in the first year or two? Furthermore, there's no stock to buy for resale and no sales tax to worry about, because you're selling a service.

If you like prestige, the employment agency business has got it. When customers leave your office after you've performed your services, they are impressed by your business because you provided them the means to earn a living! Not many businesses enjoy this kind of public stature and still show tall profits.

At one time or another everyone has to hunt for a job. Locating the right position to fit individual qualifications and desires is not easy, but there are many ways to search for employment—some of which are far more productive and expeditious than others.

The most effective way for the job seeker to find the exact position he desires at a salary commensurate with his qualifications is to secure the services of a private employment agency. The owner of such an agency is handsomely rewarded for the services provided— the profits are high, the cost of entering the field is relatively low, and a supply of experienced help is easily and consistently available.

A DEFINITE NEED FOR AGENCY SERVICES

The days are rapidly disappearing when the well-qualified worker seeking a new position could find a satisfactory new situation without help. True, newspapers will always carry Help Wanted ads, but in today's employment market the company seeking a worker through such advertising must be prepared for an enormous response. Some recently queried companies have received 200 to 300 responses to a single job opening in the Help Wanted columns. Such a response was highly unusual as recently as five years ago. The companies also felt that the caliber of applicants has dropped significantly. As many as 85 percent do not even come close to meeting advertised qualifications.

Processing large numbers of applicants to determine who qualifies is costly and time-consuming for employers. Obtaining the services of a private employment agency to handle the details can be advantageous to an employer in terms of time and money.

From the applicants' viewpoint, advantages to working with the help of an agency include being relieved of the task of investigating every colorfully worded ad found in the newspapers and thereby saving transportation costs and endless hours. Of course, applicants can and frequently do apply at state-operated employment offices where services are provided free to both employer and applicant. This approach has advantages for certain workers, but it is limited when compared to the range of individualized services offered by a privately owned employment agency.

INVESTMENT

The investment required to open a brand-new agency, as opposed to buying an existing one, is relatively low. The most important thing is to create a good public image through the quality and location of the offices. Applicants coming in to register may be doubtful of the agency's abilities and professional standards if they find dreary offices in an old building, furnished with odd pieces of worn equipment. We found that the offices doing the greatest volume looked very professional, with an attractive, well-furnished waiting room and comfortably equipped adjoining counseling rooms, at least 10 by 12 feet, with provisions for privacy.

While many private employment agencies are located in the midst of questionable business surroundings—some prefer the fast-traffic areas around shopping centers—the most successful are located in a professional atmosphere, in buildings that house doctors, lawyers, investment counselors, and insurance agents. This gives an immediate impression of professionalism—a highly desirable image.

Through the years private agencies have suffered the same problems as many other semiprofessional services in trying to achieve professional recognition from the general public. Before state licensing and supervision began (now applicable in nearly every state), there were many fast-buck operators in the employment business. Ethics were practically nonexistent: applicants could be overcharged, billed for placement fees when no fee was due, or knowingly placed in positions unsuited to their qualifications. The resulting bad name given to the industry has taken years to overcome, but it has been overcome thanks to the efforts of agency owners who saw the need and formed a national association to improve their image.

PROFIT POTENTIAL

There are an estimated 11,000 private employment agencies in this country. About 2,500 of the more progressive agencies have formed the National Association of Personnel Consultants, a Washington, D.C., organization in favor of strong collective representation with government regulating agencies and aware of the benefits obtainable through group-sponsored public relations efforts.

A recent survey sponsored by the NAPC indicated that in one year private employment agencies placed 4,120,056 job seekers in new jobs. An average of 374 applicants were placed by each agency. Many agencies—whether one-person operations or well-staffed, efficiently operated nationwide agencies—are asking up to 60 percent of the applicant's first month's salary.

The success of your own operation will depend on the caliber of the placement counselors you hire, the experience and abilities of your manager, and other factors such as local and national economic and employment conditions. Thus it is difficult to project a gross income figure for a new private agency. But we can tell you that not a few established agencies, with their first year behind them, and functioning with the facilities our plan outlines, are topping $100,000 a year gross!

Start-up Manual #51 is available on this business. See page 378.

JANITORIAL SERVICE

High net profit B/T:	$65,000
Average net profit B/T:	22,000
Minimum investment:	1,500
Average investment:	2,500

Society has classed the janitor on the low end of the professional totem pole. Janitors—or "maintenance personnel," as they prefer to be called—are still on the low end of the income ladder, drawing from minimum wage up to $4 per hour for their services. In some cities, of course, the unions have changed that, with wages running from $5 up to as high as $7 per hour.

In contrast, the building maintenance industry itself is not on the bottom of the income pile. It is a multibillion-dollar industry.

There are only 10,000 building maintenance contractors in the United States; the average gross per contractor was $200,000. A properly run operation should net about 20 percent before taxes, plus a decent salary for the owner/operator.

For example, take a typical glass-clad, 40-story high-rise office building. This structure may require the services of 80 full-time employees just to keep the floors and windows clean, trash cans and ashtrays emptied, furniture dusted, and bathrooms spotless. The cost for these services may exceed $1 million per year.

In 1950 the industry grossed only $92 million. But the tremendous growth of the last 30 years has made multimillionaires out of men who started with only a mop bucket and a vacuum cleaner as their investment.

GREAT GROWTH RATE!

The Building Service Contractors Association predicts that the industry will continue to grow at the rate of 15 percent per year, which will create openings for many new entrepreneurs.

Also, a person can still start out with as few tools and as little money as anyone 20 years ago. May we offer a word of warning, however: Over 50 percent either quit or fail during the first year of operation!

The reason for failure is the quality of service offered. Ask any businessperson who has an office or store. They will usually tell you that they have contracted for maintenance with many janitorial services only to discover that they must hire two or three before finding one that is reliable and does acceptable work.

Generally, this is not because the workmen do poor work, but because they are given a limited time in which to get their job done.

MOST OPERATORS ARE INCOMPETENT BUSINESSMEN!

This conclusion points to the business incompetence of the owner. Most operators attempt to secure jobs based on price. In other words, they do not sell quality.

We interviewed a prospective contractor and showed him through the offices, pointing out what we wished to have done and how often. The contractor then sat down, figured for a few minutes, and announced: "That will cost X dollars per month!"

Is it any wonder that less than 10 percent of these contractors survive for five years! They would probably have difficulty selling dollar bills for 75 cents too!

All of them seem afraid to talk about what they are going to offer the customer for his money.

GOOD SALES PITCH

Essentially, all a janitorial service sells is labor. A successful contractor explained and demonstrated the sales approach in this manner: "I can do a speedy cleanup job that will look fairly good if you do not inspect it too closely. The monthly cost for a once-per-week service will be $75. Or I can do a really thorough job that could pass your white-glove inspection, for $125 per month. Some people are not as concerned with the appearance of their property as others, but I prefer to do a thorough job that I can be proud of. Which service would you prefer?"

Before making his closing pitch concerning prices, he spent several minutes inspecting every nook and cranny, walls, floors, windows, and bathrooms. He then pointed out a windowsill where the paint was cracked and chipped. He stated that it would be impossible to clean the sill thoroughly because the cracks in the paint would trap the dirt and water.

He also took out a piece of steel wool and a bottle of chemical from his pocket and scrubbed a small spot on the tile floor of a hallway.

After scrubbing the spot vigorously, he explained that several coats of wax had been applied over a dirty floor. In order for the floor to look clean, it would have to be stripped before new wax was applied.

NOT AFRAID TO ASK FOR MONEY

"In order to get the office in proper shape," he said, "we will have to spend considerable time on our first visit. There will be an additional charge of $45 for this, but after that there will not be any additional charges and you will have a bright, clean office."

Analysis of his sales pitch reveals these key points. First, by showing concern about details, he emphasized his conscientiousness. When he said he would do a thorough job, it was believable because of his thoroughness in explaining the maintenance problems. Second, by offering to do a speedy cleanup each week at a low price, he indirectly indicated the kind of service the business person could expect from low bidders, and thereby removed them from competition.

Start-up Manual #34 is available on this business. See page 378.

PET HOTEL AND GROOMING SERVICE

High net profit B/T:	$75,000
Average net profit B/T:	25,000
Minimum investment:	3,600
Average investment:	72,000

Reservations for animal boarding facilities can be as difficult to obtain as hotel reservations. In researching this report before a major holiday, we had to call six establishments before finding one that would accept a pet. Five dollars per day was the rate for a German shepherd. For a toy poodle the price was $3.50.

Since our dog was beginning to take on a shaggy appearance and hadn't had a bath in a month, we asked that it be bathed and clipped—"groomed," in the trade parlance. That added $15 to the bill. For a typical weekend stay, Saturday and Sunday night, the bill was $30 for a large dog.

The hotel's cost per day to feed a dog is approximately 50 cents. It takes a good groomer less than one hour to bathe and clip a dog. The groomer usually gets a commission of half the grooming fee, making $7.50 per job.

Thus the expenses for the dog's visit probably do not add up to more than $9. That leaves a gross profit of 70 percent on the $30 bill.

$1,300 GROSS PROFIT FOR THE WEEK

In an interview with the establishment's sole employee, the dog and cat groomer, he disclosed that the gross for a holiday week, which started on Monday and ended on Sunday, came to $1,674. This included 31 dogs that were brought in for grooming only.

JUST AN AVERAGE OPERATION

The groomer pointed out that holiday weeks usually run about double the normal volume. A gross of $800 was considered an average week for this operation. Since it had only been in business for eight months, we were unable to establish annual figures. After investigating several other operations across the country, we concluded that the one we were checking was grossing slightly above average.

We came across services that were grossing close to $100,000 annually; some, over $200,000. The average "good" operation grossed between $50,000 and $60,000. Many small operators admitted to only $20,000 annually. We say "admitted" because much of the business is on a cash basis and is not always deposited or reported.

Cashwise this is an easy business to get into. Thirty-six hundred dollars is minimum, but an investment of $72,000 is needed in order to start a well-equipped facility with management planned for and an absentee owner.

MOST SERVICES HAVE POOR FACILITIES

Our investigators, all pet owners, have come to the conclusion that the adjective "dumpy" fits most of the facilities we viewed. We are sure that many animal owners who occasionally board their dogs or cats feel the same way, and that this is hurting the business in general.

The operations grossing the most money offered the cleanest, best-kept buildings. We saw some high-class operations in Chicago, New York, and Los Angeles, located in exclusive neighborhoods, which we would describe as "super plush." Of course, their rates are four to six times as high as the average.

A clean, well-kept facility is the first criterion for success in this business, as your prime responsibility is to keep the pets healthy.

Start-up Manual #33 is available on this business. See page 378.

PARKING LOT STRIPING SERVICE

High net profit B/T:	$50,000
Average net profit B/T:	25,000
Minimum investment:	600
Average investment:	1,200

There are few legitimate, proved businesses you can start with little cash and no special talents, and yet grow into something stable and permanent.

Parking lot maintenance is one of them—a business you can start with about $600, on a part-time basis, and build up to an annual profit of $25,000 or more.

Unfortunately, it doesn't lend itself to full absentee owner operation at the beginning. But it is not complicated to set up.

Parking lot striping is the way to enter the business. We have several histories of operators beginning at this end of the business and eventually becoming full-fledged paving contractors, handling lucrative new-construction contracts.

Most businesses of any size have parking lots. Depending on climate and usage, these lots must be restriped from once every five years to once a year. Eighteen months is the average interval.

The average restriping contract exceeds $200, with a gross profit margin of over 65 percent. The price for striping alone would be about one-half as much, but other things will need attention, such as resealing asphalt and filling holes. Also, numbers, names, and parking instructions will need repainting.

All this work is simple: anyone of average intelligence can become proficient literally overnight.

UNLIMITED MARKET

Your market is not limited to retail business parking lots. Factories, schools, apartment buildings, motels, airports, churches— anywhere cars are parked off-street—may require your services.

Some small towns, for example, do not own striping equipment of their own, but contract out the painting of traffic safety lines on streets.

Large shopping centers may have parking spaces for 2,000 to 5,000 cars; a striping and repair contract may run above $10,000. Usually the job goes to the lowest bidder—and that could easily be you.

The aisles of factories and warehouses are often striped. In fact, OSHA safety laws require striping around machines, conveyors, and the like. Tennis courts are another lucrative field calling for lining, as are fields for baseball, basketball, handball, etc.

WEATHER AND TIRES QUICKLY WEAR OUT STRIPING

As you drive around, you will be amazed at the number of off-street parking lots; yet, checking the Yellow Pages in cities across the country with populations from 200,000 to 300,000, we seldom found more than one or two contractors listed. And in half the cases they were paving contractors.

Asking the price of restriping only for a 50-car parking lot, we were quoted some outrageously high prices. It was obvious that most contractors were not interested in such a small job.

LOTS OF ROOM FOR THE LITTLE GUY!

In interviews with over a dozen contractors, we found the reason for this attitude. Most contractors were concerned with obtaining new parking lot contracts, including engineering, paving, striping, bumpers, and marking. Their overhead was so high that small jobs were not worthwhile.

The market is wide open to a newcomer who is willing to make personal calls on prospective customers. You will find little or no competition for the small jobs, and due to your low overhead you can usually be the low bidder on large striping jobs.

CASE HISTORY NUMBER ONE

We found a man who started in the winter removing snow from merchants' parking lots. At the end of the winter, he realized he could stay in business year-round by repairing and restriping the lots.

As starting equipment he bought a small eight-horsepower tractor with a snow-thrower attachment for $1,250, making a $300 down payment. He used the money from contracts made during the summer repairing and striping parking lots to build up an equipment inventory of three large tractors for use in winter; his *new* income was $23,500 the next year.

FIRST JOB—HIS EMPLOYER!

Another operator began by obtaining his first restriping contract from the factory which employed him. He bought the striping machine on a Friday, completed the job on Saturday, and earned enough to pay for the machine before his down payment had time to clear the bank.

Every evening after work he drove around the city looking for lots in need of repair and estimated the cost of the work to be done. The next day, during his lunch hour and coffee breaks, he phoned the owners of the lots. The work he obtained was done on weekends and evenings when the lots were not in use. On the first job he taught a teenage neighbor boy how to handle the striper, and eventually instructed him in all other phases of application and surface repair.

Within 30 days the owner was averaging two or three jobs per week, which gave him the confidence to quit his job and go into business full time. After two years, he employs four men full-time and operates two trucks every day.

Start-up Manual #31 is available on this business. See page 378.

Start-up Manual #31 is available on this business. See page 378.

_____New Idea_____

STATUE REPAIR

Finding a need and filling it is what business is all about. Consider for a moment how many garden statues there are in your town. After a few years the paint peels, chips and cracks appear, and weathering really shows. Unable to find aid for her own ailing statuary, a Texas woman began Statues Alive to restore indoor and outdoor statues.

Jeannine Williams will tackle any kind of statue: plaster, cement, bronze, lead, china, or marble. She cleans and repairs statues, using plastic cement to sculpt new parts. Then they're painted and weatherproofed. In the past two years she has restored over 130 statues for individuals and organizations.

There's not a town in the country that doesn't have businesses and people who decorate with statues. Some are historical items, relics from days when garden ornaments were popular. Besides statues of gatekeepers, Greek gods, and animals, there are thousands of birdbaths waiting to be refeathered. Dirty, peeling statues will sell the service, since attractiveness is the reason for their existence.

Ms. Williams experimented for a year on her own collection before she opened for business. If you don't want to wait for the trial-and-error method, contact local art schools, tradesmen, and suppliers for information on best methods of repair. Tradespeople are listed in the Yellow Pages under their specific field, such as "Marble" or "Enamel/porcelain."

Advertise in newspapers, and be sure to tell garden clubs, historical societies, and the specialists who can spread the word. Work out of the backyard to keep overhead low. Get an apron and some tools, and you can sculpt yourself a profitable and fulfilling business.

RENT-A-PLANT

High net profit B/T:	$48,000
Average net profit B/T:	30,000
Minimum investment:	1,000
Average investment:	9,000

The overwhelming fad for green plants in homes, offices, and businesses has created a new area of services—caring for these plants. The fad is now a full-fledged trend paralleling the "back to nature" and "back to the good old days" trend for antiques in design, furniture, clothing, camping, and natural homemade and homegrown foods.

Experts who study buying trends expect this cycle to continue indefinitely. The projected growth of high-density living quarters, such as apartments and condominiums, is a major factor.

Businesses, as well as individuals, are responding to the tremendous demand for plants. This is especially true of businesses such as restaurants and banks, where appearance is vital to attracting customers; but company offices are also following the trend and decorating with greenery.

Suppose you own a dark, cozy dinner restaurant. To be "in style" you must add lots of green plants. Who will be responsible for caring for these plants—the hostess, the chef, the headwaiter? Probably none of them knows a fern from a philodendron!

Besides, one of the major requirements for the livelihood of a plant is natural light. That means it won't be long before your dark cozy restaurant is full of dead and drooping plants.

If you assign an amateur the task of caring for your plants (even if you have sufficient light) you're probably going to have trouble. Every plant has different light, watering, and food requirements.

In addition, to get optimum decorative effects, designers and architects may pick poor locations for particular plants. Sooner or later, the plants will get sick.

THE ANSWER TO THIS . . .

There is an answer to all of these problems, though—professional care. No businessman is going to let a carpenter try to repair his computer or cash register. Plants are expensive, especially the large ones demanded by business for the best visual effect. A Boston fern with a three-foot spread sells for about $25 plus the cost of the pot and hanging paraphernalia. A five-foot-high palm (a favorite for foyers) sells for up to $250.

A restaurant may have as many as 40 or 50 expensive plants—a sizable investment that must be cared for regularly. A bank with the usual high ceilings may have 12 to 15 very large plants.

For the most part, the employees or owners of the business service the plants, often with poor results. They rely on advice from the shop where the plants were purchased, advice which is usually insufficient because it is difficult for the plant-shop owner to prescribe at a distance. So many businesses conclude the nuisance is not worth the decorative value.

Some larger plant shops have realized that extra income can be generated with a plant service department. We interviewed eight shop owners offering this service; two of them have two full-time service people each, who are booked eight hours a day.

Across the country we found dozens of "plant doctors" and service people who did not own or have any association with plant shops, though several did have small greenhouses next to their homes. Three had what we considered an ideal business situation, with a low investment. One establishment, only a year old, was netting over $3,000 per month before taxes—and it was run by one person.

THE IDEAL SETUP

One operator concentrated her efforts in a high-income community, charging a monthly service fee to wealthy homeowners and apartment dwellers for weekly plant maintenance.

On the outskirts of this community were many dinner restaurants to which she leased or rented plants on a service contract basis. Also, within and near this community were several office complexes. Many of the companies in these complexes leased plants from her. Three banks and four savings and loan companies either leased plants from her or contracted her weekly service.

Another entrepreneur did none of the plant maintenance himself but employed two women who worked a few hours per day servicing his contracts. These women were homemakers whose hobby was plants. They had gained a wealth of experience and knowledge by caring for their large collections of plants and reading most of the books available on the subject.

He was a full-time salesman for a building products manufacturer. By spending an hour or so each day selling his plant service instead of building products, in 11 months he built his gross to $2,800 per month from service contracts, plus additional profits from leasing plants.

LEASING PLANTS

Leasing is the most profitable area of the plant business. If you grow the plants yourself, you should get your money back on a plant in two to three months. If you buy from a wholesaler, your costs will be covered in five to seven months. The 100 percent return on your investment in less than a year is excellent—and you still own the plants.

Some plants draw an even higher return if they are susceptible to illness in the environment in which they are placed. A Boston fern, for example, becomes sick quickly under dry, low-light conditions and is difficult to revive even when moved to an optimum environment. Plant leasers usually request a 50 percent premium over their regular rates under these conditions.

RATES

Most plant-leasing companies structure their rates according to wholesale price. The average monthly rate is 15 to 20 percent of the wholesale price, which is usually a little over one-third of the retail price. In other words, a plant that retails for $25 will wholesale for $10 and rent for $1.50 to $2 per month.

The rental fee is based on a plant with a standard clay or plastic pot. If the renter wants a more decorative container or hanging fixture such as macrame, he must pay for it (at retail) at the time of installation (more profit for you, at a 50 percent margin).

SERVICING

Free weekly service is included as part of the rental fee unless there are only a few plants. Then the rental fee is raised to cover the cost of the weekly visit. Plant lessors also guarantee that each plant will remain healthy and attractive.

In a dark restaurant most of the plants will be exchanged each week or two for new plants. The original plants are taken back to the greenhouse for recuperation, and returned when the replacement plants begin to suffer. A higher rental fee is usually charged to offset the extra handling cost.

It is obvious that the more plants leased to one location, the higher the profit margin. For example, if a location has 12 plants and it takes one hour weekly to service all the plants, including travel time, the service cost per plant per month will be about $1.25. But if another lessee has 36 plants and service time per week is two hours, the monthly service cost per plant drops to about 83 cents.

Start-up Manual #49 is available on this business. See page 378.

INSTANT PRINT SHOP

High net profit B/T:	$75,000
Average net profit B/T:	22,000
Minimum investment:	7,800
Average investment:	15,000

Until a few years ago the printing business was dominated by people with technical skills in printing. Also, in order to make any real money you had to invest a large sum.

With the advent of automatic plate-making cameras such as ITEK and offset duplicators designed to make good prints when operated by anyone of average intelligence, the printing industry saw a new idea catch on: instant printing.

KEY TO SUCCESS

In the instant-printing business, location is the major key to your success. Most of the jobs a small shop does are for the small businesses and run under $50. With so little money involved, you won't find many people running all over town getting bids; they go to the most convenient printer available.

Picking a location is easy. Find a spot with plenty of small offices, factories, and other businesses. If your shop is on a well-traveled street near all these businesses, you will have a ready-made market and orders will start to flow from the first day. Large companies are not good customers: either they have a small press of their own or they order such large quantities that you can't compete with high-volume printers.

FREE INSTRUCTION!

Every equipment dealer we approached offered to instruct us and anyone working for us on all aspects of running a small offset press and any other equipment used in an instant print shop. They also offered to provide free technical advice at any time afterward. The reason is that most dealers also sell supplies; they want to keep you as a customer.

One thing is clear, though: you would be a fool to do the printing yourself. Skilled pressmen are plentiful, and you should remember that you are investing money to make money; not to turn yourself into a laborer.

Most instant print shops are operated by the owner, who works as the printer, bookkeeper, salesperson, sweeper, etc. There's a very old saying which applies here: "Most people are too busy making a living to ever make any real money."

In other words, as it applies to the instant press business, if you plan on doing all the work yourself, don't ever expect to make more than an average salary from it.

NO COMPETITION!

Fortunately for you, most small print shops are run this way, which will give you a big advantage. After talking to many small printers, we realized that there was very little competition because of the way people who owned print shops ran their businesses.

From statistics we have learned that the small instant print shop grosses under $60,000 annually, and nets less than $17,000 before taxes. Yet we know of three shops where the owners never touch their presses and gross over $250,000 with net profits around the $60,000 mark before taxes (in fact, one exceeds $75,000).

SELL EVERY KIND OF PRINTING

This business has many interesting aspects. For example, you can take orders for any kind of printing—not just "instant" printing. You do this by utilizing "trade printers"—printers who do work for other printers only. This includes thermography (the simulated engraved or raised printing used on fancy business cards and letterheads), engraved wedding invitations, carbon interleaved forms such as invoices, full-color brochures, and catalogs.

Some of these trade printers may not even be in your metropolitan area, especially the wedding invitation engravers and business card thermographers. You do all your business with them by mail. They are geared for this type of orders and will service your account quickly and efficiently.

Most of these companies will supply you with illustrated catalogs, samples, order forms, and a retail price list. All you do is take the order and mail it to them, and they will ship the finished product direct to you or anywhere you wish. Your profit will range from 30 to 50 percent of the list price, depending on the item.

Trade print work often contributes heavily to your income. One entrepreneur claims that he averages 150 orders per month for thermographed business cards. The average profit per card order is $5; that's an extra $750 per month.

Some shops do well with engraved wedding invitations, shower invitations, fancy announcements, etc. The average order here is about $100, and four or five of these every month will bring in another $200 profit.

A lot of businesses use custom-made, carbon-interlaced snap-out forms. This is a very lucrative service to push, and the average order will usually exceed $200.

Every business uses rubber stamps, and you make money just for writing out the order. A business we visited averages in excess of $150 in stamp orders each month.

THEY WON'T STEAL YOUR ACCOUNTS!

All the trade printers will protect your accounts; in other words, they won't attempt to go direct to your customer and cut you out. In fact, most of them will deal only with fellow printers, and won't sell anything direct to the consumer.

Four-color printing for catalogs, brochures, and the like is a little more complicated than run-of-the-mill black-on-white work. First you must take the items that will appear in the catalog to be photographed at a color studio (listed in your trade magazine). The studio will process the photos and make color separation negatives. These separations are what you must take to the trade printer, along with the copy layout.

It may seem like a lot of running around, but color jobs are not expected to be cheap. Rarely will you see a job for less than $700; the average is about $3,000. You should be able to make 20 to 30 percent on the deal, which will make the procedure worthwhile.

PHOTOCOPYING—VERY PROFITABLE!

Photocopying is another area rich in profits, but it has a bigger hidden advantage. About half of the people coming in for photocopies are small businessmen. They are very heavy users of instant-printing services, and once they are accustomed to coming to you for their photocopies, it is only natural that they will bring their printing to you as well.

The average shop in a good location that advertises photocopying service for four or five cents a copy does around 30,000 copies per month. Some shops we found, however, were doing close to 200,000 per month, and one in a downtown area turned out a half million every four weeks.

Machine and paper costs run between 3 and 3½ cents per copy, so this can be a very lucrative part of your business. In our opinion, no print shop should be without this service.

Start-up Manual #13 is available on this business. See page 378.

WINDOW-WASHING SERVICE

High net profit B/T:	$42,000
Average net profit B/T:	15,000
Minimum investment:	300
Average investment:	900

A few years ago a young man came into our office offering to wash our windows.

Our offices had a 50-foot front with windows all the way across. So we were amazed when he told us he would do the outside of all the windows for $15. It looked like an all-day job.

After about 30 minutes, though, we realized that he was almost finished—and the windows were sparkling.

His technique was the secret of his speedy finish. No Windex or paper towels for him. Instead he used a long-handled brush and a pail of sudsy water. After sponging the glass, he picked up a squeegee on a long handle, and by sweeping it back and forth across the window, within seconds he had the entire surface clean, dry and crystal clear. He wiped the squeegee and the windowsill with a rag and was ready to take on the next pane.

After he was finished, this speedy window jockey came into our office to explain that since we were close to the ocean the damp, foggy air would cause our windows to get dirty fairly quickly. He offered to come by every two weeks to take care of them, and the office manager told him he had a deal.

FAST GROWTH

We interviewed him a year later and during the course of our meeting he related that he had four people working for him, and was grossing $6,500 per month.

He explained that after graduating from college with a degree and teaching credentials, he found that jobs in his profession were few and far between. Desperate and without any ready cash, he invested a few dollars in a handful of supplies and went into business for himself. His route grew slowly but surely into a successful, stable business.

His current operating statement revealed that after office and vehicle expenses, telephone, advertising, supplies, insurance, and wages (including a full-time bookkeeper/office employee), he was netting $3,200 per month before taxes—easily twice as much as he would ever have earned as a teacher.

LOW INVESTMENT

The initial investment needed to start a window-cleaning business like this is ridiculously low—brush, squeegee, pail, stepladder, liquid dishwasher soap, rags, and towels. The total minimum outlay, including printing and a business license, comes to $300. Consequently, all it takes to get started is a short walk down any business street to present each establishment with your business card and ask if they would like their windows washed.

Start-up Manual #12 is available on this business. See page 378.

CROSS-COUNTRY TRUCKING

High net profit B/T:	$40,000
Average net profit B/T:	27,000
Minimum investment:	4,200
Average investment:	23,400

With all due respect to Jackie Gleason, Burt Reynolds, and "Smokey and the Bandit," you don't have to run bootleg booze across state lines to make a living as a cross-country truck driver. In fact, if you are a good businessman as well as a competent driver, you can net up to 30 percent before taxes on a gross of $100,000 for a year's work.

Cross-country trucking is more than truck stops, CBs, and country music. It's a multibillion-dollar market that's getting bigger every day and offers opportunity for the sharp, aggressive person who likes the freedom of the outdoors and wants to be his own boss, jockeying an 18-wheeler across the 42,000-mile interstate highway system.

BIG PROFITS

Being on the road for a typical independent trucker we talked to was worth $27,000 before taxes on a gross of $93,000 and 200,000 miles. For another, it was $35,000 before taxes on a gross of $100,000 with about the same mileage. The average was between $25,000 and $30,000 a year on start-up investments that ranged from $18,000 to $36,000.

FOUR BEST WAYS TO BREAK IN

For the enterprising entrepreneur who is interested in travel there are four different ways to enter the industry. The hardest way is to become an independent owner/operator and haul your own freight. This requires you to obtain an ICC authority. It will take longer to get into the business this way, especially if a protest is entered by a competitor.

A second, more practical approach is working under a contract basis for one of the larger freight companies. This eliminates the need for an authority, and part of your insurance and other costs are picked up by the freight company. You still own and maintain your own rig, but the freight company generates much of your business.

A third way to enter is as a furniture mover for one of the larger companies. North American was the only company we found that offers a school for the potential trucker, but other van lines like Mayflower and Allied have programs.

A fourth way is to hire on as a dockworker for one of the larger freight lines, get to know the trucks and loading and unloading procedures, move on up as a "second carrier" (the truck-driving equivalent of a copilot), and finally obtain your own rig. This takes the most time, but the experience is valuable, and it allows you to "test the water" first.

PERSONAL INDEPENDENCE

Few businesses in the country offer the independence available to the men and women who push rigs across the country night and day. It is a rough life, but one in which you can accumulate a lot of capital in a short time. Many truckers have used the road as a stepping stone into other businesses, worked their way through college, or accomplished other goals.

Living expenses can be minimal on the road; you live out of your rig and move from one truck stop to another 50 weeks of the year. If you work it right, a fat bank account can be the result of the trucking life.

TAX ADVANTAGES TOO

There are substantial tax advantages available, because all expenses are deductible as business necessities, from depreciation on the truck/trailer to fuel, maintenance, insurance, and truck payments; even food and lodging are write-offs.

Start-up Manual #157 is available on this business. See page 379.

FOOD

---------------------------New Idea---------------------------
BREAKFAST IN BED

Imagine waking up to a cozy breakfast in bed prepared by a gourmet chef, complete with fine china, crystal stemware, silver, and linen.

A luxury once reserved for the elite who stay in the finest hotels is now available in your home and prepared in your kitchen by a staff of cooks who come early in the morning and bring their own equipment.

An elegantly served omelette or eggs Benedict is sure to beat burnt toast, cold oatmeal, and a glass of what could charitably be called juice.

We've seen services like this in Los Angeles and New York, but many other cities could support a small operation on low overhead. Especially at rates like $60 per couple, which is the common tab.

It's a natural extension of existing services by caterers, exclusive restaurants, and others in the food business. You'll need to advertise in theater programs and slick urban magazines to attract the affluent clientele necessary to make a go of it.

---------------------------New Idea---------------------------
MUSHROOMING BUSINESS

Button mushrooms account for almost 100 percent of U.S. mushroom consumption. Unfortunately, they're almost as expensive to produce as they are to eat. Now a new umbrella of profits is opening up with oyster mushrooms and you can get under it from the beginning.

Oyster mushrooms, so called because they look like oyster shells, grow wild or from pure cultures. They originated in the Orient. Until recently they could not be easily grown in quantity. Dave Kummer of Wonderland Mushrooms has found a way to spawn them that slashes production costs and increases profit margin.

The source of oyster mushroom profits is in the readily available raw material—one of the problems with buttom mushroom production. Wonderland says its formula will supply 1,500 pounds of mushrooms weekly or 78,000 pounds yearly.

Oyster mushroom production uses proved methods of mushroom growth plus innovations in microbiology, an efficient growth system that keeps production costs stable, and genetic control. Oyster mushrooms grow in aseptic conditions; a simple rinse is sufficient to clean them.

Yet the surging demand for mushrooms allows a retail price of over $4 a pound. Besides that, oyster mushrooms are a better value than button mushrooms. Because of low water content, one pound of oyster mushrooms has four times the volume of a pound of buttons.

Wonderland wants to set up a network of independent mushroom growers. Kummer estimates that initial investment is relatively low. The burgeoning costs and scarcity of button mushroom production herald the spread of a mushroom market over several varieties. With demand for mushrooms increasing nationwide, oyster mushroom farming could be in the forefront of the market. For information, write Wonderland Mushrooms, P.O. Box 271, Elburn, Illinois 60119.

MOBILE RESTAURANT

High net profit B/T (two units):	$75,000
Average net profit B/T:	30,000
Minimum investment:	500
Average investment:	5,500

When the morning coffee break bell sounds in thousands of factories throughout the nation, some 25,000 drivers of mobile restaurants, sometimes called catering trucks, or sandwich trucks, pull up to the gates and swing open their doors to expose urns of hot coffee, cold juices, milk, cold drinks, and a variety of other goodies ranging from candy and cookies to sweet rolls and sandwiches.

Again at lunchtime and the afternoon break the drivers appear for five to ten minutes to dispense an annual total of $1.2 billion of ready-to-eat foods.

Factory and office managers usually cooperate in setting break times so one driver can serve lunch to as many as 12 stops. Astute operators can net $150 per day on a well-scheduled route, if they prepare their own sandwiches—yielding about $3,300 per month before taxes.

MANY AREAS UNTAPPED

This business was started during World War II to serve war

plants that were far from restaurants and snack bars. It has been spreading slowly across the nation; many smaller cities have never heard of the service. A city of 100,000 can easily support 20 catering trucks.

The business is highly competitive in southern California, but many major cities have plenty of room for newcomers. Very large factories and offices usually have their own cafeterias, but the most people in this country work in facilities with less than 20 employees, which is usually considered the minimum necessary to support an in-house cafeteria.

FEW INDEPENDENTS

Industry surveys show that over 50 percent of the catering trucks are owned by companies with ten or more trucks, some employing as many as 100 units.

Most companies do not hire crews of drivers, but assign specific routes to drivers. The company supplies the truck and the route, for which the driver puts up a deposit, usually $500 to $750. The driver gets a fully stocked truck which must be restocked daily from a company commissary for cash at wholesale prices (40 to 50 percent off retail). The driver also pays the company $25 to $35 a day for the use of the truck. The company pays for repair of the vehicle, insurance, health department permits, and a business license. The driver pays for gas and oil. A driver can net $10,000 to $25,000 per year, depending on the volume of sales.

If you own your own truck, most companies will give you a route in return for a guarantee that you will buy all your food from them. However, they still require a cash performance deposit of up to $500. The truck owner/driver will net from $15,000 to $30,000 per year.

Start-up Manual #56 is available on this business. See page 379.

LOW-CAL BAKERY

High net profit B/T:	$75,000
Average net profit B/T:	50,000
Minimum investment:	10,000
Average investment:	14,500

Most people are concerned about being overweight. The perennially skinny are definitely a small minority. Many people have a constant weight problem, especially after the age of 30.

Those with weight problems who have a sweet tooth encounter double trouble. The craving for sweets, pastries, cookies, cakes, pies, and candy, is overpowering to many; they surrender to their desires, get fatter, and endanger their health.

Besides the large weight-watching sector of the populace, there are those afflicted with diabetes, who are strictly forbidden sugar-containing foods.

THE ANSWER—SUGAR-FREE/LOW-CALORIE

Several years ago Helen Burton started the Thinnery Corporation, a bakery designed to cater to diabetics. She found almost immediately that most of her customers were not diabetics, but people with weight problems. Her business grew by leaps and bounds.

For a while the Weight Watchers franchises recommended her establishment and posted her baked-goods list in their meeting rooms. A disagreement followed, and Mrs. Burton and Weight Watchers parted ways. This did not slow the Thinnery's expansion or affect its sales. Today there are over a dozen operating stores plus a central commissary where all the baking is done.

PROFIT IS PHENOMENAL!

The average sales per shop of a business of this type usually exceed $15,000 per month. The gross profit is an astounding 50 percent (before advertising costs and office salaries). Note that most low-cal bakeries do very little advertising.

Not having to advertise depends on choice of location. Stores should either be in shopping centers or on heavy shopping streets where foot traffic is heavy.

STILL A GROUND-FLOOR OPPORTUNITY

The Thinnery is no longer alone in attempting to attract dieters, diabetics, and hypoglycemics to low-cal bakery delights. In one major metropolitan area we counted 75 low-cal bakeries and restaurants with descriptive names like the Slender Touch, the Trimmerie, the Slim Way, the Thin World, Skinny Haven, and Rikki's Inn to Be Thin. But with more than 70 million overweight people in America, plus 10 million diabetics, there is room for continued development of diet bakeries and restaurants.

A BAKERY IS A SIMPLE OPERATION

When the word "bakery" is mentioned, we found, some people conjure up a picture of a complicated, mechanized business. But it connotes something far simpler to those who have baked pies or cakes at home. If you look into the workroom of a bakery you will see a plain assortment of ovens, mixers, tables, racks, a refrigerator, and a few common tools and pans.

A bakery is not much different from your kitchen—everything is just on a larger scale. Instead of making one pie at a time, you bake a dozen or more. And bakers can be hired in every city at annual wages from $8,000 to $15,000.

Ironically, one shop doesn't even have a baker, per se. Instead, it employs a home economics graduate who supervises the production of baked goods.

HOW TO MAKE PASTRIES WITH NO SUGAR

To make low-calorie, nonsweet bakery goods is not complicated. Saccharin is substituted for sugar, nonfat milk replaces whole milk, and dried stale white bread is ground up to replace flour.

Ricotta cheese or nonfat milk (both low in calories) is combined with flavoring extracts to create the creamy fillings. Many items have fruit fillings which are naturally low in calories.

HOW MUCH INVESTMENT?

Under the right conditions you can open a nonsweet bakery for $10,000, but $13,000 to $16,000 is more realistic.

WHERE TO START: LOCATION

A medium-sized or large shopping center is the best choice; the closer you can locate to the supermarket in the shopping center, the better your sales will be. Remember, pastries and sweets are impulse items.

The more foot traffic in your area, the higher your sales. So besides a shopping center the best bet is a retail street that draws plenty of traffic. Middle-class neighborhoods are fine; if there is a wealthy section nearby, you will attract even more customers.

Start-up Manual #62 is available on this business. See page 379.

_____ **New Idea** _____
CHIP SHOP

Imagine people lining up five deep at your counter, willing to pay you a buck for four ounces of potato chips. This is what Ron Kaiser found when he opened his first Lips Chips store.

Taking advantage of the trend toward food specialization that paid off handsomely for cookies and yogurt, Lips Chips sells only chips and dips. Three kinds of chips are featured, salted, unsalted, and spicy Hot Lips. To accompany the chips, Kaiser offers exotic dips.

Kaiser deep-fries his chips on the premises in open kettles, imitating the original 1853 cooking process.

Potato chips are so easy to prepare that all it takes to go into this business is imagination and a good location. Your best bet for a moneymaking site is a mall or shopping center with heavy foot traffic. An alternative is a state fair or other tourist attraction with impulse buyers afoot.

Since the cost of the product is minimal (potatoes can be purchased for a few cents apiece), you should spend most of your money on production. Put your chips in an attractive eye-catching container to create a gourmet food item.

With a pretty package you can expand your base of operations. Sell the snack to retail outlets. Push the gourmet chips angle and stores may include them in their catalogs. As your product becomes known, include area groceries in your marketing plan.

COOKIE SHOP

High net profit B/T:	$120,000
Average net profit B/T:	60,000
Minimum investment:	18,000
Average investment:	54,000

There's a fortune in cookies—and we don't mean the Chinese kind! "Old-fashioned" *anything* in today's mechanized world of artificial, red-dyed foods promises old-fashioned success—especially when selling an old favorite staple: the cookie.

The Original Cookie Company, Inc., which opened its first shop in the Fox Hills Shopping Mall in Los Angeles, is opening stores in shopping malls nationwide. Pretax profits per store are running at $72,000. During peak hours the best stores sell close to a pound of cookies per minute at 45 cents apiece, or $3.60 per pound. The average sales of the shops exceed $20,000 a month. One 45-cent cookie contains about 10 cents' worth of ingredients, a 77 percent gross margin.

Ex-theatrical agent and high-school dropout Wally Amos created his Famous Amos chocolate chip cookie originally as a hobby or a "kind of therapy." He gave them away at business meetings as a gimmick and people gradually got "hooked." Helen Reddy and Bill Cosby are among show business notables who backed Amos, and

$25,000 later the hobby had turned into a lucrative, full-time business with five stores and a giant wholesale business.

HE MANAGES A COOKIE

Wally's prime Sunset Boulevard store has grossed as much as $40,000 in a week. Famous Amos chocolate chip cookies are noted for their "crisp, nutty rich flavor" and one southern Californian sends seven pounds weekly to relatives in the East. The 39-year-old entrepreneur owes his success, though, to a flair for publicity he learned while promoting rock stars.

"Now I manage the cookie," he says, grinning. His promotional gimmicks include Famous Amos bumper stickers, T-shirts, lapel buttons, posters, and gold-plated chocolate chip pendants. The walls of his stores are plaqued with letters of enthusiastic appreciation from his customers, who gobble his cookies at the rate of two tons a week.

A New York department store manager declares, "The Famous Amos chocolate chip cookie has replaced the Gucci briefcase as a status item." The American people consume a whopping $340 million worth of chocolate chip cookies alone, making it the number one sweet in North America. The Commerce Department states that the value of shipments in the cookie industry is expected to exceed $6 billion by 1985. That is a growth average of 8 percent per year.

The May Company, which has opened a store in Cleveland, Ohio, ordered five tons of Famous Chocolate Chip cookies and sold out immediately. Bloomingdale's in Washington, D.C. sold $2,000 worth of Famous Amos chocolate chips in one Saturday.

The trend toward old-fashioned foods like mother used to bake, coupled with the American phenomenon of fast takeout foods, ensures that the cookie industry will remain a stable, high-profit area for many years.

KEY TO SUCCESS: THE SMELL

When you walk into one of the malls where the Original Cookie has a shop, you immediately encounter the pleasing odor of freshly baked cookies—even though you can't even see the cookie shop yet. Some shop owners secretly vent their ovens into the mall enclosure, or out their front door. Mall managers and the fire department definitely resist this approach, but it certainly attracts the attention of every passerby.

The real key to creating a permeating smell from baking cookies is use of pure vanillin, the aromatic essence of vanilla, rather than synthetic vanilla flavoring.

We cannot hammer home with too much emphasis the power of pure vanilla extract; it has a staying power that, when circulated through your ventilation system, creates the irresistible smell of fresh hot cookies—as tempting a come-on for any shopper, tourist, or ambler as can be imagined. There are few so hardy that they can resist the overwhelming scent of pure vanilla, butterscotch, chocolate and peanut butter.

THE MOBILE COOKIE

Cookies are an impulse item, so go where there is heavy foot traffic: shopping malls, and tourist attractions such as outdoor art shows, beaches, swap meets, flea markets, and parks, high-density (downtown) office areas, high auto traffic streets to which there is easy access, college campuses, etc. You can even christen a van "The Mobile Cookie" and go where the action is, seasonal or otherwise, after baking a batch at home.

Our investigator visited the plush indoor Fox Hills Mall for a look at the Original Cookie Company's first store. We counted 56 people buying cookies in fifteen minutes—at 3:30 p.m. on a Tuesday (the slowest day of the week).

Start-up Manual #83 is available on this business. See page 379.

FRYSTICK SNACK SHOP

High net profit B/T:	$66,000
Average net profit B/T:	53,000
Minimum investment:	1,000
Average investment:	40,000

A new snack-food craze is sweeping the country. There hasn't been anything this hot since the chocolate chip cookie turned fast-food. Like the cookie, the frystick, or churro, is a low-cost, high-profit-margin item which offers the chance to make a million from the American public's amazing sweet tooth.

The pennies-apiece product is incredibly simple to make. Tasty dough is shaped into long sticks which are deep fried, rolled in confectioners' sugar, and flavored with vanilla, chocolate, or cinnamon. Neither adults nor children can resist the wonderful aroma of fresh-cooked frysticks. Our researchers found customers standing six deep, money in hand, waiting to pay 75 cents for snacks that cost about 5 cents to make. In one hour at this location over 12 dozen churros were sold.

Don't make the mistake of confusing these fried doughsticks with doughnuts. The only similarities are the dough and the cooking procedure. Churros appeal to a different market, a dessert or fun snack—unlike doughnuts, which are usually a breakfast item.

The most successful frystick operations are found in shopping malls, craft fairs, and swap meets: any location with high foot traffic and a fun atmosphere. The beauty of the business is its simplicity—if you can't open a full-fledged food outlet in a fancy shopping mall, you can shoestring a churro stand from the back of a van for as little as $1,000.

Whopping profit margins of 35 to 40 percent are to be expected. You can gross up to $200,000 before taxes in a prime location with an initial investment of about $40,000.

THE MARKET IS WIDE OPEN

Fried dough sticks have been around for centuries with different names in different cultures. (Italians call them zéppoli.) But until recently they were only found in ethnic neighborhood restaurants and occasionally at a state fair or swap-meet booth. Frysticks never hit the mass market because they were considered a regional or ethnic food and were handmade instead of being mass-produced.

This is a ground-floor opportunity. Our researchers searched far and wide and came up with only a handful of people selling churros full-time.

One operation has cleverly trademarked its product Whimsys and has decorated its store with fanciful cartoon characters. It's a traffic-stopping show that lights up kids' eyes and the cash register at the same time. A miniature train brings cinnamon logs from the Cinnamon Forest, vanilla snow from Vanilla Mountain, and chocolate bars from the Chocolate Mine.

Another operation, developed on a down-home country theme, spent $5,000 on design and $25,000 to build a delightful set of animated characters who make Vittlestix and Moo Joos. You can achieve a similar effect at lower cost, but gimmicks like these pull customers into the shop as a carnival barker draws customers to a sideshow attraction.

MAKE 'EM IN A FLASH!

Automated frying machinery makes cooking frysticks easy and fast. Custom-made churro machines are being developed, but you can set up a high-speed operation using only equipment commonly found in doughnut shops.

One California manufacturer has built a machine which cooks up to 64 churros in four to five minutes. The proof box allows you to store batches so you can even out the production workflow and keep up with the demand at high-volume locations.

You can start your frystick empire with one full-time worker in the back doing the frying, one full-time counterperson, and one part-time reliefperson. Peak weekend and holiday crowds may necessitate hiring an extra helper.

Remember, these yummy snacks sell like hotcakes to young and old alike. We watched two young entrepreneurs sell 1,900 frysticks one afternoon at 50 cents apiece for an impressive $950 gross. But we recommend selling them for 75 cents—a fantastic markup of 1400 percent.

Start-up Manual #164 is available on this business. See page 379.

SHRIMP PEDDLING

High net profit B/T:	$100,000
Average net profit B/T:	20,000
Minimum investment:	2,300
Average investment:	13,000

Want to make up to $30,000 net profit for a few weeks' work? Peddle seafood in landlocked areas of the country! Several layers of greedy middlemen stand between the boat captain who catches shrimp, or lobster, and the hungry consumer.

Cutting out most or all of these middlemen can mean incredible profit opportunities for anyone with enough moxie to seize the chance! Being a peddler may not be a glamour business, but we've talked with some who "cry all the way to the bank" about what others think about their livelihood.

What these smart operators do is buy shrimp, lobster, and other popular delicacies in quantity, priced well below wholesale, and sell direct to the public off the tailgate of refrigerated trucks. We talked with one operator who banked $20,000 net profit from one truckload. And he makes five or six "runs" a year!

We watched one peddler from Alabama sell $500 worth of shrimp and lobster in a Los Angeles suburb in one hour. He was parked in back of a local bowling alley, had no signs on the street and an unmarked truck. His sale had been advertised in advance in small ads in the food sections of local papers. All he had was crude cardboard signs, a display table, and a full cashbox!

HUGE SEAFOOD MARKET

Shrimp and lobster have been favorites for many years. Many people who say they don't like fish will name a shrimp cocktail as their favorite appetizer. Fresh shrimp is a popular topping for salads, and always goes quickly at holiday buffets. Restaurants have served fried shrimp and fresh boiled lobster for years. The total value of seafood consumed by hungry Americans totals about $8 billion annually.

Our research for this report took us into gourmet fish markets and big chains in many areas of the country. We found that retail prices for shrimp range from $4.50 to $11.50 per pound in places like Wichita, Denver, and Salt Lake City. Lobster tails were selling for $12 to $15 per pound!

Shrimp and seafood lovers willing to pay such prices in stores for the delicately flavored menu favorites will jump at the chance to buy in quantity and stock up at prices below normal retail. And that's how you make big bucks, peddling to them! You profit on the spread between dockside and retail market prices.

ABOUT THE SEAFOOD BUSINESS

This fascinating business has several levels of distribution. The boat captains usually catch 4,000 to 5,000 pounds of shrimp in a single run, return to port, and sell their shrimp to packing company representatives for cash.

Packing companies sort, clean, and freeze the shrimp, usually in five-pound boxes. Frozen shrimp is whole in the shell, headless in the shell, or headless, peeled, and deveined. Most shrimp is brown, white, or choice pink—it all cooks up pink, but there are flavor differences.

Within these categories there are grades of quality which also affect prices in the marketplace. If a peddler deals in the poorest grades, sales will suffer the next time around in a particular area. So we've based our prices in this report on no. 1 and no. 2 grade shrimp.

Packers will sell frozen shrimp or precooked lobster to brokers who are located most often in major port cities like New Orleans, Brownsville, Texas, and Gulfport, Mississippi. Broker prices vary widely from one area of the country to another—and even within one state. We've found differences of $1 per pound between brokers in the same city.

Brokers sell to wholesalers and/or distributors around the country who sell smaller quantities to local retailers. With prices at dockside of $1.20 to $1.50 per pound for small shrimp, and retail prices as high as $11 per pound for larger shrimp, it's easy to see the potential profit in this business!

CUT OUT THE MIDDLEMEN!

The most successful peddlers work directly with the packers wherever possible, and negotiate for the best price, using a quantity buy as leverage. While most packers claim they will sell only to brokers, most of those we questioned admitted they would sell direct to peddlers—when large quantities like 10,000 to 20,000 pounds were involved.

After acquiring experience in the business it may be possible to do even better by dealing directly with boat captains. Many modern shrimp boats have on-board quick-freezing and packing equipment. Shrimp bought this way is whole, unsorted "boat-run" shrimp. Smart peddlers get some boat-run shrimp at $1.20 or less a pound, advertise it at superlow prices to attract buyers, and then "sell up" buyers to better grades at higher prices. This is not illegal "bait and switch" as long as the boat-run shrimp is actually available at the advertised price.

INCREDIBLY PROFITABLE

We found brokers in New Orleans selling shrimp at $2.50 to $4.50 per pound, depending on size and quality. The terms "jumbo," "medium," and "small" are relative, but usually there are 15 to 20 jumbo shrimps per pound, 30 to 35 medium shrimps (which sell best in the marketplace), and 40 to 45 small or cocktail shrimps.

Assuming a $2.50 per pound average cost for a variety of shrimp skillfully purchased in a truckload buy of 10,000 pounds, your product cost is $25,000. At retail, you can expect to sell for as high as a $6 per pound average, depending on grade and area of the country. Your gross profit for one truckload of shrimp can be $35,000!

Your margin on whole precooked lobster, lobster tail, and certain other delicacies, can be even better! So most peddlers we investigated were offering these products too.

You don't have to start buying by the truckload. Many peddlers buy in much smaller quantities and run the business as a weekend sideline, or as a summer job during school vacation. All you need is a small van and a relatively convenient source of frozen seafood at an attractive cost.

Of course, the profits will be lower. You will have to pay higher prices for 500 to 1,000 pounds of shrimp and lobster—in the range of $3 to $4 per pound. And you will have to pay up front; brokers and others usually won't offer terms on small orders.

A 500-pound buy will cost you $1,500 at $3 per pound. If you sell it all at $5 per pound you've made $1,000 with virtually zero overhead. Not bad for a few weekends' work!

Start-up Manual #127 is available on this business. See page 379.

ICE-CREAM PARLOR

High net profit B/T:	$300,000
Average net profit B/T:	70,000
Minimum investment:	30,000
Average investment:	100,000

Ice cream is an American institution—over 400 million gallons are consumed annually. One of the hottest ice-cream trends is a return to good old-fashioned flavors made from real natural ingredients. The ingredients may not be secret—but they are the secret of success.

Old-fashioned ice-cream parlors all over the country average gross sales in the $130,000 to $300,000 range. They're often small as well as nostalgic. One store started with 300 square feet and grossed $105,000 its first year. Four years later there are 20 stores dipping a total of close to $2.5 million a year. One of its units is even netting $300,000.

The most successful operators combine ice-cream knowledge with marketing and professional savvy and are able to bring in pretax nets of 20 to 30 percent without the use of mass production.

WHY OLD IS BETTER THAN NEW

Americans are leaning more than ever to natural, nonadditive foods. By federal law a gallon of ice cream must weigh at least 4½ pounds. If you follow the adage "A pint's a pound the world around," a gallon of ice cream should weigh eight pounds. This would be decreased by large quantities of air, which most commercial dairies pump into their ice cream. That's why more people are turning back to the good old-fashioned recipes with more ice cream than air.

SWEETEN PROFITS WITH MARKET SELECTION

The market for natural ice cream is anyone from 3 to 103 with a well-developed sweet tooth. We've found that the lion's share of the market is in the age brackets from 12 to 19 and from 23 to 37. Zero in on these customers and you'll get the lion's share of profit margins.

Be sure to zero in on the right site too. A good way to get started is to convert an existing structure to your needs, adding the old-fashioned parlor atmosphere that supplies the charm you'll be selling with your ice cream.

The moment customers enter your ice-cream parlor, take them back to the good old days of strawberry phosphates and band concerts in the local park, Sunday afternoon walks and porch swings. This can be done with a little flair, a little more investment, and plenty of imagination.

Though your atmosphere may reflect the mellow days of a bygone era, your layout has to be geared to 20th-century efficiency in cost and operations. Get a good equipment package for making and serving old-fashioned ice cream. Your space-age technology will be in your office operation in back of the parlor.

POPULAR FLAVORS MAKE THE DIFFERENCE

Don't be intimidated by competition from 31- and 54-flavor ice-cream conglomerates. There are thousands of recipes in the public domain, and what the pros do is test these recipes until they find ones that appeal to their customers.

Choosing flavors should be the most pleasant part of your market research during the start-up phase. After you do that, move out of testing into production. Control costs all along the way so you can sell off your inventory.

The best part is the numbers game. Your markups from wholesale ingredient purchase to scoops of ice cream can be as high as 500 percent; yet you'll still be giving ice-cream lovers a good buy.

DOUBLE SCOOPS OF PROFIT AHEAD

Many small ice-cream stores have failed because of two business factors—bad management and bad product. That should be a clue. Get a firm grasp on your day-to-day operations, and sweeten your management expertise with the best-tasting ice-cream dishes in the world.

It's not complicated, once you get a firm grip on what your customers want. Risk can be high, but profit potential is even higher.

Make sure your homemade ice cream contains only the finest ingredients. Set a standard for yourself and maintain it, and you'll find yourself setting the standard for the industry.

Experts predict that old-fashioned ice-cream stores will continue to prosper through the '80s. As more and more Americans experience the taste difference between artificial ice cream and the old-fashioned kind, you'll get a steady flow of customers, and piles and piles of revenue.

Start-up Manual #187 is available on this business. See page 379.

CONVENIENCE FOOD STORE

High net profit B/T:	$90,000
Average net profit B/T:	50,000
Minimum investment:	27,500
Average investment:	70,000

Next time you rush into your local 7-Eleven store for a carton of milk or pack of cigarettes, take a good look around. You stopped there for convenience, and that convenience is creating the hottest growth industry of the decade—the convenience food store.

Annual sales are topping $10 billion, and there's no end in sight. We discovered one store operating out of 400 square feet that grosses $250,000 annually. Another dynamic store we investigated averages 900 customers a day with daily sales of more than $1,300. The highest-volume store we found, with 2,400 square feet, grossed almost $1 million in 1979.

At $1.50 per average sale nationwide, this type of operation depends on the largest possible volume. But keep in mind that you are selling a product that everyone needs three times a day or more—*food*.

ROOM FOR EVERYONE

Convenience food stores are a product of a nation on the go. In 1957 there were around 500 with total sales of $75 million. Today there are more than 3,000 grabbing almost 6 percent of the total grocery shopping dollar.

Even major oil companies are jumping on the bandwagon, setting up stores in company-owned and -operated service stations. The newest competition with the well-known 7-Eleven stores is the AMPM Mini Market, which is waging an advertising campaign guaranteed to give the 7-Eleven chain a run for its money.

There's still room, though, for the little guy to make a splash. Fifty-three percent of the firms belonging to the National Association of Convenience Stores are small, operating fewer than ten outlets. With careful cost accounting and good management you can be looking at a pretax net of 10 to 14 percent—after your salary has been paid!

HAPPY TO PAY MORE

Convenience food stores have the ideal customer. Your average customer is *buying, not browsing.* Not only that, he is happy to pay for convenience! The average shopper visits the store four to five times per week and spends an average of four minutes shopping. This describes customers in a hurry—customers willing to pay a few cents more for a can of baked beans rather than fight the hassle of a big supermarket. One shopper we interviewed said it was worth paying an extra 30 cents for his favorite bottle of soda pop at his local convenience store; he didn't have to drive in heavy traffic, and he could get in and out quickly.

SETTING UP SHOP

Your most important decision will be where to set up shop. We found convenience stores operating profitably out of single-store locations, strip shopping centers, congested downtown areas, even converted gasoline stations. They all had one thing in common: they were located in densely populated residential areas with massive consumer traffic.

Remember, 80 percent of your customers will live or work within one mile of your store. Look for a highly visible spot that can be seen from at least two directions. Providing parking is essential. You should have parking for at least ten cars, preferably right in front of the store for easy in-and-out shopping; you're selling convenience as much as food and other products.

YOUR SHOPPING LIST

What's the secret of choosing a good product mix? Experts we investigated gave this advice: Know your customers, and trust your own judgments.

The stores we investigated had an inventory of 2,800 to 3,200 basic consumer items. In order of volume, the more successful convenience stores sell the following items: tobacco, beer and wine products, groceries, soft drinks, nonfoods (magazines, charcoal briquettes, etc.), dairy products, candy, baked goods, and health and beauty aids.

Once you decide upon your beginning inventory you will have to find suppliers. You will be dealing with three main types of suppliers: wholesaler, co-ops, and route vendors.

THE PRICE IS RIGHT

Accurate, competitive pricing will be the basis of your success. Most stores shoot for a 29 to 30 percent overall gross spread out over their line. Bread and milk generally have only a 3 to 4 percent markup, while cigarettes and beer can carry a 40 to 45 percent markup.

High-markup items include sandwiches, coffee, and snacks. Many convenience stores are turning to the sale of fast foods to raise their total profits and increase store traffic. The customer in a hurry will gladly pay $1 for an egg salad sandwich which cost you as little as 30 cents.

Nonfood items such as magazines and periodicals generally provide you with a 40 to 45 percent markup and they are returnable to the supplier, so it's basically a "gravy proposition."

GENERAL OPERATING EXPENSES

Because you're dealing with food, you will need to be licensed by the board of health, and if you sell alcoholic beverages you must be licensed by your local beverage control board. Insurance is another necessity. Since your store is open long hours (82 percent nationwide are open 24 hours a day, 7 days a week), your electricity consumption will be high.

Qualified, trustworthy help is worth paying for. Most stores we investigated were managed by an owner and one or two employees.

All in all, convenience food stores are a recession-proof business that can pay off big for the entrepreneur who wants to work and be independent.

Start-up Manual #173 is available on this business. See page 378.

SUBMARINE SANDWICH SHOP

High net profit B/T:	$78,000
Average net profit B/T:	40,000
Minimum investment:	8,000
Average investment:	18,000

How would you like to make a product for 60 cents or so and sell it minutes later for $2.25? Sounds intriguing? That's what sandwich shop owners all over the country are doing, racking up annual grosses of over $250,000 with basic operations you can duplicate in your city.

For years, the sandwich has been king at lunchtime. Millions are sold every day, ranging from peanut butter and jelly to pastrami on rye with a hundred variations in between. Last year 500 million sandwiches were sold over the counter in America, not counting the ho-hum hamburger.

BIG PROFITS

Nationwide, our researchers found that gross sales in simple takeout sandwich shops with limited seating ranged from $100,000 to $500,000. Crisp management and low product cost can yield net profits in the 26 to 31 percent range. That's a bottom line of $26,000 to $75,000 or more, and well-run places can do that the first year.

GOOD LOCATIONS EVERYWHERE

There are many sites where a sandwich shop will do well, in communities of almost any population. For highest volume and profit, however, look for a site surrounded by as many people as possible at lunchtime. An urban high-rise business/shopping district can be ideal, drawing heavy lunchtime traffic from office and shop employees in the area. A nearby urban college campus is an added plus.

We've seen profitable sandwich shops in the basement of high-rise office buildings or apartment complexes serving tenants only. We've also seen owners doing quite well in isolated suburban offices or industrial parks. In either case, you must be "the only game in town."

START ON A SHOESTRING

Some sandwich restaurants spend hundreds of thousands of dollars on elaborate theme decor and fully equipped kitchens before they open their doors for business. This is not necessary.

Under the right circumstances, you can start with as little as $8,000. Twenty thousand dollars should be considered the maximum for opening. The low end assumes that you take over the lease of a failing restaurant, take over payments, and redo the premises. We've seen high-profit sandwich operations follow losing restaurants into the same location.

Of course, you need to know why the previous owner folded. The best location won't cover the mistakes of a poor businessman. If the location is sound, then go for it.

The simplicity of the operation and the easy availability of equipment means you can set up in nearly any storefront site without high renovation costs. You won't be cooking on site, so grills, fans, and vents aren't a problem. About all you need is a small work area, a service counter, and a few tables.

Start-up Manual #156 is available on this business. See page 379.

SOUP KITCHEN

High net profit B/T:	$300,000
Average net profit B/T:	150,000
Minimum investment:	15,000
Average investment:	50,000

Soup is hot! And soup kitchen restaurants we researched, selling little besides soup, are grossing $400,000 to $1 million a year. One outfit selling only chili, clam chowder, and salad grosses over $300,000 annually!

Soups are traditional in the diets of all nations as appetizers, side dishes, even as main courses. In the U.S., soup gained tremendous importance during the depression, when it was about the only nourishment some people could afford.

Now soup kitchens are back bigger than ever. Instead of providing nourishment for the down and out, they're appealing to young workingpeople who are seeking something new and inexpensive for lunch and dinner.

The cafeteria-style soup kitchens we researched are doing fantastic business! We visited one in the midst of a downpour while it served 600 people during the 11:00 a.m. to 2:00 p.m. lunch rush—many customers sat at umbrella-covered tables on a rain-soaked outdoor patio!

HOT MARKET

Our researchers report that soup kitchens get phenomenal patronage whether it rains or shines. Lunchtime business every day of the week is astonishing, and although the dinner crowd isn't as large, it warrants staying open to 8:00 or 9:00 p.m.

The lunchtime crowd at these innovative restaurants is about 70 percent female, mostly students and office workers grabbing inexpensive meals during the lunch break. After 1:00 p.m. the crowd becomes older and more sophisticated—businessmen and housewives linger over soup, salad, and a glass of wine while conducting business or taking a break from shopping.

Lunch menus are typically limited to a selection of soups and salads, bread or rolls, desserts, and wine, beer, espresso, and other beverages. Some served quiche—a cheese pie. This kind of menu appeals to the hurried schedules and eating practices of female students and office workers—as much interested in waistlines as they are in a quick cheap meal.

BOWLFUL OF PROFIT

Soup kitchen outfits are finding huge profits in items which most restaurants fail to exploit—soup and salad, items which are very inexpensive to prepare and require little overhead to serve cafeteria-style. Patrons are willing to spend as much as $2 for a bowl of soup and a roll, $1 for a simple dinner salad, and 75 cents for a glass of wine.

There's nothing magical about a soup kitchen operation. All it takes is good location, proper atmosphere, keeping overhead low, and maintaining superior product quality.

The product cost for a soup kitchen is 23 to 25 percent; labor should be 20 percent or less; and overhead is about 25 percent. That translates into a handsome profit margin of 30 percent or more for you. A full menu restaurant with a similar seating capacity has about the same sales volume, but sales and overhead costs may be 20 percent higher!

FIND A DYNAMIC SPOT

Proper site selection is especially important for a soup kitchen restaurant. Most of your revenue will be generated during the lunch rush, and this means you have to go where the workers are! Office workers on limited lunch schedules don't have time to drive across town.

Locating in a high-rise business district is ideal, especially if department stores, boutiques, antique shops, and other businesses that attract crowds, especially female crowds, are nearby. You will be able to attract a capacity lunch crowd, as well as draw late afternoon shoppers.

Once you've zeroed in on the right location, make sure the local zoning and health departments will give you their blessings. This is especially important if you plan to convert an existing structure.

You'll need a location big enough for at least 100 patrons: 2,500 to 3,000 square feet—or a 1,500-square-foot location is enough if there is an outdoor patio area for seating. Keep future expansion needs and capabilities in mind too.

A 1,500-to-2,000-square-foot soup kitchen with a seating capacity of 100 to 150 can be opened with a budget as slim as $15,000, under the right circumstances. Investing $40,000 to $60,000 should allow you to open a well-planned specialty restaurant in a fine location.

Start-up Manual #128 is available on this business. See page 379.

PUB/NIGHTCLUB/DISCO

High net profit B/T:	$100,000+
Average net profit B/T:	20,000
Minimum investment:	10,000
Average investment:	40,000

Through war, drought, and depression—interrupted only once by Prohibition—America's taverns, lounges, and bars have survived. And they have continued to provide the twin assets of good drink and fellowship to customers. The bonus is potentially high profits for the owners.

Well-managed bars, which are often recession-proof, require persons with many talents. Granted, they're hard work to get going, but the profits are well worth it. We found bars grossing $900,000 their first year. We also found bars that folded in the first six months.

One bar in a town of 26,000 can average $900 a night in gross receipts. Another bar in a town of 75,000 banks weekly receipts of only $9,000. Why?

With the potential for high profits also come risks. A bar is highly regulated by government—you always have federal, state, county, and sometimes city officials looking at your operation. Another thing to keep in mind is that bar customers are fickle, quick to investigate the "new kid down the block" and take their patronage (and your profits) out the door with them.

FOUR WAYS TO GO

Your first step is to decide what kind of bar you want to set up. There are four broad categories: neighborhood tavern, pub, nightclub, and disco. Each has different start-up costs, setup and location decisions, and marketing plans. Avoid locating a tavern where a disco would be a better bet.

Size up your local market. To open a profitable drinking establishment you have to know the habits and spending tastes of your community inside and out. Find out the average age, family size, type of occupation, income, and other data in your area.

After you've done your nuts-and-bolts research, narrow in on a site. But be advised: a nightclub or a disco will need not only a different address from a tavern or a pub, but different physical attributes.

PLAN THE LAYOUT OF YOUR BAR

Just as you have to know where your market is, you're going to have to decide on the right decor. The environment sets the mood, and you want to get people in the mood to sit in your place and have a few friendly drinks together.

Don't be afraid to get top-notch equipment. In any bar today, space-age bartending is the way the smart money is going. You need high tech to go with every point of proof in your booze. State-of-the-art computerized bartending can make a neighborhood pub owner an efficiency expert.

You're going to be coping with problems like bouncing out drunks, repairing the ice machine, and tracking down a customer's favorite label. Plan ahead for special drinks of the month to help your customers try out new tastes. That's also an intelligent approach to racking up a higher markup.

INSIDE SECRETS OF ALCOHOL CONSUMPTION

A neighborhood bar can be established for as little as $10,000. How can it be so little? A new bar owner can buy an existing license on time and take over the lease on equipment that's already in operation. Our research has revealed that it's possible to turn a shoestring investment into a $100,000 return the first year. What is needed is correct planning. Sometimes all that's required is a new sign and fresh promotions—not to mention shrewd customer relations.

As you would expect, pubs or nightclubs require higher start-up costs than neighborhood bars. Discos, with their elaborate decor and lighting needs, can sometimes cost in the millions. But when you talk markup in the alcohol business, you're talking in the hundreds of percent, not to mention all the "extras" of some setups.

The more exclusive you make your bar, the more people will want to get in. There's even profit in such things as plain old coffee for nondrinking friends of drinkers, not to mention the happy hour crowd. And with entertainment packages come cover charges of anywhere from $2 to $8 per customer!

TOMORROW'S BAR SCENE

Statistics indicate that the tendency for adults to meet in establishments to drink and socialize will continue through the years. In recession years, prospects are even brighter. As tastes become more sophisticated, the successful bars will keep in step with innovations, new services, new drink sensations—and more profits.

Start-up Manual #186 is available on this business. See page 379.

HEALTH FOOD STORE

High net profit B/T:	$75,000
Average net profit B/T:	48,000
Minimum Investment:	27,000
Average Investment:	42,000

You can capitalize on the phenomenal boom in "natural" foods by opening a health-food store! We've found smart operators grossing $750,000 a year and more selling "organically grown" fresh fruit and vegetables, "natural" foods, and a myriad of vitamins, lotions, and potions—designed to keep us healthy and grocers wealthy and wise!

Health-food stores have been around for years, but they no longer cater only to eccentrics, vegetarians, and the like. The "back to nature" '70s changed all that. The stores we researched for this report were crowded at all hours with health-hungry shoppers of all ages, shapes, and sizes.

Adverse publicity about chemicals, additives, and sugars in foods has made Americans more and more aware of what they eat. And our research has shown that once the decision is made to go natural, the zealous convert will make few exceptions. So the health food store becomes the *only* place a devotee shops for foodstuffs!

HEALTHY PROFIT MARGINS

Savvy retailers are using healthy markups on inventory carried in their stores, from 54 to 100 percent on most items. Perishables like organically grown vegetables and fruit carry up to 300 percent markup to cover spoilage losses.

Markup, as a percentage, is the increase above basic product cost you add to cover expenses and profit. *Margin* is the gross profit percentage of selling price you obtain by doing so. Thus a $1 item marked up 100 percent will sell for $2, and yield a 50 percent gross profit margin.

With markups averaging 54 percent to 100 percent, health-food stores are getting gross profit margins of 35 to 50 percent on most items. Produce must be marked up even higher because of spoilage losses. Tomatoes you buy for, say 18 cents a pound carry a selling price of 69 cents. In this case the markup is 283 percent and the gross profit margin 74 percent.

120

The smallest store (1,500 to 2,500 square feet) will stock between $10,000 and $20,000 in inventory, and turn it over eight to ten times a year—for gross sales ranging from $360,000 to $600,000. Net profits pre-tax are in the 9 to 10 percent range at most established stores, with cost of sales about 68 percent, and overhead a skinny 20 to 25 percent.

These margins are enough to turn the typical chain grocer green with envy! Chain grocers are lucky to realize a 2 percent net profit. And the health-food store that's carefully located won't have to go "toe-to-toe" with the major chains and do discounting, or have contests or other costly promotions that eat away at this bottom line, either!

THRIVING MARKET

Our research shows that the health-food store appeals to an amazingly diverse market. Everyone from teenagers and office workers to upper-class housewives and business executives is shopping in these stores, using them as full-service groceries as well as a place to pick up a snack or a bottle of vitamins.

While health-food stores attract a wide spectrum of shoppers, they do best in a community large enough to support at least 20 conventional grocery stores, with a minimum population of 200,000 in the vicinity. The experts allow one grocery store for every 10,000 in population.

In large cities, avoid low-income areas where tight family budgets allow for only spot or occasional purchases of higher-priced health food items.

What you're looking for is full-service female shoppers—people willing to spend the extra money to buy meat, fruit, vegetables, and dry goods free of insecticides, chemical additives, dyes, artificial flavorings, and other food treatments.

Vitamins, nutrients, and "organic" and "natural" foods are expensive, but this doesn't mean that you must locate only in very affluent areas. Middle-class communities, as well as neighborhoods appealing to students and "counterculture" types, can support a health-food store just as well. We've noted a surprising number of elderly people shopping in these stores too.

Our researchers report that there is no age or sex barrier when it comes to health consciousness. And operators of health-food stores inform us that healthy eating is simply a question of priorities.

Record sales of health magazines like *Prevention,* health-food cookbooks, organic gardening manuals, and how-to books on the proper use of vitamins and herbs are further validation that increasing numbers of Americans are thinking twice, reading ingredient labels carefully, and becoming more discriminating.

WHERE DOES YOUR GARDEN GROW?

The ideal location for a health-food store is a densely populated residential shopping area where middle- and upper-class communities converge, preferably not far from the local college or university. Look for a growing neighborhood that's "young thinking." Over 50 percent of the revenues will come from residents within a five-mile radius of the store.

Start-up Manual #125 is available on this business. See page 379.

SALAD BAR RESTAURANT

High net profit B/T:	$170,000
Average net profit B/T:	72,000
Minimum investment:	8,000
Average investment:	25,000

You can turn real lettuce into the green stuff that folds into your wallet. How? By opening a salad bar restaurant. It has worked like magic for owners of "saladerias."

We've seen hundreds of people go through the cafeteria-style restaurants that specialize in salads during a single lunchtime! And the idea is as fresh as the "fixin's" they toss in their bowls. The timing is perfect for this kind of specialty restaurant nearly anywhere in the country.

Millions of people are health- and diet-conscious. The phenomenal boom in natural foods, coupled with bad publicity about junk food and additives, means that more people are becoming concerned about what they put in their stomachs.

PROFITS GREEN!

A salad restaurant in the 90- to 120-seat range should gross from $250,000 to $500,000 per year. One of the most successful we found projects $600,000 to $750,000 gross. That's about the same as a well-run coffee shop the same size, but simplicity and operating economies result in higher than 25 percent net profit pretax for its owners. That's $150,000 to $187,000 on the bottom line.

One operation we saw is ideally located in a business district with a heavy lunch and dinner trade. It serves from 800 to 1,000 people per day at an average of $3.50 per meal, in a 100-seat storefront of only 3,000 square feet.

Another medium-sized operation we observed seats 100 and has served up to 500 people a day in its 7,000-square-foot store. Its owners project $400,000 in gross revenues from this newly opened restaurant at an average meal price of $4.25.

Gross volume potential depends on location, the number of daily customers, and average price of a meal. Seating capacity is an important variable.

Food costs for a salad bar restaurant are 22 to 27 percent, labor is 23 percent, and operating costs are 27 percent. We believe that some food and labor costs can be trimmed. So pretax profits of 23 to 28 percent can be improved somewhat. A smaller restaurant or coffee shop of the same size can expect higher operating costs (35 to 54 percent) and food costs (35 to 40 percent)—resulting in lower net profits of 15 to 18 percent.

HUGE MARKET

Our researchers conducted traffic studies at salad bar locations and found that the lunchtime business they do is phenomenal!

Most of the customers are healthy, weight-conscious executives, office workers, and shoppers. They have little time or money and want to eat light and run, between 11:00 a.m. and 2:00 p.m. At the later hours, patrons tended to be leisurely lunchers who lingered over salad, wine, and cheese or carrot cake.

Dinner trade was lighter, but more than justified staying open till 8:00 or 9:00 p.m. Couples and families would come in for soup, salad, and quiche (a baked cheese pie), and the adults often had white wine or beer along with their dinner.

KEEP FRONT-END INVESTMENT LOW

Some operations we investigated have spent as much as $150,000 before opening, but it is neither necessary nor desirable to invest this much up front. You can start with $8,000 to $13,000 under the right circumstances; $35,000 should be considered maximum for start-up costs, net of operating capital.

The low end assumes you can take over the lease and equipment of a small restaurant that's gone broke. Here you just pay the rent and redo the premises to suit your needs. You can renovate and increase seating in a location as small as 1,500 square feet.

The simplicity of this operation and the easy availability of used equipment means you can set up in nearly any good storefront without high renovation costs. All you need is a small "Pullman" kitchen area with a minimum of hardware and equipment. The salad bar, tables, chairs, and decor can complete the picture.

Start-up Manual #119 is available on this business. See page 379.

HOMEMADE-CAKE SHOP

High net profit B/T:	$84,000
Average net profit B/T:	31,000
Minimum investment:	550
Average investment:	22,000

Baking cakes with rich, natural ingredients in your home oven may seem an unlikely way to make $30,000 a year, but a woman out in California is making close to twice that much. It's easy to see how it can be done if your cakes sell for $8 or more and your product ingredient cost is kept considerably under the average 30 percent. All you need to get started in this business is an oven, a recipe for a tasty product, and a brochure mailing list.

The company we investigated started out just this way. The reasons for its success are that people everywhere are sick of mass-produced, tasteless bakery products. They miss the delicious home-baked cakes "like mother used to make." They are eager for the personal touch and delight in telling their friends that a real person baked their cake.

Today, more and more women are working and just too busy to bake anything beyond an instant mix. They and their families make up a huge market waiting to be satisfied.

SUPER INGREDIENTS MAKE A SUPER PRODUCT!

A woman in California opened one store selling homemade cakes and was soon able to start a second. Her success is based on the sale of seven homemade cakes made from natural ingredients that set them apart from the artificially flavored, dyed, and preserved commercial variety. Compare the ingredient list of a store-bought fudge cake with those of a homemade one:

Commercial	Homemade
Sugar	Sugar
Butter	Butter (more)
Flour	Flour
Eggs	Eggs (more)
Cocoa	Chopped walnuts
Whey	Pure vanilla

124

Milk
Monodiglycerides
Buttermilk
Baking powder
Corn syrup
Cornstarch
Vegetable gum
Pectin
Polysorbate 60
Artificial flavors

Unsweetened chocolate
Instant chocolate
   pudding and pie filling
Soda
Salt
Ice water

The taste comparison between the two cakes is dramatic!

The concept of the now famous chain House of Pies and of the renowned Marie Callender Pies began in the home. The cake company we investigated (though it is not franchising yet) or your own "Grandma's Homemade Cakes" (a great name idea) could be the "House of Cakes" a few years down the road.

One cake company we investigated is open six days a week and sells an average of 40 cakes a day. That's 240 cakes per week, cash and carry. At an average $10 per cake, sales are $2,400 per week, $10,320 per month. Costs of material, labor, and overhead total 40 percent, which leaves a fat pretax profit of $6,192 per month.

With the proper location, a good grand opening promotion, and some follow-up advertising, your shop should begin to return a healthy profit within a few months. Your profit margin will depend on two factors: keeping your overhead down to 15 percent and your labor down to 15 percent. The labor cost can be kept down by using moonlighting bakers part-time, or by doing the baking yourself. The overhead percentage will slide on a scale relative to your volume. Rent won't be a heavy factor because of the image you wish to maintain. Your customers will expect to see a nice woman in small, simple, even funky—but clean—quarters. They won't believe the authenticity of your product if you have an elaborate, plush location.

The key to pricing a specialty item like this is to aim high for snob appeal. In our world of mass production people expect to pay high prices for a handmade item. They feel it is more exclusive, and this is important, especially when it comes to the type of customer you want to attract.

Start-up Manual #94 is available on this business. See page 379.

YOGURT BAR

High net profit B/T:	$62,000
Average net profit B/T:	30,000
Minimum investment:	8,000
Average investment:	38,500

A decade or so ago a young man set up a frozen-yogurt stand in Bloomingdale's department store in New York City. Skeptics said he wouldn't have a chance—there weren't that many people interested in yogurt.

The skeptics were wrong. Today there are hundreds of successful yogurt shops throughout the country. With the right location, a good product, and proper management, a yogurt shop is a solid investment. The top shops are grossing as much as $750,000; the average established shop is taking in over $100,000. Location is the key to the highest volume, but the net profits of even the average stores are exciting—30 percent and more, depending on volume and excluding owner's salary.

THE DAIRY QUEEN OF THE '70s

During the '50s we saw a sudden proliferation of soft ice-cream drive-ins and shops like Dairy Queen. Soft ice cream was billed as the hottest new fast food. Yogurt became the dairy queen of the '70s and is becoming one of the staples of the fast-food scene in the '80s. Surprisingly, no big chains have moved into this yet—the chance to build your own looms high.

WHY YOGURT?

For ten years America's consumption of yogurt has grown as we have become increasingly more health-conscious, with strong trends toward physical fitness and health foods.

In 1967, $25 million worth of yogurt was sold nationally; in 1975, 200,000 tons passed over the counter, selling for $300 million. Recent sales have topped the $500 million mark. Surveys show that the majority of yogurt eaters are women from 18 to 34 years old. It is estimated that even today, over 70 percent of the population has never tasted yogurt.

The difference between commercially produced yogurt and the

custom-made variety sold in these new shops can be compared to the difference in taste between commercial ice cream and the custom-made product available through chains like Baskin-Robbins—a dramatic difference.

Custom yogurt is dispensed through a soft ice-cream machine and looks very similar in consistency. Honey is used to sweeten it, and it tastes like custard. All yogurt shops offer small free samples—their key to expanding the market.

A SUPER LOW-CAL DESSERT OR SNACK

A four-ounce serving of custom-made vanilla yogurt contains only 90 calories; yet it contains 7 grams of protein and 25 grams of carbohydrates (and only 2½ grams of fat). With 25 million adults dieting each year, the health-conscious populace is your primary target. One advantage of yogurt is that unlike many specially prepared low-calorie foods, it tastes good even to the uninitiated.

The date of the creation of yogurt is unknown, but we do know that the Turks used it 1,500 years ago as their sole source of an inebriant, fermenting it into a liquor.

YOGURT IS MADE VERY SIMPLY!

Like cheese, yogurt is made from milk to which bacteria are added, causing the mixture to jell. Yogurt is produced by adding the *Lactobacillus bulgaricus* and *Streptococcus thermophilus* to warmed skim milk. The warm temperature is maintained for several hours, and the result is yogurt.

You won't be making the stuff in your store, however. Milk companies can supply the yogurt in bulk containers. Most shops put the yogurt into a soft ice-cream machine which adds air, keeps it cold, and dispenses it in an attractive swirl.

You will offer frozen yogurt in cones, cups, and dishes, just like ice cream. A 3½-to-4-ounce cone sells for 60 cents (average); a 6-ounce dish for $1.25, and an 8-ounce dish for $1.50. Sundaes are made by adding fruits and nuts—bananas, peaches, strawberries, walnuts, pecans, raisins, dried apples and dates, carob chips, shredded coconut, almonds, cashews, or granola—and sell for at least $1.75.

Most shops have two dispensers with two flavors each. Shakes can be made from frozen yogurt by adding a little skimmed milk and putting the mixture in the usual shake blender. Shakes sell for 90 cents to $1.50, depending on the size and thickness of the mix.

Many yogurt bars also offer pure vegetable and fruit juices on their menus: carrot, celery, orange, grapefruit, and the like.

Start-up Manual #79 is available on this business. See page 379.

HOTDOG STAND

High net profit B/T:	$75,000
Average net profit B/T:	20,000
Minimum investment:	2,000
Average investment:	8,000

A hotdog stand that grossed $3,185 in one day! Unbelievable, but it happened at the grand opening of a Der Wienerschnitzel stand in Chino, California. That's the Wienerschnitzel chain's record and probably a record for hotdog sales for one day by one shop.

HOTDOG POPULARITY COMING BACK!

During the Roaring '20s hot dogs outsold hamburgers by a hefty margin. That's when the famous Coney Island and Nathan's Famous Hot Dogs were in their primes—what's more, dogs held that margin until after World War II; then hamburgers began edging past with continued impetus—until now.

Recently the giant A&W chain realized that hot dogs were gaining ground on the burger, and in some areas hotdog sales began matching hamburger sales.

TRENDS AND CYCLES

That trends follow definite cycles is accepted today. Historians analyzing interests during the last century can point out many examples in every area of our life-style. For example, baseball was once the most popular spectator sport; now it's football. Clothing and furniture often have even shorter cycles of popularity, yet here we are returning to decorating our homes and wearing clothes much like people 40, 50, and 60 years ago.

Perhaps a chain of hotdog stands will become the McDonald's of tomorrow. We have witnessed the success of little chains in every major city—a ground-floor indication that hot dogs may be moving up again.

EVEN IF WE'RE WRONG

A lot of money is being made in hot dogs, which still constitute one of the lowest-investment areas of the fast-food business. Around every city we found little hotdog stands giving their owners a before-tax net of $25,000 to $30,000 a year. Savvy owners able to land good financing have started with a couple of thousand dollars.

THE HOTTEST NEW HOT DOG

A few years ago Dave Barham opened a stand called Hot Dog on a Stick. It was an immediate success. He now has 40 units, each of which grosses nearly $10,000 per month. The hot dog is stuck on a stick, dipped in cornmeal batter and dropped in a deep fryer for a minute.

Until a few years ago, all he sold was this simple hot dog and handmade lemonade. Then he added a cheese stick: a one-inch-square by five-inch-long lump of mild cheddar cheese dipped in the same cornmeal batter and deep-fried. The hot dog, the cheese stick, and the old-fashioned lemonade are 75 cents each.

PROFIT POTENTIAL

Most small independent fast-food operations gross $1,500 to $2,500 per week. There are many exceptions to this rule, though, and we'll try to point out how to become such an exception.

The average food costs are 39 percent of gross sales; however, smart operators try to pare this down. Labor costs can be held low by using part-timers during the rush periods. Your percentage of profit is affected by volume and control of labor costs.

For example, if one person handles $36 worth of business in an hour, the labor cost is 5 percent. However, if volume is only $10 during that hour, labor cost rises to 19 percent. Labor costs of 15 percent or more are very hard to survive.

Overhead is usually the same regardless of volume. Assuming a $1,000 monthly overhead, the fellow with a $5,000 volume pays 20 percent to overhead, while a $10,000 volume pays only 10 percent.

If a stand does a healthy volume, it often nets the owner 40 percent gross before income taxes—plus his wages, if he works. As you can see, $3,000 monthly profit is not unusual for a little hotdog stand.

AVERAGE SALE PER CUSTOMER

We surveyed 20 small independent hotdog stands and found the average sale per customer to be $1.65. Some were registering over $2 consistently. So, a stand that grosses $10,000 per month feeds about 200 people per day. Not many when you consider that an average McDonald's may handle over 3,000 customers in a day.

Start-up Manual #73 is available on this business. See page 379.

HOMEMADE-CANDY STAND

High net profit B/T:	$25,000
Average net profit B/T:	18,000
Minimum investment:	100
Average investment:	2,000

There's an entrepreneur we've met in the course of our travels who nets about $500 every weekend, and our guess is he doesn't even pay taxes on it. That's equivalent to $900 of regularly taxed earnings for the average person, and he does it on an original investment of $100.

He sells candy made in his own kitchen by his wife and daughter. Preparation takes about ten hours of their time each week.

Amazing? Perhaps, but you've seen roadside candy vendors along the highway. We found some of them who have used the same roadside spot for over 15 years. They all use the same merchandising system with crude, prop-up signs placed every mile or half mile down the road in both directions: "Homemade Fudge," "Grandma's Saltwater Taffy," "Peanut Brittle," "Pralines," "Walnut Penuche," "Almond Butter Crunch," and "Pecan Turtles."

MARKUP IS FANTASTIC

Good quality ingredients that cost about 30 cents will make an eight-ounce tray of fudge that sells for $3.50. The aluminum foil tray and cellophane wrapper and label cost 10 cents. At the minimum wage, labor is about 5 percent, or 17 cents. Even if you pay $5 per hour, labor is only 8.6 percent.

YOU DON'T HAVE TO MAKE YOUR OWN CANDY

If making candy yourself is too much bother and you are willing to take less profit, you can buy your stock from "Candy Manufacturers and Distributors" (see the Yellow Pages) at about 50 percent off normal retail prices.

A GIANT ROADSIDE SUCCESS

Probably everyone has seen the Stuckey's candy shops in the southern and western states. Stuckey started after World War II just as we described it above. Today there are several hundred Stuckey's shops—all of them out in the countryside along major highways.

People traveling or joyriding on weekends develop a sweet tooth at the sight of these roadside signs. Buying is on impulse.

To presell you, the vendors use one of the most effective techniques in advertising—message repetition to build expectation: "Only 5 Miles, Grandma's Famous Homemade Pecan Log Roll" . . . "Only 3 Miles Ahead," etc. This gives your taste buds time to respond and you can almost taste the stuff by the time you reach the vendor.

Start-up Manual #70 is available on this business. See page 379.

DOUGHNUT SHOP

High net profit B/T:	$75,000
Average net profit B/T:	25,000
Minimum investment:	13,000
Average investment:	39,000

Here's a way you can turn a sweet tooth into a healthy profit! Sell doughnuts! It's so profitable, in the right location, that we found some owners of high-volume doughnut chains who were looking for the kind of tax shelters that doctors need.

These stores can be big money-makers because of superrich margins and relatively simple operation. Automation and dirt-cheap product costs can mean gross profit margins of 75 to 80 percent! That's because even the fanciest doughnuts cost pennies apiece to produce in quantity, yet they sell for 20 to 45 cents apiece, or even more, to hungry buyers—one at a time or by the boxful!

Operating expenses for a good high volume location are almost as small as the holes in the doughnuts you'll sell. Keeping expenses in the 50 to 56 percent range means net profits on the bottom line of 20 to 25 percent before tax.

BIG BOOMING BUSINESS!

Last year 663 million pounds of cake and yeast-raised donuts were sold in the United States alone! Donuts sold outside supermarkets were valued at $1.5 billion, yet the market is far from saturated. In 1978 the combined gross sales of the 15 largest franchisors were just under $500 million, and doughnut shop sales generally show no sign of reaching a peak.

Industry research proves a trend toward more and more eating out by in-a-hurry Americans. During the '80's experts project that two out of three meals will be prepared or eaten away from home. This is the result of a combination of factors: more singles and workingwomen; smaller families; more leisure time; on-the-go life-styles; and increased spendable income.

VOLUME IS KEY TO PROFIT!

There are thousands of small, struggling doughnut shops around the country barely making it, grossing $50,000 to $60,000 a year. The failure rate in this business is quite high, as a result.

Yet we found independently operated shops, and small chains run by absentee owners, grossing $100,000 to $150,000 a year. Some were grossing as much as $225,000 in tiny storefront locations!

One of the most successful new operations we found opened only two years ago in a tiny store behind a gas station. Phenomenal growth based on high quality has led the owner to open his ninth store recently. Average gross volume in each store is estimated at $100,000 plus!

One of the highest-volume single-store operations we found is owned by a former pharmacist, who now offers donut shop consulting services. His 900-square-foot location grosses $200,000 per year!

As an absentee owner he spends about eight hours a week in his store supervising baking. He told us that he nets almost 25 percent, and could do even better if he chose to work in the store every day himself!

We repeat, the secret of success in this business is volume. To gross $150,000 a year you need to make and sell 125 to 150 dozen doughnuts, or more, per day. This takes into account 20 percent of sales from beverages.

Owners enjoying the highest returns in this business were doing everything possible to bulk up retail sales volume. They had carefully selected a site for their shops, and were not afraid to stay open around the clock by staffing lean.

A good location will make its "bread and butter" at night—well worth the extra effort of staying open. Booming shops had a surprising number of patrons through the night, from midnight snackers to night workers.

Business in some stores was especially brisk after the bars closed, when night people were looking for a place to go and unwind over coffee. Many of these patrons would buy "takeouts" for a tasty breakfast.

In high-volume operations, product costs get smaller and smaller. It costs from 5 to 15 cents to make decorated doughnuts which will sell for three times that amount. The cost of making 150 to 200 dozen decorated doughnuts is $75 to $100, or 4 to 5 cents apiece.

The successful stores we investigated for this report had overall product costs of about 25 percent of gross sales. This depends on the price paid for and the quality of mixes, frying shortenings, and toppings.

The monthly expenses of running an all-night doughnut shop are $4,400 to $4,900, or 41 to 46 percent of gross. Before tax and owner's takeout this will bring monthly net profits of $3,100 to $4,400. That's $37,000 to $52,800 a year, selling doughnuts! Well-located shops netting $75,000 a year to absentee owners were found.

FIND A SWEET SPOT

Doughnuts are most popular as a breakfast, midmorning, or late evening snack food; they are usually served with a cup of coffee. While a doughnut store can be profitable in nearly any high-traffic location, the most profitable ones we found were in blue-collar areas.

Start-up Manual #126 is available on this business. See page 379.

GRANDMA'S BREAD SHOP

High net profit B/T:	$104,000
Average net profit B/T:	56,000
Minimum investment:	58,000
Average investment:	82,000

The back-to-nature movement of the '70's is a powerful trend in today's market. And you can capitalize on it with that basic staff of life—bread. We've found a handful of operators who've created a winner by selling high-margin exotic breads in a nostalgic, old-fashioned bakery atmosphere.

At California's 1980 Renaissance Pleasure Faire, people waiting to spend 55 cents for a thick slice of plain, unbuttered whole wheat bread formed longer lines than those waiting for pastries and soft drinks. And our researchers have watched people lining up to buy hot, crusty loaves two at a time, as well as buttered slices to nibble while shopping in malls and other high-traffic areas. After just two years, one retail chain is grossing $250,000 and more per store. The largest we found topped $800,000 *the first year*. The best part: Net profits ranged from 20 to 25 percent!

THE NOSE HAS IT

The secret of the success of these operations is smell. Physically and psychologically, nothing stimulates sales of tasty bread like the smell of a freshly baked loaf hot from the oven. Before shoppers see the store, the aroma grabs them by the nose and pulls them inside for a taste. The smells of bread conjure up not only hunger pangs and childhood memories, but high profits! Yes, you can make a living on bread alone, *if you have a very high volume.* This means building your bread output to over 1,000 loaves a day. Aim for 35,000 loaves a month after four months. We have witnessed much larger volumes in San Francisco and Chicago, where one bakery sells over 15,000 loaves a week. It has a superior and unique product, and people come to buy its special breads.

GET YOUR SLICE OF THE MARKET

Your location will dictate the types of bread to sell. Nationally, whole wheat is the most popular bread, with natural grain and granola breads expected to show the greatest future growth. Your product mix will depend on how much of a purist you want to be, and how much your customers like natural foods. Many bakers use only natural ingredients with no preservatives or chemicals, but remember: health breads with no preservatives last only a day.

For mass appeal, don't get labeled as a health-food operation. Owners of successful shops take regional preferences into consideration, but still try to accommodate everyone. We've seen outlets with over 30 bread varieties plus a complete range of rolls and buns.

Before beginning, survey your market. Significant preferences for bread exist. The age, income, and ethnic background of your customers are very important when you are deciding what breads to bake.

THE BEST LOCATIONS

A good location is vital to achieve the high volume needed for high profits. Get a store with good exposure, parking facilities, and very heavy foot traffic—ideally, a mall or shopping center. Shop identity is quickly built in large enclosed malls, since thousands of people see your store daily and can be drawn into it. Just as eating bread is a strong habit, so is shopping at a favorite store!

Getting in a mall can be difficult, though, and the start-up expense is higher than at other locations. Strip centers adjacent to malls can be equally profitable if they have very high foot traffic and good parking access. The strip center is popular with bread-shop owners, who pay less than half the typical annual mall rent of $18 per square foot.

GOOD HEALTH—GOOD PROFITS

The growing emphasis on health and nutrition is a potent ally for specialty bakers. Avant-garde nutritionists say that your typical market-bought, mass-produced white "wonder breads" are great for cleaning lampshades and suede shoes, but they're not fit to eat. This is where you come in. Americans are growing more aware of the ingredients of foods and tend increasingly to buy ethnic, gourmet, and health foods. Singles and young marrieds aged 20 to 38 are your best customers. Older consumers are another key target, because they will spend money on a good loaf of traditional pumpernickel.

NO-HASSLE RECIPES

Don't think breadmaking is complex. Bread is made by baking a mixture of flour or meal, water or milk, and a few other ingredients. The craft dates back to the ancient Egyptians. Batters are the simplest doughs, and whole wheat bread requires neither sifting nor kneading.

Ingredient suppliers or flour companies will provide you with bread bases, blended mixes, and advice. Once you gain experience you will be able to cut back some expensive mixes and experiment with your own specialties. The difference between your bread and the ordinary loaf will be in the special ingredients you add; you will probably want to have a few of your own recipes along with the formula recipes from suppliers and cookbooks. A specialty bread shop yields not only high profits, but the personal satisfaction of self-expression. Bread is the ideal product. It's not only a daily staple, but an impulse item. With the right location and a fresh, tasty product, your breads will sell as fast as you can bake them.

Start-up Manual #158 is available on this business. See page 379.

_____ **New Idea** _____

CASH IN ON CORN

There's something inherently American about popcorn—like baseball and the Fourth of July. A Downey, California, man has taken our national penchant for this treat and merchandised it in a way that would make Uncle Sam swell with pride.

Ron Sartin's *Culpepper* offers 18 varieties of popcorn. Cheddar cheese and carmel corn lead the list of favorites, but taco flavored, sour cream and onions, peanut butter crunch, butterscotch, licorice, and coconut all have their followers. Culpepper doesn't overlook fruit flavors either—lime, lemon, orange, pineapple, and, of course, strawberry.

It makes its own coatings from scratch, and the smell of all these flavors plays a big part in attracting customers. The small shop, with its even smaller kitchen, pops and coats about 300 pounds of the exotic corn a day!

The popcorn is sold by the bag, in the shape of balls, cakes, animals, and in six gallon tins which are mailed all over the world. The store sells 5,000 to 6,000 during the Christmas season alone.

This should be an easy-to-duplicate business that would do well in a mall. Equipment needs are small—just a popper and pots for making the coatings. Quality control is everything, though—that and letting an enticing smell drift from the shop.

NO-ALCOHOL BAR

High net profit B/T:	$175,000
Average net profit B/T:	75,000
Minimum investment:	18,000
Average investment:	34,000

A surprising number of people can be found in local bars or night-clubs who go there for the chance to socialize, for the entertainment, or for the inviting atmosphere—without drinking anything stronger than a Coke!

There are a number of reasons for this. Some are ex-drinkers and others can't imbibe for health reasons. Or they don't like what liquor does to them, or they have religious beliefs that don't allow alcohol.

We've investigated an operation that has all the makings of an overnight success story like this—a nondrinkers bar designed specifically to appeal to those who don't drink, but who want an exciting place to go for "action." One bar we checked out draws patrons from as far as 100 miles away—in fickle southern California!

AMAZING PROFITS!

A nondrinkers' bar can produce greater profit margins than an alcohol bar, and there's no need for an expensive liquor license—which can cost from $20,000 to $60,000 in some communities.

Original-recipe nonalcoholic drinks are sold for the same price as their alcoholic counterparts, but with less ingredient cost. And you don't need to stock $3,000 or more in booze inventory, either.

A nondrinker's bar can legally remain open 24 hours a day. But to optimize profits while maintaining a manageable overhead, we recommend operating, at least at first, with two shifts, opening around 11:00 a.m. and closing at 2:00 a.m. or whenever other local bars shut their doors.

This schedule lets you pick up the afternoon crowd for light lunches, drinks, and the use of game machines, pool table, and jukebox before the evening's bar and entertainment business gets under way.

Serving 400 to 500 drinks a night to regulars and to those who have one or two at the bar and leave without going to a table produces a daily income of $700 to $900. An "in" bar will do even better; it isn't uncommon for a packed night spot to gross $1 million or more a year!

Profits will fluctuate daily, with weekends and certain weeknights "hotter" than others. If the bar is open seven days a week, with good entertainment and lots of things for customers to get involved in, weekly profits can be high and quite consistent.

Making an average of $700 nightly results in gross revenue of $255,500 a year. Even at $500, gross revenue of $182,500 can be expected!

In the evening, charging a $2 minimum per person at the tables (but not at the bar) isn't so stiff as to turn customers away, yet protects against those who nurse one drink all night long.

A straight cover charge or entry fee may not work, unless it is common in your area and you have good entertainment. An option is a two-drink minimum.

Taking over an existing alcohol bar with equipment is the best way to start a no-alcohol bar. In addition to a monthly lease of $1,500 to $2,500 for 2,000 square feet, basic improvements, including minor equipment changes, shouldn't run to more than $45,000.

Second best is to renovate a small coffee shop or restaurant. This can be more costly than leasing an existing bar, when you consider that bar equipment, fixtures, and furniture may have to be bought and money spent for plumbing, electrical, and carpentry improvements.

A rule of thumb of bar equipment distributors and designers is to allow $300 to $500 per seat investment for new bar equipment. This is a heavy investment, but most distributors will provide financing with as little as 20 percent down.

KNOW YOUR MARKET

The market for a nondrinkers' bar has much in common with that of an alcohol bar, but there are additional needs. Like a regular saloon, your nonalcohol version should be near the entertainment and shopping areas of a community, where there is a naturally heavy flow of "with it" people after work and on weekends.

Because the no-alcohol bar represents an alternative form of entertainment, you must locate in a community with a population large enough to include a substantial non-drinking element.

While an alcohol bar can be profitable in a tiny community, the no-alcohol kind should be considered only in a metropolitan marketing area with a population of at least 500,000.

You won't have to reeducate or convert the public. In any large metropolitan area there are a large number of men and women who are nondrinkers. Besides the million alcoholics actively involved in the Alcoholics Anonymous program, there are 18 million recovering alcoholics in the U.S., according to the National Institute of Alcohol Abuse.

HIPSTERS TO EVANGELISTS

A nondrinkers' bar can do well in diverse locales—from trendy metropolitan areas where "hip" residents seek the latest innovation in evening entertainment to dry counties where liquor is illegal—even in the Bible Belt of the South and Midwest, where Christian temperance still has clout, with strict liquor laws to match. In these areas you can get by with a smaller population base.

Social psychologists state that the lower middle and lower classes use alcohol as an escape from the daily struggles of existence, while the upper classes increasingly tend to frequent expensive trendy nightclubs with "snob appeal."

The middle and upper classes are the segment of society who will patronize your no-alcohol bar. They have the discretionary income to frequent a nightclub, and also are into current self-improvement and health trends like bicycling or jogging.

YOUR VITAL "REGULARS" WILL BE EX-DRINKERS!

The people who will make you a success in this business are recovering alcoholics and their families. Along with the friends they bring with them, these people will be your regulars, because only you can offer them the environment that they desperately miss—and a place to go to have fun without the tortured worry about falling off the wagon.

It is essential to do everything you can to cultivate this market. With all your efforts to attract a wide-spectrum nondrinking clientele, never lose sight of the fact that these regulars are your bread and butter.

Visit local Alcoholics Anonymous clubs to spread the word about your new "safe house" before you open for business. Hire members of these clubs as your bartenders and waitresses. This will not only help solidify your relationship with the vital AA community, but provide you with reliable employees.

Word should spread quickly within the tight-knit AA group, and ex-drinkers will come from miles around to your bar, especially on weekends. (Weekends are a particularly depressing time for recovering alcoholics because they have lots of time to kill and few places to go that are congenial and "safe.")

Make sure that members of local AA clubs are free to hold meetings at your place—or to come over afterward for a bite to eat and some conversation with friends.

Start-up Manual #124 is available on this business. See page 379.

COFFEE SHOP

High net profit B/T:	$300,000
Average net profit B/T:	100,000
Minimum investment:	11,000
Average investment:	66,000

The National Restaurant Association claims that coffee shops are enjoying a 10 percent growth rate per year in sales. In 1975 gross sales jumped to $39 billion from $33.8 billion in 1973. Industry officials expect continued growth to extend well into the '80s.

This startling projection can be attributed to three factors. First, restaurant menu prices have risen only about 20 percent, compared to a 30 percent increase in the price of food purchased to eat at home. Second, each year more mothers enter the job market; it's reported that by 1990 two of every three mothers will be working outside the home. With one million women per year entering the work force in the '80s, there'll be less home cooking and more eating out. And third, more people are living alone. Many of them prefer dining out to eating alone at home.

The average 100- to 125-seat coffee shop will get its share of the market, and will gross about $12,000 per week. Many 24-hour operations collect more than $1.5 million per year—in fact, the Denny's and Norm's chains use this figure as the criterion of a good location.

Profit margins increase dramatically with volume. A high-volume operation nets in excess of 25 percent before taxes and depreciation; an average shop will net about 15 percent for an absentee owner.

INVESTMENT VARIABLES

For an absentee owner the optimum-size coffee shop is one with 125 seats. An owner/operator, however, can make a 50-to-60-seat shop profitable. The lowest range for cash investment is between

$10,000 and $30,000, but some have invested over $100,000.

The minimum $10,000 investment is in the restaurant that has gone broke, where the landlord has acquired the equipment in lieu of the lease default. The new operator simply pays rent, cleans up the building, erects a new sign, and stocks the pantry. This happens more often than you realize, but mostly with smaller shops seating 20 to 30 customers.

We do not suggest a coffee shop with fewer than 50 seats, because your per-seat labor costs will be too high. One cook and one busboy/dishwasher can handle 50 to 60 seats. With fewer seats than that, they can loaf.

INVESTMENT RANGE

If you purchase used equipment with a 50 percent down payment and find a building for rent that requires very little structural or exterior modification, you can open a 100-seat coffee shop with $30,000 to $55,000 in cash. This is often done by independents. Most new restaurants built from the ground up are built by chains, who are prepared to dish out $350,000 or more (even on leased land).

From an investment standpoint a 100-seat coffee shop requires only a few thousand dollars more than a 50-seater, because they require the same basic outlays for major equipment.

THE KEYS TO SUCCESS

We asked an executive of a chain of coffee shops what he felt are the most important secrets for a very profitable shop. His answer was threefold: location, location, location. Of course, a restaurant must be well managed, but from our surveys, we tend to agree with the chain executive. Other important factors for independent operators include moderate prices and quick, 24-hour service.

ESTABLISHING AN IMAGE

In and around every city there are a few restaurants that are well known for one specialty item: "The Biggest, Juiciest Hamburger"— "Rare Roast-Beef Sandwiches Sliced and Piled High at Your Table"—"The World-Famous Texas Tom's Chili"—"Anderson's Homemade Pea Soup"—"Home of Jacques's Famous Crepes"— "Granny's Clam Chowder"—the list is endless. One high-volume shop, The Pantry, is known for "Huge Portions of Country-Style Food."

MAKE YOURSELF FAMOUS

First you must choose a food item on which to base your fame, whether it be falafel or Greek lasagna or "mother's apple pie." Advertise it prominently on your signs and menu. Marie Callender is primarily a coffee shop, but the chain became famous for its pies. People buy what they are sold—if you say you produce "The Famous Joe Doe's Whatever," people will try it just to see why you claim it is famous. If it's good, they will believe you really are famous for "whatevers" and tell their friends. Thus you improve the reputation of all your foods.

Start-up Manual #59 is available on this business. See page 379.

New Idea
HOT DOG GOES FRENCH

There isn't much you can do to a hot dog—or is there? Lee Burns, a Napa, California, resident, has come up with what looks like a major change in the great American frankfurter. His store is called Le Hot Dog and it should do wonders for Franco-American relations, not to mention Burns' bank account!

His extra-long hot dogs start out ordinarily enough: he steams them in a steamer. But there the conventionality ends. Burns takes long pieces of sourdough, slits them in the center, then skewers them on an upright Teflon-coated spike. In one step the inside of the sourdough bun is hollowed out for the forthcoming hot dog and toasted to a crisp, golden tan.

Finally Burns gives the inside of the bun a squirt of Dijon mustard and insets the hot dog. He wraps the finished product in a paper with his trademark—Le Hot Dog—emblazoned on it, and hands it to customers who are waiting, mouths watering.

Burns claims that aside from the delicious taste of a sourdough bun wrapped around the hot dog, his innovation forever ends the problem of mustard-coated fingers and yellow stains on new jeans.

The marketing concept is a master stroke—giving the American-born hot dog a gourmet touch. Burns is gearing up for nationwide franchising.

FRIED-CHICKEN TAKEOUT RESTAURANT

High net profit B/T:	$150,000
Average net profit B/T:	50,000
Minimum investment:	20,000
Average investment:	60,500

A well-run chicken takeout restaurant in the right location can net upward of $150,000 annually before taxes—and it doesn't have to be a Kentucky Fried Chicken restaurant!

The Colonel franchises over 5,000 locations throughout the nation. We found a small chain in practically every major city making as much profit as the Colonel per outlet, with only 2 to 24 locations.

Have you heard of Church's Fried Chicken? They had 40 locations in 1969. Now they have over 1,000 restaurants nationwide.

The reason these companies can compete so successfully with the Colonel is that a fried-chicken takeout will draw most of its customers from no more than one to three miles away. That leaves a lot of gaps for competition practically everywhere.

When Church opened a restaurant in Orange County, California, where the chain was completely unknown, gross sales for the first week were only 11 percent below the average opening in Texas, where the chain is well known. This convinced us that anyone can open a fried-chicken takeout in a good location and make an exceptional profit, if a steady program of advertising is used.

A COMPARISON

Church's average first-week sales per location exceeded $7,000, only a little below the Colonel's for a similar area.

THE KEY TO SUCCESS

The chains have become experts in location choice. After many years of seeing some locations gross $3,000 per week and others $8,000, thorough studies of these failures and successes were made.

Church executives found they needed 20,000 to 30,000 people in the area, with the majority of the adults being young—aged 20 to 31. The location should be free-standing on a street heavily traveled by local traffic and it should be near a local shopping area.

THE PERFECT LOCATION

The perfect location will gross fairly close to $8,000 per week, but the ideal location is not always available. A store that grosses $4,000 to $5,000 per week can still be quite profitable, but of course it has the same labor, overhead, and advertising costs as the higher grosser.

Nevertheless, the net for an independent, absentee owner/operator rarely drops below 30 percent before taxes, and obviously the percentage goes higher with greater volume.

YOUR OWN SECRET FORMULA!

The Colonel claims his chicken is so good because of "18 secret herbs and spices" added to his flavoring. We had a chemical analysis performed on his batter to find just what we had suspected—the slogan is merely an advertising gimmick.

Sure, the 18 ingredients are there—and he does keep them a secret. All his store managers and franchises must buy the mix direct from the main office.

We had a top-flight chef try the formula our chemists prepared and there was no difference in taste or appearance between it and Kentucky Fried. You are free to call it your own secret formula. You might call it Atlanta Fried Chicken or Georgia Fried, or Tennessee Fried, or simply Real Southern.

Start-up Manual #55 is available on this business. See page 379.

POPCORN VENDING

High net profit B/T:	$40,000
Average net profit B/T:	20,000
Minimum investment:	1,000
Average investment:	5,000

Not many products offer the tremendous markup of popcorn. A plain 50-cent box costs the seller 5 cents for materials. The box costs almost as much as the ingredients, because 90 percent of the product is air.

This is an easy business to get into, since a good used popcorn machine can be purchased for less than $350. Our investigation turned up one small unit in good condition for half that, in a used restaurant equipment showroom.

Another $150 spent on corn, oil and bags or boxes will buy your supplies. Your health department will probably want to inspect your machine before issuing you a permit, but that's a simple procedure. The permit fee is usually less than $25. Another few hundred dollars spent on such items as a countertop, cash register and your rent or space fee puts you in business.

Selling popcorn is easy once you have a good location. The aroma of the product is a great salesman. Any spot where there is lots of steady foot traffic will provide you with a nice profit. The higher the traffic count, the higher your volume and take.

We investigated a variety of locations and found the possibilities amazing. And we found most operators had little promotion experience. It's easy to slip into this business and immediately start making money.

Potential locations are practically unlimited, since all you need is a lot of foot traffic. Concessionaires, as they are called in this business, often like to move from spot to spot, following high-traffic gatherings such as sporting events, trade shows, and fairs. We found one who specialized in high-school and college football, baseball, and basketball games and covered every little league in the area.

We found another whose specialty was shows: home shows, boat shows, auto shows, and trade shows. Another operator worked nothing but concerts, fairs, charities, and auctions. And many concessionaires sold anywhere they could expect a crowd.

60 TO 70 PERCENT NET PROFIT

Most "popcorn" events are one-day or one-night attractions, but a gross of $1,000 is not unusual—a gross that makes it worthwhile to set up for one day.

Several factors control your gross at one-night events: the volume of foot traffic, the age distribution of the crowd, how close you are to the full stream of traffic, the proximity and number of other food concessions, and the type of event and time of day.

The type of event will indicate the activity of the crowd. A football game will generate 50 percent less volume per 1,000 spectators than a boat show, because the boating crowd is continuously moving about.

The time of day affects sales of popcorn, which is a snack item consumed between meals. If you are serving an after-dinner crowd, your sales won't start rolling for a couple of hours.

Any other food concession should be viewed as your competition, even if it isn't selling popcorn—and it shouldn't be if you've made the proper agreement with the promoter of the event. Most popcorn vendors agree that it is a disadvantage to have all the food concessions grouped together if the crowd is always moving: try to get as far from your competitors as possible. But if the spectators are sedentary, say at games or concerts, try to locate in the general concession area where they can find you.

An age distribution of mostly mature adults or people nearing retirement age will produce less sales than a crowd of families with children.

Negative aspects don't always mean you must stay away from an event, but you should consider them, for example, in determining the size of your crew for each event. Peak sales periods for your snacks will be different from those for hamburgers. Even if it means your crew is not working hard during some hours of the day, you must have enough help to handle the peak volume periods.

USING SLOW PERIODS EFFECTIVELY

Smart operators prepop the corn during the slow periods, and store the popped corn in tightly sealed plastic bags, ready for a simple rewarming at peak demand times.

$70 PER THOUSAND PASSERSBY

Since most concessionaires are small operators and pocket some of their cash sales, our normal investigative procedures produced less than exact results. Information obtained from raw popcorn wholesalers, however, provided a useful base for more accurate sales statistics, since pound for pound, raw popcorn will produce about the same quantity of popped corn every time.

Sales for a site with constantly moving traffic were $35 per thousand people (low), $50 (average), and $70 (high). Almost every concessionaire sold cold drinks along with the popcorn; many sold several other snack-food items, including caramel-covered popcorn, cheese-flavored popcorn, snow cones, and cotton candy.

One small operator claimed that he worked about 25 events per year, totaling about 80 days, and grossed over $50,000 last year. His job as a salesman for a tire manufacturer gave him the time and freedom to book the concession, and he relied on a crew of three who operated the stand for him. His net before taxes was over $24,000.

Start-up Manual #25 is available on this business. See page 379.

GOURMET CHEESE AND WINE SHOP

High net profit B/T:	$90,000
Average net profit B/T:	40,000
Minimum investment:	16,500
Average investment:	60,500

The trend toward the "good old days" has filled everyone with nostalgia, affecting home, furniture, and clothing design, entertainment—in fact, every aspect of our lives, including the food we eat.

For example, sourdough bread, the staff of life for early pioneers, has become a national favorite. The nostalgia trend plus an increased interest in health food has fostered interest in other primitively made grain products, including stone-ground, whole-grain bread, biscuits, and crackers.

Wine sales are up. Between 1965 and 1975 they climbed almost 100 percent. Imported cheese, once a rarity like caviar and other gourmet delicacies, is racking up high sales.

Picnics, once annual company, club, or church affairs—or occasionally a family event—have made a comeback as a frequent social activity. This is substantiated by the sales of picnic paraphernalia such as special picnic baskets, coolers, and related items, which have increased 50 percent in the past decade.

Today, as always, the desire to be youthful is a major preoccupation of the adult from 25 to 75. Naturally, along with cosmetic attempts to rejuvenate themselves, people adopt some of the current youthful ideas and trends—from bicycling to disco dancing—to forestall Father Time. Health foods, old-time breads, cheese, and wines fit in with this trend.

HICKORY FARMS MOST SUCCESSFUL

The big successes in capitalizing on the trend toward old-time foods are novelty food retailers like Hickory Farms of Ohio and Swiss Colony Cheese Shops, Hickory Farms is by far the most successful, with stores in almost every state. Average monthly gross sales per store exceeds $25,000; some outlets gross over $50,000.

HIGH MARKUP—LOW INVESTMENT

Unlike supermarkets, where the markup is very small and a net of 2 percent on gross sales is a good profit, novelty food stores use markups of 100 percent and more. Net profit before taxes of 15 to 20 percent of gross sales is normal. Profit margins on wine are 25 to 40 percent (occasionally up to 60 percent), depending on how cheaply you buy the wine. Typically you should mark up a bottle or case by 50 percent.

The initial investment for equipment and inventory can be under $7,150, unless you have to build the store from stud walls, as in some new shopping centers. Hickory Farms stores used to be mainly in tourist attractions. Now, they—along with Swiss Colony and a few other smaller chains—have met with tremendous success in shopping centers and malls. Independents are doing very well in local shopping areas not supported by the shopping center's or mall's mass advertising concept.

Start-up Manual #19 is available on this business. See page 379.

HAMBURGER STAND

High net profit B/T:	$75,000
Average net profit B/T:	20,000
Minimum investment:	2,000
Average investment:	8,000

So you think your product has a good markup? Your cost is a dollar, and you sell it for $2. Well, that's peanuts. Let's take a super king-size quarter-pounder loaded with tomatoes, lettuce, onion, and a pickle—a hamburger. The average restaurant pays 50 cents for the ingredients. The selling price for the hamburger will range from 95 cents to $2.50, depending on the restaurant, with an average selling price of about $1.75.

To make it a double-decker with a half bun in between, reduce the weight of each patty by a few ounces; the result is that your cost increases by only a nickel. A regular run-of-the-mill hamburger will cost you only about 40 cents.

Of course we haven't included labor costs or overhead such as rent and utilities in these prices. These costs can only be charged to the product when you know the volume sold. Let's assume your rent, utilities, and all other business expenses—except labor—are $1,050 per month, and let's say you are selling 125 orders a day, seven days a week. (This isn't many, considering that the average McDonald's pushes 2,000 to 3,000 orders across the counter every day.) Your overhead, based on these figures, is less than 29 cents per order.

As for labor, let's assume you're open 14 hours a day—from 11:00 a.m. to 1:00 a.m.—and that you have one person working each shift. With wages at $4 an hour, including all payroll taxes, your total labor cost should average out to 45 cents per order.

Now, throw in a 35-cent Coke, which with paper cup, straw top, ice, and carbonated water costs you 7 cents. Your total cost for the king-size hamburger with all the trimmings and a Coke comes to $1.31, leaving you a net profit before taxes of 54 cents. And you didn't even have to put on an apron.

WHY HAMBURGER?

What is the attraction of the hamburger? Nobody seems to know, but whatever it is, burgers outsell all other sandwiches put together. McDonald's sells a billion hamburgers every 3½ to 4 months in the U.S. Since there are 220 million people in the country, that averages out to over a dozen hamburgers a year for every American man, woman, and child—for just one company. And that's just a drop in the burger bucket. Americans consume 112 pounds of beef per person and 50 to 60 percent of this is in the form of ground beef. This represents about 250 quarter-pounders a year.

Where could you find a better seller than that? Sure, there seem to be hamburger restaurants everywhere you look, but more than 80 percent make healthy profits relative to their investment.

THE BEST CHOICE—MAKE THEM BETTER!

The key to competing, when the product is universal and strongly in demand, is to make it cheaper, or make it better.

Making a cheaper hamburger has been exploited to death by chains such as Royal Castle, White Castle, Henry's, and McDonald's. But making a bigger, juicier, better-tasting hamburger, loaded with extras, has not yet been overpromoted. In almost every city in the U.S. you can find one quaint little hamburger stand that is known all over town for its big, juicy hamburgers. And think a minute. How many places do you know of where you can buy a half-pound hamburger? Probably not many.

So raise your price and put up a sign: "See the World's Largest, Juiciest Hamburger." People won't stop and eat a hamburger unless they are hungry, so capitalize on their hunger and hang up another sign: "Homemade French Fries—No Chalky, Frozen, Precooked Spuds Here. We Hand-cut Them Every Day and They're Fried Fresh." Give twice as many fries as the usual order and charge more. For instance, some places get 55 cents for a quarter-pound of fries. Give a half-pound for 55 cents and you'll build a reputation overnight. Your cost for the potatoes plus oil and packaging? Fifteen cents.

CASH-IN-ON-NOSTALGIA BINGE!

Nostalgia is in, so a "homemade" approach will make your product desirable. And here's another sign for you: "French Fries, 100 Percent of the Nutrients Left In."

To leave them in, simply scrub the potato and instead of peeling it, slice off the outside in big chunks. This will leave you with a rectangular block of clean potato and four sides with the skin intact. Cut up the heart and use it for regular french fries orders. Slice the outside pieces and fry them with the skins intact, and you have your staple.

THE ANGLE FOR A LOW INVESTMENT!

This is not an expensive business to get into. But if you take an empty building and set it up from scratch you may spend thousands of dollars just for used equipment. The inexpensive alternative is to take an existing hamburger stand—either a takeout-only or a takeout/sit-down type.

When you find one for rent it will usually be fully equipped. All you have to do is bring your food, hang up your signs, and you're ready for business. Naturally you'll be paying a higher rent than for an empty building, but start-up costs will be as low as possible.

Start-up Manual #16 is available on this business. See page 379.

PIZZERIA

High net profit B/T:	$90,000
Average net profit B/T:	35,000
Minimum investment:	5,500
Average investment:	23,000

It may surprise you, but one of the largest chains in the world is a pizza parlor chain, with almost 4,000 units in the U.S., Canada, Australia, West Germany, and Mexico. It is Pizza Hut.

The operation grossed over $317 million in 1977 with 2,820 units. That's an average of $112,000 annual gross per store, according to the figures turned in by the franchisees. A $3,000-per-week gross is not unusual for an average-sized pizzeria.

In 1958 Frank and Dan Carney—both in their early 20s—were working on degrees in college. They borrowed $600 to open their first Pizza Hut, more as a part-time lark than as a serious business venture. Within three months the regular take was $1,000 per month, so they decided to open their second store and get into business seriously. The rest is history.

The brothers are not Italians, and claim they never cooked anything, much less a pizza. Their mother had obtained some recipes from Italian friends. Some experimentation in the oven at home, and they were on their way. They say their mother was busy and didn't help.

The food service business is one of the few that you can start with very little cash, and still have the potential of becoming a millionaire. Look around and you will see little chains growing every day, in every city, in every type of food business.

Running a "to-go" pizzeria by yourself with a couple of helpers and grossing $1,500 per week, you should net about $600. As in most food businesses, the markup is high. Your material cost for a $4 pizza is about $1.60.

Pizza is one of the fastest-growing food items in the country. In 1978 pizza orders increased 15 percent, putting pizza ahead of hamburgers in growth. People are eager to try new varieties of pizza like Chicago or Sicilian style; every time a new version comes out, hungry Americans flock to buy it.

It isn't necessary to make the pizzas yourself, or even to run the store. Experienced pizza cooks are plentiful and are paid an average of $5 per hour. Some operators train high-school or college boys and pay a dollar less per hour.

In case you're worried about making pizza—don't be. You will be amazed at how simple it is. Try one in your home oven, and you'll see how easy it is and how good it tastes. You can expect considerably better pizzas baked in a commercial oven.

Start-up Manual #6 is available on this business. See page 379.

RETAIL

PLANT SHOP

High net profit B/T (before taxes):	$200,000
Average net profit B/T:	15,000
Minimum investment:	11,000
Average investment:	25,000

It has taken about ten years for the "return to nature" trend to catch the full attention of the nation. An offshoot of this trend is the potted-plant business.

STATUS SYMBOLS

Over the past years, decorating magazines and other publications have implanted, nurtured, and confirmed the notion that having plants in your home is a sign of good taste and good decorating; if you don't have any, it is implied, you are cold, insensitive, unfriendly, unsophisticated, and probably not very intelligent. It is hard to believe that this phenomenon was not dreamed up by some public relations firm.

FROM ART GALLERY TO PLANTS

A young artist-artisan with a small storefront gallery/studio in the hippie section of a city decided to add some plants to his shop to pick up a few extra dollars. The plants began selling better than his artwork, and it wasn't long before the fellow gave up his grand artistic ideals, found a new, larger store in a better area—and he probably hasn't painted a stroke since.

Now he is grossing over $700,000 a year with a projected net of $200,000 this year before taxes. Not bad for a young man with no starting capital to speak of and no business experience.

He did know one thing about plants, however: people like and want the unusual. He has plants potted in everything you can imagine, from spittoons to rusty old coffeepots. He pays young kids 50 cents an item to hunt out and bring back potential pots from junkyards, city dumps, or wherever. Using this system, his profit margin is beautiful. His cost for the plant in the old coffeepot is $1.25, and for the pot, 50 cents. The planting takes all of about five minutes. The retail price is $8.95.

The interior of his shop illustrates an unusual concept which,

153

because of his success, has been copied by many shops in the area.

Driftwood, antiques, waterfalls, and slabs of sand-blasted red-wood stumps have been combined into interesting islands covered with plants. Bark and sand cover the floor. The ceiling and walls are loaded with more plants and antique memorabilia. Walking through this giant 5,000-square-foot shop is like strolling beneath thatched treetops through a forest with babbling brooks.

PARKING ATTENDANTS FOR YOUR CAR

Today this shop has become the most famous plant shop in Los Angeles and is something of a tourist attraction! There is so much action that on certain days he has parking attendants, like those used at restaurants, to park his customers' cars.

CASE HISTORY NUMBER TWO

Another shop owner doing a similar volume has copied his interior layout to a degree, but he has also capitalized on the public's ignorance of the proper care of plants to build his own success. Most plant customers have problems keeping their greenery healthy, so this operator promotes free classes in plant care. He holds these seminars daily and nightly for his patrons or anyone who walks in.

To provide the best possible assistance, he convinces salesmen from nurseries, pottery companies, seed companies, and the like to give lectures. He borrows films from the Department of Agriculture to show on some nights. When he hires salesclerks he picks people who love plants and know a lot about them.

These employees hold casual instruction sessions free to anyone who comes in during the day. In the evening, the owner has a regular course for 20 students, three nights a week for four weeks. There is no charge for classes. As instructors he hires anyone who qualifies as semiexpert on plant care; usually foremen from nurseries, college instructors, and such. He pays these "experts" $20 per night for a two-hour session.

The shop owner advertises consistently in the local newspapers, pounding on his two key sales drums: We have the most unusual pots and plants in the world, and we give FREE lessons on how to care for your plants. Attend our free classes daily.

COULD BE A TEAHOUSE, ALSO!

To add to the colorful setting, he gives away free wine, cheese, tea, coffee, and cookies to his patrons. And throughout the store he has paintings, sculptures, macrame, and other crafts which he takes on consignment from local artisans (no investment, free decoration for his store—and a nice profit).

The store that we've just described, doing a half-million gross a

year, has an average inventory of $18,000; however, a small
can be opened with as little as $11,000 worth of plants, pots,

Start-up Manual #2 is available on this business. See page 378.

MOPED SHOP

High net profit B/T:	$150,000
Average net profit B/T:	62,500
Minimum investment:	33,000
Average investment:	44,000

If skyrocketing gas prices and shortages have you thinking of other
means of transportation than your car, yoou're not alone. That's why
mopeds—the bicycle with a motor—are selling like the proverbial
hotcakes. Moped sales are increasing nationwide at a rate of 60
percent a year, and the end is nowhere in sight!

When mopeds first hit the American market in 1975, only
25,000 were sold annually. By 1979, over 350,000 were sold. After
all, anything that gives good short-haul transportation and provides
150 miles per gallon is bound to be a winner.

One dealer we found sold 240 mopeds in just three days!
Another is averaging sales of more than 60 a month for an annual
gross of $360,000.

The moped business has four profitable areas: initial sales,
backup service, accessories, and rentals. Combining them can result
in hefty pretax nets of 35 to 45 percent.

MOTOR REPLACES LEGS

The word "moped" is a shortened form of "motorized pedaling
machine." It got its start in Europe more than 50 years ago. The idea
was to combine the economy of a bicycle with a tiny motor that
would eliminate the need for constant pedaling.

A simple two-cycle engine was developed which ignites by pedal
motion. Once the engine is running, there is no need to pedal. Today
there are more than 80 companies manufacturing mopeds with
speeds ranging from 17 to 35 mph. These speeds make mopeds the
ideal machine for short commuter hops.

YOUR TYPICAL BUYER

The gas crunch of 1978 caused a notable shift in the moped
market. The first mopeds were purchased by the 17-to-21-year-old
crowd, since they offered cheap transportation without the hassles of

special motorcycle licensing. By 1978, 70 percent of mopeds were being sold to men and women 25 and over to be used as primary sources of commuter transportation.

Now, as the dust is settling, the typical moped buyer is male, 18 to 35, with an annual income of $12,000 or more. Since mopeds cost $500 to $750 (and as high as $1,200), they are well within many people's income. The bottom line is that anyone with reasonable credit and a desire to have cheap, fun transportation is a potential customer.

GO WHERE THE ACTION IS

A population base of 50,000 is necessary to support a moped dealer. Our research shows that potential customers will travel up to ten miles to see these machines, which gives you a potential market area of 100 square miles.

We found dealers in isolated industrial areas and on streets with high foot traffic. We suggest that you locate centrally in an area that has a population of young, active people. Locations close to colleges, business schools, or residential areas of young marrieds are ideal.

Depending on your area, you should be able to rent a location for 50 cents to $1 per square foot. To open the kind of dealership we recommend, 1,200 square feet will be adequate.

THE KEY TO LAYOUT

In planning your layout, allow space for three main operations: showroom, office, and service-parts area. Planning the showroom layout is vital; experiment with several methods.

The most successful moped dealers have an active, well-planned service program. Often these programs can add as much as 30 percent to annual gross income. One dealer we found orders $2,500 to $3,000 wholesale in repair parts each month. By the time he has added his markup, his service area accounts for a gross of $45,000 annually.

YOUR "PEDDLE POWER"

Your employees are your peddle power. None of the operators we interviewed believed that a moped dealership would allow absentee ownership. However, as the moped craze expands we believe that absentee ownership will be possible if you hire the right general manager *and* a service manager.

The first qualification of your general manager should be excellent promotion and sales skills. Your service manager should be able to quote chapter and verse on servicing mopeds.

You will also need one or two hotshot young salespeople on the floor during rush hours. The best type of moped salesperson we found was young, dynamic, and most of all, a moped "freak," someone who can sell the glamour of your product.

ADVERTISING: YOUR PRIMARY INGREDIENT

Your best advertising will come from sponsoring and promoting moped events such as moped races and free moped rides.

An ad in the Yellow Pages is a must. Be sure to spell out services, hours, and the brands you carry. Next, plan a sale at least once a month promoting an item at discount. All print ads should feature both the fun and economy of owning a moped.

THE TWO-MOPED HOME

As the energy crisis continues we feel that more people of all classes and economic levels will turn to the moped as an alternative form of transportation. Almost every region in the country has experienced an increase in sales, and a trend to more than one moped per home is increasing. It's a business where you can still get in on the ground floor.

Start-up Manual #179 is available on this business. See page 378.

T-SHIRT SHOP

High net profit B/T:	$200,000
Average net profit B/T:	25,000
Minimum investment:	600
Average investment:	10,000

Everyone seems to be wearing a novelty T-shirt these days, and there seems to be no sign that the trend is abating. The sale of T-shirts carrying a design or saying has become as dependable as sales of blue jeans—the backbone of the casual apparel business. T-shirts offer comfort and style (they go perfectly with a pair of jeans), and low cost.

Individual customizing—accomplished 90 percent of the time by a pressing machine and a five- or six-color heat transfer—can turn an otherwise ordinary shirt into a unique treasure. One shop owner comments that most of his customers use the slogan or pattern to indicate preferences, identify with some group, or express a facet of the wearer's personality. And most purchasers are back time and time again—for something different or newer.

EASY TO START

The equipment and product list is simple: a heat-sealing machine, a few dozen assorted styles and colors of shirts, and 30 to 100 patterns. As you open a store your requirements are minimal (and hence, inexpensive). All you need is 300 to 400 square feet of floor space, some shelves for the shirt inventory, a few racks for display of shirts, and a dressing area with a mirror.

Depending on conditions, your cash investment need be only $600 to $2,400. A more elaborate permanent setting may take up to $30,000.

Customers will pay a premium price for a T-shirt or sweatshirt that has been imprinted with a decal of their choice. The cost of the heat transfer to provide the specific pattern is less than $1.00.

While most shops advertise that the design is applied free of charge, prices for the shirts reflect the decaling work. The mark-up on an individual item, with transfer, is usually to three times the cost. Most stores show a gross profit of 50 to 65 percent, which is fantastic for the clothing business. In a high-volume area a shop may make 50 to 100 sales per day, at an average of $5 to $6 per sale. One store in the poshest section of Los Angeles grosses up to $1,500 per day on the sale of shirts and transfers. It employs a full-time manager, two salespeople, and two pressers who operate their fully automatic heat transfer machines all day long.

"ONLY" $275 PROFIT PER WEEK

The lowest-volume shop we found was grossing an average of $823 per week. Even with this low volume the store was netting an absentee owner about $275 per week. And keep in mind that the higher the volume, the higher your percentage of profit.

We found a young man selling these shirts at a flea market on weekends and netting an average of $155 for two days. So, as you can see, anyone can get in and make money with this business.

Most buying of designed shirts is done on impulse. Some volume, however, can be attributed to specialized work, to athletic teams, clubs, and businesses. Certain prints will appeal to your customers more than others. Naturally, the more variety you offer, the higher your sales potential. Heat transfer manufacturers throughout the country have come up with over 1,000 designs that should fit every taste, fulfill any whim. When starting with limited capital, ask the manufacturers for a list of their hottest sellers. As you progress you can add the slower sellers out of your profits.

DESIGN YOUR OWN

If you are creative, the business will give you an opportunity to try your hand at creating decal designs. Most of the stores we visited had about 10 to 15 percent of their patterns custom-made to their specifications. Often these would be nothing more than a transfer made from a color photo of a rock star, an album cover, or some other design that would appeal to buyers in their particular markets.

Any transfer manufacturer can take an original piece of artwork and make a transfer from it. Normally the only requirements is a minimum order of 25 units.

Start-up Manual #43 is available on this business. See page 378.

WOMEN'S APPAREL SHOP

High net profit B/T:	$300,000
Average net profit B/T:	15,000
Minimum investment:	18,000
Average investment:	42,000

The Hula-Hoop came—and it went. So did 3-D movies, backyard bomb shelters, and the Edsel. While the sales of many products fluctuate with time and the economy, this is not the case with ladies' ready-to-wear. A report in *Dun's Review* in September 1976, for example, indicated that while the recession of 1974-75 was taking its toll on many other kinds of businesses, womenswear stores continued to maintain a respectable profit margin.

Come rain, snow, inflation, depression, or recession, people continue to shop for attractive clothes, and as long as women continue to buy clothing the opportunities for profit in the womenswear world run high.

Thus a ladies' clothing shop is one of those good old reliable kinds of markets. But the true entrepreneur looks for the fiery opportunity—the chance to go wild with success—the hottest product on the market. An average American couple in west Texas has proven that womenswear can be just that—and more.

About ten years ago W. R. (Dub) and Virgie Cook borrowed $20,000, rented a tiny building in a south Amarillo shopping center, and launched themselves as entrepreneurs. In so doing, they also launched themselves from obscurity into fame and fortune. In their first year of ownership they grossed an unexpected $200,000 in their tiny store, and celebrated with the opening of a second. Now they have a chain of women's clothing stores (in a city of just 150,000 people).

The comforting jangle of cash registers in five stores last year totaled out at a nice fat $1,500,385 with a profit before taxes and their salaries of over $350,000. The Fashion Corners of Amarillo, Inc., now supports about 50 full-time employees plus as many part-time workers during the busiest seasons. The corporation also maintains three automobiles, a truck, and a tractor for full-time company use, and two of its locations are now owned rather than leased.

The Cooks have moved into a splendid new home; they have been featured in their city's Sunday supplement magazine, and each of them drives a luxury car. A Dallas retailing expert has said that their success and fantastic growth rate has never been equaled in the retail world. Theirs is, indeed, a true American rags-to-riches story. And it's one that can be told time and time again.

Only one of the five Fashion Corner stores is located in a building that was originally intended for that kind of business. Two were former meat markets, one was once a service station, and another was just an empty shell of a building. The Cooks have taken unlikely buildings, often even grubby ones, and transformed them via paint, carpet, partitions, and plenty of elbow grease into attractive, workable stores. As a result they are able to get a much lower rental rate than usual and put more of their money into merchandise. They have been very careful, however, to locate each of the stores on a major traffic artery. They found that good advertising of their two independently located stores attracted as many customers as the shopping center locations. They say, "The important thing is to make the building serviceable, to use the space well, and to keep down overhead."

Certain basic guidelines should be followed to help you choose an ideal location in your town. Like the Cooks, you will want to locate on a heavily trafficked, two- or four-lane street. You must also consider the parking facilities; anything less than a 25-space off-the-street lot will hurt your chances for success. An adjacent lot plus abundant on-street parking is ideal.

When you are considering a location it is important to be sure to match the merchandise you plan to carry with the neighborhood you're in. An up-and-coming neighborhood with workingwomen will require different merchandise—and pricing—from an older area where the women stay at home. In order to coordinate your merchandise with your future customers, analyze the area: the type of homes and their costs, the age of the residents, whether or not there are career women in the area. Also check the type of customers frequenting other businesses on the same street.

Start-up Manual #107 is available on this business. See page 378.

GIFT SHOP

High net profit B/T:	$94,000
Average net profit B/T:	26,000
Minimum investment:	13,000
Average investment:	30,000

Owning a beautiful gift shop can be either the fulfillment of a dream or a very rude awakening. Even though gift shops have the third-highest failure rate among retail businesses, new ones are being opened at a rate of 50 a week. The primary reason for the dismal failure rate is that too many people enter this type of business motivated by a love of giftware merchandise, but with only a vague knowledge of the business realities involved.

While we don't hesitate to tell you this is an extremely risky business, it can prove to be a satisfying, challenging, and profitable one as well. If you are seriously considering investing your hard-earned money in a gift shop, a we advise you to come back down to earth and take a hard look at the business side.

PROFIT

Many little gift shops operated by the owner gross as low as $40,000 annually and give the proprietor $10,000 in profit and salary. A gift shop in a good, high-traffic location typically grosses between $100,000 and $200,000, with some larger ones exceeding $400,000 annually. Usually the percentage of profit will edge up slightly as the gross accelerates.

LOCATION—MOST IMPORTANT!

Location plays a particularly important part in determining the success of a gift shop. Not only is it a key to success, but the amount you "invest" in your location will be directly related to your future sales volume. Keep in mind that a gift shop, unlike most retail operations, is usually without an effective means of advertising. Capital which would otherwise be earmarked for advertising must, therefore, be put into obtaining the best location possible.

The basic rule is: A retail store paying $1,000 a month rent will do twice the sales volume of one paying $500, if the rent has been determined realistically.

There are certain ideal locations for a gift shop, the best being a spot in an enclosed regional shopping mall. Although your rent will be high, and building preparation expensive, you are practically guaranteed a profit from opening day. Mall locations now charge up to $4 per square foot, guaranteed against 2 to 3 percent of your gross.

Another ideal spot is on a business street or shopping area with heavy foot traffic, with adequate parking facilities and close proximity to public transportation a must. Your rent will be only slightly less than the rent in a mall, and the percentage of the gross will be the same.

SIZE DEPENDS ON YOUR CAPITAL

Tourist attractions produce a high volume of business, but, unfortunately, most have only four- or five-month seasons. Don't let this stop you. Many produce enough profits in the short season so you can take the rest of the year off. Rent, again, will be based on a percentage of your gross (3 to 5 percent), and unless it is a new attraction, building preparation will be low.

The size of your shop may be determined by the area in which you hope to locate. A spot in a downtown hotel will ensure a very high sales volume with as little as 600 square feet, while a suburban shopping area location may take 1,500 square feet to do as well.

Basically, the size of your shop will be determined by the variety and size of merchandise you can carry and by how much you will have to invest in fixtures, equipment, and inventory.

Start-up Manual #106 is available on this business. See page 378.

DO-IT-YOURSELF FRAMING SHOP

High net profit B/T:	$87,000
Average net profit B/T:	25,000
Minimum investment:	18,000
Average investment:	30,000

You don't need to be a Picasso or live on the Left Bank in Paris to become an important member of the art world. It doesn't take the money of a J. Paul Getty, either. With a little training and a lot of learning by doing, you can open a do-it-yourself framing shop in your community.

Owners of framing shops are hardly starving artists living in cold-water flats. We found do-it-yourself framing shops grossing

$250,000 a year or more and netting as much as $87,000, or 35 percent before taxes.

Nationwide, Americans are going on an art-buying binge unrivaled in recent history. Well-to-do collectors and average citizens are buying original oils, limited edition prints, and other framables at record rates. Over $100 million is spent annually in framing shops getting artworks ready for the wall.

TAKE ADVANTAGE OF THE DO-IT-YOURSELF CRAZE

Custom framing shops have been around for centuries, and framing has been considered an art form with a rich history and its own group of "old masters' for just as long.

Do-it-yourself framing represents a break for this tradition; within the framing industry, it has been as controversial as the development of fast-food franchises in the food business. Old-timers see it as a gimmick or fad at best and a prostitution of their artistry at worst. Newcomers see do-it-yourself framing as a way to bring better quality framing to the public, increase awareness of fine art, and capitalize on the boom in art and do-it-yourself crafts at the same time.

A do-it-yourself framing shop is set up so that customers can make their own frames with help and advice from experienced staffers. Customers select from hundreds of different molding patterns and mat colors, putting together their own frame for the fun of it—and saving up to 40 percent of what they would pay a custom framer.

Some shop owners offer only do-it-yourself (or "d-i-y" as it's called in the trade) and devote their entire operation to the concept, but most d-i-y shops offer customer framing as well. Custom work generates higher gross and net profit returns per customer. Also, many customs buyers will try making their own frames after exposure to the concept. Others will feel that the savings are not worth the effort; these people will come back for custom work next time. Thus they are "sold up" to the higher-margin customer work.

HANDSOME PROFITABILITY

The gross revenue in most established d-i-y shops is split on a 60/40 basis between do-it-yourself and custom-framing work. With material costs between 26 and 32 percent, gross profit falls in the 68 to 74 percent range.

Labor averages 25 percent, and overhead at well-managed shops is usually in the 20 to 25 percent range, resulting in net profits monthly of $2,500 to $2,900 pretax at a store grossing $120,000 annually. Several stores gross $21,000 monthly and net 35 percent pretax, or $7,350 monthly!

VERY LITTLE COMPETITION

Many parts of the country are wide open, and the demand for framing exceeds the supply of available shops. This is particularly true in the Midwest, according to industry studies. But there are some surprises. We learned that there are less than a dozen such stores in New York City!

Start-up Manual #144 is available on this business. See page 379.

ANTIQUE STORE

High net profit B/T:	$100,000
Average net profit B/T:	20,000
Minimum investment:	1,500
Average investment:	33,000

A young woman, walking through a house whose contents were being sold by the heirs to pay off inheritance taxes, spotted a cane-backed walking-stick rack.

The rack apparently had been kept in the attic, was grimy, and had a loose joint that needed to be reglued. She guessed the date of its origin as around 1900. The price tag read $2. Earlier, while browsing through the kitchen of the house, she had purchased a three-tiered salad colander for $1.

As she returned to her car with her prized possessions, a gentleman—who was just arriving at the sale—approached her and offered to purchase the walking-stick rack. His first offer was $25, which she declined. She weakened, however, when he stated that his final offer was $55.

He inquired what she planned to do with the colander. She replied that it was to be used as a three-tiered planter for green plants and hastily added that she had no intention of selling this item. Refusing his offer of $25, she happily returned home with a $52 profit and another prize for her antique collection.

The gentleman was an antique dealer, and this kind of story is commonplace in the antique business—a field that practically anyone can enter with some basic knowledge of antiques and a minimum of cash.

PROFITABLE HOBBY

Recently we came across a housewife at an auction. She had developed antique collecting into a very profitable hobby. Starting with a $50 investment a year ago, she has completely furnished her home with antiques whose retail value exceeds $10,000.

Each afternoon she packs the kids in the car and they go off to explore auctions and estate sales, and to answer classified ads in the newspaper. Occasionally she rummages through junk shops in the poorer section of town.

Every other weekend she places her own classified ads for the items she has purchased, using her garage as a showroom. The first weekend her sales were $308 on items for which she had paid $42.

This amateur collector-dealer's profits have ranged from a low of $50 to a high of $820 for her biweekly sales.

She began with very little knowledge, so she carefully researched the history of each item she purchased. Today she has an extensive collection of books on American antiques and is as knowledgeable as most dealers. Learning about your antiques is essential to success in this business.

Antique dealers have congregated in the same area or along the same street in most cities. Now a new phenomenon has been born—the antique shopping center. Many of these exist across the country. Two noted ones are Village Square Antiques, Bergen Mall Shopping Center, Paramus, New Jersey, and the Manhattan Art and Antique Center, 1050 Second Avenue, New York City.

Along the roads leading to the Catskills resort area in an 84-square-mile area in the Hudson River valley there are over a hundred dealers' shops.

Merchandisers with huge outlets are getting into the act. There are several in the New York City area whose showrooms are as large as football fields.

A THREE-ACRE ANTIQUE SHOP!

The Guild Antique Center, in Los Angeles, took over an old bakery warehouse with a floor space covering three acres. Using mass-merchandising techniques, they advertise on radio and TV and in newspapers and magazines, drawing people from as far as 300 miles away to this gigantic showroom where some items are priced as high as $10,000.

The nostalgia craze and antique fever are making the general public well aware of the possible value in old items. Consequently, dealers are finding it increasingly difficult to purchase antiques at the "right price."

"ANTIQUE CON MEN"

Antiques are hot. Even semiantiques are hot. With nostalgia for the good old days the "in" trend, buyers are traveling into the oldest rural sections of the country, buying and stealing anything and everything from the 1940s and earlier.

The raiders aren't leaving a stone unturned—literally. Practically every ghost town in the West has fallen to these scavengers. They don't leave much behind—some historical sites now require additional 24-hour security police to protect them.

The attic-hunting raiders do best in small towns and rural areas. They approach old homes, which are frequently owned by widows and old couples living on Social Security. Flashing a lot of cash, they represent themselves as members of a historical society looking for old memorabilia. All they want to do is look at the junk in their attic. The raiders offer to buy anything that is not wanted and tell stories of paying people in a nearby town as much as $2,000 for some items of historic value.

These raiders are often very successful in conning the people and usually pay about a twentieth of the real value of the items they purchase.

We've had reports of some operators in the South who approach the owners of large old homes and mansions telling them that the "historical society" is a nonprofit organization. The raiders promise to list homeowners' names as contributors in the society's annual yearbook or report. Their angle is that any "junk" people donate can be deducted from their income tax at today's value.

The raiders give out authentic-looking appraisal sheets and receipts and walk away without paying a cent for merchandise worth thousands of dollars.

Start-up Manual #32 is available on this business. See page 378.

WEDDING STORE

High net profit B/T:	$200,000
Average net profit B/T:	28,500
Minimum investment:	33,000
Average investment:	55,000

Formal weddings are back! The rising divorce rate has only added to the increasing number of new marriages every year, and today's young people have embraced the traditional rituals celebrated by their parents and grandparents, rejecting the "do-your-own-thing" attitude of a few years ago.

Sociologists claim that the weddingless days of the '70s reflected a general distrust of society as a whole, and that young couples were put off by a society that they didn't like or understand. The shift back to formal weddings began, some experts believe, in early 1977 when more couples opted for a formal exchange of vows, and interest in traditional dress, receptions, and showers was revived.

MARRIAGE IS BIG BUSINESS

Marriages made in heaven are paid for in hard cash right here on earth. In 1979 there were an estimated 2.3 million formal marriages at an average cost of between $3,000 and $6,000—that's over $10 billion. This total doesn't even reflect the cost of wedding gifts!

Many businesses are profitably in step with the wedding march. We found tuxedo rental shops grossing more than $1 million a year. Some wedding photographers are averaging $700 to $1,000 for a one-hour ceremony. Wedding chapels gross $2,000 a day and are booked months in advance.

ONE-STOP WEDDING SHOP

The secret of a successful wedding shop is simple. The ritual steps to a formal wedding are complex and time-consuming, running for a period of six to eight months. Choosing a bride's dress and trousseau, arranging receptions, showers, buying rings, mailing invitations, selecting music, choosing a location for the wedding, planning the ceremony, and arranging for the honeymoon are just a few slices of the traditional wedding cake.

Formal weddings create a tremendous burden on families who are emotionally tense from all the pressures of the upcoming nuptials. So smart entrepreneurs are combining many services under one roof. We are witnessing the creation of "one-stop shopping centers" for the soon-to-be-wed.

PROFITS ARE HEAVENLY

A relatively low investment of $50,000 will get you started turning dreams into dollars. Net profits range between $28,500 and $200,000 before taxes and there's even money to be made acting as a "wedding consultant." You are little more than a coordinator steering brides and grooms to the proper services. One consultant charges a flat fee of $1,000 per wedding and handled more than 800 weddings last year for a gross of $800,000!

So, along with your wedding dresses and tuxedo rental service, there are plenty of profitable activities to pursue. Look at the cost breakdown of a $6,000 wedding: $400 of that will go for a wedding dress, $500 for bridesmaid and maid-of-honor dresses, and $300 for tuxedo rentals. That's $1,200 in revenue coming through your door and $4,800 going past it. An average of $500 to $700 will be spent on photography, so why not add the services of a local free-lance photographer to your wedding package? Many operators pay a photographer a flat fee of $200 to $300 for a wedding, mark it up 100 percent and pass it on to the customer.

Six hundred dollars will go for flowers and other decorations. There's no need to open a flower shop; just work out a co-op arrangement with a flower shop where they provide the service and you take a percentage. Likewise with invitations, catering, limousine service, and even honeymoon travel plans.

One operator explained his $1.2 million gross as follows: wedding dress sales, $400,000; tuxedo rentals, $350,000; photography and videotaping, $65,000; floral contracting, $35,000; catering, $102,000; equipment rental, $109,000; musicians, $72,000; invitations and other printing, $82,000.

GOOD SERVICE IS THE KEY

The wedding industry is highly competitive and there are many major companies going after the bridal dollar. But successful shop owners are proving that it's not size that counts, but service. A small shop that caters to all aspects of a wedding ritual can be more profitable than a big store that sells only wedding gowns.

Start-up Manual #182 is available on this business. See page 378.

VITAMIN-NUTRITION STORE

High net profit B/T:	$100,000+
Average net profit B/T:	17,500
Minimum investment:	30,000
Average investment:	45,000

There's a billion-dollar business behind that vitamin pill you washed down with your juice this morning. In fact, if you're like millions of Americans, you probably took more than one. And you'll take more before the day is over. The one-a-day vitamin of the past has given way to an assortment of vitamin and mineral supplements. Our researchers have found retailers all over the country pushing pills in nutrition centers—or vitamin stores, grossing as much as $1 million in a single location.

Vitamin stores have been around for years, but they no longer cater just to health nuts or little old ladies looking for herbal remedies. The back-to-nature movement of the 1870s changed that by increasing emphasis on health, nutrition, and exercise, an important long-term market trend.

Our research shows that last year's sales of vitamins alone tapped $1 billion with little sign of a letup! And don't think that you have to be a big retailer to make it big in vitamin-nutrition stores. The little stores are also raking the profits in, when they are well run.

HEALTHY, WEALTHY, AND WISE

We found stores crowded with nutrition-minded shoppers writing checks for as much as $100 for the vitamins, supplements, and herbs they need to stay healthy—and make wise store owners wealthy. The best part of the business is that once a person becomes a zealous devotee of nutrition, there's little backsliding, and the only place a true believer can get the natural vitamins and supplements he needs is a specialty store carrying the specific types and potencies he requires. Such buyers scoff at the synthetic, commercial one-a-day style carried by drugstores and supermarkets. They want the real thing, *and they're willing to pay for it.*

A MARKETER CAN CLEAN UP

The average independent nutrition-vitamin store grosses between $150,000 and $200,000 a year, providing a modest return on investment for the usual devotee-turned-businessman. Contrast this ho-hum performance with the numbers turned in by Groff's Nutrition in Seattle, Washington, where "Vitamin Virg" Groff pulls a million bucks a year out of two tiny, 1,000-square-foot mall locations, banking a healthy pretax net estimated at over 15 percent. The average industry-wide is 10 to 12 percent.

And these aren't isolated cases. Our researchers turned up several other operators who started small and built miniempires through hardheaded marketing and promotion. That's what brings the cream to the surface in this business. Knowledge of nutrition and a commitment to good health are vital to success, but so are good business sense, merchandising skill, and buying savvy.

A DIVERSE MARKET

Women aged 40 and over will be your primary market. Seventy-five percent of your business will come from this market segment. But don't overlook younger women, aged 25 to 40, who will often be doing the shopping for the family. Our researchers have found young athletic men buying wheat germ standing elbow to elbow with senior citizens stocking up on herbal remedies and supplements. But even though more males are getting into nutrition, women still do most of the shopping. Vitamin stores that do best cater to this market in a metropolitan area large enough to have vast numbers of women in the right age groups surrounding their location or within a reasonable distance.

MALL LOCATION THE BEST

A large enclosed shopping mall does the best job of delivering the foot traffic you need to achieve highest volume and profitability. Mall shoppers are predominantly female, are in the age groups you are seeking, and have the money to spend. If you cannot afford a mall site, the next-best location is a densely populated residential area where middle-class to upper-middle-class communities converge.

The customers you are looking for are entirely different from health-food store customers. Don't mistake the two markets. Young trend setters are important as customers, but you need the mature female buyer more. Keep this in mind when decorating your store.

BEST-SELLERS

Inventory is a complex problem for the beginning vitamin store owner, but certain line items are essential and will be best-sellers overall. Experts recommend that beginning nutrition retailers carry only two or three of the five national brands. The sharpest retailers avoid putting in an entire line, even from major manufacturers, carrying only the items that sell best off the shelves. Most manufacturers, by the way, provide training programs on nutrition for retailers and their employees.

PROMOTE THE HEALTH OUT OF IT

The promoters are the ones making fortunes in this business, and you should do all you can to build interest and awareness in your marketplace through aggressive advertising and promotion. Developing an image as an expert in nutrition is important; customers must look to you for advice.

Plan to invest as much as 5 percent of projected gross sales on advertising, especially while you are getting established. With the right location, well-trained employees, aggressive marketing, and attention to details, you'll have a very healthy business on your hands.

Start-up Manual #169 is available on this business. See page 378.

CHILDREN'S APPAREL STORE

High net profit B/T:	$57,500
Average net profit B/T:	22,500
Minimum investment:	20,000
Average investment:	35,000

Here's a business in which "growth" has a double meaning, and both meanings lead to high profits for the smartly run store.

How would you like to own a store that sells items that will be obsolete in a month or two? What's more, the customers who bought those items will be back for newer ones that will also be replaced in a couple of months!

If this sounds appealing to you, the children's apparel business is the one for you. Many well-managed stores are realizing gross sales in the $100,000-to-$300,000 range, with the industry average over $200,000.

Careful buying and healthy markup coupled with a selective market can realize a pretax profit between 19 and 26 percent. Our researchers found one phenomenally successful five-store chain grossing over $1 million per year!

KEY TO SUCCESS: SPECIALIZE

A large part of the children's clothing business is captured by discounters who appeal to mothers shopping for price. Because the bulk of discount business is done by large chains such as K-Mart and Sears, you should keep away from this end of the business. Your share of profits from the children's market will come from going for the upper-end market. By handling exclusive, fashionable children's clothing, you don't have to worry about Sears carrying the same outfit for a few dollars less. Your customers will be shopping first for quality fashion, not low price.

Specialization is the key to success in today's fashion market. There is a sizable segment of the population that wants high-quality, fashionable children's clothing and is willing to pay a premium price for it. These largely upper- and upper-middle-class customers think of their children as extensions of themselves. The way their children are dressed and the degree of stylishness directly reflects their own sense of taste. They buy boutique-priced fashions for themselves and want the same for their children.

THE RIGHT LOCATION

In this business, location is vital. Open your shop in a neighborhood composed of young upper- or upper-middle-class families with children. Most successful children's apparel shop owners told us that 90 percent of their business comes from a five-square-mile area around their shop. This is something to keep in mind when advertising. Local newspapers and fliers, your least expensive form of advertising, should be all you need.

Look for a location with stores that promote browsing— bookstores, men's clothing stores, and specialty shops such as jewelry and antique stores. Make sure the area has heavy foot traffic.

Keep in mind that it pays to take advantage of evening shopping. With more and more mothers holding down jobs, the morning hours aren't as important as before.

IT PAYS TO BE DIFFERENT

The best way for a person to be successful in this business is to be different. If you create an unusual atmosphere, your customers will enjoy shopping.

Our researchers found several stores that used theme decorating. Popular themes are the circus, superheroes, and cartoon characters. The aim of these motifs is to make your shop pleasant and appealing. Proper designing of a store with 1,500 to 2,500 square feet should cost from $8,000 to $15,000. However, by working with skilled free-lance designers and woodcrafters you should be able to design and prepare an innovative interior for less.

A large, highly visible sign is one of the best investments you can make. Your sign and your window are your store's first contact with consumers.

MARK IT UP

Our researchers found that the largest portion of business in children's apparel is in the two- to four-year-old age group. Within this group, the largest amount of business—about 60 percent—comes from color-coordinated outfits. Your major stock should stick to the traditional pastel colors, but don't be afraid to try the new "hot" colors. Whatever you try, don't be afraid to take high markups! Because you are aiming for the quality market, you should stock items that won't be found in budget basements and large discount stores. You will often have exclusive items that can't be found anywhere else, *and people will be willing to pay for them!* Our researchers saw designer children's jeans in one store selling for an incredible $35 a pair!

When you've got an exclusive item, don't be afraid to take a healthy markup, which means pricing it as much as three times the wholesale cost. For example, if an item costs you $10, you will sell it for $30, a 200 percent markup. Of course, you won't be able to do this on every item.

MARK IT DOWN

Most retailers wait far too long to mark down slow-moving merchandise. If you have items that aren't selling quickly, you shouldn't hesitate to mark them down. Generally, 7 to 9 percent of your stock will be marked down.

PERENNIAL GROWTH

With more and more futurists predicting we are on the verge of another baby boom, the children's apparel industry is gearing up for a new period of growth. Innovative, promotional entrepreneurs will be assured of a large chunk of the business by specializing and carrying exclusive fashion lines, and by continually devising new and exciting means of promoting your business.

Start-up Manual #161 is available on this business. See page 378.

LIQUOR STORE

High net profit B/T:	$200,000
Average net profit B/T:	150,000
Minimum investment:	26,500
Average investment:	65,000

Looking at consumption figures for alcohol in this country, you might get the impression that we are running on booze instead of gasoline. Only 30 percent of the adult population say they have never touched a drop. The other 70 percent consume over 4 billion gallons of beer, wine, and distilled spirits every year, which figures to be 168 quarts per person.

Demographic studies and marketing research results indicate that the average middle-class family drinks less than a poor or a wealthy family. Men under 35 drink more than those over; the opposite is true of women.

Status-conscious, ambitious young professionals consume more spirits and wine than any other group. Married people without children consume almost twice as much as those with children at home. Single adults imbibe almost four times as much alcohol as their married neighbors. Beer consumption was not included in these studies, so that's extra.

It's easy to conclude where the best location for a liquor store is: an area with few children and a lot of single adults.

COMPLEX LAWS
If you are in one of the 32 states where the state government doesn't monopolize liquor revenues, owning a liquor store can be very profitable. We found a few stores netting close to $200,000 before taxes. The average low-volume store grosses around $100,000 per year; the average successful store, $300,000 to $400,000; and the really savvy operator, $500,000 to $1 million or more.

BUSINESS BROKERS
In some large cities we found business brokers who specialize in liquor stores and bars. Their knowledge of the state's laws is com-

prehensive, so if there's one in your area, this is who to talk to. Next best is a present owner of a liquor store, and next a lawyer.

If you have decent credit, we found that you can get a liquor store started in some states with as little as $26,500. Average start-up costs were $65,000 cash, with 80 percent of the fixture cost financed.

The average minimum down payment for buying an existing business is one-third, with the bank supplying from 30 to 50 percent and the seller holding a subordinate note for 15 to 35 percent of the total price. A rule of thumb used to determine the selling price of a liquor store is three times an average month's gross.

THE MOST PROFITABLE LOCATION

At the beginning of our investigation we conferred with many wholesalers and manufacturers across the country. We wanted to know what kind of independent operation turns the most volume and profit. Experienced people in the industry told us that a young, outgoing, affluent neighborhood is the best spot for the highest volume. Stores in some disadvantaged or ghetto areas also do well.

Good parking facilities are especially important in the suburbs. A corner location is always a good bet. The most successful stores are on free-standing locations.

WINE—THE KEY TO BETTER PROFITS

The type of store that produces the best sales figures is one that delivers, has charge accounts, provides a small selection of grocery staples and toiletries, and carries a good selection of wines.

Three outstanding stores, we found, carried a complete line of party goods and would allow the customer to taste any wine before purchase. Their wine sales were over 30 percent higher than those of comparable stores. The wine-tasting gimmick had to be the reason.

People drink for various reasons, but drinking is usually associated with entertaining. Consequently, selling party goods and offering gimmicks is a wise move. It may add only about $15,000 a year to the gross, but it fosters the feeling of a one-stop store for entertaining supplies.

Some successful stores had self-service cheese counters, offering 40 to 60 domestic cheeses. They had a shelf of exotic and gourmet-type canned goods, ranging from smoked oysters to caviar.

The markup on party goods, cheese, and gourmet food is 100 percent, so they make a worthwhile addition to your profit picture.

In a prominent spot in these stores was an elaborate display of snack items ranging from potato chips to prepared hors d'oeuvres. This kind of setup is a proved method of increasing gross sales and profits.

Start-up Manual #24 is available on this business. See page 378.

LINGERIE SHOP

High net profit B/T:	$62,500
Average net profit B/T:	15,000
Minimum investment:	18,000
Average investment:	35,000

Here's a way you can capitalize on a hot new trend before the rest of the marketplace catches on. Frilly feminine lingerie is coming back strong, and we predict that sales will explode over the next ten years.

We're not talking about the standard, ho-hum bras, girdles, and panty hose. The public is clamoring for items that are sexy, sensual, and more fun to wear—lacy camisoles, fancy slips, satin knickers, merry widow foundations, French garter belts, and silk stockings. Sales have increased by over 20 percent in the past year with no sign of letting up.

Our researchers watched customers pay $12 and more for lace-trimmed brassieres and as much as $300 for a pure silk peignoir set which includes a floor-length nightgown and jacket. Our research shows the average purchase is $20 in specialty lingerie shops, but $200 sales are frequent. This is well above the average sale in a standard department store.

BIG PROFITS POSSIBLE

By opening small specialty lingerie shops, we found, you can realize a net profit before taxes of 25 percent during the second year, based on $150,000 in annual sales. One owner/operator, who stocks an incredible array of intimate apparel, has a 1,500-square-foot shop that's constantly filled with customers. Women and men buying gifts yield a gross in excess of $200,000 annually and she's been in business for only four years. Her net profits are close to 29 percent before taxes.

Another owner/operator, who opened his 700-square-foot lingerie boutique a year and a half ago in a supersized shopping mall, grossed $120,000 the first fiscal year with 16 percent net profits before taxes. He expects to reach $200,000 in sales with a 35 percent net profit margin. There are only a handful of stores like this, so the market is virtually untouched.

CASH IN ON THE TREND

The upsurge in lingerie sales is partly due to recent fashion trends in womens wear—dresses and suits are being designed with femininity in mind. And to complete the "total look," women are buying complementary intimate apparel. Some style-setters are even using items like camisole tops and knickers as outerwear to deliberately emphasize femininity.

LOW INVESTMENT

You can open a lingerie shop that caters to these women for as little as $18,000 as a shoestrong operation. This will be profitable if you carry a tight inventory of specialized merchandise and emphasize personal service. We found one tiny 500-square-foot shop that opened three years ago in a busy suburban shopping center. The owner/operator started with a $14,500 investment and is now grossing $50,000 a year.

However, figure on an opening investment of $35,000 to $45,000. This gives you the advantage of a larger inventory and the vital opportunity to develop your store's image—an important ingredient for success in this business.

HUGE MARKET

All women wear lingerie in one form or another, including nightwear and lounge clothes. However, the market to focus on for non-traditional intimate apparel is young women between 18 and 30 years old. Those over 30 make up a substantial secondary market you shouldn't overlook.

The customers who frequent a specialized lingerie store are contemporary women who are very much aware of themselves and current fashion trends. They reject everyday underwear in favor of sexy lingerie—regardless of price.

Impulse buying is strong, too. Customers we watched rarely picked out a single bra, for example. At least one or two pairs of coordinated panties were also selected.

Men enjoy buying beautiful lingerie for their wives or girlfriends as much as the ladies enjoy wearing it. When it comes to gift buying, money is no object. We observed a store where one-third of the customers were men purchasing lingerie as gifts. They were often spending $75 or more on sexy negligees or classy silk camisole/knicker combinations.

The market for nontraditional lingerie is definitely there; it just hasn't been tapped. So a fast-moving entrepreneur can build up a lucrative business by attracting a young, progressive clientele of style-setters.

Start-up Manual #152 is available on this business. See page 378.

BICYCLE SHOP

High net profit B/T:	$150,000
Average net profit B/T:	20,000
Minimum investment:	5,000
Average investment:	23,000

For many years bicycles have been the vehicles and toys of children. In 1969 only 12 percent of the bikes sold in this country were of adult size, and the majority of them probably went to teenagers.

Today, however, the Bicycle Institute of America reports that adults buy about 50 percent of all the bikes sold, for their own use.

The bicycle binge has not reached its peak, and with a continued gas crunch there isn't any indication that it will within the next few years. Right now the retailer's biggest problem is getting enough merchandise and, especially, parts for repairs.

The two-wheeler boom started in 1971 when sales jumped an unprecedented 22 percent, from about 7 million units the previous year to about 9 million. In 1973, sales reached a high level of 15.2 million units. Bicycle shops began popping up everywhere in the country as other retailers started adding bicycles and related gear to their lines.

In 1978 sales reached 9.4 million units and in 1979 10.8 million. Industry sources believe that this is not like the fuel shortage of 1974, when people soon turned back to cars and bike sales dropped sharply. The consumer is now convinced that a gas problem is here to stay. With the trend toward energy conservation and more and more people looking to bicycles as a means of transportation, sales should easily top 12 million units yearly in the early 1980s.

It is true, however, that bicycle sales have closely followed the economic climate and are susceptible to tight money. A free-spending economy greatly influences bicycle sales. When a recession hits and sales start to slide, many shops may fold. But there will be those who maintain steady and profitable sales figures for years to come. The ones with the best locations and with efficient repair departments will probably survive.

LOW MARKUP

Unfortunately, bicycles don't receive what we feel is a reason-

177

able markup. Thirty to 32 percent is the average margin of profit on a bike, though the more deluxe models and accessories offer a fair 50 percent margin.

Currently, 91 percent of all bikes sold to adults are geared bikes. A ten-speed may be purchased for as little as $90 in some discount stores, or up to a high of $700 for a fancy European racing model. The average cost is $115. Shops in more affluent areas sell more ten-speed units in the $140-to-$170 range. Accessories will add an average of $18 to the total sale.

NOT AN ABSENTEE OWNER BUSINESS

Dealers have shown excellent sales figures; two we found were grossing almost $1 million and the low was $50,000. Annual gross sales of $200,000 were typical, but the average net was only 18 percent before taxes and the owner/operator's salary.

The average cash investment exceeded $20,000 and many had better than $30,000 tied up, with another $10,000 in financial obligations.

ASSEMBLING BIKES—LOTS OF FUN!

Another unfortunate part of being a bike dealer is that you receive your stock from the manufacturer "KD"—knocked down. In other words, assembly is required. That means that on top of your wholesale price, you must add, just like an automobile dealer, "dealer preparation costs," or 1 to 1½ hours of labor.

SCHWINN DEALERSHIP'S THE SAFEST

Schwinn, which runs a carefully monitored operation and is quite rigid in selecting dealers, requires an investment of $20,000 to $30,000; but for this the dealer gets a protected territory, the best sites for stores, and thorough management and repair training along with strong assistance in sales promotion. Other manufacturers made verbal overtures in the same direction, but with them, according to comments we received, action was slower than words.

Most distributors or manufacturers provide service and parts manuals when you stock their line. But don't expect a lot of help from the service end of the manual.

The National Bicycle Distributors Association (NBDA) source book contains a list of bicycle tool and repair stand suppliers. The manual has two parts, one for pricing and one for repairs. If you come across a problem not covered in the manual, just give the NBDA a call.

REPAIR HAS THE BEST FUTURE GROWTH

The NBDA manual states that you can make up to $15 an hour

just repairing bikes. Dealers throughout the U.S. are charging $6 to
$18 per hour for repair work, with a $10 average. If you are going
into the rental business only, the NBDA book would be a worthwhile
investment, since you must maintain your rental fleet. In addition,
with the manual many rental operators have found it profitable to
open part-time repair businesses in their homes and garages for extra
income.

Some further facts and figures to help you along: This is not an
absentee owner-type business, because of the low profit margins.
You should be mechanically inclined and able to assemble bikes as
they come from the factory, make minor adjustments, etc. The odds
are that you will have to train your servicemen yourself.

Start-up Manual #22 is available on this business. See page 378.

FLOWER SHOP

High net profit B/T:	$150,000
Average net profit B/T:	27,000
Minimum investment:	16,000
Average investment:	25,000

"Say it with flowers" is a phrase that has changed the meaning of
giving. A brilliantly colored bouquet of chrysanthemums or a single
red rose sent to a friend as a gesture of gratitude can mean more than
the most heartfelt words.

The flower business has never been better. Over the past five
years retail flower shop sales have increased from $2.3 billion to $3.6
billion a year. Men and women send flowers for weddings, births,
deaths, and simple "thinking of you" gifts because flowers represent
nature and give pleasure.

Florist revenues are expected to increase more than 10 percent
annually over the next five years. And there is room in this growing
business for you—as the owner/operator of a flower shop.

HEALTHY PROFITS

In the right location, a well-managed flower shop can easily
realize gross profits of $150,000 a year and net profits of 18 to 24
percent pretax.

We found 16 established shops with individual gross sales of an
unbelievable $1,000,000 a year. But it is realistic to figure that a
small two or three-year-old shop in a good market area will average
$150,000 annually and has the potential to provide the owner with

approximately $25,000 in earned income. This is a substantial living for the entrepreneur who enjoys working with flowers and has the ability to capitalize on this talent.

A minimum investment of $16,000 will put you into an 800- to 1,000-square-foot flower shop with a workable opening inventory. However, the best bet is to figure on $22,000 to $30,000 in capital. This allows you to rent a prime location and be more flexible when ordering your opening inventory.

The smallest shop we found is 600 square feet and is located in a small, suburban "strip" center. The owner/operator opened the shop five years ago with a shoestring investment of $13,500 and is now grossing $110,000 a year based on a large telephone clientele.

THE MARKET IS BOOMING

It is necessary to know and understand the flower-buying market to reach and maintain top-line volume goals. In the past the market has changed drastically from a primarily upper-income buyer to a casual, more expressive middle-income customer. Flowers have become an appropriate gesture for many occasions other than formal events. The most successful owners have changed their business policies accordingly by developing a contemporary atmosphere in their shops to attract this new breed of buyer.

There are many categories of flower purchasers, from the impulsive nature lovers who buy flowers regularly for friends and for their own enjoyment to those who rarely buy for reasons other than a birth or a funeral. The majority of buyers are between 24 and 45 years old, generally well educated, with a middle to high income. They are active in business and social events and consider flowers a part of their lifestyle. A recent study by the American Florists Marketing Council indicates that the mix between female and male buyers is close—54 and 46 percent respectively.

Young, unmarried people are becoming regular flower buyers. In many cases these men and women are career-oriented and find flowers the perfect gift for new business friends and associates. A large and relatively untapped market is children and teenagers, who often have a little money to spend on gifts.

Start-up Manual #143 is available on this business. See page 378.

TROPICAL FISH STORE

High net profit B/T:	$51,000
Average net profit B/T:	20,500
Minimum investment:	12,000
Average investment:	36,000

Remember the goldfish bowl you won at the state fair? Or that first little aquarium with a couple of angelfish and a tiny castle submerged under five gallons of water? While no one was watching, the tropical fish industry has grown into a $600 million-plus business. Over $20 million was spent last year by fish fanciers on aquariums alone.

Tropical fish spawn fans at a phenomenal rate, and the hobby is second only to amateur photography in consumer sales. Capitalizing on this booming hobby by opening a tropical fish store can easily net you $20,000 to $35,000 a year before taxes. You won't just be "keeping your head above water," either.

A tropical fish store takes hard work and determination to reach profit goals. It isn't enough to love fish; this is a competitive business that requires skill in buying, displaying, and maintaining livestock. But it is well worth the effort.

We found owner/operators of tropical fish stores grossing as much as $150,000 pretax with healthy profit margins of 27 to 34 percent including income from servicing home and office aquariums. The average volume for a small shop is $75,000 yearly. Most owners started with small inventories of high-quality livestock and have built a reputation for quality and service that draws customers from miles away.

Enthusiasts regularly visit stores seeking different breeds of fish, the latest equipment, and supplies. Store owners selling what they desire reap rewards to the tune of 18 to 27 percent net profit before taxes.

FAST GROWING HOBBY

Tropical fish store customers spend an average of $8 per visit for accessories and food. And aquarium setups can cost between $25 and $1,000 depending on size of tank, fish species, and decorating accessories.

The boom in tropical fish is the result of several factors: easier care, lower costs, and improved shipping conditions for transporting fish from distant waters. Industry officials estimate there are more than 20 million aquariums housing over 390 fish in this country. Fish don't take up a lot of room, eat very little, never need to be taken for walks, and are a beautiful addition to any home.

Projections indicate that sales of aquariums, accessories, food, and fish will increase by a dramatic 154 percent over the next ten years. Markups consistently average 90 percent over wholesale cost for dry stock and up to 200 percent for exotic fish and other livestock.

We have seen some stores that were started on a shoestring budget of $12,000 to $15,000. The owners/operators stocked only a basic working inventory of equipment, supplies, and fish at the beginning, and built the business into successful operations by expanding as profits grew.

One owner/operator we spoke to opened a 1000 square-foot store three years ago with $6,000 for equipment and inventory and $1,000 for building improvements. He has more than doubled his inventory since that time and is now expanding into a vacant store next door.

However, opening a well-stocked store in 1,000 square-feet will cost between $22,000 and $28,000. It is better to install top-quality aquarium equipment to minimize replacement expenses later. Plus, you have the advantage of opening as a "going business" rather than a low end operation.

HOT NEW TREND: SERVICING TANKS

We have found owner/operators who have started in the tropical fish business for much less money by servicing home and office aquariums for those who want the beauty of fish without the work. The initial investment on this side of the business can be as little as $300 to $500. After several years they have set aside enough capital to open their own retail store.

Several store owners have successfully incorporated this new concept into established operations. The service business, either as a start-up venture or sideline activity in a going retail store, can be exceptionally profitable if run properly. Some operators net up to 35 percent per year pretax due to service contracts with affluent homeowners, businessmen, and professional people. These contracts go for $10 to $50 per month plus the cost of equipment, which is usually paid by the customer.

FIND A GOOD SPOT

We have found tropical fish stores in unlikely locations doing quite well. In most cases, these stores are well established and were pioneers in the field. They are highly regarded for top-quality livestock and knowledgeable personnel.

In order to guarantee the highest possible volume, it is best to locate in a middle-class area in a city with a population of at least 300,000 people. Even though you will attract hobbyists from 30 or 40 miles away, you need a strong base of customers in the immediate vicinity.

A highly visible storefront near heavy auto traffic and parking are key location factors, but foot traffic is important to any retail operation and a tropical fish store is no exception. First-time browsers will not jump at the thought of spending $50 to $200 to set up an aquarium. But if the store is accessible and your sales ability is convincing, it won't be long before browsers become interested in raising their own fish.

Start-up Manual #141 is available on this business. See page 378.

GOURMET COOKWARE

High net profit B/T:	$125,000
Average net profit B/T:	62,500
Minimum investment:	18,000
Average investment:	45,000

Last year men and women in this country spent over $400 million on specialized cookware, kitchen gadgets, and serving items. Sales are expected to increase by 40 percent during the next year! Here's a way you can enjoy a generous helping of these national sales—open a gourmet cookware shop in a good location and cook up gross profits of up to 52 percent before taxes.

We have seen small gourmet cookware shops whip up appetizing annual sales in the six figure category. One 600 square-foot shop currently grosses $120,000 a year, and nourishes the owner with net profits of 21 percent before taxes. We found an owner of three shops in Virginia whose combined annual sales surpass the million-dollar mark. The smallest of the shops is 1,200 square-feet and the largest, which has a large cooking school setup, is 2,000 square-feet.

The potential is here for an owner/operator with a knowledge of gourmet cooking to make annual net profits of between 22 and 33 percent before taxes, based on a minimum inventory of $17,000. Adding cooking classes at $10 to $20 each class per person boosts gross profits by as much as 12 percent.

One major attraction for owners of gourmet cookware shops is the profit margin on merchandise. Basic cooking and serving products are generally marked up 105 percent. Unique accessories are slightly higher, and items like specially blended teas can go as high as 300 percent. Customers can't wait to buy. Industry studies indicate that $15 is the average national purchase in a gourmet cookware shop. Participants at store cooking classes generally spend up to $100 for the purchase of items used in each session.

GOURMET INTEREST GROWING

Business is booming for several reasons. The high cost of eating out is bringing people back to the kitchen, and as a result, home entertaining is once again in vogue. Gourmet and ethnic cooking has become a hobby for thousands of men and women, and attendance at food preparation classes has nearly tripled in the past three years. Graduates flock to gourmet cookware shops in search of exciting new gadgets, cookbooks, and tools of the craft.

A minimum investment of $18,000 will put you into a small 500 square foot shop with excellent profit potential. This includes equipment, building preparation, and a well-rounded opening inventory. One owner/operator we spoke to opened an 800-square-foot shop with $19,000 two years ago. Last year's sales volume reached $168,000 and volume is expected to increase dramatically this year.

Figure to open a shop in a prime location. Although the merchandise required is basically the same in any size shop, more available capital will improve your working inventory. Keep in mind that an annual inventory of $27,000, turned between four and five times, will result in net profits of $25,000 to $30,000 before taxes in addition to the salary you would draw as an owner/manager by running the shop yourself.

INGREDIENTS OF SUCCESS

The most successful shop owners are those with an in-depth knowledge of their market. While the gourmet craze is touching every socioeconomic level, the primary market is the well-educated, upper-income man or woman who on investing approximately $45,000 has the discretionary dollars to spend on innovative cookware and generally is into exotic cuisines.

The typical customer is 35 to 45 years old, has a family, and is a middle- to high-income homeowner or apartment dweller who enjoys the challenge of creating new dishes and the intimacy of entertaining at home. There is a fine balance between the number of male and female buyers. One owner noted that 40 percent of his regular customers are men.

An important secondary market is the increasing singles population. Ages vary, but generally these people are young professionals with incomes of $12,000 and above. They are usually interested in products to simplify meal preparation and save time in the kitchen;

they buy convenience items like food processors and blenders dustry experts predict that as more and more women return to ... job market, convenience products will become a mainstay in the American kitchen—and in the profit picture of gourmet cookware shops.

Start-up Manual #142 is available on this business. See page 378.

New Idea

SELLING OLD BARN SIDING

The trend in interior decor is going back to a rustic, natural atmosphere, and there's a lot of money to be made recycling old weathered barns into authentic interior wall coverings.

Din Kir Van of Washington has no trouble finding barns to tear down on weekends. Ever since barn siding has become popular as an interior decor item, the market has been flooded with barns for sale.

Kir Van pays $300 to $800 for barns. He and two employees dismantle the barn board by board. According to Kir Van, only 25 to 30 percent of the boards are salable, but they go for a hefty $1 to $1.80 a square foot.

The more weathered the boards and the knottier the wood, the higher the price. Unbelievably, the highest prices go to the boards with the most moss on them.

Kir Van says there is a great demand for barn siding to use in home interior wall treatments and in restaurants, hotels, and department stores. Architects and designers are eager to buy authentic barn siding.

The veteran barn hunter advises you to buy abandoned barns. Those recently inhabited by livestock keep that barnyard smell, making resale more difficult.

CHRISTMAS TREE LOT

High net profit B/T:	$10,000
Average net profit B/T:	5,000
Minimum investment:	10,000
Average investment:	18,000

Last year, over 30 million natural-cut Christmas trees were sold in this country. Cheerful operators of Christmas tree lots filled their stockings with net profits as high as $10,000 before taxes. *During a four week sale period!* And you can be part of this growing $350 million retail business by setting up a Christmas tree lot this season.

Business has never been better. Sales are expected to soar over the next few years as people hunger for the real spirit of the holidays. And a tree lot will break even during the second week of operation—the rest is gravy.

Several small retailers we found sell an inventory of 700 trees and walk away with gross profits of $5,000 to $7,000. An exceptional harvest for one month's work! And they are netting close to 18 percent before taxes. Tree lots with larger inventories of up to 1,500 trees average sales of close to $30,000 and can net from 25 to 32 percent for the season—even more under the right circumstances.

The secret is the markup on trees, which runs between 200 and 300 percent. A six-foot Scotch pine, for example, may wholesale for $7.80, including delivery, and retail for close to $20. If the tree is flocked, there's a 65 percent increase in gross profit. And the consumers *will* buy—regardless of cost.

THE FRESH SMELL OF SUCCESS

Studies by the National Christmas Tree Association say people will flock to the lots this year to capture the old-fashioned feeling of Christmas with a real tree. They are leaving artificial trees in the closet and opting for the fresh, seasonal sight—and smell—of natural-cut trees.

For as little as $10,000 you can "shoestring" a small tree lot, staff it with your family, and still be home in time for Christmas. This assumes a minimum of 700 trees in a good residential location.

Many operators work on a permanent seasonal basis. Every year they set up in the same location, building a faithful clientele that returns year after year for their trees. So the option is there to turn a one-time venture into a thriving annual business that will make every Christmas bright and green.

The successful Christmas tree lot operator boosts sales by knowing the market and choosing a location accordingly. It is a big market, which is growing as more and more people get tuned into nostalgia in today's fast-paced world and want Christmas "the way it used to be."

CHRISTMAS ORNAMENT STORE

High net profit B/T:	$46,000
Average net profit B/T:	14,000
Minimum investment:	10,000
Average investment:	20,000

Every year, most retail store owners look forward to the Christmas selling season with visions of profits dancing in their heads. Why? Because 50 to 80 percent of their annual sales take place between October and December.

We've found a way for you to wrap up a tidy share of these profits without the hassles of a year-round business. You can open a seasonal Christmas ornaments business in a good location, realize net profits of $20,000 before taxes, based on markups as high as 350 percent, and work only four months a year! You open in October and close in January.

Christmas ornaments have changed over the past decade. The basic lights, balls, and tinsel have been augmented by European baubles, handcrafted tree toys, and delicate blown-glass decorations. Theme trees decorated with bows, feathers, or tiny stuffed toys have also become popular.

Creativity has become the password for decorations as women—and men—select new ornaments every year to add to the family collection. Supplying these people is a fun and lucrative business that you can be a part of this Christmas or next year! An investment as low as $10,000 will get you into the Christmas ornament business with a basic opening inventory. To avoid major restocking and a bare-shelf look during the season, however, it is best to figure on an investment of $15,000 to $30,000. This will give you a well-balanced inventory of standard and exclusive ornaments to see you through the season, and a strong cash base for decorating and outfitting your store.

Seventy percent of all ornament buyers are women between the ages of 20 and 45 years, although sales to men are increasing every year. The majority of your customers have children and buy anywhere from 3 to 12 new ornaments a year.

One seasonal owner we talked to has a net profit before taxes of 14 percent. We have found other store owners netting profits of 20 to 25 percent and grossing $200,000 while open only 3½ months a year. Net profits before taxes for these operations are as much as $40,000 to $50,000.

One thing is certain: IF you know how to set up your Christmas ornaments business, where to locate, and what stock to carry, you should have an excellent chance of giving yourself one of the best Christmas presents of all—money!

Start-up Manual #140 is available on this business. See page 378.

FURNITURE STORE

High net profit B/T:	$150,000
Average net profit B/T:	45,000
Minimum investment:	20,000
Average investment:	50,000

For many years some furniture stores have been big money-makers, including the high line—very fine, expensive furniture; the middle line—good furniture; the low-to-middle line; and the low line.

The high line usually means a large investment—from $65,000 to over $100,000. It takes a lot of time to build a clientele and become profitable.

The middle line has a larger market to draw from. With an average investment of $55,000 and a healthy advertising budget, these stores become profitable sooner.

Low-line operations don't require a large investment, but they demand expertise in credit selling and lots of hard salesmanship. They are most effective when they carry their own contracts. Financing your own credit instruments requires a tremendous amount of capital, but the profit margin is very high.

The best operation is a combination low- and middle-line store. The initial investment is the lowest and it is the simplest store to operate. Aside from the information in our start-up manual, an experienced salesperson—and there are many—is all the expertise needed.

A 5,000-square-foot store spending $2,000 a month on advertising should gross $25,000 per month within 90 days. The net should be approximately $5,000. Within a year the gross should climb to a monthly average of $40,000 and the net to $8,000—an excellent return on investment.

UPHOLSTERED FURNITURE IS CUSTOM-MADE

An upholstered furniture store is simple to set up and run. The advantage is that you don't sell anything from the floor. Every piece of furniture in your store is merely a sample on which you take orders. The upholstered furniture is custom-made for the customer by the factory and delivered direct. This system has resulted from the need to maintain floor space and inventory investment.

The Levitz chain has become nationwide and successful doing the opposite. Unbelievable quantities of upholstered goods are stocked in each location. They must maintain a high gross margin to ensure a satisfactory net. This also means they must charge for delivery.

Naturally they advertise that they have the lowest prices in town, but this is not true. Any low-to-middle-line operation can beat their prices and still give free delivery—and profitably.

If you are in a town where Levitz has a store, price and delivery will be your selling points. We know of one store that blatantly claims in their ads that they will beat Levitz's price and give free delivery, plus more personalized service. This store is doing over $40,000 per month.

T.O. SALES SYSTEM DOUBLES CLOSING RATE

Most low-to-middle-line stores use a T.O. sales system. (T.O. stands for "takeover" or "turnover.") It works this way: If the salesperson cannot close the sale, he or she finds out what the customer's objection is and then calls in another salesperson to take over, presenting the salesperson as the sales manager, decorating expert, buyer, or the like.

Even though the takeover person tries to answer the customer's objection and often does—thereby closing the sale—he or she impresses the customer with the power to make a deal in order to make a sale. A special deal is offered, dropping the price as an enticement to buy now. The precentage of sales at this point is high, and the procedure saves a lot of sales.

The theory is that it is better to take a small profit than none at all. In the furniture business, the number of people who promise to come back and do so is very low. An explanation is included in our start-up manual.

There is plenty of latitude for price-cutting, since furniture of this type is generally marked up 100 percent plus 10 percent. (Most store owners add the 10 percent to pay advertising costs.) That is, a sofa that cost the dealer $100 sells for $200 plus $20, or $220. The lowest drop allowed the T.O. person is a "half number" or is 25 percent of the total price—in this case, $55. The customer's special price is now $165. In the trade, this is called a fullnumber markup and a half-number drop.

SPECIALIST FOR THE BIGGEST MARKET

The highest volume of furniture sales is in upholstered goods—living-room sets and accessories. Bedroom furniture runs a slow second in volume, with bedding sets and miscellaneous pieces coming in third. Dining-room sets are fourth.

Once a salesperson has closed a sale for a living-room set, usually the value of the sale can be doubled with add-ons: tables, lamps, etc. Most customers finance their own purchases, and an additional $5 to $15 a month doesn't seem like much to them when they visualize a completely new living room. Also, bedroom, den, and dining-room furniture are easily promoted once the initial sale is made.

Start-up Manual #11 is available on this business. See page 378.

HOBBY SHOP

High net profit B/T:	$110,000
Average net profit B/T:	11,000
Minimum investment:	13,000
Average investment:	52,000

Here's a business where you can be paid handsomely while surrounded by the stuff that dreams are made of! At one time or another most of us have daydreamed about being an ace fighter pilot, Grand Prix racer, sea captain, or locomotive engineer. And a hobby shop is the place where these fantasies can come true—in miniature.

Scale modeling, whether pastime or passion, has never been more popular than it is today. Hobbyists building or collecting model planes, railroads, racing cars, sailing ships, and the like are flocking to hobby shops for wish-fulfilling kits and other supplies they need. Total retail sales exceeded $1.7 billion in 1977 and topped $3 billion in 1979. So there's no question the market is there and it's growing!

Hobby shops can be "models" of profitability, too. We found several owners grossing $500,000 and more, netting as much as 22 percent pretax. The average pretax hobby shop, however, grosses about $100,000 and has a 38 percent gross profit margin. Many small stores net in the 10 percent to 12 percent range, once established, and provide a modest salary and takeout for owner/operators satisfied with devoting their days to a hobby-turned-business.

You can be as succesful as the owner who is able to spend most of his time in the store, just building models for display—if you remember that it took initially many years of hard work and low income to get to that point.

Hobby shops are not "get-rich-quick" operations. In the first year or two, most owners put profits, except for "eating money," back into their stores to satisfy inventory needs. A supplemental income, or substantial operating capital going in, may be necessary at first.

We found some owners who opened stores on a shoestring and built them into very successful businesses. One opened a few years ago, with only $5,000, which does not include the $4,000 put on inventory and $1,000 on fixtures for a 2,100-square-foot store. Now he grosses $320,000 a year and has between $50,000 and $60,000 in inventory.

Another started in a tiny storefront with borrowed capital, and over several years built up a five-store chain now valued at $1 million! So the opportunity is there for impressive long-term financial success—or a comfortable living, depending on what your goals are.

KNOW WHO THE BUYERS ARE

The most successful hobby shop owners have a clear understanding of the real maket for their products; it is primarily male hobby enthusiasts in the late 20s to early 40s. The majority are middle-income homeowners and family men, although a growing number of single men are involved in hobbies.

Buyers are most often skilled workers, professionals, or businessmen who have the leisure time and the income necessary to make larger-than-average purchases for themselves or their sons.

Preteens and teenage boys are the second key market. But average purchases by kids and teens are smaller when they buy for themselves. By the midteens many youths set aside their desire to build airplane kits or tinker with model trains—about the time they get interested in dating.

A FINAL WORD

Opening a hobby shop filled with fantasy-fulfilling kits, a model railroad empire, or dogfights between suspended biplanes can be a dream come true. Very few individuals are able to make a delightful hobby their life's work; for those who do, financial success is often secondary.

Start-up Manual #132 is available on this business. See page 379.

DISCOUNT FABRIC SHOP

High net Profit B/T:	$81,000
Average net profit B/T:	37,800
Minimum investment:	20,000
Average investment:	60,000

Operators of fabric shops across the nation have discovered that in this business, you can reap from what others sew! Today, 25 percent of all women's clothing in the U.S. is made in the home. Over 50 million women—half the female population—are sewing everything from simple shifts to men's suits.

Retail sales of home sewing goods in 1977 totaled $5.1 billion. Over 600 million articles of clothing and other items are made by home sewers annually and nearly 50 percent of all fabric sold to the consumer is purchased in fabric shops.

As a result, small yardage stores we researched are grossing between $150,000 and $250,000 a year. One national retail chain specializing in home sewing supplies grossed $177 million in 1977. That's an average of over $600,000 in sales for each of the company's 280 shops. But the highest gross and net profit on this business go to small fabric discount shops.

Small fabric discounters, we found, nearly always buy substantially below wholesale—often for as little as 10 cents on the dollar. Gross profit margins of 80 percent, which means a markup over cost of 400 percent, are commonplace!

Their trick is to specialize in seconds, irregulars, end cuts, and closeouts from the mills, distributors, clothing manufacturers, upholstery and drapery companies. Skillful buying allows substantial savings to the consumer, while these fabric discounters can compete successfully even with the largest retail fabric chain stores.

A discounter obtains these leftovers or high-grade seconds for a fraction of the wholesale price that a retailer must pay. So a fancy fabric that sells for $9 down the street or across town in the "high-rent" district can be sold for, say $5 per yard to cost-concious patrons, at higher gross profit margins.

THE LITTLE GUY CAN WIN BIG

The huge retail chain operations move slowly, and miss out on the majority of great buys in fabric seconds and closeouts, while the smaller independent discounters aggressively canvass the nation's garment districts and textile company buying offices in search of high quality merchandise at dirt-cheap prices!

An inventory of $60,000 to $100,000 in goods, turned over two or three times annually, nets established discounters between $3,100 and $6,700 before taxes monthly. That's 25 to 32 percent of sales, based on a $150,000 to $250,000 annual gross in a 3,000 square-foot fabric shop.

Galloping inflation has made women's clothing prices nothing to laugh about. And the home sewing industry anticipates a continuing pattern of record growth. Best estimates predict an increase of sales of 40 to 50 percent through the 1980's.

In addition to reacting against inflation, a growing number of women and men are making their own clothing, drapery, and furniture covering as a means of self-expression.

As prices of food and durable goods continue to soar, the economics in home sewing will become even harder for consumers to ignore. And with the four day workweek on the horizon, increased leisure time promises to give added impetus to this practical hobby.

A dramatic example is the "Sew-ins" now being held throughout the country. Recently, over 100,000 people attended a "Sew-in" held at the Houston Convention Center. Classes and demonstrations were held on home sewing techniques, fabrics, patterns, and notions.

THERE'S ROOM FOR YOU

The "typical" home sewer is female, 38 years old, with two children, and an annual family income of $13,000. She makes 13 garments a year. About 40 percent of these women visit a home sewing shop at least one a week; approximately 50 percent learned sewing in school.

So the market is definitely there for a small discounter. In 1967, only about 2,300 retail home sewing centers were scattered across the nation. Today there are over 20,000. But with record growth forecast for the coming decades, there's plenty of room for a smart operator.

Department stores and retail chains specializing in inexpensive fabrics constitute the greatest competition. But their service and product quality are characteristically poor. We found small discount fabric shops providing *top-quality* fabrics (seconds and closeouts) and accessories, with expert personal service existing quite profitably alongside major retail chain operations in the same area.

Women are shoppers and rarely buy without checking around first. Locating near a large impersonal chain and featuring quality goods and services can work to your advantage.

YOU MUST KNOW THE BUSINESS

You have to know what you're doing to compete effectively in this business. Merchandising fabric goods requires a thorough knowledge of sharp buying techniques, pricing, and inventory control methods. Technical knowledge of fabrics is not a requirement, but a working knowledge of types of fabrics, and how to buy them, is critical. Many small fabric stores are opened by individuals with sewing experience and a love of fabrics and fashion.

With careful attention to detail, and application of sound business sense, there's no reason you can't become another rags-to-riches success in this pleasant business!

Start-up Manual #133 is available on this business. See page 378.

_____ **New Idea** _____

RECORD PEDDLER

The kid standing on the corner selling bunches of flowers to passing motorists may have a Continental parked just down the block. But the newest form of street peddling puts the flower vendor to shame. The new generation are pushing records, and their profits have them dancing all the way to the bank.

Although we've yet to see it in America, record peddling in the streets is sweeping England. The only operating expense besides your inventory is a newspaper-boy type bag. The bag is slung over your shoulder and the records are stuck inside.

People have always been fascinated by the street vendors, and combining this fascination with the current explosion on the record industry seems a real winner. Of course you'll have to buy your stock from legitimate distributors, unless you've got a reliable bail bondsman. You'll also want a peddler's license, to avoid singing "Jailhouse Rock."

Beyond that it looks like a winner. One London lad told one of our researchers he's pulling in between $60 and $80 for four or five hours' work. Wonder how much he claims for income!

PAINT AND WALL COVERING STORE

High net profit B/T:	$140,000
Average net profit B/T:	48,000
Minimum investment:	23,000
Average investment:	42,000

Color your world with paint and wall covering! Last year American homeowners spent $3 billion in paint and wall covering stores. You can get on the bandwagon in this booming business, and add the green—as in profits—to your life. How? By opening a service-oriented paint and wall covering store in a good location.

The specialized paint and wall covering store is an invaluable asset to the growing numbers of do-it-yourself decorators in the nation. Sales personnel provide assistance with paint selection, as well as helpful information about preparation of surfaces, color coordination, and application techniques. In return, store owners are realizing high annual sales with solid markups 1.7 times inventory costs, based on $8,000 to $15,000 in stock.

A small independent paint store with average annual sales under $150,000 can realize a gross profit of 40 to 50 percent during the first three years with no problem. We have seen tiny operations, run by the owner/operators in good locations, grossing $125,000! And netting 25 percent before taxes. Established companies with more than one location are pulling in $150,000 to $200,000 annual gross sales at each store.

Government studies indicate that the profitability is here to stay. Total sales volume in decorating products for the past ten years was up 382 percent, surpassing total U.S. retail sales increases by 171 percent—dynamic, solid growth. Based on growth figures and trends for paint and wall covering stores from 1976, one study projected a 79 percent increase in expected sales figures by 1982—just around the corner.

HOME IMPROVEMENT BIG BUSINESS

Despite inflation, or perhaps because of it, more and more American men and women are trying their hand at do-it-yourself decorating. Even children are taking an interest in improving their surroundings as awareness of styles and trends starts at an earlier age than ever before. People are spending a greater portion of their free time and discretionary dollars on home improvement.

For as little as $23,000 you can set up a shoestring operation. This approach is profitable if you maintain a basic, workable inventory and emphasize customer service. We found one store cleaning up in a small suburban shopping area. The owner/operator had opened less than four years before with a $9,500 investment and soon was grossing $80,000. An investment of $30,000 to $40,000 is more common.

Most stores operate on a 40 to 46 percent profit margin for paint and wall coverings. Brushes, rollers, and other supplies, called sundries in the industry, operate on even higher margins. The sundries are impulse items and can account for one-third of your store sales. In addition, they provide the customer with one-stop shopping which is a very important aspect in this service-oriented business.

FIND THE BUYERS

Profitability depends largely on knowing your market in the paint-store business. An increase in the number of home shows and decorating clinics across the nation indicates that the market is there. We know it is increasing steadily!

There is a new interest among apartment dwellers in personalizing their environment. No longer is institutional white an acceptable backdrop to people who settle into a rental situation for $1\frac{1}{2}$ to 4 years. Apartment dwellers currently make up approximately 40 percent of the population and are important customers to consider.

Contractors and decorators also make up a large portion of a store's trade. A survey of independent store owners shows that an average of 40 percent of total sales was to smaller painting and decorating contractors in 1977. There are over 25,000 independent painting contractors in the United States today. They generally purchase volume amounts of paint and/or wall covering, and can play an essential role in your inventory turnover goals.

Annual retail per capita spending in specialty paint and wall covering stores is about $14. So, you can figure that in a community of 20,000 homeowners and apartment dwellers, your total store sales will easily reach $125,000 per year, counting on only half of the available decorating dollars for the area. Keep in mind that the cost of paint and sundries per room can vary from $15 to $50 depending on the type and amount of paint used.

Start-up Manual #134 is available on this business. See page 378.

DO-IT-YOURSELF COSMETIC SHOP

High net profit B/T:	$126,780
Average net profit B/T:	31,800
Minimum investment	26,000
Average investment:	70,000

Here's a way you can get in on the $6 billion cosmetics business and its fat profit margins without spending millions as Charles Revson, Helena Rubinstein, and other makeup moguls did.

You can open a do-it-yourself cosmetics shop, acting quickly on the hottest merchandising phenomenon to hit the cosmetics industry in 30 years. We've found tiny 400-square-foot cosmetiques, as they're called, reaping colorful six-figure annual sales with only two employees on staff. They sell private label cosmetic lines, purchased direct from manufacturers, at prices marked up as much as 600 percent over their cost, and still save the consumer 40 to 50 percent of the cost of big name-brand items. An ordinary lipstick, for example, will wholesale for 50 cents and retail in a cosmetique for as much as $3. Highest margins in this business are on the retail end, rather than manufacturing.

Cosmetiques are doing so well because they don't have to spend millions of dollars on product development and research, package design, and heavy brand advertising to make it big. And they use innovative yet proved merchandising techniques.

The most successful of these new operations is headquartered in New York City and was started by a husband-and-wife team in 1977. It now has 11 locations. Industry data show that stores this size can gross as high as $300,000, depending on location, and net over $126,000 pretax.

You don't have to be in chic, downtown Manhattan to use their brilliant merchandising approach and achieve the same kind of profit margin. This is a business that can succeed wherever there are women who want to enhance their beauty. Whether the latest look is natural, sophisticated, or Egyptian, cosmetics play a major role.

LET BUYERS EXPERIMENT

The cosmetiques we found completely change the way cosmetics have been marketed in the past. What they feature is a display smorgasbord of unpackaged products, opened for customers to play with to their hearts' content before they buy.

This violates traditional industry thinking, in which name-brand items are offered to patrons over the counters of department stores, and recommended by aggressive salespeople—without the chance to do much more than sniff or dab.

A woman looking for a certain shade of lipstick, for example, will often find that the color just doesn't look the same as it did at the store. So it joins a costly group of "orphans" in the bathroom drawer—usually never to be used again.

In a cosmetique, on the other hand, women have a chance to sample as many colors as they want, get guidance from expert staff, and find colors that look as good on as they do in the pot. There is no pressure from "pushy" commissioned salespeople, and no need to visit various shops in search of a particular color, or to pay inflated name-brand prices.

MARKET IN THE MILLIONS

There are about 76 million women over 18 years of age in the United States who are likely to react well to such a store in their area. Marketing studies have estimated that 76.9 percent of them use lipstick or gloss, and 88.4 percent use facial makeup. Just over half of them use some type of eye makeup too, if only a dab of shadow.

A shop like this will attract any woman, but the typical customer is 25 to 55 years old. Those under age 25 are a secondary market; the natural look doesn't require much makeup. But when the aging process sets in, use of treatments and cosmetics increases, as well as average purchases in a shop like this. Some stores report purchases of $25 to $50. The more spendable income a woman has, the more makeup she buys, according to industry data.

Clearly, the ideal market segment for a cosmetique is middle- to upper-class women in the age range given. Characteristically, these are workingwomen and housewives with financially stable life-styles.

While at the beginning you'll be catering to women, the male market currently is between $560 million and $1.2 billion in yearly sales and is growing twice as fast as the women's market. Male products include lotions, astringents, bronzers, shampoos, and conditioners, as well as scents.

In market areas with heavy concentrations of blacks, appealing to this significant market segment can be a wise move, as the black cosmetic market is currently estimated at $500 million to $750 million.

LOVELY MERCHANDISING

One cosmetique displays over 200 shades of lipstick, 108 eye shadows, and 23 shades of foundation makeup laid out on long tables and wall "palettes." You can expand on this concept by including a shampoo, lotion, oil, and fragrance bar too. In one cosmetique we found, patrons filled their own containers with shampoo from spigoted kegs!

The success of these shops is tied to psychology. Customers are free and unrestricted in these shops (within obvious limits). This merchandising approach generates higher sales and bigger profits than the conventional marketing method.

Start-up Manual #135 is available on this business. See page 378.

PIPE SHOP

High net profit B/T:	$140,000
Average net profit B/T:	20,000
Minimum investment:	27,000
Average investment:	39,000

Only college professors and tweedy types smoke pipes? Wrong! We've seen tiny shops grossing $700,000 a year selling pipes, tobacco, and related smoking paraphernalia to men and women from all walks of life!

Hundreds of people are drawn into these modern-day curiosity shops by window displays of lovely hand-carved briar and meerschaum pipes, masculine gift items and the pleasing aroma of exotic tobaccos.

We were surprised to find patrons ranging from stylish young women interested in small opera-style pipes and foreign made cigarettes to burly construction workers purchasing hand-carved Danish briars at $175! Between 10:00 a.m. and noon we counted 60 paying customers in one small shop!

MARKET GROWING

Almost $2 billion worth of pipes, tobacco, cigars, and related gift items will be sold in the U.S. this year at net profit margins better than 20 percent.

Once male sanctuaries, pipe shops now cater to both sexes. There are 4.1 million pipe smokers in the U.S. and as much as 20 percent of annual sales stem from women. During the Christmas holidays when 25 percent of all sales characteristically take place, 80 percent of revenue derives from women. And not all female purchases are for gifts. Women are smoking pipes and cigars!

Still, year-round clientele is predominantly male and takes pipes and tobaccos quite seriously. Pipe smokers own an average of 7 pipes. This allows the pipes to "rest" between uses so they smoke well. Pipe smokers also tend to be collectors. Many own 25 to 100 and more—each to suit a particular mood.

Once a person is sold on the idea of smoking a pipe, he tends to become a connoisseur, visiting the local pipe shop frequently in search of "expert" advice, new pipe designs, and various "private label" blends of tobacco. One small pipe shop we checked out sells seven tons of pipe tobacco a year!

HOT PROFITS

Profits in the pipe shop business depend on proper location and providing customers with expert service and advice. Establishing yourself as the local authority on pipes, cigars, and tobacco can lead to astounding success! While most pipe shops we checked out grossed between $80,000 and $300,000 annually, we found several grossing over $650,000 a year!

Markups on pipes generally provide a 50 percent gross profit margin. Pipe-shop operators enjoy a larger markup on tobacco, for a 60 percent gross profit margin on bulk tobacco, cigarettes, cigars, snuff, and chewing tobacco. You can expect about one third of your business to derive from cigarettes (foreign and domestic) and cigars. Snuff and chewing tobacco generally are slow movers; they depend on the market area.

Margins on smoking paraphernalia like lighters, pipe tools, leather tobacco pouches, pipe racks and humidors average around 66 percent. Savvy pipe-shop operators we encountered derive nearly 40 percent of their profits from masculine gift items. These include German beer steins, English ale mugs, leather wine pouches, walking sticks, and figurines.

Typically, well-run pipe shops keep overhead down in the 25 to 30 percent range, which combined with an average cost of goods sold of 50 percent, provides a net profit pretax of 20 to 25 percent. Put that in your pipe and smoke it!

EASY START-UP

Pipe shops are simple and relatively inexpensive to set up. Depending on location, rent for a 1,000 square-foot storefront location should range between $500 and $1,000.

An initial inventory of $13,000 to $16,000 covers everything from cigarettes, pipes, tobacco, and cigars to lighters, pipe tools, humidors, and general gift items.

Fixtures and equipment (most of which are available used for savings of 50 percent or better), including glass display cases, display islands, wall shelving, cash register, tobacco scale, and walk-in cigar humidor, should cost between $4,000 and $5,500.

Including decor, equipment, furnishings, and a full product inventory, this business can be started for as little as $27,000. Investing $40,000 to $45,000 would enable you to open an extremely well-planned and decorated pipe shop, which should pull in patrons as smoothly as well-made briar draws smoke!

Start-up Manual #129 is available on this business. See page 378.

USED-BOOK STORE

High net profit B/T:	$45,000
Average net profit B/T:	10,000
Minimum investment:	4,000
Average investment:	9,000

Book stores are most often started by book lovers who want to turn a lifelong passion into a profitable business. Often a personal collection accumulated over the years with loving care becomes the basis for opening inventory.

Romantic dreams of whiling away the hours conversing intellectually with other bibliophiles, reading a steady supply of good books, or finding a first edition Dickens in someone's attic *can come true*. And have, for some owners.

But the risks are high for those who don't recognize going in, that running a book store is a business. Established book stores are stable and do provide a moderate living for the owner/operator after two or three years of operation. Those who succeed, however, must shelve pipe dreams and concentrate on "minding the store."

NEW OR USED?

Risks are highest and profit thinnest in selling new books, and we don't recommend that you try it without experience and great chunks of capital up front.

Specialty book stores carrying only children's books, occult, or science fiction titles spring up from time to time—but usually die in the vine when the public tastes shift to a new craze.

A used-book store has several advantages over new or specialty bookshops. You deal only in books that have established track records in the marketplace. You pay a lot less for them, so inventory expense is lower.

GET FIRSTHAND EXPERIENCE

An intense love of books is a must. But not everyone loves books—and those who do rarely share the same tastes. A prospective bookseller should work in a used-book store for a while to get practical experience and a feeling for the tastes of the buying public.

KNOW YOUR MARKET

Before scouting for a specific location, do some research on the market in your area. You should evaluate population, size, growth rate, turnover rate, lifestyle, income, education and age levels. Competition should be considered.

Our researchers found that only 1 out of every 13 Americans buys books. Thus a sizable community—50,000 minimum—is required to support a used-book store. Even more important is the profile of the typical book buyer—you must seek out the book readers.

The greatest amount of reading—for pleasure and otherwise—is done by college students, and by college-educated adults with higher-than-average incomes. You should try to locate as near to a university or college campus as possible, preferably with a surrounding community of literate, middle-income, *mobile* apartment dwellers. (A common reason given for selling books is moving.)

NEW GIMMICK: EXCHANGE

An old practice in used-book stores was trading of paperbacks—on a two- or three-for-one basis. There are some problems with this: Paperback prices vary and the customer will not always have similarly priced books. Also, two for one isn't attractive to you financially, while three for one is resisted by the customer. Many store have given this up in favor of a new concept: *exchange.*

The exchange works on the basis of credits. There are some paperback exchanges that give credit slips for 25 percent of the list price, provided that the book is quite new and in mint condition. These credits can be used to buy other paperbacks for 50 percent of list. This is a handsome markup but the volume must be quite large to make it financially viable, because on a $2 paperback the owner will make only 50¢ per book. In a conventional used-book store a $2 paperback will make the owner 75¢ to 85¢.

The exchange or credit-chit approach is very popular, new, and an excellent way to build volume—especially when promoted among the dollar-conscious college crowd. It's also cost-effective to the bookstore operator because he can acquire new stock without using precious cash.

WHAT YOU CAN EXPECT TO MAKE

We found an established store, in a good location, with bottom-line numbers that are typical of smaller stores that have been in business five or more years.

The store is open six days a week, Tuesday through Sunday, from 10:00 a.m. to 9:00 p.m. (to 5:00 p.m. Sundays.) The owner closes for two weeks a year, and on some holidays like Christmas and New Year's Day.

The average gross is $175 per day or about $50,000 per year. Rent for the store is $450 per month. Utilities, phone, and so forth add another $100 to this. Salary expense varies; the owner has added as many as eight part-timers—most are teens who work for minimum wage with parents' permission. Average weekly salary expense rarely exceeds $200 per week or $10,000 per year.

The owner is just now taking out a salary. For the first year he was just taking out his expenses while trying to get rolling. Gradually his take rose to $500 per month, then $800, and it's still on the rise.

Balance of the store's income goes to replacing and increasing stock—he depends heavily on exchanges, and plans to add a mail-order section soon. He hopes this will add 50 to 100 percent to his gross. Added income will be spent on the stock and more employees so that he can have more free time.

Start-up Manual #117 is available on this business. See page 378.

MATTRESS SHOP

High net profit B/T:	$50,000
Average net profit B/T:	30,000
Minimum investment:	16,000
Average investment:	35,000

People in the United States spent over $2 billion last year for mattresses and foundations. It is a business which few of us notice, but let's face it—everyone needs a place to sleep.

Surprisingly enough, major brands do not entirely dominate this market. In fact, almost 25 percent of the mattresses were produced by smaller local companies. The six largest, and their percentage of the market: Sealy, 24 percent; Simmons, 14 percent; Serta, 13 percent; Spring Air, 9 percent; U.S. Bedding, 9 percent; and Stearns and Foster, 7 percent.

Furniture stores, department stores, and national mail-order businesses sold about 65 percent of the bedding in this country in 1978. Specialty sleep shops handle about 10 percent of the market but are gaining on these large stores with competitive prices and personal service.

Specialization and steady advertising are the reasons for their growing share of the market. A specialized business of this type is simple to run because small inventories are required in only one basic product. Few employees are necessary: most shops employ only two people. They are ideal for absentee ownership.

HIGH PROFIT

The average independent sleep shop grosses over $150,000 a year for a net before taxes and depreciation of $30,000 for an absentee owner.

Around every major city small chains of sleep shops have developed with 2 to 30 units. Gross sales were much higher than that for a single store—$175,000. The net averaged over $35,000.

The reason the chains gross higher is primarily a larger advertising budget—$23,400 annually per unit compared to $18,200 for the single-store owner. However, individual store operators spending more on advertising were registering higher sales.

The highest-grossing shop, one of a ten-unit chain, had $377,124 in sales during 12 months. That gross will provide the absentee owner approximately $42,000 pretax profit before corporate overhead and salaries. The entire chain netted $203, before taxes last year.

MARK-UP HIGH

Some operators only mark up their merchandise 60 to 85 percent. The smart ones, we found, sell at 100 percent over cost. A mattress set with a wholesale cost of $100 will be marked $185 by most operators. But the most profitable operations add on an extra 10 to 15 percent to absorb part of the advertising cost.

Start-up Manual #72 is available on this business. See page 378.

PET SHOP

High net profit B/T:	$80,000
Average net profit B/T:	24,000
Minimum investment:	25,000
Average investment:	71,000

Sell a parakeet for $15 and make a $20 profit. Sell a cat for $12 and net $20 profit. No matter how you figure it, it doesn't figure.

Or does it?

A little girl looks up at her mother imploringly. "I want a parakeet for a pet, and they're only $15."

Okay—with today's prices, $15 isn't much, so to the pet shop you go. The girl picks out the bird she wants . . . and now the fun begins. "The "add-ons."

For you see, naturally she'll need a birdcage, complete with swings, bells, feeders, and a birdcage cover, a quantity of seed, vitamins, and a book on the care and handling of birds.

That $15 parakeet has ended up costing her mother nearly $50, and it could have topped $75 if she had bought the fancy birdcage that the girl was eyeing.

Now those figures in the opening paragraph make more sense. The pet-shop business has been around a long time, but few outsiders realize how lucrative it can be.

BIG PROFIT IN DOGS

Birds make up only a small part of the pet-shop owner's business. The big money is in dogs. The average pedigreed dog sells for $250—while costing the pet shop $100. Not a bad markup, and the dog buyer will spend another $25 to $50 for add-ons: dog beds, leashes, brushes, food, vitamins, collars, books, and other goodies. The average gross profit on the accessories comes to 50 percent.

A well-run pet store with absentee ownership will net 25 percent before taxes. In a shopping center or mall, the average gross usually exceeds $25,000 to $30,000 per month for a $75,000 to $90,000 annual net before taxes.

These figures are based on a 2,000-square-foot store carrying only animals—no fish. If fish are added and the space is increased, the gross and net will also increase.

Christmas is a profitable time for many pet shops. Some owners have reported grosses from $60,000 up during the month of December.

START-UP COSTS LOW

The minimum cash requirements for a pet shop is in the $25,000 range. More realistically you can expect to invest at least $50,000 to set up. Mall locations, especially those where no building preparation has been completed, will be closer to $75,000 to $100,000.

KNOWLEDGE NEEDED

You will need an experienced manager who is also a pet fancier. Unless you are located in a very small town, managers are easy to find and not expensive. From $15,000 to $18,000 a year seems to be the average salary.

The rest of the staff will be very easy to find, and will work for minimum wages just to be around animals. Many shop owners find that giving a small commission on sales to the other personnel is worthwhile. An assistant manager ($800 per month to start) and two part-time workers are all that you will need. Total annual wages should not exceed $60,000.

Start-up Manual #7 is available on this business. See page 378.

Start-up Manual #7 is available on this business. See page 378.

New Idea

CAT PARAPHERNALIA

Since the time of the pharoahs, cats have been revered by groups of worshipers. Today, thousands of years later, cat lovers are still legion. A New York entrepeneur has opened a store catering to this mania called Purrfection.

Purrfection is a cat lover's heaven, offering sculptured wax cats, Morris pillows, Siamese cats wrought in porcelain, and a library of books about felines. Pictures and paintings of the lovable pets dot the walls. The store also does a bustling mail-order business by advertising its catalog (no pun intended) in national magazines.

We can see this working in any medium- to large-size city. Gift shows will provide a wealth of cat-oriented items. We can also see the same idea applied to dogs, frogs, and owls—each of which has a notable following of admirers.

If you don't want to take the full plunge, test-market the idea at a flea market or swap meet. Booth space at some meets goes for as little as $20. Take a nice selection of pet gifts, and you'll get an idea of the public's response. Be sure to take names so you'll have a mailing list when you announce the opening of your shop.

To get an idea of what Purrfection sells, send for their catalog. It's 50 cents, and you can get it by writing Purrfection, 1584 First Avenue, New York, New York 10028.

SHELL SHOP

High net profit B/T:	$50,000
Average net profit B/T:	10,000
Minimum investment:	12,000
Average investment:	35,000

You don't need to be a pirate to make a fortune from the high seas! Instead you can find your treasure in the lovely jewels of the ocean—seashells. People everywhere are fascinated by these collectibles and decorative gift items and they're willing to pay a bundle for the privilege of owning a beautiful pink conch shell or rare cowrie.

For as little as $12,000 you can open a shell shop and stock a variety of shell crafts, decorative and collectors' shells, and other marine delights. We've found tiny shops in such landlocked spots as Minneapolis and Denver capitalizing on these hot-selling items.

Shells range in quality from souvenirs priced at under $1 to gem quality exotic varieties with prices of $1,000 or more.

Annual sales in these shops range from $80,000 to $250,000. One we uncovered was no bigger than a hotdog stand—84 square feet—yet it grossed $90,000 in a shopping mall. Net pretax profits for well-run stores are in the 20 percent bracket.

THE BEAUTIFUL LURE

Shell shops are really specialty gift shops, and they must be geared to the typical gift buyer. By locating your shop in a prime area and making the interior and exterior displays as attractive as possible, you can easily attract the typical gift buyer and promote impulse buying.

The ideal exterior should establish a theme for the store. Most successful shops have a casual, slightly weather-beaten look that makes the customers feel as if they are at the beach. Shells virtually demand some sort of nautical or Davy Jones's locker decor. Your inventory will sell itself if it is properly arranged. A good layout invites browsing and the "joy of discovery," which is just the effect to aim for.

OTHER ITEMS RAISE PROFIT MARGINS

Dangling capiz-shell lamps and custom shell-craft mirrors are big sellers. Seascape paintings and shell collages and graphics will increase your profit potential. One owner we found uses a collection of shell prints (hand-colored lithographs) from the 19th century to add to the decor and the sales flow.

Jewelry is popular and profitable to carry. A 25-cent shell can easily be made into a $5 handcrafted necklace or pendant. We've seen customers buying five or six shell rings at $3 apiece for use as gifts.

You should also stock shell design stationery, napkin rings, clocks made from shells, mobiles, fossils, and mounted shells on stands. These items have markups up to 50 percent or more and can really boost profits!

SUPPLY IS PRACTICALLY ENDLESS

There are shell wholesalers who will provide you with a perpetual stream of shells of almost every variety, from the lowliest "bargain shells" (which sell in packages for about $1 each) to high-priced and valuable collectors' shells like the Cypraeaguttata and Rare Spotted Cowrie, which sell for thousands of dollars.

You can obtain an initial inventory at half the normal cost by carefully selecting your suppliers. Regional and national varieties are necessary to maintain an interesting mix of shells, but foreign wholesalers provide a much wider selection, and their prices are often half those of nearby dealers.

DIVERSIFY YOUR MARKETING STRATEGY

Shells are a natural mail-order product. We found one shell shop which increased its gross sales by 40 percent through a simple catalog direct mail campaign!

Because of your shells' beauty, they will be in demand as a display item for other local shops like bath boutiques and fine jewelry companies. You can offer shells to them on consignment with a simple placard crediting your store.

You can shoestring your initial inventory and lower your start-up costs by accepting finer shells on a consignment basis from collectors and hobbyists. This is a good way to attract local business through word-of-mouth advertising. Once the news gets around that you're accepting items on consignment, you'll find your best customers are those who bring something in to sell!

Start-up Manual #163 is available on this business. See page 378.

VIDEO STORE

High net profit B/T:	$300,000
Average net profit B/T:	52,000
Minimum investment:	27,000
Average investment:	39,000

There is a revolution in entertainment going on in the United States. The VCR, wide-screen TV, and related accessories are the greatest explosion in home entertainment since the advent of television.

And the industry is still in its infancy!

In the mid-'70s, we predicted that videocassette recorders (VCRs) and related video equipment were going to find a giant market. What has happened? More of a growth in the video industry than we imagined.

Retail stores specializing in video entertainment equipment are grossing $250,000 to $500,000 a year in major metropolitan areas. One six-store chain in an affluent neighborhood has more than $10 million in sales.

TUNE IN ON PROFIT PROJECTIONS

This isn't just another TV retail store. We're talking about expensive electronic equipment. A complete home entertainment system can include a VCR, a wide-screen television to screen videotapes, a videotape camera and lighting equipment to record state-of-the-art home movies, and a library of current and vintage feature films.

With a 25 to 30 percent markup on large volume and a variety of video equipment, you can expect profits of $40,000 to $75,000 a year. Your best bet is to focus on a staff of commissioned salespeople.

LET'S MAKE A DEAL—IN CINEMASCOPE

Most VCRs have been selling for about $1,000, although manufacturer's list prices vary. Your sales advantage is that electronic video equipment is a mystery to most people. They expect to pay high markup prices for complicated equipment. For that reason you can sell VCR accessories, or accessories on wide-screen TVs, the way you would sell the extras on a luxury car. The consumer will need the advice of a professional—you—to make the machines look easy to operate.

You'll have mostly sample units to demonstrate to customers. They can pick up their purchases from the selection they see in your store. Be careful of your inventory: don't get stuck with a lot of outdated merchandise.

WIDE SCREEN—NARROW MARKET— PINPOINT LOCATION

Why pay a hefty mall rental and deal with foot traffic? You're going after people who can afford to pay for the best in electronic entertainment. Prescreen your customers; locate where committed buyers will seek out you and your video equipment.

Display your wares in a spick-and-span contemporary setting in keeping with your space-age equipment. Let your customers make themselves comfortable while you demonstrate the TVs and recorders. But you've got the secret. You don't need much technical knowledge, because you're going to get plenty of help from the manufacturers in selling video equipment.

THE FUTURE IS NOW IN VIDEO TECHNOLOGY

Stock a variety of VCRs in your shop. As customer demand increases, start planning to expand, because the biggest potential for profits is in a small chain.

Take good care of your customers. Show them everything you have to offer. When salespeople start explaining the different capabilities of the units, customers will be thinking about which model they like best. You've got them by then; they're not wondering whether they should invest in a home video system, but which one they should buy!

With videodiscs spinning onto the market at thousands of technological revolutions per minute, the video market is clearly a high-growth one. Every month brings innovation into the industry, and customers are constantly adding to their existing systems.

The cost of an entire video system—including wide-screen TV, videocamera, and VCR—can run from $3,500 to $10,000. During one hour of our research in a video store we watched a half-dozen customers order complete layouts!

FOCUS ON BIG SALES

Sony introduced the first VCR—the Betamax Model 7200—in 1975. During the next three years 200,000 units were sold. That doubled by 1978; currently more than 2 million American homes own a videorecorder, and industry experts predict more than 15 million American families will have these devices by 1985.

American habits are changing, and video systems are part of that change. Americans are buying more than 17,000 VCR units per month at an average price of more than $1,000 per unit. With the gas crunch more people are staying home, making the home entertainment market grow at epic rates.

Start-up Manual #167 is available on this business. See page 378.

RETAIL PHONE STORE

High net profit B/T:	$82,000
Average net profit B/T:	37,600
Minimum investment:	23,000
Average investment:	42,000

Do you own that telephone on your desk? Probably not. Yet that telephone may be the secret to starting your own thriving business—a retail phone store.

One shop rang up a hefty $25,000 in Christmas sales in its first year. Another operation is moving $600 worth of phones and answering machines every day. Three outlets in New York are closing in on $2 million in annual sales—taking a big chunk out of Ma Bell's revenues.

What are the odds of your operating a successful phone store? You don't have to be an engineering whiz kid. You'll need about 25 percent knowledge of phones and 75 percent marketing savvy.

ARE THERE ANY LEGAL HASSLES?

Not at all, although you may find yourself spending half your time explaining the legalities of private ownership to your customers. Here are the facts:

1. The FCC says that telephone network lines are a common carrier and that any FCC-approved equipment may be plugged into the network.

2. A telephone subscriber can now buy his own phone—just as he would buy a toaster.

Your retail phone store helps customers stop paying that rental fee to the telephone company month after month. Emphasize these points in your marketing program, and you'll succeed.

YOUR SALES PITCH

Telephone customers pay as much as $60 a year to rent one phone—which gives them no equity. By renting just one phone at $5 a month for 20 years, your customer may have dumped $1,200 down the drain—and extensions cost even more.

You're offering permanent ownership of an instrument that should have been the customer's property all along. Besides, he's getting just the phone he wants.

YOUR INVENTORY IS KEY

One retail phone franchisor suggests a $10,000 opening inventory that gives a good mix of decorator phones and answering machines. Retailers we interviewed said that if they had it to do over, they would have bought leaner. That means you can probably come in low to start.

In no other retail operation is there so much variety of price. Phones retail at $14.95 to $4,000. The market is constantly changing, which means you can negotiate for the best wholesale price.

Common sense is the watchword for inventory selection. Be sure your inventory mix is aimed at your particular market.

LOCATE WHERE YOU CAN SELL THE MOST

The right location is crucial to your success. High-foot traffic areas like malls can be a dead end; such areas often attract browsers instead of buyers.

The most successful phone stores are found in strip shopping centers in a middle- to high-income district. Stores in older, well-settled communities are just as profitable as stores in the modern, affluent communities. Top-of-the-line models are bought by luxury apartment dwellers and single-family residences alike.

Inside the store, offer a mix of personal phones, business phones, and communications systems. You're aiming for an upper-income client with discretionary dollars to spend on unique, fanciful items.

AFFLUENT CLIENTELE WILL PAY FOR PERSONAL SERVICE

Your personal attention and sales pitch will motivate your customers to buy the most distinctive phone models in the store. They're after plenty of personalized attention and are willing to pay for products that prove they've got it.

You don't have to be connected with General Telephone or the Bell System to cash in on this $1 billion market. Don't be fooled by the big TV ad campaigns of Sears and Radio Shack. They're going after the lower-income customer with a product that will sell for $50 tops. Your average sale will probably start at $60.

Selling the uniqueness of phone style, color, and most of all permanent ownership can really pay off. One phone mart sold an

$1,800 silver and marble candlestick phone for a wedding present. But that was only the beginning. The young couple loved the phone so much that they came back to the store. By the time they had finished buying decorator phones for use as gifts, they had spent an additional $3,000—all in one hour!

A phone mart has all the pluses of a modern business—good profit potential in a growth market, no experience required, and minimum investment requirements. It's not unusual to find a retail phone store that sells fast-moving phone models grossing from $150,000 to $350,000 in the first year.

Start-up Manual #171 is available on this business. See page 378.

RECREATIONAL
SPORTS

SOCCER SPECIALTY STORE

The latest concept in sports merchandising in America is the soccer store. Aim at the youthful market with soccer equipment and you can build a foundation for future sales.

Soccer is the most popular sport in the world. Only in the U.S. does it rank behind football and baseball. And it's growing in popularity with young people because it's now being offered in schools.

A soccer equipment store should do well wherever soccer is taught in school. And you'll be building an adult market as the soccer-playing youngsters get older. Studies have shown that adults stay interested in the sports they played as children.

A soccer store can offer everything from low-cost socks to heavy equipment such as goals and nets. Soccer outfits, similar to rugby uniforms, come in many styles. You'll want to have several available to outfit competing teams in your region.

In addition, soccer supplies include balls, goalie gloves, and soccer shoes.

Soccer World, a franchisor of soccer specialty stores, has begun operation on the East Coast. Independent retail operations are beginning countrywide as soccer increases in popularity in America.

The magazine *Soccer Monthly,* published by the U.S. Soccer Federation in New York, should put you in touch with what's happening nationally in the sport. Contact local and regional soccer leagues to establish yourself as the major soccer supply outlet in the area. By saving school soccer teams the trouble of having to order from soccer suppliers a continent away, you'll be the one to score the profits.

ROLLER-SKATE RENTAL SHOP

High net profit B/T:	$50,000+
Average net profit B/T:	25,000+
Minimum investment:	2,500
Average investment:	18,000

Roller skating is enjoying a tremendous resurgence in the United States. Skate sales are booming; more than 45 million Americans have taken to wheels. The number of roller rinks has jumped from 500 to 3,500 in just ten years and the industry projects another 300 to 500 rinks this year. There seems no end to American's fascination with this sport.

Books and movies focusing on roller skating and skaters are beginning to turn up all over, and in a true reflection of skating's popularity, skaters are showing up in TV commercials.

Many skaters are combining the fads of skating and disco. The disco craze combined with the current physical fitness mania has turned skating into the fifth most popular participation sport among teenagers. Polls show that skating gets more votes than tennis or skiing.

BIKE PATHS WILL BECOME SKATE PATHS

We predicted years ago that with the advent of the new urethane skate wheels that make rougher surfaces skatable, the bike paths crisscrossing the country would become multipurpose paths devoted also to roller skating.

The last few years have seen an ever-increasing interest on the part of more and more people to engage in activities that are healthy, noncompetitive, and ecologically sound. Witness the rise in the popularity of skateboards, bicycling, surfing, jogging, frisbee tossing, etc. Capitalizing on the increased interest in personal forms of fun exercise, along with concern for husbanding resources and respecting the environment, a spin-off business idea called Cheapskates surfaced in Venice, California, several years ago, when a young entrepreneur opened a roller-skate rental business on the beach promenade.

It was an immediate success, so much so that there are hundreds of imitators in the business. Jeff Rosenberg, father of Cheapskates, is helping people set up successful skate rental outlets. His business has grown to eight rental shops in Los Angeles alone.

The skates are rented for $1.50 per hour or $5 per day. On sunny weekends or holidays there are customers lined up waiting to get to the counters. Cheapskates' initial cost for the skates is rapidly paid for by the first weeks of rentals, and thereafter the return is very high since the same merchandise is used over and over.

Those young people who have opened skate rental operations working out of vans or small trucks are a spin-off of the roller-skate rental business.

Just about everybody roller-skated on the streets of their hometowns when they were kids, just as most people rode bikes as children. The tremendous growth in adult bike riding that has swept the country in recent years appeals to the same desire for exercise and nostalgia that mark potential customers for roller-skate rentals.

The most promising aspect of this blossoming fad is that it attracts such a wide range of people—from kids who are new to skating to older people who want to recapture the fun they had long ago.

So your market in the skate rental business is larger than you think. It is not an activity that is limited to children. What you want is a population base ranging from youngsters through people in their late 30s who are looking for fun and relaxation, who have time on their hands. Your potential customers are in beach communities, resorts, parks, and other locations that attract vacationers or local people out for a day of family fun. There is also a good market near high-school and college campuses.

Single females are the largest group of renters, but there is also a brisk interest on the part of young men, as well as couples. The growth market to target is people from 17 to 30.

WHAT CAN YOU EARN?

Cheapskates averages 50 to 75 rentals per day on weekdays and other winter days and up to 350 rentals per day on sunny weekends and holidays. When it first opened, hourly rentals were about 80 percent of the total. Today 50 percent of the rentals are by the day. A low-side calculation of 50 $5 rentals on 325 weekdays and 200 rentals on 40 sunny weekends and holidays produces a yearly gross income of $121,250.

Not every business is going to generate that much volume: a lot depends on your competition. We've left out the substantial income potential from selling rolling skates, so while your gross may be lower than the figure we gave it could also be higher.

Start-up Manual #88 is available on this business. See page 379.

HOT-TUB/SPA FACILITY

High net profit B/T:	$200,000+
Average net profit B/T:	74,000
Minimum investment:	70,000
Average investment:	275,000

Hot tubbing is the hottest new status symbol for everyone from young singles to middle-aged executives. You can get into hot water and come out making a handsome profit by renting time in a hot tub to devotees who haven't bought their own.

Hot tubbing and spa soaking first became popular in northern California. Since then, "hot-tub fever" has spread across the country. Resorts, backyards, and bathrooms everywhere are filling with hot tubs and spas. The benefits of this drugless tranquilizer are not just physical, but emotional as well.

Sales of hot tubs and spas are approaching the billion-a-year level. But dropping your derriere into a hot tub is getting dear. Having one installed at home can run to $10,000, if you count all the extras most people want. Visionary entrepreneurs are capitalizing on escalating cost—and on the craze itself—by setting up "rent-a-soak" operations. Hand-over-fist profits are often the result of careful planning and attention to detail.

IT PAYS TO RELAX

The business is so new that only a handful of people are in it, but our researchers have uncovered operations grossing over $1 million a year. They offer patrons the chance to take a relaxing soak at hourly rates of $4.50 to $20. The average gross for smaller operations is $150,000 to $350,000 a year, with pretax net in the 35 to 45 percent range!

There are only a few spas yet, but we've found them in San Francisco, Los Angeles, New York City, and several smaller communities, as well as in snow country: Chicago, Colorado, and Utah. There's plenty of market potential nationwide and lots of room for growth—even franchising. But you need to select just the right community. The best bet is to find an area where hot tubbing and spas are growing in popularity.

LOCATE NEAR YOUR MARKET

You may think that heavy hot tub or spa sales will keep people from renting from you—but that's not true. Sales of hot tubs do not represent competition; they are a strong advantage.

Your customers are not the same as the typical hot-tub buyer. You'll be catering to younger people between 21 and 35 who cannot afford a tub or spa—and who still crave the experience of a relaxing soak.

Hot tubbing is not just a fad; it has a real therapeutic value. So don't overlook senior citizens' groups, residents of nearby retirement communities, and convalescent homes. One very successful technique was used by an operator who sent letters to all local physicians about his operation and achieved an increase in business because the physicians began prescribing healthful soaks on a regular basis.

THOSE SENSUAL OVERTONES

Even though communal bathing—and hot tubbing—has been around since the days of the Babylonians in one form or another, you can have image problems with city authorities unless you counter with a strong offense. Before you invest important money in this business, it is vital to have the city fathers on your side. With a new concept like this, which can be controversial because of the sensual overtones, you should be prepared for plenty of advance legwork and selling to get your idea across.

Basic to getting the approvals you need is a businesslike sales presentation of your idea, stressing the family image, the relaxation angle, and the fact that you are going to be running a straight, clean operation.

A BUBBLING SUCCESS

Our researchers have come up with a concept that gets you started in this business for a lot lower investment than some advocate. Rent an older home with some charm, located in an area that is zoned commercially. In small college towns or resort areas, such pieces of property abound.

The minimum number of tubs for a beginning operation is six. We have seen giant setups with as many as 26 spas in private rooms, each with a sauna in the room as well as a fireplace! But you can expand once you are up and running.

The hot tub or spa is only one part of the story, of course. You need ancillary equipment to get the hot water you require, maintain constant temperature, and filter the water so that it remains clean. Experts in the business warn that it is vital to work closely with your local health department about meeting or exceeding their code requirements.

SPLASHY PROMOTION IS VITAL

Because a hot-tub rental operation is so unusual and new in most of the country, there are a number of dynamic promotional ideas that can draw thousands of dollars' worth of free publicity from editors of newspapers, magazines, and radio and TV stations. Promotional devices should fit your hot-tub theme. Consider contests, discounts, and presenting your news releases to the media in a splashy way. You can work with a radio or TV station on a remote broadcast from one of your hot tubs! Supplement your promotional gimmicks with solid advertising in local newspapers, and on the radio (if costs permit).

With an energetic staff, good management, and a sharp eye for dynamic promotion, you can set up in this business while it is still wide open, and tell the people who said it couldn't be done to "go soak their heads!"

Start-up Manual #176 is available on this business. See page 378.

ATHLETIC SHOE STORE

High net profit B/T:	$85,000
Average net profit B/T:	35,000
Minimum investment:	36,000
Average investment:	78,000

Since President Kennedy's physical fitness campaign in the early '60s, interest in keeping in shape has grown by leaps and bounds. The number of participants in almost every sport from mountain climbing to gymnastics has increased rapidly. In fact, 59 percent of adult Americans participate regularly in some formal physical activity. (Only 24 percent considered themselves active in 1961.) Many inactive people intend to start this year.

Joggers are out in force; sports like racquetball have grown in popularity. The boredom of repetitious running leads many fitness buffs to seek their exercise elsewhere.

Formerly a pair of tennis shoes was sufficient footwear for most sports. But today the only place a tennis shoe is acceptable is on the tennis court.

Nowadays if you play baseball you must have "spikes" (baseball shoes). If you like to jog, you should wear jogging or track-type shoes. To play football you'll want a pair of "cleats" (low-cut football or soccer shoes). There are even shoes for flopping, a special high-jump style. It seems, in fact, that every sport has its own special breed of footgear—and if you participate you must have a pair, or you'll appear out of style next to your fellow enthusiasts.

Special apparel doesn't stop at the ankle. You'll find a plethora of socks, shorts, sweat pants, and other paraphernalia peculiar to your sport. And of course, you'll have to carry all this gear around in your Adidas bag.

THE BIG NAME

In case you're not familiar with Adidas, they're the French sportswear manufacturers who, through giant publicity campaigns tied to the Olympics and subsequent advertising and publicity throughout the U.S., have become *the* top name in athletic shoes and sportswear. They seem to have sold as many tote bags with their name imprinted on the side as they have shoes.

The company has long been successful in Europe, where people have traditionally been more conscious of physical fitness than the average American, at least until recently.

Sporting-goods sales in the U.S. are booming, with almost a $17 billion annual market. For the last few years sales have risen 10 percent each year, with the trend expected to continue.

STATUS IN SPORTS

In the '50s you might have seen a group playing touch football dressed in old jeans, T-shirts, and sneakers. Today it is more common to find them decked out in sleek jerseys, matching shorts or sweat pants, and regulation cleats.

It is a simple case of status moving into the field of sports.

While many sporting-goods stores sell all kinds of sportswear along with sports equipment, specialization is the current trend: golf shops, ski shops, tennis shops, jogging shops, and lately, athletic shoe shops.

One chain in southern California specializes just in tennis shoes. Just imagine it, rows of tennis shoes and socks, but no equipment. And they are opening more stores every year.

SHOES—THE BEST-SELLERS

A group operating in Pennsylvania has almost 300 stores throughout the U.S. and overseas, specializing in athletic footwear of all types. Although this chain also carries an extensive line of sports clothes, shoe sales are 65 percent of their gross. Another Florida-based chain has almost 150 stores cross-country. The store we investigated is in a new shopping center. Its average gross has been $24,845 per month during the first six months of operation, and the net profit has been $4,200 per month.

Naturally, as the gross goes higher, the percentage of profit will rise. A $400,000 annual gross with a 20 percent net is considered par for a healthy, well-run store in this field.

A specialty operation of this type will have a steady growth in volume for several years before reaching a plateau, due to saturation of the potential market area.

SHOPPING-CENTER LOCATION

A specialty business can survive successfully in any area that enjoys easy access. You don't have to set up in an enclosed mall. One store we investigated in a shopping center was close to a sporting-goods dealer who carries a complete line of footwear and clothing as well as the usual sports gear—yet business didn't seem to suffer.

This store is in an area populated by lower-middle-class wage earners (average male wages, $11,400). Within six miles there is a higher-income area (male average about $20,000) which contributes to the store's volume.

You can still buy tennis shoes for $10 or less, but the sophisticated weekend athlete is looking for professional quality and is willing to pay for it—an average of $30 per pair of running shoes. If he is active he will wear out that pair within six months and be back for replacements. Sports styles last for years, so there's not much worry of getting stuck with outmoded items.

Sixty percent of the sales in our sample stores are made to young men and boys 14 to 30 years old. (Boys under 14 contribute only about 5 percent.) The over-30 group generates 30 percent of the sales (buying many bigger-ticket items). More and more people in their 40s and 50s are jogging, so sales to this age group are expanding. These figures were developed in a three-store marketing study.

Start-up Manual #5 is available on this business. See page 379.

WIND-SURFING SCHOOL

High net profit B/T:	$150,000
Average net profit B/T:	50,000
Minimum investment:	2,000
Average investment:	6,000

(These figures are based on schools now operating at capacity in Europe. U.S. totals will be significantly lower.)

Wind surfing is one of the hottest new sports sweeping across Europe, where there are many thousands of enthusiasts, and the sport is just beginning to catch on here in the States. There are over 1,000 wind surfing schools overseas, and at least 40 manufacturers of free-sail craft, as they are called. Predictably, wind surfing magazines are springing up to capitalize on the new craze.

Devotees in the business believe that free-sailing will eventually become as important a sport as skiing, and are betting that its wildfire acceptance overseas is a solid predictor of major success in the multi-billion-dollar U.S. recreation market. Already the sport has spread up both coasts from southern California and Florida beginnings; schools and dealers are opening up inland too, in major recreation areas.

WHAT'S WIND SURFING?

It's a challenging activity that combines sailing and surfing on a narrow 12-foot craft similar to a surfboard, with a simple mast and sail unit. A universal joint at the mast base allows a standing sailor to tip the mast/sail unit forward, backward, or sideways to change speed or direction. Upward thrust allows speeds in excess of 30 knots by producing lift, as in hang-gliding—you can skim across the tops of waves and be airborne for a few feet at a time.

Lightweight and responsive, with no rudder or complex rigging, a free-sail craft in the hands of a skilled sailor using body movement can outperform other single-man centerboard sailboats like the near-legendary Fin, Laser, or Sunfish. Many enthusiasts race their free-sail craft in weekend regattas; national and international competitions have been held, and wind surfing is now an Olympic sport.

MARKET ADVANTAGES

Because of its surfboard qualities and use of the craft in heavy surf, "wind surfing" is a name that's stuck. Actually, only a small percentage of enthusiasts do this—it's roughly equivalent to "hot-dogging" on snow skis. Most owners use their craft as they would a small shallow-draft sailboat. So all that's needed is a light wind and water; sailors don't need to live near or travel to a heavy surf area to have fun. This flexibility should mean greater acceptance on the East and South coasts, where surf conditions are poor, and on inland water recreation areas.

Easy breakdown and assembly in minutes, as well as light weight (40-60 pounds), mean that the craft can be car-topped anywhere, towed behind a bicycle, or carried under the arm. Unbreakable materials, negligible maintenance cost, and relatively low price (about $1,000 retail) are advantages over the typical sailboat.

The craft is unsinkable and easily righted. When you fall off—inevitable while learning—it capsizes and stays nearby, unlike a surfboard, which flies away and can injure the unwary swimmer. In fact, safety is a big plus and the U.S. Coast Guard doesn't require a life preserver. A flotation belt is recommended for those who aren't strong swimmers; a harness can be attached to the sail boom. The harness aids in maintaining footing and provides added support that reduces fatigue.

Fun, challenge, portability, safety, and low price lead early entries in the industry to speculate that free-sailing may parallel skiing over the long run as a family activity with broader market appeal than either sailing or surfing.

PROFIT POTENTIAL HIGH

If European market acceptance is an indicator, profits can be phenomenal. On the Continent you can't buy a free-sail craft without a long wait, and you have to be certified first by attending a school.

Two-day classes are fully booked, at an average tuition of $40 per student. And classes of 20 or more students at a time are common. That's an $800 gross per class; some schools are running seven days a week and have long waiting lists.

A school will normally rent part of its fleet for varying rates: retail sales of the craft at $900-$1000 on a wholesale cost of $650-$750 add significantly to gross and net profits. Accessories, like surfing daggerboards, custom sails, wet suits, and other wind surfing paraphernalia usually amount to 20 percent of the sales for a going school "over there."

School/dealerships in the States, where growth is just beginning, are nowhere near that level yet. The most successful school we found is in San Francisco and gets 10-12 students in a good week—the average is 10 by appointment—for an average monthly gross tuition income in the $1,000 range. Rentals average three or four boats a weekend, adding $190-$250 to monthly totals. But sales to new devotees average 30 boats a month—a margin of $250 apiece yields $7,500 monthly in gross profits. Add $1,500 or so monthly for accessory sales and you arrive at a monthly gross income of $10,000 during the peak summer season.

Start-up Manual #109 is available on this business. See page 379.

_____ **New Idea** _____

ARCHERY—RIGHT ON TARGET

Neil Burger tells us that the next sports craze to sweep the country may be archery. Burger should know, since he's staking his future on the idea by opening New York's first archery club—the New York Archery Centre.

The club will have 22 Olympic-length archery shooting lanes, which you can use for $10 an hour. Equipment and instruction will bring the hourly tab up another $6. This Big Apple entrepreneur has included a restaurant—the Longboe Cafe—in his plans.

With the emphasis on health and athletics, archery is worth taking a good look at. It has the right elements: competitiveness, clean fun, and an upper-class feel.

This idea should work in large urban areas, especially in well-to-do neighborhoods. Socializing is a good part of the sport's appeal, so a lounge (with a fireplace, perhaps) is a good idea.

One thing that appeals to us is the relatively low start-up costs involved. There's very little building modification and practically no inventory expenses—just initial equipment outlay. This idea may be a big one; time will tell.

PHYSICAL FITNESS CENTER

High net profit B/T:	$140,000
Average net profit B/T:	95,000
Minimum investment:	44,000
Average investment:	77,000

Americans used to hate exercise; at least, they were bored by it. Maybe they still are, but the fitness mystique has grown to such proportions that health clubs have become one of the country's hottest growth industries. People don't exercise just to become more fit; they also do it to lessen stress, become sexier, improve their skin, and most of all, become thin. The battle of the bulge has become big business.

Americans spend more than $20 billion a year joining clubs with machines that stretch them, pound them, shake them, and make them firm and lean, smoothing, and flattening telltale bulges.

A small club in Georgia run by a husband and wife team is grossing $1,500 per week. An executive health club in Louisiana brings in $500,000 per year and is getting bigger all the time. Every successful club we investigated—whether a simple gym or an elegant health spa—shared one thing: hefty pretax nets. Some even hit the 45 to 50 percent range.

The self-improvement movement has led not only to a healthier America, but to some healthy profits for fitness center operators.

HEALTH-CLUB JUNKIES

A recent study done by an audience-testing house confirmed that 90 percent of the public doesn't like the way it looks. Some 40 million Americans are estimated to be overweight and out of shape, and they spend over $60 billion annually on diet and weight reduction drugs, fad diet books, reducing machines, and health courses. More important, they lay down hard cash to join clubs that will give them that lean, hungry, glowing look.

Almost every community in America is a prime market for your health club, even if other clubs are operating. Our research shows that health-club junkies have a notorious lack of club loyalty; they will investigate and join any new operation in town that offers more for their money.

We asked the president of one of America's leading health-club chains to describe the size of the potential market. His answer: "How many Americans are there? Anyone who is breathing and between the ages of 14 and 80 is a potential customer."

THE COED APPEAL

Given a choice of working out in an all-male or all-female environment, most people would choose coed. After all, the bottom line of your business is selling sex appeal, so why not capitalize on it?

Coed or not, you don't have to start off with a fancy spa. Many operators started small, just offering workout equipment and shower facilities. As profits increased, they added other profit-making amenities like saunas, steam rooms, jacuzzis, health-food bars, massages, retail outlets—even discotheques. Until you get a good membership, however, we suggest you keep your operation simple, and thus more immediately profitable.

Coed clubs have common areas as well as separate workout, shower, and locker-room areas.

LOCATION: A WEIGHTY DECISION

When choosing a site for your health club, consider population density. Experts in the industry look for a population base of 50,000 to 75,000, both residential and transitory (office workers, students, etc.).

We found health clubs in a variety of locations, but most of the profitable ones were in strip shopping centers. Rentals in strip centers can range from 60 cents to more than $1 per square foot. Don't be afraid to pay for a good location: exposure and convenience are important.

ADVANCE SALES

Advance sales is the name of the game. The professionals we investigated all said the same thing. Start selling memberships the minute you sign the lease. Your biggest job, along with the details of starting up, buying equipment, and getting off the ground, is to aggressively sell the benefits your club is going to offer—*before it opens*.

Advance membership fees can pay for most of your equipment. We found a club in San Francisco that sold 500 advance memberships at $300 each and paid for its equipment in full before opening.

SALES TIPS

Hard, realistic selling is the key to your success. Skilled professionals use every sales technique—advertising, exciting promotions, fliers, direct mail, phone calls, and hot-air balloons—to guarantee large numbers of members up front.

All your sales pitches must feature the *implied* benefits of your club: good looks, a great time, a leaner, more attractive customer. In other words, sell the sizzle, not the steak.

TOMORROW'S LOOKING GOOD

We predict that the market for profitable health clubs is just being tapped. Exact figures aren't available, but annual membership fees nationwide are estimated at $5 million to $6 million, which still leaves a healthy market share open. This is one of the few recession-proof businesses we've uncovered. There doesn't seem to be any letup in America's preoccupation with looking and feeling good.

Start-up Manual #172 is available on this business. See page 379.

SAILBOAT LEASING

High net profit B/T:	$175,000
Average net profit B/T:	42,000
Minimum investment:	31,000
Average investment:	55,000

Here's a way you can really become captain of your own fate. Catch a ground-floor trend we've spotted in the boating business and you'll sail to high profits.

Over 50 million Americans are boaters, and they spend plenty of money on their habit. Last year *$6 billion* was spent to buy, equip, and maintain boats in the United States. Sailboaters—the most avid fans of all—number almost 10 million, and more than 1 million sailboats ply America's waterways and coasts.

The numbers are growing fast, but imagine how many more people would get into sailing if they could afford it. Sailing, especially with larger craft, has been restricted to the upper crust of society by the price of the average boat: $22,500 for a new 25-footer, and almost as much for a used one. That doesn't even include docking fees and maintenance costs, which are skyrocketing along with the prices for the sleek craft themselves. Prices are escalating at 18 percent annually, and almost $200 million is spent every year maintaining sailboats.

HOT NEW CONCEPT

A handful of bright entrepreneurs have applied the time-sharing concept from the computer industry to sailing. It's simple, really. Use of a sailboat for a specified period of time, say one week per month, is leased to several sailors by the fleet owner. These customers are then entitled to call and reserve their time on the boat, based on a point system.

The lease contract lasts up to 12 months. The customer, or time sharer, is charged an average monthly fee of $150 to $200. Seven months' fee is paid up front; the rest is paid off in five monthly installments. Options are given for six-, three-, and one-month plans. But at $2,080 for six months, $1,900 for three, and $1,700 for one, the yearly plan is a bargain!

HIGH PROFITS DOWNWIND

Smart owners across the country are grossing hundreds of thousands of dollars with sailboat leasing. With careful control of expenses, many are netting a phenomenal $75,000 or more annually and showing 25 to 35 percent pretax profits.

We investigated the operation of one entrepreneur who is working out of a one-bedroom apartment with a 24-hour answering service to handle calls. He has been in business for five years and owns 20 boats—10 of which he acquired in the last 18 months! His net earnings this year will exceed $175,000!

He knows how to make use of every hour his boats are free. When they are not scheduled, he fills the unused time by chartering, and taking visitors on short excursions at an hourly rate.

YOU CAN DO THIS ANYWHERE

You have three basic requirements for locating your business: water, people, and moderately good sailing weather. If you are on the East or West coasts, Great Lakes, Mississippi River, or Gulf Coast, or have any decent-sized lake at your disposal, sailboat leasing can be for you. You don't need to be near a sea marina.

BUILD YOUR BUSINESS WITH OTHER PEOPLE'S MONEY

You don't need extensive capital if you start with two boats. You can grow gradually. The beauty of the boat-leasing system for you, the owner, is that the business is built with other people's money. On the yearly contract program each customer pays for seven months of sailing from the beginning. You receive more than $1,000 from each customer before the boat sets sail on its business venture.

With only 11 customers you can finance a $15,000 used sailboat, or put a hefty down payment on a new boat costing $25,000-plus. By constantly reinvesting money, owners quickly build their fleets.

Start-up Manual #149 is available on this business. See page 378.

TENNIS AND RACQUETBALL CLUB

High net profit B/T:	$300,000
Average net profit B/T:	200,000
Minimum investment:	10,000*
Average investment:	50,000*

*based on limited partnership situations.

(Profits before debt service. Investments are based on a limited partnership situation.)

A dozen years ago there were only a handful of tennis clubs that were sheltered from the weather and open all year. By 1975 tennis was booming and thousands of indoor tennis facilities were built throughout the country.

Many of the promoters and owners of these clubs made fabulous profits. But since 1975 tennis has peaked and many tennis clubs are showing losses. Savvy operators have turned the situation around and are converting their underused courts to racquetball or opening multipurpose recreational clubs.

Sports are fads. People take up a sport with a vengeance, are enthusiastic for a while, and then drop out, leaving club promoters looking at empty facilities. These promoters have learned that no recreational theme, be it bowling or skateboarding, maintains a high rate of interest over a long period.

With this in mind, experts warn us that building a large unipurpose club is not always viable. Instead, the most profitable clubs have indoor tennis and racquetball courts, outdoor tennis courts, women's and men's exercise rooms, jogging tracks, a pool, a nursery, a snack bar, a pro shop, and other amenities. We heard of one club like this grossing $2 million, but it is a veritable social and recreational arena.

RACQUETBALL vs. TENNIS

In recent years racquetball has taken over from tennis in the race for the "soles" of court-game aficionados. Racquetball is different from tennis in that you bounce the ball off a wall rather than over a net.

In 1971 there were only a few racquetball clubs. Today, there are over 1,000 nationwide, with projections of 2,000 clubs in another year. The sport claims almost 10 million American devotees, up from only 75,000 "wall bangers" in 1970. In New England five new facilities open each month. Industry enthusiasts predict 20 to 30 million zealous converts by 1985. Club promoters are capitalizing on the phenomenal growth of the sport by offering members easy access to courts and, often, the chance to play their favorite game in lavish surroundings.

MARKET—TENNIS

A broad spectrum of the population has been attracted to racquet sports. From the local garbage man to the executive, almost everyone, including an abundance of kids and housewives, has at one time or another tried his or her hand at a game.

This segment of the population is expected to grow by 49 percent in the next decade. Tennis is most popular with those aged 35 to 44. There are definite indications that the game is gaining in popularity with preteens, especially young girls, and college students—as well as with the over-50 set who are becoming more health- and exercise-conscious. Women are particularly enthusiastic and appear to be more inclined toward tennis than golf.

Due to its relative expensiveness, tennis players are mostly middle or upper-middle class. It's estimated that the average tennis club member spends $550 a year to play.

MARKET—RACQUETBALL

Millions of tennis players are switching to racquetball, which is now considered one of the fastest-growing sports in the country. The reason for this growth is that racquetball is easier to master than tennis, provides a quicker workout, is good exercise, is a great couples game, and is fun. Racquetball players tend to be younger than tennis players, 18 to 35 rather than over 35. Women find the game much easier to cope with than tennis as it is much easier to keep the ball in play.

GETTING STARTED

There are two ways of getting into the sport-club business. Many new clubs are built from the ground up, but a few promoters have converted large industrial buildings and warehouses into indoor tennis or racquetball clubs. The lower land and construction costs when you take over an existing structure can lead to quicker return on investment and higher profits. Not everyone, of course, can find a suitable building to convert.

If you are interested in building a club, proceed cautiously and make a detailed feasibility study and market analysis. Pay attention to factors that spell the difference between success and failure.

This business depends on number of members; if there is not

enough interest in your area, the business will fail from the start. A good tennis club will gross $50,000 per court per year; a good racquetball club, $35,000. Ten mixed courts will gross $350,000 to $500,000.

While a racquetball court grosses less than a tennis court, it takes only one-quarter as much money to build, so the return on investment is much quicker.

If you study the market and build accordingly, you should realize a 30 percent return on investment before taxes and debt retirement.

Start-up Manual #4 is available on this business. See page 379.

New Idea
FEMALE SPORTS MARKET

Sally Hurlburt turned her anger over a baggy warm-up suit into a burgeoning sports business that pulls customers from as far away as Italy and Ethiopia. When she was teased one day about her ill-fitting men's warm-up suit, she took the problem to manufacturers and set them to a task.

The Women's Sports Center is one of the few stores in the country that exclusively carries equipment and apparel for women. Most women over 5 feet 10 inches tall have to wear men's warm-up suits; that means a poor fit. At the Women's Sports Center they'll find a wide selection of outfits specifically designed for their figures and height.

The Wellesley, Massachusetts store carries lightweight tennis, squash, and racquetball rackets with extra-small grips. Running shoes, ski boots, and ice skates designed for narrow female feet are also available. Finding equipment for sports played particularly by women, such as field hockey, can be a problem, but not at the Women's Sports Center, which even carries support bras.

Hurlburt plans a worldwide mail-order business. We think this is a coming idea. Women like to shop in places that are specifically designed and run by other women; witness the great success of the First Women's Bank. Catering to the needs of women sports enthusiasts can be a winning business.

AMUSEMENT GAME CENTER

High net profit B/T:	$110,000
Average net profit B/T:	30,000
Minimum investment:	3,600
Average investment:	42,000

An amusement arcade may not sound like the classiest business, but the coins pile up so fast that you'd think they were coming off a mint press.

Pinball machines have been more or less passé for 25 years, arcades few and far between, and machines stacked to the rafters collecting dust in warehouses. Now, phenomenally, they are catching the attention and favor of a new generation.

Several years ago, the management of arcades located in amusement parks and tourist attractions began to notice an increase in business. Many ordered the newest gimmicks—electronic machines—to help push the renewed interest along.

Distributors who had been depending on jukeboxes, coin-operated barroom pool tables, and children's rides in front of supermarkets began to respond to the sudden interest.

An entrepreneurial outgrowth is "the operator"—a person who owns and places coin-operated amusement devices on a 50-50 split with various businesses. This is a great way to capitalize on the new interest.

NEIGHBORHOOD ARCADES

The operator usually begins by opening a couple of small neighborhood locations to test his market. If they prove out, he concentrates on finding other people to open more arcades; he puts the machines on a split profit basis, and supplies service.

The idea first caught on like wildfire in Los Angeles. Between 1973 and 1974 over 200 new arcades opened. Southern Californians, however, are exposed to many diversions and the neighborhood arcade soon palled on them. Most of the arcades are closed now, but those located in shopping malls are doing well.

The trend today is to locate amusement arcades in malls. The amusement centers are cleaning up their act and shedding their seedy image. Shopping-center developers have found this is a profit-making way to keep teenagers, who frequent the centers, busy and controlled.

The new atmosphere demands new standards of security and operating procedures. Smoking, food, and beverages are usually banned; personnel are well trained; and strict operating procedures are maintained.

An operator in one large shopping center in southern California grosses $10,054 per month. He has one full-time serviceman for 65 machines, and two change-making managers covering a 12-hour day, six days per week. His net before taxes averages $78,900 per year. Not bad for such a simple absentee owner-type business.

We've seen another equally successful shopping-mall operation. The operator could lease only 1,200 square feet for his arcade, which limits the number of machines and people he can handle. But his volume averages $8,000 per month, and the arcade is packed most of the time.

Neither of these operators was allowed a food concession in his lease, because of nearby stores that serve food. But a smart operator will carry easily handled soft drinks, ice cream, candy, gum, and in some cases popcorn—all of which add a nice profit to an already healthy margin.

Arcades require little or no promotion to get rolling. Every one that we've looked at was jammed with local kids from the moment it opened.

MIDWEST AND EASTERN CITIES BETTER

Arcades in cities with seasonal climates, like the Midwest and East, do well. (In states with a warm climate year-round and a variety of countryside attractions, kids have a larger selection of activities to divert their attention.) One arcade in the East consistently grosses over $15,000 per month.

These pinball emporiums or family amusement centers immediately become hangouts for the 10-to-18-year-olds in the area. Don't be put off by the word "hangout"—these kids have more money to spend today than the older generation had at that age. And they spend it, playing games and munching the goodies.

Start-up Manual #100 is available on this business. See page 379.

ROLLER-SKATING RINK

High net profit B/T:	$350,000
Average net profit B/T:	80,000
Minimum investment:	100,000
Average investment:	180,000

Roller-skating rinks date back 100 years. Since their introduction they have experienced cyclical popularity. Until recently, roller skating had been on the downslide for 20 years.

During the '40s and '50s rinks were giant money-makers, packed nearly every night. About 1960 interest started to wane, attendance fell off sharply, and many rinks closed their doors.

People seemed to be losing interest in roller skating—as they seemed to be losing interest in baseball. (Both were temporary.)

One of the biggest problems rink operators had a generation ago was rowdy youngsters. Rink owners felt this was one reason for the decline in popularity.

Now roller skating is back. The great search for leisure-time activities has interested the older (over 35) market again. The novelty of skating to rock and disco has attracted the younger market.

The old profit potential is back. If you add a variety of new supplemental income sources, roller rink ownership is again a terrific opportunity.

With the image cleaned up, rink operators are cashing in on the roller-skating boom. It's true that the health-conscious public is finding skating a most pleasurable form of exercise, very relaxing, relatively cheap and a great way to meet other free-wheeling types. But the real impetus behind the skating revolution is the newly designed and improved skates.

The Roller Skating Rink Operators Association of America (RSROA) reports over 1,600 members, up from 500 members less than ten years ago. They estimate that there are now over 3,500 rinks in the country.

Small family-run operations are realizing a 15 to 20 percent return on investment, but well-run, larger rink operations get net profits of as high as 35 percent. Many rinks have total annual incomes of $300,000 to $500,000. One large rink in Florida is reputed to be making close to $1 million a year gross.

MARKETS

An estimated 42 million Americans skate once a week or more in indoor roller rinks, a figure that has jumped from 28 million two years ago. Rink attendance is up almost 50 percent in one year.

The industry sees the increase in rink attendance as an effect of the increased popularity of outdoor skating. The millions who are skating outdoors for fun and health look to rinks for nighttime skating or for use when the weather is bad.

NEW CYCLES HAVE NEW FACES

When an activity returns to popularity, there's a change, whether in clothing or furniture (slight) or bicycles (dramatic).

Consequently, any rink created today should not copy old-fashioned rinks, but be designed for today's market.

Music is important in a roller-skating rink. Most adults over 40 and occasionally some young people prefer oldies and waltzes while skating. But most younger skaters prefer current rock music.

Many rinks have giant 15,000-square-foot floors. Why not divide them into two 7,500- or 5,000-square-foot rinks with two music systems?

HOW MUCH MONEY CAN BE MADE?

Several factors contribute to profit projections. The square footage of the rink area will control your maximum gross. Figure a minimum of 20 to 25 square feet per skater. A 10,000-square-foot rink can hold 400 to 500 skaters. Figuring 30 to 40 percent of the customers will be off the floor at any given moment, taking a break, eating, and so on your total capacity is 500 to 700.

In the '60s a 20,000-square-foot facility, with 10,000 feet of rink, might gross $150,000 to $200,000 per year, with 25 percent net profit before taxes. Today the same rink has a potential gross (excluding daytime rentals) of over $300,000, with 35 percent net profit.

INCOME DISTRIBUTION

The RSROA states that nationwide, 65 percent of gross income comes from admissions and skate rentals and 35 percent from extras: snack bar (19 percent), pro shop (8 percent), and games and lockers (8 percent).

SUPPLEMENTARY INCOME

Your extra income sources, which produce a third of your gross, must be as carefully planned as the rink itself. The snack bar should feature a simple menu with low preparation time, high unit return, and low waste rate.

The pro shop probably has the greatest potential for growth. Roller-skate sales are booming; retailers are unable to get enough stock to meet demand. Skate sales are 300,000 pairs a month and new suppliers are beginning to take business from the top three or four manufacturers.

Chicago Roller Skates, the largest manufacturer of skates sold in rinks, reports a 250 percent increase in sales in a year! Sure-Grip Skate expects to double its 1978 sales of over $5 million. Roller Derby Skate Company projects similar increases.

Obviously, if you maintain a well-stocked pro shop and hit hard on sales, you can cash in on the trend toward buying skates.

A pinball-electronic game room can generate another $10,000 to $30,000 of profit. Most rinks have only a few games. We suggest 30 to 40 games to generate the true potential profit from this area.

Start-up Manual #90 is available on this business. See page 379.

AUTOMOTIVE

MUFFLER SHOP

High net profit B/T:	$120,000
Average net profit B/T:	54,000
Minimum investment:	13,000
Average investment:	22,000

One muffler shop we've seen grossed $348,000 last year and netted the absentee owner $118,000 before taxes. And that's not unusual! A major franchisor claims an average shop grosses a minimum of $270,000 a year. Franchisees, however, pay substantial amounts for a franchise and equipment—$80,000 to $125,000; they also return 10 percent of their gross to the franchisor as a royalty and advertising fee. The franchisor owns the property and building, and leases it to the franchisee. Still, average net is 17.3 percent before taxes, after a $15,000 salary to the owners.

In the past few years the whole muffler shop concept has changed. You can get started, with help from some muffler manufacturers, for as little as $13,000 in cash.

The reasons are the development of a machine called a pipe bender, and standard mufflers that can be used on different cars. Before these, a muffler shop had to stock as many as 1,900 different tailpipes and 400 different mufflers to handle all cars. The required warehousing space added tremendously to rent or property expense. The huge inventory made start-up costs outrageous for a small business.

Now 30 expandable nipple mufflers fit all American cars. A small number of each of six diameters of straight tail pipe is all that is necessary to complete your inventory.

The pipe bender is exactly that—a simple hydraulic press that bends pipe to any angle or radius necessary. It flares, flanges, and can deform the pipe opening for a slip connection.

When a car comes into the shop, the mechanic pulls a card for that model car which shows what setting to use on the bender. He makes the setting, activates the bender, and in six to ten minutes the header and tail pipes are ready to install.

What's even more attractive is the cost. The tail pipe of an average Plymouth wholesales for about $13—for a Cadillac, about $17. But with a pipe bender you can make either one for about $4, including material and labor.

Pipes for foreign cars, trucks, and some older cars are hard to get, and vehicle owners usually had to wait several days or even weeks for the part—and then pay a premium for it. The pipe bender has eliminated all that.

NEW LOW MATERIAL COSTS

Standardized mufflers cost much less. The average wholesale price for a Chevrolet muffler is $16—for a Cadillac, $30. These are original equipment mufflers. A standardized muffler of equivalent quality costs $8 to $9, with better-quality mufflers costing $10 to $14. If you can buy in large quantities from a small muffler manufacturer direct, you can cut even these costs a couple of dollars.

KILL COMPETITION!

You can undercut the market and still make a high profit. The average retail price for a single muffler job on a Chevrolet is $60—on a Cadillac, $100. Of course, cars with dual pipes cost double.

A major's franchisor's average ticket is $65 for a muffler installation. As you can see, one of the best-known names can't compete with your prices.

THE MARKET

Parts replacement on autos is called the "automotive aftermarket." Mufflers and tail pipes rank third in sales after tires and batteries. Last year the public spent over $3 billion replacing exhaust systems. Exhaust service lines up right behind tune-up and ignition repair, as the second largest segment of the automotive service business.

Industry surveys indicate an 11 percent annual growth for the muffler business, as, out of the 130,000,000 registered vehicles, 4 out of 10 will need some type of muffler or exhaust work each year.

A muffler only lasts 1½ to 4 years. In colder climates, because of corrosion from salt used to melt ice on the street, they last even fewer years.

Over 60 percent of the cars on the road today are from three to nine years old—that's 80 million cars that are potential customers. What more could you ask?

With over 1,000 shops, Midas, the leading franchisor, claims only 8 percent of the market. Several authorities in the field have told us they doubt that Midas can retain even that share of the changing market.

NO REAL MERCHANDISERS

From media and visual surveys and conversations with muffler distributors and manufacturers we concluded that there are few hard-hitting merchandisers in this field. Low-price come-ons are common, especially in the tire and battery business. The only merchandising by price we found was by Sears and K-Mart.

Almost everyone at the wholesale distribution level agreed that any shops that offered and promoted discount prices on muffler installations had to be a winner. Distributors directed us to only a handful of shops in the country that were aggressively selling this way. The ones we interviewed were grossing higher than their competitors.

From that standpoint we feel it is an open market, ripe for anyone who wants to sell by price. And you can sell quality equivalent to anyone in the business, too.

Start-up Manual #44 is available on this business. See page 379.

CONSIGNMENT USED-CAR LOT

High net profit B/T:	$96,000
Average net profit B/T:	60,000
Minimum investment:	2,000
Average investment:	11,400

Last year about 10 million new cars were sold in this country. Over 30 million used cars changed hands, which means that over three times as many people buy used cars as new ones.

People in the used-car business have made snide remarks about the new concept of selling cars on consignment such as "It's a poor man's car business." They are right! It's the cheap way to get started. But our conclusion is, the consignment lot owner won't stay poor very long.

We found one operation selling 50 cars per month with an average gross profit of $150 per car. That's $7,500 per month before expenses. The net profit was over $3,500. Not bad for a business that a person can start for as little as $2,000. Why so little? A unique money-making part of consignment auto sales is that someone else's capital enables you to make big money with zero risk.

The principle of consignment is easy to understand. It means selling merchandise and paying for it afterward. You are an independent agent for the party supplying the merchandise. People consign their automobiles to you with the agreement that they will receive a certain amount of money when the vehicle is sold. You make a reasonable profit when you sell the automobile off your lot at the best price you can get!

THE CONSUMER IS WISER

Inflationary pressures are causing the consumer to watch his dollar more closely. Also, he is becoming more aware of how the system works. He realizes that when he trades his car in he gets the wholesale price, if not lower, and buys his next car at the retail price. Obviously there is a big gap.

All dealers subscribe to regional publications of the retail and wholesale prices of used cars. In the West it's called *Kelly's Blue Book*. In the East, the National Auto Dealers' Association publishes the book.

Suppose the *Blue Book* retail value of your car is $6,000. If you trade it for another car, you will get the wholesale price, which the *Blue Book* says is about $5,200. The car that you trade for has an average retail price of $9,000—which you pay. That car cost the dealer about $7,200, if he was a good buyer.

REVERSE THE SYSTEM IN YOUR FAVOR

If you could sell your car a couple hundred bucks under the regular retail price, let's say for $5,750, and buy your next car at a couple hundred over wholesale, let's say $7,400, you would save $2,150. That's a lot of money to anyone.

The consignment dealer does just this. When you go to the dealer, you will discuss how much you want to get for the car and what condition it is in. Once you have agreed on a selling price, he tells you that he will add $150 or so to the price as his commission. In other words, you will get your rpice, and he will make money for his trouble.

MAKE MONEY FROM BOTH ENDS

Then the dealer asks what make, model, and year car you are planning to buy to replace this one. You tell him, and he announces that he "will get it for you wholesale."

Sounds like a pitch, doesn't it? Not quite! The dealer explains that there is a weekly or biweekly auction where other dealers bring cars to sell to each other. The cars at the auction come mostly from new-car dealers who are overstocked on used cars. Or perhaps a sports-car dealer will bring in regular passenger car trades that he doesn't want to handle, and vice versa. But unless you are a licensed dealer, you cannot buy cars at the auction.

TAKE CUSTOMERS TO THE AUCTION!

The dealer tells you that he will take you to the auction and buy a car for you, charging you just $175 over his cost. He explains that the auctioneer gets $45 per car sold, so he's only making $130 for his trouble.

You can test-drive the car before the auction and check it out thoroughly. In fact, you can look at all the cars there and pick the one you want. When the auction starts you can stand beside the dealer and stop him if the bidding is going too high.

We learned about this new business from an insurance agent who recently bought a 1974 Continental Mark IV for $2,700. The car was clean and sharp with only 46,000 miles on it. *Kelly's Blue Book* quoted $3,220 as the average retail price in California and $2,350 wholesale, and the consignment dealer made $500 on this one.

Consignment selling is a fantastic concept still in its infancy. An operator in Pennsylvania has a new twist: he opens his lot only on weekends. He rents a parking lot on a main thoroughfare and puts up a banner-type sign. His clients leave their cars with him on Saturday and Sunday for him to sell.

Start-Up Manual #18 is available on this business. See page 379.

DO-IT-YOURSELF AUTO REPAIR SHOP

High net profit B/T:	$100,000
Average net profit B/T:	40,000
Minimum investment:	7,800
Average investment:	30,000

There are about as many automotive breakdowns each year as there are cars on the road. Worse yet, the auto repair business is rife with unethical operators. Although many state legislatures have enacted licensing and control methods for consumer protection, the rip-offs continue.

Unfortunately, the majority of consumers never realize that they have been taken. Those who do have begun to educate themselves about their automobiles. Many are discovering that some repairs necessary to keep their cars in proper condition are so simple that they can do the work themselves.

A market study done for various companies in the auto industry by J. P. Powers and Associates of Los Angeles revealed that over one-third of the small-car owners were do-it-yourself service and repair buffs.

Now, with increased inflation, everyone is becoming more conscious of every dollar spent.

NO TOOLS HINDER DO-IT-YOURSELFERS

Many drivers have found that they can save 40 to 80 percent of service and repair costs by performing the work themselves. Unfortunately, as anyone who has ever attempted to work on an auto has discovered, special tools are required—most of them too expensive to buy for one-time use.

This has led to the establishment of do-it-yourself auto repair centers across the nation. The centers rent garage space and every tool imaginable to accomplish any repair job, up to a complete engine overhaul.

The rent-a-bays provide, free of charge, service manuals for all cars, which give step-by-step instructions for the repair or replacement of every part. Most centers have a professional mechanic who will give additional assistance, if necessary.

For as little as $3 to $7 per hour, customers may use any or all of some 800 automotive tools. The centers offer all the professional tools except, possibly, those used in servicing automatic transmissions and radiators.

WIDE MARKET

Teenagers and adults, workers and professionals alike, men and women, have started repairing their own cars.

One shop has had over 11,000 customers during its first three years of business. Most of the successful shops average 25 to 40 customers on a good day, 10 to 12 on slower days. Customers spend an average of three hours making a repair.

As an added inducement, profitable shops offer to obtain parts, rebuild engines and transmissions, and do machining or radiator repairs at 20 percent below the going retail price.

AMATEURS ARE MAKING IT!

What amazed us about these shops was that many of them had reached a profitable level with little advertising and promotion. They relied mostly on word of mouth. This leads us to believe that a good businessperson with sufficient capital and a well-planned advertising campaign can make this into a very lucrative business.

MORE VOLUME NECESSARY

We have determined that few of the existing do-it-yourself centers are very profitable as business investments. Increased volume could make them very lucrative business because most of their operating costs are independent of the volume.

A center is easy to start. It is a viable business that will be around for some time, and it is virtually recession-proof.

In shops we saw that had been in operation over six months, gross profits were $700 to $1,000 per week. Only 50 percent of revenues were derived from rentals, the other 50 percent coming from profits on parts, machining, etc.

Start-up Manual #35 is available on this business. See page 379.

_____New Idea_____
PARKING LOT CAR WASH

We've reported on entrepreneurs who visit people's houses to wash their cars. Now a company has improved on the idea by visiting parking lots to tap the large number of potential clients.

Contract Car Wash works in association with garages. The garages put up a sign telling customers that wash services are available. In return, the garages pull in 25 to 50 cents per car washed. Contract Car Wash pockets the difference.

The service charges $4 to $6 depending on the service provided. With gas costing over $1 a gallon, the service puts an end to wasting gas by driving to the car wash. It saves time, too, because the cars are washed while the owners are at work.

Most people wash their cars irregularly. But with this service, people sign up for regular washes once a week. Bumper stickers are used to identify cars to be washed.

This is an easy business to get into, and the front-end investment is low. All you need is pails, washing mittens, and detergent. Contract Car Wash also uses 50-gallon drums of soapy water and two vans, but these can come later.

Finding parking lots willing to advertise your service shouldn't be any trouble, since they're going to get a percentage of the take. Try to stick to lots that are close to each other, as in downtown areas, so you can cut down on driving time.

TUNE-UP SHOP

High net profit B/T:	$60,000
Average net profit B/T:	30,000
Minimum investment:	13,000
Average investment:	27,500

This is the age of specialization. Gas stations no longer perform all the tune-ups, brake jobs, and work on mufflers, tires, transmissions, etc.

Nationwide there are more and more shops that specialize in brakes, mufflers, tires, and other important services.

The main reason why specialization is so successful is that in today's confusing maze of technology, people prefer doing business with someone who they feel knows everything about one subject—the subject they are concerned with at the moment.

The tune-up specialist is like a heart specialist—the ignition is the heart of your car. There is nothing more frustrating than a poorly tuned, rough-running, hard-starting engine. People imagine all sorts of complications when their car is in need of a tune-up. Hence to look up a specialist is only natural.

From the businessman's point of view, specialization has the key advantage of control. For the absentee owner or chain operator, rigid control over every aspect of the business is a must. With one product or service, a simply structured system of operation is easy to set up and maintain. Wasted motion is easy to spot and eliminate, unprofitable or low-profit activities can be restructured or cut out; and you don't need a computer to tell you where your profit is coming from and where your expenses are going.

A FORMULA FOR SUCCESS

We analyzed a tune-up specialist's operation for the key ingredients of his successful formula, and found that the promoter is not an average gas-pump jockey grown up into a mechanic. His system is simple but sophisticated, and shows much business experience behind it.

Though it isn't necessary, he is constructing his own building at each location—a simple double garage with overhead doors on each end so cars can drive through.

The operation is like an assembly line. Cars line up as though entering a car wash and come out, one by one, on the other side. Two cars fit into the garage side by side: only 15 to 30 minutes are spent on each car. Most people wait while their car is being tuned.

FIRST KEY INGREDIENT

Do ignition work only. Do not include rebuilding carburetors. The only thing done to the carb is to run some cleaner through it to remove the varnish buildup, and then to adjust the gas-and-air mixture and idle.

If the customer needs to have his carb rebuilt, the necessary tune-up is completed and a recommendation is made to the customer that he take his car to a carburetor rebuilder (another specialist).

Experience has shown that the customer appreciates honesty and the fact that the shop won't just take his money and do a halfway job. Most people fear that auto mechanics will take advantage of them, and this procedure dispels their fear.

What does a tune-up entail? The whole ignition system is checked electronically and all poorly operating parts are replaced. All tune-ups include engine diagnosis, chemical carburetor cleaning and adjustment, timing set, check and cleaning of smog control valve, and replacement of the following parts if necessary: plugs, points, condenser, rotor, air filter, fuel filter, distributor cap, and spark-plug wires. If the customer needs a new generator, alternator, voltage regulator, coil, battery, battery cables, or starter, it is charged for extra.

IMPORTANT

An automotive trade-school professor told us that the tune-up done by Tune Masters is not a full-fledged tune-up, but a "pep-up." Here is where a smart angle comes in for making a profit. Tune Masters gives a flat guarantee that your car will stay in tune for six months. They don't replace every doubtful part—only the ones the mechanic feels are absolutely necessary. Every car gets points and plugs. Only a few receive new condensers, rotors, and distributor caps. And occasionally an air or fuel filter is so clogged that it can't be blown clean. The parts cost per car averages $7 to $8. (Returns for retuning are less than 5 percent.)

Start-up Manual #9 is available on this business. See page 379.

AUTO PARKING SERVICE

High net profit B/T:	$54,000
Average net profit B/T:	26,000
Minimum investment:	450
Average investment:	2,000

A prestigious attorney recently told us that he had put himself through college and law school and financed the opening and furnishing of his law office by parking cars at fancy dinner restaurants. He said, in fact, that some of his first clients were people whose cars he had parked regularly.

But that happened 20 years ago, and times have changed. In most cities big operators provide parking attendants for restaurants on contract. This would lead you to believe that the service is so tied up that competition can't get a foothold. For example, Valet Parking Service, one of the giants, is a multimillion-dollar company.

But often when a company in a service field becomes big it grows more vulnerable to competition than when it was small. Several factors cause this: each contract becomes a number, and the personal touch is lost, which can only decrease customer loyalty.

WHY DO THE RESTAURANTS CONTRACT FOR THIS SERVICE?

Why wouldn't a restaurant hire its own parking attendants rather than contract for a parking service? Some do! But there are several reasons why they shouldn't. First—hiring, supervising, and ensuring you have someone on the job every night is a headache for the restaurateur. What if his parking attendant doesn't show up on Friday night—the busiest night of the week? Many restaurants have limited parking space and on busy nights cars must be double-parked to facilitate the heavy flow of diners. You can see that without an attendant parking will be chaotic; and some customers, who can't find a parking space, will go to another restaurant.

The biggest problem with hiring attendants, though, is the quality of people attracted to the job. Most are students or young people with low stability. On the spur of the moment they may change their minds about coming in to work; they may decide to take a trip. And because young people are active, finding a substitute on such short notice may be difficult.

Also, the restaurant's liability insurance rates increase when their employees drive on the job.

But for the operator of a parking attendant service, it's easy to have on call six or eight attendants who check in every day to see if you have work. The restaurateur would find it annoying to have to contend with these calls every day. And soon, if he didn't have work for those on call, they would cease calling. You are operating several parking lots, so you will find this necessary evil easy to handle. The restaurant manager has other problems that are important to him. Thus many restaurant owners are eager to contract valet parking services which will eliminate parking problems and save the parking attendants' wages as well.

BUT HOW DO YOU MAKE ANY MONEY?

One of the simplest ways you can make money is to take a percentage of the parking attendant's tips. However, recent state labor laws prevent this practice in some states. Where governed by new law, operators pay attendants the minimum wage, and the attendants keep any tips received. Under this approach, operators charge customers one dollar or more for parking and/or negotiate a deal with the restaurant or business owner.

If labor laws allow, use the following method: auto jockeys normally get $2 per hour, or $12 for an evening plus 33 percent of tips after the first $20. A popular 50-table restaurant parking lot will bring in $320 per seven-day week in tips. Wages are $84, commissions $59.70, and lease fee about $50. That leaves $115 for overhead and profit.

These figures do not include lunch and Sunday brunch business, which will usually add another $75 to $100 profit. Some large popular restaurants double the figures given. Restaurants that have a dance band and attract the late evening singles crowd to their lounge will increase profitability even more. Many high-volume establishments need as many as six attendants to handle the traffic on busy nights.

Start-up Manual #48 is available on this business. See page 379.

New Idea

CAR-CARE CO-OP

A recent poll shows that the service most consumers are dissatisfied with is auto repair, because of high prices and the feeling that unnecessary work is done. In Tulsa, Oklahoma, a group of people have fought back by opening a cooperative car care club.

Members of the Car Care Club of Oklahoma have hired their own mechanics who only do necessary work and don't charge inflated prices. The annual membership fee of $39.50 per car provides operating capital for rent and the mechanics' salaries. Parts and supplies, such as oil, are sold to members at wholesale cost. The club anticipates that members can save up to 50 percent on yearly maintenance and repair through the organization.

This is a capital idea that can go over in any area as a profit-making venture. The more members, the better, since their fees pay for the services. With such a good deal, finding participants won't be a problem. Locate garage space in an industrial or warehousing section of town to keep rent low. Search auctions and used-equipment outlets (ones that maintain quality) and haggle for supplier discounts on tools. Start with one or two mechanics and expand only as membership grows. Knowing exactly the number and type of cars will help control inventory and indicate the type of equipment and mechanical skills needed.

Begin advertising in the newspaper and on the radio, and be sure the AAA knows about the business. This deal should prove so popular that word of mouth will do most of the advertising.

AUTO-PAINTING SHOP

High net profit B/T:	$115,000
Average net profit B/T:	85,300
Minimum investment:	10,000
Average investment:	18,000

Most business "kings" in the United States aren't born, they're made. They attain royalty because they've been sharp enough to take an idea, incorporate it into a working plan, and mold it into a money-maker.

If you live in a city that has an Earl Scheib Auto Repainting Shop—there are over 200 of them nationally—you are near a neat, workable, and efficient example of the ultimate success in this industry. Although he has many competitors who take delight in pointing out his shortcomings, Scheib has, over the past 35 years, formulated a business plan that attracts price-conscious consumers en masse. And that's the name of the game in business today.

Close examination of the auto painting business reveals a wide variation in prices between shops outside the Scheib chain. They advertise low up-front prices, but when you take your car in you find that only painting is covered by the attractive quote—you face added charges for the preparation and bodywork usually necessary before the first burst of the spray gun is triggered. And the price you pay is drawn from a scale determined by what kind of car you're driving. The old mechanic's maxim "If he can afford a big car, he can afford a bigger price" is nowhere more evident than here.

There is nothing wrong in trying to make a profit. But how you price your work will ultimately affect your repeat business and referrals. For example, we took two cars to three shops. One was an economy car, and one a rather expensive small sports model. The economy model had a two-inch dent on the hood trim and a couple of supermarket parking lot scratches on the doors. We were quoted prices ranging from $125 to $235 for preparation, bodywork, and painting with a standard off-the-shelf paint. The same shops quoted the same job—bodywork on a 6-inch square rough spot and same paint—from $175 to $275 for the sports car.

We tried the same test at three Earl Scheib paint shops, specifying the $69.95 paint job in all cases. Bodywork on the economy car was $60 to $65, and on the sports car $45 to $50—for totals of $130 and $120 respectively. Some people might explain the differences between Scheib's prices and the others' by detailing variations in the quality of the paint job, but that's not the point. The average car takes 3/4 to 1½ gallons of paint, depending on who's doing the job and how well it is applied—hardly enough to justify such a variation in charges.

PLENTY OF ROOM FOR COMPETITION

In many cities we saw higher priced auto painters competing with Scheib and doing very well. We surveyed these cities and found many locations that would not be in direct competition with Scheib.

Since people usually choose to have their car painted near where they live or work, we believe all cities could support more low-priced paint centers. In fact, we found several shops that had duplicated the Scheib formula and price structure very successfully.

If the average, better Scheib shop does 15 to 20 cars per day—and we took the mean at 18—this means 5,616 cars in a 12-month period, with doors open 6 days per week. Not all cars will require bodywork, so the average sale will come to only $90.50 per vehicle. Each shop should show gross sales of $500,000 annually.

Using a 12-car-per-day-average, the shop would net about $85,300 for an absentee owner. This is allowing a $25,000 salary for a manager. So even on the low end of the scale, with a $30,000 annual advertising budget, it is a very profitable business.

Start-up Manual #50 is available on this business. See page 379.

AUTOMOBILE DETAILING

High net profit B/T:	$60,000
Average net profit B/T:	30,000
Minimum investment:	1,100
Average investment:	5,000

Ever wonder who puts the mirrorlike showroom shine on all the cars at the dealership down the street? If you're thinking it's someone who makes minimum wages for back-breaking labor, guess again. Small auto detailing or reconditioning companies do this, and some *net* over $60,000 a year!

This little-known but vital part of the huge automobile industry is a "sleeper" that can be incredibly profitable. Detailers "prep" new cars for sale and recondition used cars taken in trade on a volume basis for car dealers. But the highest profits per car come from performing high-quality, cosmetic maintenance on automobiles owned by proud private parties.

Most auto detailers are craftsmen, not businessmen. Few promote their services aggressively; many are in out-of-the-way locations such as alley garages and parking lots. Not many realize the true potential for profit.

HUGE PROFITS FROM A TINY INVESTMENT

Even under these circumstances, average gross profits for this loose-knit industry are $75,000 with net profits pretax in the $30,000 range. This is a whopping 37 to 41 percent of sales! These lucrative margins result from very low operating expenses for shoestring operations. We found that it is possible for a bright operator with marketing savvy to get into the business for as little as $1,100.

MULTIBILLION-DOLLAR MARKET

A person who parks a car and walks away from it will invariably turn around and take a final look sometime before the car is out of sight. (Test yourself if you don't believe it.) Psychologists who have studied this curious habit know that it comes from pride of possession and affects all of us.

For the 120 million-plus people who own vehicles from Cadillacs to clunkers, an automobile is a prized necessity. Manufacturers and dealers know this and play on pride and ego when making a sale. Who'd buy a dirty car? Who'd want to be seen driving one if they could help it?

That's why every new or used automobile is prepped by dealers prior to sale. Most cars will be thoroughly reconditioned cosmetically at least once during their lifetime; many will be detailed three or more times.

LEADS TO ADDITIONAL PROFITABLE BUSINESS

There are a number of services performed by detailers when prepping a car for sale or reconditioning a used car. Depending upon the condition of the vehicle, some or all of the services may be provided to the dealer or individual who requests the work.

Basic to the business of detailing a car is a thorough cleaning inside and out, including the trunk or other cargo space. For an extra charge, some detailers will clean the engine and engine compartment; some will paint the engine as well. The final and most visible step is polishing the exterior of the car.

Detailing does not include bodywork, painting, mechanical repair, or upholstery work. Nor does it normally include vinyl or convertible top repairs. This work is done by other tradesmen.

Providing detailing services by contract to dealers is a full-time task for many operations. All but the highest-volume dealers, who often have their own staff do the work, will farm it out to independent detailers. The detailer who does the best work at the lowest price per car will get plenty of work.

HARDLY ANY COMPETITION

The consumer market is vast and virtually untapped by most detailers, so almost any city in the country is wide open. Even in the areas where several detailers now operate, a good marketing plan can easily overwhelm unsophisticated competition. Most operators are not promoters; they are often low-key individuals who don't want to grow much more.

Only a handful of detailers are going after the consumer market now, and they usually focus on owners of luxury imported or domestic automobiles like the Mercedes and the Cadillac. In part this is because the average price for a thorough inside and outside detailing job can be as high as $150. These detailers build a regular clientele of affluent customers who have their cars gone over periodically. Pickup and delivery service or on-site work from a mobile van or truck is frequently part of their service for busy executives without the time or desire to get involved with maintenance.

The average middle-income car owner doesn't have this option. He can only go through a car wash for a hot wax job that lasts between washings or spend a weekend rubbing and buffing his car with off-the-shelf products. Neither approach really restores paint or chrome to its original luster for any length of time. Even the best commercial products last only about 45 days in good weather.

YOU CAN LOCATE ANYWHERE

So you can see there is much more opportunity in this business than simply polishing cars. As profitable as detailing is for those in business now, it becomes even more exciting when you consider what a bright, promotion-oriented marketer could do.

One reason detailing involves so little initial investment and generates such high margins is that you can do the work almost anywhere. We found one operator who worked in an alley behind a parking lot—and grossed $60,000 a year. His office was a portable tool shed, and in the evening he packed his equipment in the trunk of his car and drove away.

We found several shoestring operators making an excellent income working out of their homes using the garage, driveway, and nearby streets as their work area. Others set up an answering machine on their home phone and work out of a van or car detailing in the customer's driveway or parking lot. This is an excellent timesaving approach for the executive market.

Start-up Manual #146 is available on this business. See page 379.

CAR WASH

High net profit B/T:	$200,000
Average net profit B/T:	62,000
Minimum investment:	22,000
Average investment:	90,000

In 1914 two young fellows in Detroit opened the world's first car wash—The Automated Laundry. The cars had to be left all day since they were pushed through the "system" manually, and even brass parts were removed for polishing by hand.

Twenty-five years later the first crude "automatic" conveyor car wash was opened in Hollywood, California, by two gas station owners. On busy days as many as 40 men splashed in the tunnel soaping, scrubbing, wiping, and drying cars as they were pulled through.

Today, there are over 20,000 automatic car washes, many of which can completely wash and dry a car in about one minute without it being touched by human hands. With more than 120 million passenger cars on the road in the U.S., it is possible to find a car wash handling 20,000 cars per month and netting over $200,000 a year before income taxes. Net profits of $50,000 to $75,000 are common.

Your out-of-pocket cash investment isn't out of the line with the return, either. You can set up a small-scale automatic exterior wash with $22,000, but the big profits will come from a larger operation in a prime location—figure $50,000 to $65,000 down, with bank loans of $75,000 to $150,000.

WHAT HAPPENS WHEN IT RAINS?

That seems to be the first question prospective car-wash investors ask. Taking national weather figures, look for 250 days without precipitation. Also, night or morning rains don't hurt business. In fact, the day after a heavy rain, business is usually better than normal in car washes because autos get muddy and sloppy driving around.

Car washes in northern climates do much more business during the winter because car owners are concerned with keeping their cars free of the corrosive road salts used for melting snow and ice.

Nationwide the car-wash industry does less business during June, July, and August, because people wash their own cars more during these warm months.

On the other hand, southern California—which usually has fewer than 20 rainy days a year—grosses more per car than any other part of the nation. No one seems to have an explanation for that! Most of their car washes are full-service operations, unlike other parts of the country which may have 50 to 90 percent exterior-only washes.

We conclude that it is the buying attitudes that are different—a factor you must consider in the area you plan to evaluate.

More people are using car washes, however. A 1975 Louis Harris poll on the car-wash industry showed that usage had increased from 20 to 38 percent since 1971. In these days of high inflation, car owners view their automobiles as investments; thus they spend more money on preventive maintenance and care. The car wash is definitely a growth industry.

TYPES OF CAR WASHES

Coin-operated spray washes are for the do-it-yourselfer. These units have proliferated nationwide in the past ten years, and the market is currently overbuilt in many areas, although there are a few virgin spots left. We expect many of these to be replaced shortly by coin-operated rollover wash equipment. Some vandal-resistant units are available already.

Rollover washes are easily installed in a standard coin-operated bay by simply bolting the unit to a footing and installing the plumbing and wiring lines.

This system with it's $1.50 to $2.00 price is, for the money, a viable alternative to automatic car washes. Drying must be done by hand. Coin-operated paper chamois dispensers and vacuum cleaners allow the customer to do a thorough job.

Maintenance of the rollover units is expected to be negligible because of the simplicity of their design.

Automatic exterior washes are the most popular nationwide, primarily because the units can be operated by one or two men. Car owners simply pull up to the floor conveyor and ride their cars through the tunnel, where blowers air-dry the car at the end. No handwork is done.

The exterior washes are almost always coupled to gas sales, and are perfect for the absentee owner. A manager and one employee per shift will do, unless gas sales or traffic is very high.

A few oil companies are very active in converting regular gas stations into automatic car washes, because the change usually triples the sales of gasoline.

Full-service car washes offer interior window washing and vacuuming, along with hand drying—for a higher price—to customers who want a thorough cleaning without exerting personal effort.

A new feature is being added to many full-service operations which generates even higher profits—automatic application of a high-quality wax and high-speed automatic buffing. The additional price for this service is $3 to $4 and the quality of the wax job is much better than you would expect. Custom wax jobs can range from $15 to $75.

Most of the full-service operations will soon be replaced with *menu services,* offering a choice between full service and exterior-only service.

Every car wash that has been converted to menu services has achieved higher volume. Hanna Industries, the giant of the car-wash field, has been successfully promoting additional services in their menu such as carpet shampooing, a buffed wax job, rust inhibitor application, tar removal, vinyl top dressing, and interior shampoo detailing on request.

Truck and bus washing, once ignored by the industry, is now being actively pursued. The most lucrative area is truck washing and cleaning. The semitrailer truck business is promising; many areas of the country do not have sufficient facilities yet to take care of the demand.

THE CHOICE: TO BUY OR TO BUILD?

You have to be more careful if you are going to buy an existing car wash. It is very important to unearth the real reason for the sale.

After about five years the maintenance costs for car-wash equipment start getting high. Perhaps the owner foresees some large expenditures for replacing major components.

Also, many areas change gradually to a point and then change explosively: the current population moves away in droves and people with different buying habits move in. Usually only the people who live and work in an area are sensitive to the subtle changes that precede an exodus.

Car-wash books can be easily manipulated to hide high maintenance costs and to reflect higher earnings than those actually received. If there isn't a water reclamation system, sometimes you can correlate the water usage of the system (available from the manufacturer) with the gallonage on the water bills to arrive at the number of cars being washed. If your figure is much lower than that claimed by the owner or shown in the books, something is wrong, because water usage should go up slightly as the equipment wears.

Start-up Manual #76 is available on this business. See page 379.

TEN-MINUTE OIL-CHANGE SHOP

High net profit B/T:	$40,000
Average net profit B/T:	36,000
Minimum investment:	6,500
Average investment:	16,000

This is the end of an era for the full-service gasoline station. In a few years stations that do all kinds of automobile service will have practically disappeared. Most will be replaced by self-service stations, either operated by a cashier overseeing the station from a remote change booth, or by self-service pumps activated by coins or credit cards.

All the major oil companies have been quietly testing these concepts under unknown names on the stations, such as Quickie, Jiffy, Go-Go, and Economy.

The self-service stations offer discounts up to 10 cents below full-service prices. Because of federal price laws governing the petro leum industry, the major companies are forced to set up subsidiary or independent corporations in order to offer these low prices—this explains the new names. Once a major company has 30 to 40 stations under one name, it creates a new company name for the next 30 to 40. The gas is the same in the discount stations as it is in the full-service ones.

THE REASON FOR CHANGE

Several things have encouraged this new marketing concept: inflation, the oil shortage, franchise laws, specialization, public buying attitudes, and the realization that marketing today is much different from what it was in the '40s and '50s. The main reason is simply that the oil companies are not interested in repair work because they don't make any money on it. Until now it has been a necessary evil in running gasoline stations.

Gulf Oil found that when they converted a station pumping 300 gallons a day and doing repair work to a discount operation with no repair work, their gas volume immediately jumped to 3,000 gallons per day. That's a strong argument!

Standard Oil and Texaco found that if they replaced the repair bays with a small, free automatic car wash, gas volume jumped five to ten times its original level.

WHAT DOES ALL THIS MEAN?

Where will you go to have your car repaired when most stations have been converted to strictly gas-dispensing operations? To specialists: tire dealers, brake shops, tune-up shops, transmission shops, diagnostic multirepair centers, and single-purpose service facilities.

A NEW SPECIALIZATION

A car needs an oil change every 3,000 to 6,000 miles. Several years ago an auto repairman realized that a person who wanted a simple oil change either had to leave his car at a gas station or wait from a half hour to three hours for the work to be done.

He reasoned that a shop doing only oil changes could, with two workers, do the job in less than ten minutes and at the same time do a grease job, replace the oil filter, check and add rear-end lubricant, transmission, power steering, and brake fluid, blow out the air filter, check the radiator level, and clean battery terminals and add water.

Today this man has a number of Quick Oil Change shops; several competitors have copied his idea. Most shops handle 100 to 200 cars per week at $15.95 each, minimum. Average gross sales per shop are about $1,800 per week. The average net for an absentee owner is over $500 per week. The average owner-operated shop should net $36,000 before taxes annually.

LOW INVESTMENT

The total cash investment if you convert an existing gas station can be only $10,000, and effective use of financing can lower this figure to $6,500.

THE ANGLE

If you buy your oil, transmission fluid, and other oil products in quart cans, you won't be able to sell your services at $15.95. The angle is to purchase oil products in bulk—55-gallon drums. The cost per quart drops by one-third.

The oil is hydraulically pumped directly to the crankcase through a metering gun. The same is done with rear-end grease, automatic and standard transmission lubricants, power-steering fluid, and filtering grease. Instead of taking several minutes to fill a crankcase from individual cans, five quarts of oil can be pumped in within a minute.

THE REASON PEOPLE BUY THIS SERVICE

Speed, convenience, and expertise are what ensure the success of this business. Everyone is anxious to make auto maintenance a less time-consuming and complicated affair.

Ignorance also contributes to the success of the quick oil-change shop. We took a minisurvey and found, to our amazement, that seven out of ten drivers were not aware that their local gas station would change their oil free—that is, for simply buying the oil.

The average good grade of oil sells for 90 cents to $1.20 a quart. Multigrade, 10W to 40W, sells for about $1, tax included. Most cars take five quarts to fill the crankcase. So you see an oil change can cost only $4.50 to $6. Of course, if you need lubricants in the transmission, power steering, rear end, or brake cylinder you will pay extra. A grease job is a thing of the past, because most cars made in the last five years don't require this service (another fact of which many drivers are not aware).

Start-up Manual #54 is available on this business. See page 359.

MANUFACTURING

HANDICRAFT MANUFACTURING

High net profit B/T:	$60,000
Average net profit B/T:	10,000
Minimum investment:	1,100
Average investment:	4,400

Even if you have no artistic ability or special knowledge, you can join the entrepreneurs who transformed simple handicraft manufacturing into a billion-dollar industry.

There are dozens of people grossing $100,000 or more annually by selling their crafts at craft fairs, retail stores, and swap meets, and by direct mail. These operators report nets in the 35 to 45 percent range.

Start-up costs can be as low as $1,100 and the materials used can be anything from tree bark to broken mirrors. We found one man who had converted old tin cans, wax, and cotton string into a profitable candle business. Just by selling at swap meets and fairs, one woman was grossing $400,000 every year with her hand-tooled belt business. Then there was the shrewd operator who was importing wooden boxes at a cost of 50 cents each, decorating them with tole painting, and selling them for $15.

SIMPLE TO MAKE

The fascinating aspect of handicrafts is the simplicity of the manufacturing process. Even if you're all thumbs you can learn how to make any of the hottest crafts on the market today. These are *the* money-makers—all of them are super-easy to make, require little front-end capital, and can be safely transported to any marketplace.

Our research uncovered these crafts as tops: glass staining, country pine, silhouettes, tole painting, mirror sculpture, patchwork wall hangings, wooden toys and games, glass etching, and bread-dough artifacts.

Surprisingly, even the most crudely constructed crafts can bring home the bacon—just replace the word "crude" with "primitive" and you'll understand that the natural-looking non mass-produced items are the big movers.

HANDMADE IS IN!

The reemergence of handicrafts is due to the fact that today's

Americans are tired of the "factory-produced" look. People want to decorate with items that reflect their individual tastes—they don't want their homes to look just like everyone else's!

The nostaliga trend has led people to reject the anonymity of mass production. They yearn for the good old days of Yankee ingenuity and craftsmanship. This accounts for customers paying $100 for a country pine medicine chest that costs $30 to produce, or paying $50 for an old tin bucket decorated with tole painting.

MARKETS ARE EVERYWHERE

By mastering a few inside secrets of selling at fairs and swap meets, you can negotiate for the prime locations and boost your sales over those of your competitors. There are more than 6,000 craft fairs held each year where handicraft wares are sold. Along with this marketing network there are county fairs, state fairs, gift shops, boutiques, swap meets, and major department stores as potential outlets for your goods. The possibilities are practically endless— anywhere people congregate, you'll usually find someone selling crafts.

MARKET RESEARCH REVEALS TASTE

In conducting your own market research, you should always ask yourself these questions: (1) Is there a need for my particular craft? (2) Can I make this unique, compared to other versions of the craft? (3) Can I profitably sell the craft?

One shrewd operator in Iowa answered the questions yes. He wanted to make candles because of their popularity and simplicity of design, but he wanted a gimmick. He thought up the idea of personalized candles that would commemorate some important date: a graduation, a birthday, a wedding anniversary, or a promotion. He got some old lead type forms from a printer, filled them with wax, and produced a good inventory of letters and numbers. He simply glued these onto his standard inventory of candles and sold the result for $10. His product cost? A mere $2.

BUILD YOUR CAPITAL AS YOU BUILD YOUR CRAFTS!

A big advantage to selling crafts is that this kind of business is often self-amortizing. If you begin with $100 worth of lumber for country pine items and create $1,000 worth of products, you can then buy $700 or $800 worth of lumber and greatly increase your production.

One of the leading tole painters in the country started with $80 worth of wood, $20 worth of paint, $10 worth of brushes, and in less than two months made over $900! Today, the profits from her books on tole painting, her lectures, and her finished product are in the

$75,000-to-$100,000 range and are growing 20 percent per year!

Regardless of the craft you choose, it should be possible to get started for $1,100, which includes initial supplies, tools, and preparation of a work space.

Start-up Manual #177 is available on this business. See page 379.

See page 379.

_____ New Idea _____
MINIATURE FURNITURE

Miniature furniture is bigger than ever! Dollhouses are no longer kid stuff—adult collectors have swooped down on hobby shops, flea markets, antique stores, and thrift shops in search of these tiny domiciles, buying them up as if they were the latest real estate gambit.

Decorating these tiny homes calls for even tinier furniture, and there just isn't enough of it around these days to satisfy the growing demand. Manufacturers and dealers can't keep up with the orders!

Perhaps reacting against a world obsessed with grand dimensions, dealers and collectors are crying out for suppliers. The field is growing rapidly.

If you're imaginative and good with your hands, consider building miniature furniture. Copy the designs of contemporary furniture makers, or research period pieces. Basic books on furniture making are readily available; simply reduce the dimensions.

You can manufacture a complete line of miniature furniture, including beds with real mattresses, upholstered chairs, china cupboards with pullout drawers, tables, ottomans, stools, bureaus, and curtains.

SCULPTURED-CANDLE MAKING

High net profit B/T:	$32,000
Average net profit B/T:	18,000
Minimum investment:	2,000
Average investment:	3,000

We stood in line for 35 minutes at a small shop in Lahaina, Hawaii, to pay $15 for a candle that stands about 12 inches high. The material cost for this beautifully sculptured work of art was about $1.

In 35 minutes the lady making the candles grossed close to $300. Since we were all tourists from the mainland and elsewhere, each customer asked that the delicate item be placed in a cushioned carton. This naturally slowed the line and the volume of sales.

At a flea market near Seattle, our reporter watched an operator sell 14 sculptured candles in one hour. This candleman had three sizes: 8-inch, 10-inch, and 12-inch. His prices ranged from $10 to $22.

In Palm Springs, California, a young lady has a shop in the high-rent area specializing in multicolored hand-carved candles. These are isolated examples. The market for these candles is just waiting to be tapped.

LOOKS COMPLICATED, BUT IT'S NOT!

The appearance of the candle makes it look complicated, but actually it isn't. For those of you who don't know the first thing about candlemaking, here's how it works:

Paraffin or wax is heated to the temperature suggested by the manufacturer. Pigment or color is stirred in. Next, the wick is dipped progressively in and out of the hot wax until the size and shape desired is achieved.

Our carved, variegated candle is made similarly with a few variations.

A stock candle is dipped in one color until it is about 1½ inches in diameter, then four sides are shaved off with a hot knife to create a tall pyramid shape.

Now the candle is progressively dipped from one color to cold water to another color to cold water to a third color and the sequence repeated until the finished size is reached.

Next, sculptor's wire carving tools are heated and the sides of the candle shaved and hand-rolled to create the curlicues and design.

When the carving is finished the candle is sprayed or dipped in a glaze. Dipping is most effective, using Johnson's Wax Versacryl 766 or clear liquid varnish. This gives the candle a porcelainlike appearance. The carving takes the least time—only about 5 minutes. Dipping can take up to 15 minutes for the largest candles.

THE MARKET IS UNLIMITED

This business can be started from your home. Flea markets are a good spot to start. Art shows are equally lucrative. A net of $200 to $500 per weekend can be expected if the foot traffic is good.

Tourist attractions are ideal locations, but your start-up investment will be higher. Do your dipping and carving right in the window to attract passersby. You've probably seen the attention glassblowers attract. You'll do the same and make even more money.

WHOLESALE MARKET UNTOUCHED!

Gift shops, boutiques, and department stores are ripe markets, but you must be ready to manufacture in quantity and have enough capital to produce the products and then wait up to 60 days for your money. The standard discount is 40 percent to retailers but some big chains will hold out for more.

Start-up Manual #120 is available on this business. See page 379.

———————————— **New Idea** ————————————

NAME THAT SCARF

Ever think that writing your name on a scarf would be the beginning of an up-and-coming business venture? Charlotte Dillas of Tarrytown, New York, annoyed at high retail prices for designer labels, bought a solid-colored scarf and wrote her own name on it. A neighbor wore one and brought back 25 orders; another friend returned from a club meeting with 25 more. And the orders haven't stopped coming in!

Although Dillas initially ran into difficulty from wholesalers who didn't want to sell to an individual not affiliated with a major corporation, Charlotte persevered and found a supplier of solid-colored polyester scarfs. There are several brands of ballpoint paint tubes that write on fabric; Dillas uses Vogart's liquid embroidery. The scarfs she sells are available in a multitude of colors and are machine washable and colorfast. A 24-inch square sells for $4; a 27-inch square and a 12-by-54 inch oblong scarf go for $5.

Charlotte finds that proper names are the most popular, although requests for nicknames, initials, and special sayings such as "numero uno" come in. The width of the pen compensates for less-than-perfect penmanship, and each scarf takes only a few minutes to fashion.

This is an excellent business to operate from the home, with low overhead and no experience needed. Most people look for ways to express their individuality, and personalized accessories are a popular way of doing so. Neighbors, work associates, and clubs are natural buyers for the scarfs. It might also be possible to make arrangements with gift, clothing, and department stores to display a few samples and take orders, but be sure this method doesn't cut into profits too much.

Dillas is so sure of a large market for the scarfs that she is offering to help others get started in the business and is interested in inquiries from salespeople. If you want to contact her, send a stamped, self-addressed envelope to Charlotte Dillas, Dept. IE-7, 15 John Street, Tarrytown, New York 10591.

CUSTOM RUGMAKING

High net profit B/T:	$36,000
Average net profit B/T:	20,000
Minimum investment:	400
Average investment:	1,100

It's not often we come across a low-investment business that can be successfully operated from a person's home—even on a part-time basis. Also, it's rare to find ground-floor opportunities that have possibilities of growing into large, solid, profitable enterprises.

Even though this business is new and as yet unproved, we feel it is one of those rare situations on which you can capitalize. If we are right, in a year or two the market may be flooded, but anyone starting now will have such a strong base that they won't be hurt by competition.

Until recently, hand tufting of custom rugs was a tedious, tiring, time-consuming chore. A two-by-three-foot rug took at least ten hours. Now an electric tufting tool reduces the time by 25 to 40 percent and eliminates the tiring wrist action that usually produces sore, numb arms in less than an hour of tufting.

THE PROFITS

The rug described above retails for $75 to $100. Material costs are $15 to $25, depending on your buying power for supplies. The average time, from start to finish, is eight hours, depending on the intricacy of the design. Some operators, however, with practice can turn out this size rug in six hours.

If you pay someone minimum wage, your average labor costs are about $24. If you wholesale the rug at $50 to $60, your gross profit is $11 to $21. If you retail the rug for $100, you net $51 to $61. As you can see with some quick multiplication, ten rugs per week will produce a healthy profit.

WHO WILL BUY THE RUGS?

Companies as well as individuals are big egotists. Everyone likes to see his name or logo emblazoned in a rich, new, unique way. We feel this is a virgin market. Companies are quicker to spend money in this form than individuals and are usually less concerned with price.

A lucrative market among small and large companies is developing. Most company executives can easily visualize their corporate logo, trademark, or name in the rich colors of a plush wall-hanging rug in their reception room. Manufacturers, insurance companies, banks, auto dealers, associations, unions, hotels, retail stores—practically any business, large or small, is a prospect.

Besides the corporation market, boat owners are a well-heeled group who would enjoy the name of their vessel on a rug in the cabin. Luxury and custom car owners are another set who would be tempted by monogrammed floor mats for their plush vehicles.

HAVE OTHERS TAKE ORDERS FOR YOU!

An idea we have here, which has been used successfully for many other products, will increase your initial investment but can prove to be your most lucrative source of revenue. There are heraldic crests for most European names; many companies have specialized in producing these crests, and have grossed millions of dollars through mail order—which proves the interest in the item.

Suppose you prepared a typical heraldic crest on a two-by-three-foot rug along with a sign: "Your Family Crest or Any Design or Words—Only $89.95." Take this rug, your sign, order forms, and a catalog of crests to the better gift shops and department stores in your city. Offer to place the display on consignment and give them 30 percent for any orders taken. They make no investment—and they get a new, unique item with tremendous sales potential.

A few dozen shops could provide you with a healthy income if each one only sold two or three per month. Naturally, the person who wanted a special design would have to provide the artwork, and all orders would require a 50 percent deposit. Many people will want rugs larger than two by three feet, which will multiply your income proportionately.

OTHER MARKETS

Several other markets are untapped. Gift shops would be a good choice, except that they are usually small and don't have the wall space to display more than a single rug. Custom rugs are usually used as a wall decoration rather than on the floor, and furniture stores will be an ideal market—especially for the larger sizes, such as three by six feet, four by five or six, and five-foot-diameter circles. You can display stock designs. Furniture stores specializing in contemporary or modern decor are your best prospects, and you should bring your best samples in different colors and large sizes to show to the dealers.

Owners of furniture stores and their buyers are usually tough to deal with, and will try to push you for a consignment arrangement. Hold out until the last minute for a sale with net 30-day billing. Don't forgo the consignment deal, though, if you can't do better; you may get your money just as quickly and wind up with more samples displayed. The normal discount is 50 percent off retail.

Swap meets and flea markets have possibilities, although people who attend them won't have as much money to spend and are primarily bargain hunters. Offer your rugs at 25 percent off retail.

Start-up Manual #66 is available on this business. See page 379.

STAINED-GLASS WINDOW MANUFACTURING

High net profit B/T:	(Variable)
Average net profit B/T:	(Variable)
Minimum investment:	$ 400
Average investment:	2,500

The nostalgia trend has created an unbelievable demand for stained-glass windows. Less than ten years ago there were very few stained-glass artisans in the United States—only an occasional creative artist in some of the larger cities. Now, nearly every college with night craft classes offers instruction in the art of assembling stained-glass windows and other items using the same techniques. And sales of books on the subject are over the million mark. Libraries cannot keep books on stained-glass construction on their shelves.

In 1969 it was rare to find stained glass in any building other than a church. The few specialists in the trade relied entirely on religious organizations for their revenue. Today all types of buildings are having stained glass incorporated into their design—apartment buildings, offices, stores, etc.

FEW ARE MAKING BIG MONEY, THOUGH!

Yet with all the interest in this art very few of the thousands of practicing craftsmen are making healthy profits. The ones well connected with architects, designers, and decorators are making tremendous profits. The others, though, will pick up an occasional job here and there, but by and large they rely heavily on teaching classes, and on the supplies they sell their students.

STAINED GLASS—EXPENSIVE!

The reason most of the shops don't do a higher volume is that stained glass is expensive to create. People drawn to this work are interested in its creative aspects; they are people who like to work with their hands, and they are not particularly attuned to the techniques of merchandising and exploiting the commercial prospects of their trade.

The creation of a stained-glass piece is expensive, not only due to high material costs but to its being time-consuming. The price of the glass ranges from $2 to $25 per square foot, with an average of $4. The selling price for a simple window measuring two by five feet will range from $250 to $750; the average is $500.

A TREMENDOUS MARKET UNTAPPED

Halfway through our investigation we decided that there existed a tremendous market for stained glass, if the quality could be retained while cutting the price by 80 percent. This would open the item to mass-marketing techniques.

Then, quite by accident, one of our investigators found a wall or window hanging piece in a furniture store at a ridiculously low price. The quality of the construction was excellent and the colors and textures of the glass were brilliant. This 30-by-40-inch piece was selling for an unbelievable $95—cheaper than the average painting.

VIVE LA DIFFÉRENCE!

The furniture salesman finally confided that the glass wasn't actually glass, but had been simulated using polymer resins. We purchased the item and made a side-by-side comparison with a real stained-glass window. The simulated window was more impressive than the real one. The colors were actually more brilliant, the texture of the "glass" more interesting, and the weight almost as heavy as real glass. A big advantage is that this creation is not easily damaged. Regular stained glass, if dropped or struck, will usually crack or break—but not so with this polymer creation.

SELLS WELL

This small furniture store was selling an average of one of these pieces per week during the four weeks they had carried the product. Customer interest was high.

We learned that a local craftsman created the windows on weekends in his garage, and had them on display in only four stores. He had only one design and was selling five per week.

MANUFACTURING COSTS LOW

Continuing our investigation, we interviewed the young artisan. He confided that he was paying retail prices for all his supplies, yet his total material costs were only $14 for each window—$13 for the lead and a dollar for the polymer, which he cast himself. The wholesale price he charged for a window was $45.

Using very few assembly line techniques, and cramped into a crowded garage, the creator figured he spent about three hours per window—although at this point in our interview he was becoming wary of our probing questions.

We estimate that even with a low-quantity production of 12 to 15 units per day, using an assembly line and purchasing supplies at wholesale prices, the cost of a window of this size, before overhead and sales costs, would probably come to about $12.50.

GROUND-FLOOR OPPORTUNITY—WHOLESALE MARKET FANTASTIC

A little later we contacted wholesale gift salesmen, wholesale furniture salesmen, and distributors throughout the nation. We did not find anyone selling stained-glass windows. Obviously, then, this is a ground-floor opportunity in a virgin market. The interest in the product is at an all-time high, and the mass market is wide open.

Furniture stores have already proved to be a good market. Art galleries, gift shops, and decorators will naturally fall into the same category. Discount stores and department stores have an unbelievable potential, although you had better be well organized and financed before you approach these people.

Start-up Manual #61 is available on this business. See page 379.

HOT-TUB MANUFACTURING

High net profit B/T:	$125,000
Average net profit B/T:	47,000
Minimum investment:	5,500
Average investment:	38,500

In 1968 a small publishing company printed a book called *Hot Tubs,* by Leon Elder. In the past few years the book has become immensely popular and has been reprinted several times.

The book tells how the locals in Santa Barbara, California, were filling up large redwood wine casks with piping hot water and inviting their friends over for a communal bath. The trend has spread fast and hot tubs are the hottest new product on the West Coast.

Now the old wine casks are all used up, and local entrepreneurs are building redwood tubs to fill hot-tub demand. One man and his wife have a shop that sells $5,000 worth of tubs each week.

There are over 100 manufacturers in this field—however, retail business is so good that few are interested in wholesaling to an independent. With an average manufacturing cost of $400 to $600 and a retail price of $2,200 to $4,500, you can't blame them.

The tubs come in every variation of size and style, from "cuddle tubs" (which sell for $500) holding only two—very closely—to a storage tank large enough for an entire family, in fact, up to 30 people.

The common hot tubs are wood tanks, usually from five to eight feet in diameter. They are usually made of redwood, due to its durability. However, cedar is very popular now, and other hardwoods like mahogany or even cypress can be used. The tubs hold 600 to 1,000 gallons of water. A six-foot-diameter tub will comfortably bathe ten people at the same time.

Most tubs have whirlpool or air jets, which are excellent for massaging tired or sore muscles. The members of our staff who tried the tub all agreed that the effect was so relaxing that it was hard to get out.

BALNEOLOGY!

We're sure that many a sensibly conservative thinker is trying to figure out who would buy a big tub to sit in the patio or the backyard when everyone has a perfectly good bathtub already.

Or maybe you're thinking this is another far-out California fad that will soon pass. Well, we've been watching the phenomenon for several years and have seen it grow dramatically throughout the country. National magazines have printed articles which created interest not only in the intellectuals, health addicts, and the elite who are looking for something new, but in Mr. and Mrs. America.

The water bed began in the same modest fashion. Then *Playboy* did a feature on it and business boomed to unbelievable proportions.

Communal bathing has always been an important part of Japanese culture. Balneology, the science dealing with the therapeutic effects of hot baths, began in Japan. People around the world, especially Europeans and Americans, take an active interest in balneology. They visit hot springs by the millions each year.

THE MARKET IS WIDE OPEN

As a society we are becoming ever more aware of the problems of stress and how it affects health, longevity, and productivity. An essential part of stress management is relaxation; more and more people in the blue- and white-collar ranks are seeking ways to relax in comfort.

The market for health-related recreational facilities in the home is exploding. This is reflected in sales not only of hot tubs but of jacuzzis and whirlpool baths, sauna baths, home steam-bath kits, and a multitude of new products hitting the marketplace daily.

People realize that it pays to take care of yourself, and the hot tub is one of the least expensive ways to add that leisure touch to the home.

Health, relaxation, and stimulation are by-products of hot-tub use that appeal to people of all ages. Approximately 90,000 spas and 40,000 hot tubs were sold in 1979, compared to only 5,000 hot tubs sold in 1976. The total retail sales for tubs and spas has risen to close to $1 billion.

While hot tubs have a swinging image, your typical customer isn't a swinging single. Rather, fortyish homeowners will be your best customers as part of the "new awareness" among the middle class, who look to hot tubs as a means of getting back to nature, getting in touch with their feelings, and often, as a means of sexual expression. Of course, many users stress the therapeutic rather than the social aspects of hot tubbing.

Your market includes anyone who works hard, is health-conscious, and wants to relax for health and recreation. In other words, the market is everywhere and the only limit is that customers must have homes, townhouses, or apartments with patios large enough to accommodate a tub.

NORTHERN CLIMATES NOT A PROBLEM

Those who have used hot tubs in cold weather claim they are exhilarating. The air is cold but the water is hot. Northern Europeans, such as Finns, Swedes, and Norwegians, prefer to visit their hot springs during the cold winter. Many American ski lodges keep their swimming pools active during the winter, and recently a few have installed hot tubs.

Freezing water isn't a problem because all tubs have a water heater and a pump. Either the pump is kept running (running water doesn't freeze) or the water heater thermostat is kept low.

To shield the tub from wind, a plastic bubble can be erected over it at low cost. In areas where winter conditions preclude outdoor use, many tubs are moved inside for storage.

Start-up Manual #75 is available on this business. See page 379.

BURGLAR ALARM MANUFACTURING

High net profit B/T:	$100,000
Average net profit B/T:	37,500
Minimum investment (direct sales):	2,000
Average investment:	25,000

Burglary is big business! There is a burglary committed in the United States every ten seconds, 24 hours a day! That's nearly 3 million burglaries a year, and it represents a loss of almost $1 billion in residential thefts alone. Is it any wonder that more and more Americans are considering burglar alarm systems?

Most home burglaries are not committed by members of organized mobs. They are pulled off by teenagers. In fact, 85 percent of those arrested for burglary are under 25! More than half are under 18. A few have sophisticated methods, picked up on the street or during a term in a correctional institution, but most just break and enter. And as more and more women take jobs, daylight robberies increase. In one year such offenses increased 67 percent. What are your chances of recovering anything after a theft? Slim at best. Nationally only 16 percent of residential burglaries are solved, and less than 2 percent of the stolen items are returned.

FANTASTIC SOURCE OF PROSPECTS

Every time a burglary is committed, that victim and his neighbors are instant prospects for burglar alarms! These homeowners may have already been considering an alarm system, but when actual fear replaces rationalization, they will be ready for a product demonstration.

In our research, we discovered many burglar alarm representatives who were unaware of one of the best sources of information on home thefts: the police reporter. In most communities burglary information is made available to reporters covering the police departments, with the hope that public dissemination will put others on guard. This source can be a gold mine of prospects.

You can succeed in the burglar alarm business in one of two ways: you can enter the field with a direct sales organization, or you can add alarms to an existing business or line. Also, you can buy equipment completely assembled and ready to install, or components you will assemble to fit the installation. We found a few established direct sales organizations with net annual profits of $40,000 to $50,000.

BURGLAR ALARM MARKETS

No segment of the marketplace can be ignored. While the middle-income-and-above residential family is the best prospect, as the more affluent homeowner feels he has more to lose than an apartment dweller, this market profile is beginning to change. With new types of professionally installed systems of local alarms that cost only $300 to $600, the market is widening.

The affluent customer, who owns art objects, hobby equipment, antiques, jewelry, and custom furnishings, remains a prime target. This is especially true when an art collector is told by his insurance agent that his premium will be lower if he installs an instrusion alarm system.

When dealing with affluent prospects you will be thinking of complete systems, not just a preentry alarm on the front door. Doors, windows, certain "secure areas," and total perimeter systems should be a part of the package.

DRAMATIC DEMONSTRATION—THE KEY TO SUCCESS

Burglar alarms are impulse items. Prospects don't spend hours weighing the relative merits of various systems. When they are motivated by a loss or fear of a loss, they are ready to buy, and the dealer with a line of alarms that lends itself to dramatic demonstrations is the dealer who will make the sales. Choose alarm systems that sell the sizzle along with the steak.

Imagine the reaction of a prospect who merely puts his hand on a doorknob and sets off an alarm! He doesn't have to force it or even turn the knob; just his hand on the knob releases an alarm.

A system that lends itself to dramatic demonstrations is the frequency deviation alarm. There are many of these on the market. During the demonstration you walk in and out of the room and talk with your prospect in normal tones. Then you tap a coin on the side of a table, and off goes the alarm. Or perhaps after giving the prospect some basic information on the system, you slide open a squeaky drawer. Again, the alarm goes off. The system has been programmed to react to abnormal sounds in a room, ignoring the frequency range of normal footsteps, conversation, and perhaps a radio in the background. When in the middle of your sales presentation you activate the alarm by tapping your ballpoint pen on the ashtray, you will get the prospect's undivided attention.

Start-up Manual #91 is available on this business. See page 379.

TOURISM

STUFFED-TOY ANIMAL VENDING

High net profit B/T:	$18,000
Average net profit B/T:	10,000
Minimum cash investment:	300
Average cash investment:	800

You have probably observed someone on the side of a main highway, or standing beside a car on a busy street, surrounded by colorful stuffed animals—someone who made a couple of hundred dollars profit that day.

For example, there's a woman who owns and operates a permanent stand in Hollywood, California. She rents space in the corner of a service station lot on Hollywood Boulevard—*not* considered an outstanding location!

Her net profit, before taxes, is over $18,000 annually on a gross of nearly $40,000. Her investment has not exceeded $800 at any one time. She started with an inventory of less than $200. Her costs for signs, advance rent to the service station operator, and some plastic bags and receipt books were less than $50.

Anyone can do the same thing—stuffed animals sell themselves. In fact, the owner speaks very little English. We needed an interpreter to translate for us during the interview.

In our travels around the country, we have seen stuffed animals being sold in every area. Every operator we interviewed claimed that sales of $400 to $800 for a two-day weekend were not uncommon. (These stuffed animals are aptly called "plush" by the carnival trade.)

SALES GIMMICK

The best sales gimmick we saw was a sign with a large "99¢" and, painted in small letters below, the words "and up." Of course, the giant lifesize animals that really attract the attention of passersby sell from $50 to $500 with the average around $60. The 99-cent items are small "carnival toys" which cost the seller 40 to 65 cents each. The average 14- to 16-inch item sells for about $15.

Almost all purchases are made by adults, and not always as gifts for children. One entrepreneur told us that over half of his sales are made by men who purchase the plush animals as gifts for their friends. He claims that his best-selling periods are on Friday and Saturday evenings—the typical date nights.

A gift-shop owner in Las Vegas, Nevada, who does a big business in the plush trade, sells several of the maxi-size animals to "big spenders" each month, at $250 to $500 apiece, and ships them to their destination.

THEY BUY ON IMPULSE!

The cuddly, furry animals are almost always bought on impulse by people in a happy mood with a desire to do something childish. This was the opinion of a seller who travels through Florida and the South. He says the business is most enjoyable because all of his customers are happy and having fun.

Start-up Manual #39 is available on this business. See page 379.

BALLOON VENDING

High net profit B/T:	$100,000
Average net profit B/T:	15,000
Minimum investment:	600
Average investment:	1,500

During his vacation a friend's son came to our editor asking if there were any summer jobs available. Our editor told him he had a better idea. Did he think his father might be willing to lend him about $500 for a few weeks? This lad replied that it would probably depend on what he would be doing with the money, so the editor briefly explained what he had in mind.

Recently, he spoke with this young fellow again. He learned that the boy had not only repaid his father, but spent $50 a week on himself and still put almost $4,000 in the bank. Not bad.

What was the key to his successful summer enterprise? During those ten weeks, the student had grossed over $6,900—simply by selling balloons on a beachside pier.

BALLOON CONCESSION NETS $100,000

The young man was told about the businessman who owned the balloon concession at Disneyland. He sold, on the average, 1,000 balloons a day. During the summer months the figure often exceeded 3,000 a day. A little calculating shows that 360,000 balloons a year at an average of 50 cents apiece yields a gross of $180,000.

The colorful 11-inch balloons he sold cost about 4 cents each in the quantities he purchased. He paid about $30 for a cylinder of helium which will inflate over 400 balloons, averaging out to 7 cents per balloon for gas. Insurance, labor, and related costs added up to about $30,000 a year, which included a manager's salary of $10,000.

The man behind this operation lived about 400 miles away, and visited Disneyland once a month. Before taxes, he netted around $100,000 each year—but of course, there are not many locations like Disneyland, and it's very difficult to acquire that type of high-volume concession.

7.200 BALLOONS PER MONTH

Another young fellow we met had been introduced to the balloon business by an uncle who had worked carnivals in his youth. This man landed a balloon concession in a new year-round indoor tourist attraction. His helium supplier told us that he's buying 18 tanks per month, except during the summer when he orders 28 a month. That works out to about 7,200 balloons—or $3,600 gross for most months, and $5,600 during peak summer periods.

Rent takes 15 percent of his gross, his average monthly wages come to $1,600—which includes a $600 salary to a young fellow who runs the operation. The owner spends most of his time looking for additional locations, and going to the bank each day.

PART-TIME PROFIT AT FLEA MARKETS

We also found a retired gentleman who hawks balloons at swap meets every weekend. Swap meets are the flea markets held in drive-in theater lots in California, and they draw amazing crowds—5,000 to 20,000 people per day. This old fellow empties almost two tanks of helium each weekend, for a gross of over $400.

Start-up Manual #3 is available on this business. See page 379.

_____ **New Idea** _____
MULTI-THEATERS

Cineplex 18 has opened to rave reviews in Toronto. It's a theater, and it's definitely the wave of the future. The theater is actually a combination of eight small theaters which seat from 57 to 116 people. (The average is 100.)

Each minitheater is capable of showing a different movie. This is what makes Cineplex unique. It can cater to mass-market movies and also grab the small, specialized foreign trade.

If there's a small market for an Indian film, it's played in the 57-seat theater. But if they're showing *Apocalypse Now* they can book it into all eight of their minitheaters. The beautiful part is they can cut back and show a hit in just three of their theaters during slow periods like midweek and then shift back to eight on the weekend.

They can cater to every taste—old-time silent films, Bogart festivals, John Wayne movies, and foreign films, along with popular mass-market staples. Most important, they can do it all at the same time.

Theaters are a big investment, but they can pay off handsomely. Cineplex, with its diversified bill of fare, may capture the moviegoing public to the point where it's the only game in town.

ANTIQUE PHOTO SHOP

High net profit B/T:	$116,000
Average net profit B/T:	40,000
Minimum investment:	1,000
Average investment:	7,000

Using a few chemicals, some old clothes, and Polaroid film, a man in Hawaii has developed a technique for producing 1890s-type photographs in minutes. He can also simulate the tintype famous during that era.

His timing could not have been better. The country has gone "nostalgia crazy," with anything styled antique selling faster than ever before.

With about a dozen costumes gleaned from antique shops, movie studios, and costume suppliers, he can make a man look like a Broadway Dapper Dan complete with top hat, cravat, and spats; a hardened bandit; or even an authentic reincarnation of the sheriff of Dodge City or Tombstone.

The women can become fox-tailed saloon floozies or pampered, bustled ladies. Oddly enough, he says most women want to look like the floozies seen frequently in western movies!

For a portrait of one person you can charge $9. Most customers are couples, so your average sale is $22 to $30 for group shots. Materials cost from 75 cents to $1.75 (film and chemicals) and 20 to 50 cents for the "antique" picture holder.

THEY'RE STANDING IN LINE!

The activity around another store in a shopping mall always

attracts attention; during the evening hours, there's usually a line of people waiting for their "instant antique photo."

In summer and at Christmas and Easter, the volume doubles the owner's normal sales of around $1,200 per week. The highest sales for one week topped $3,105. At the end of the first 12 months, gross sales were a few dollars short of $65,000.

All expenses—including $400 per month rent, utilities, phone, and wages for one full-time and one part-time worker—came to only $20,000 during the first 12 months. That's a net before taxes of $45,000. Not a bad bundle, considering that the owner came into this mall as an itinerant merchant for a three-week promotion, bringing four costumes, a simple backdrop, a couple of floodlights, a Polaroid camera, and several boards of display photos. This was a total investment of less than $500, although your start-up costs would be double now for a similar setup.

The response was so great that the mall manager asked if the photographer would like to take a store that was being vacated and become a permanent tenant. Taking money out of profits, the owner leisurely decorated the store with a few antique photos, bought a 50-year-old portrait camera, had the lens reconditioned, and adapted the camera to a Polaroid film pack. Today, the store looks like an 1890s photographer's studio and attracts everyone's attention.

NONE HAVE FAILED

There are over 800 such studios nationwide and more appear every year. One of our subscribers grosses $500 per day working malls, fairs, and shows.

This is a simple business to set up and is perfect for absentee ownership. Anyone can use a Polaroid camera, especially when no adjustment for differing conditions is necessary. The antique process is so simple it can be carried out by a bright six-year-old.

Using any standard Polaroid camera (not the SX-70), with a black-and-white film pack, anyone can create these antique photos. And you don't need to know anything about photography to do it. We produced antiques perfectly the first time in our office, just by following our engineer's instructions.

Start-up Manual #27 is available on this business. See page 379.

HANDWRITING ANALYSIS
BY COMPUTER

High net profit B/T:	$60,000
Average net profit B/T:	15,000
Minimum investment:	1,000
Average investment:	4,000

Hanging on a bank of "simulated computers" was a bold sign proclaiming "For Your Fun and Entertainment Only." But it didn't stop over 600 people from paying 95 cents each to have their handwriting analyzed by this so-called computer when our investigator spent a Sunday afternoon watching and counting the traffic at a local tourist attraction.

He reported that the majority of the customers walked away exclaiming how accurate their readings were!

We came across this unusual little business quite by accident in 1971, while investigating a successful tourist attraction for a large building contractor and promoter. Our client wanted to know how much rent was being paid by the various merchants in the attraction.

We were amazed to find that the highest rent per square foot was being paid by the operator of a computerized handwriting analysis booth. An operation such as this charges the merchants, the gift shops, and the other concessions a part of their gross sales against a guaranteed rent. We found the handwriting booth paid $12,000 annually for 192 square feet—20 percent of gross sales.

Even more astounding was the fact that this "computer analysis" booth was located in Niagara Falls, Ontario. The bulk of their business was concentrated in four summer months, and they were only open on weekends during the rest of the year.

Once this discovery piqued our curiosity, we searched out other examples of this business, and investigated the cost of building the "computer" and the various other facets of this enterprise.

We found a company that owns several of these handwriting analysis booths, in tourist attractions across the U.S. But, much to our dismay, they were so protective of their operation that we could acquire only a superficial view of their techniques. We did learn enough, however, to convince us that the booth in Niagara Falls, grossing $60,000 annually, was no fluke.

THE INSIDE DETAILS

We pursued our inquiries, though, and our patience finally paid off when we found an operator in a small tourist attraction in California who let us in on the details of his business.

He informed us that in eleven months at this location he had grossed over $32,000. His rent was based on a $150 per month guarantee against 15 percent of the gross, or about $4,800 for that period. One full-time worker and two part-time attendants hired at minimum wages ran the entire operation, with wages totalling around $11,000. His only other expense was for the graph cards produced by the "computer" which cost 0.012 cents each—about $408. His net of $15,792 for 11 months would indicate an annual net income of $17,227.

This location uses three "computers" which originally cost $960 for parts plus labor for assembly. Finding the parts and assembly time takes an estimated 40 hours per unit. The owner claims that he put in the three machines expecting more volume than he finally drew, indicating that two would have been enough.

THE INVENTOR OF THE IDEA

Handwriting analysis by computer is not a new idea. As far back as 1960 at a county fair in New Jersey, a man rented a booth and put in an old IBM card-sorter—his "computer"! Over 5,000 people paid 75 cents each to have their handwriting "analyzed" during the fair, and all the activity immediately attracted opportunists all over the country into this strange new business.

Today there probably isn't a state or county fair of any size anywhere in the country that doesn't boast its own handwriting analysis booth. Reliable sources indicate they gross $1,500 to $3,000 per week. A fair booking agent told us that a lot of retired couples work fairs during the three summer months to supplement their income. After traveling expenses and booking fees, they stand to net $15,000—based on a $2,000 average weekly gross. Not a bad supplement to anyone's income—retired or not!

Start-up Manual #8 is available on this business. See page 379.

FLOWER VENDING

High net profit B/T:	$80,000
Average net profit B/T:	17,000
Minimum investment:	200
Average investment:	1,650

We met a man in Montreal several years ago who was netting $80,000 a year on less than $100 original investment plus a few minutes of his time each day. Sounds unbelievable? It is true!

What was he doing? Selling roses in nightclubs and restaurants. Only he didn't do it—he had five young women who made the rounds for him, like this: Each night, five women stopped by and picked up the night's quota of 200 roses each. Then each woman visited seven nightclubs and restaurants, five nights each week (two days off).

They visited each table where women were seated, asking their escorts if they would like to buy a rose for their lady—for only $1.

They sold about 20 roses per stop, or 140 per night. And on Friday and Saturday nights they increased that to between 200 and 250. For each rose they sold they received 25 cents (25 percent minimum). The women we spoke with were making over $200 a week, and loved their jobs.

Sales amounted to at least 4,000 roses per week. Figuring 30 cents a rose, cost of sales was $1,500. Commissions were $1,000, leaving a profit of $1,500 a week.

One of the women explained that the club and restaurant owners were in favor of the operation, feeling it was an additional and thoughtful service for their patrons. The only payment the proprietors received from the girls was in roses, a dozen twice each week, which would be placed in a vase somewhere in the clubs as decoration.

The business has a universal appeal. As we all know, women love to receive flowers. A single red rose is interpreted to mean "I love you." There isn't much question about this being a successful enterprise.

OFF THE HOOK FOR JUST A DOLLAR!

A single man will jump at the chance to buy a rose for his date.

And a married man, if nothing else, feels he is getting off the hook cheaply. After all, the wife can't claim he never buys her flowers, now.

With all these factors working in your favor, it's easy to see how the club and restaurant owners allow the girls to come in. But perhaps Montreal—being a very European city with its many immigrants—has more of a continental flair than the average American city. We've traveled through partically every major city in the U.S. in the past few years, but have yet to see any flower girls. We are told, though, that flower vendors—usually older women—sold blooms during the '20s in many large cities like New York and Chicago.

Considering the fact that this has proved to be an extremely lucrative enterprise—$80,000 to $90,000 per year can't be considered peanuts—it would be worth a concentrated tryout. There is certainly no high investment to lose.

SECOND CASE HISTORY

About a year ago, in the marina area of Los Angeles, we were reminded of the Montreal flower girls when we spotted high-school boys peddling flowers at stoplights, much as they sell newspapers in many eastern cities during the evening rush hours.

The Marina del Rey area is a pleasure boat harbor, surrounded by thousands of apartments inhabited by upper-income people. Seven days a week, on the corners of key streets feeding into the area, young boys stand next to signs advertising "Long-Stemmed Roses, $1." In a one-mile strip we counted seven boys vending flowers.

Checking, it turned out that each boy sold 30 to 50 flowers per night during the week in winter months, and 50 to 80 per night during the summers with the longer daylight hours. On weekends, each boy could sell between 100 and 150 flowers per day.

$1,300 PER WEEK PROFIT!

Although not as lucrative as the Montreal operation, their gross of $2,600 to $3,000 a week cannot be ignored. The commission paid the boys was, again, 25 percent. The roses were short-stemmed seconds, but instead of one you received two or three. Their cost to the owner of the business was 10 to 20 cents each.

There were three other groups selling flowers in the city. We investigated one and found a beehive of activity at the storefront where this crew met to prepare their flowers before being dropped off at their sales spots.

Five rented U-Haul vans were parked in front, and we counted 16 teenage boys and a couple of girls making up bouquets of carnations.

The group would put a dozen blooms in a bouquet, wrap it in green cellophane, and later sell it for a dollar. This meant a 40 percent profit per sale, or about $2,000 net per week.

ANOTHER CONTEST

We found a contest in progress. One boy proudly pointed to a chart on the wall that showed each salesperson's name and the quantity sold for the last 10 to 12 weeks. The weekly prize was more realistic—$100 cash to the top man, $50 for second place, and $25 for third.

We saw that sales ranged from a low of $156 to a maximum of $523. The average sales for each three-day period hovered around $300 per seller, which figures out to about $5,000 in sales every week, less the 25 percent paid as commissions.

Carnations are colorful and attractive, but are probably the cheapest flower you can buy. The average cost, direct from the grower on a contract, is about 3 cents apiece. Of course, if you are buying in smaller quantities through the market this can get up to about a nickel apiece.

During Christmas they sell potted poinsettias; and at Easter, lilies, along with the standard bouquet of carnations.

ANYONE CAN DO IT!

The fellow behind the marina operation was a 24-year-old ex-truck driver without a high-school education. No special expertise or experience is necessary for this business.

If you want to try it, all you will need is a state resale permit (sales tax permit). Look up "Florists, Wholesale" in the Yellow Pages. In most major cities all the flower wholesalers are located on one street in one building. It may not be wise to tell the wholesalers about your method of selling at the beginning. After you buy a nice quantity regularly, they won't care.

Start-up Manual #10 is available on this business. See page 379.

DIVE-FOR-A-PEARL SHOP

High net profit B/T:	$39,000
Average net profit B/T:	18,000
Minimum investment:	8,800
Average investment:	14,300

It is generally known that jewelry has a very high markup, from 200 to 1,000 percent of the retailer's cost. A pair of typical costume earrings that cost the jeweler 25 cents will retail for $1 to $3 a pair, depending on how rich or poor the traffic is where the jeweler is located.

Unfortunately, the jewelry business has expanded enormously. For example, in a typical shopping mall with 125 stores we counted 12 full-fledged jewelry stores and 31 other stores carrying some sort of jewelry. The high profit margin is the only reason so many jewelers can compete so closely together. You can see that it doesn't take many customers to build a nice profit each day.

With so much competition, it would be wise to find an item that will make you stand out from other jewelers.

One jeweler on the West Coast has discovered that extra ingredient and used it to multiply his operation to 13 stores, bringing in a healthy six-figure profit each year. His extra ingredient is a great gimmick, but few people have realized it; and for that reason, it has not been copied much.

The gimmick is Dive-for-a-Pearl, and you may occasionally see it in a tourist attraction. Here's how it works: As a store owner, you order cultured pearls still in the oyster shell from Japan or a local distributor, who places 250 oysters in a large can of formaldehyde and ships them to your store at a cost of $3 to $3.25 each (price varies according to supply and demand and the deal you can make with the supplier).

You then install a small plastic tank in a window which is open to foot traffic. Your sign reads: "Dive for a Real Cultured Pearl Still in the Oyster. A Pearl Worth $6 or More Guaranteed in Every Oyster. Only $5.50 a Dive. The Pearl You Get May Be Worth as Much as $50; and Sometimes There Are Two Pearls in the Oyster."

Passersby are attracted by the novelty and approach the window. They are curious, but not enough to come in the store. (Few passersby just "shop around" inside a jewelry store; most of those who enter are serious about a purchase.) Make sure a clerk is waiting to serve the customer. He or she should be working with pearls and settings, seated in the window next to the tank as a companion attraction.

You'll be impressed at the crowd that gathers when someone decides to stop and dive for a pearl. People are generally bashful about doing something new and unique, but once someone does stop, a group will follow, and usually several will try it.

The clerk coaches the customer by asking him to "pick his oyster." The customer is offered tongs or a net, or the clerk can use them himself to pull the shell out of the tank. The clerk slides a paring knife into the mouth of the shell, then twists it, popping the oyster open. Then he feels around in the oyster meat for the pearl or pearls, pulls a jewel and shines it with a pinch of salt to add polish and remove the oyster film.

Next the clerk lightly washes and towel-dries the pearl(s). Placing it on a sheet of metal with various sizes of holes in it (a pearl gauge), the clerk finds the size of hole that the pearl fits into perfectly.

THE PITCH!

The clerk announces: "You are very lucky. You have a pearl that is six millimeters in diameter, is perfectly round, and is a beautiful color. Its retail value is about $20. If you will step inside the store, I will make sure of my appraisal and get a bag for you."

Inside the store the counters are full of settings for pearl rings, necklaces, bracelets, earrings, etc. The clerk remarks, "Since you are here, you might as well get an idea on how your pearl will look in a setting—perhaps as a gift for someone or for yourself. It would be a shame not to mount such a beautiful pearl and show it off."

Most customers enjoy the process because it is exciting and dramatic, especially the anticipation of waiting to see the size and color of the pearl, and then getting a valuable pearl for only $5.50. So the customer agrees that it would be a shame not to have it set in something beautiful.

Now the clerk has the customer looking at settings and quotes prices to him. He emphasizes, "We will set your pearl free. If you don't have it set by us, be sure it is someone who specializes in pearls. Don't let just anyone do it." The salesperson has got the customer coming and going. (Think about it: How many jewelers have you seen who specialize in pearls?)

PSYCHOLOGICAL PRESSURE!

Once the customer believes he's already saved about $14 on a pearl, he'll think nothing about spending up to that much to buy the setting—as much to get a conversation piece as to get an item of jewelry! Even if he doesn't have the pearl set right away, you've already made $2.25 to $2.50 on the pearl, and have probably created a future customer.

That is the key: Keep them coming back. You've got it. You're building a clientele; because, if you are smart, you'll be carrying other jewelry besides pearls.

HOW THE CUSTOMERS GET HOOKED

That $5.50 impulse "dive for a pearl" usually ends in a sale for $20 to $150, with the average sale around $45. The setting can cost you from $1.50 for a rhodium-plated ring to over $200 for an item in solid gold. But remember, you are selling the setting at three to four times your cost.

The stores investigated averaged 18 dives per day and seven jewelry-setting sales for an average monthly gross of $9,936 and a net before taxes of $3,278. None of these stores carried other jewelry besides pearl jewelry or did any advertising.

Start-up Manual #1 is available on this business. See page 379.

See page 379.

New Idea

BOOK BALLOON TOURS

There was a time when railroad or ship travel was the most elegant way to go. Nowadays our fast-paced society wants to get there quickly—except for a few folks who still want slow, elegant travel. For them, ballooning is the latest high-class way to go.

There are a handful of companies, mostly in Europe and Africa, that offer balloon tours. The most successful of these is Buddy Bombard's Champagne Balloon Tour. The two-week tour starts and ends in Paris. A train of four balloons carrying 18 people drifts down through the wine and champagne country of France.

A chase truck follows each balloon with all the fixings for picnic lunches. Participants stay overnight at some of France's finest hotels, and each time they land they are greeted by officials: mayors, chiefs of police, owners of vineyards.

Going this route costs plenty—about $3,200 per head, *not* including transportation to France.

We can see running a balloon tour like this in many parts of the

United States. How about a trip up the Grand Canyon, or down the Mississippi? Short one-day tours would work well, too. This would make a nice alternative to a camping weekend.

PUBLISHING

WHO'S WHO PUBLISHING

High net profit B/T:	$250,000
Average net profit B/T:	86,000
Minimum investment:	49,500
Average investment:	110,000

How would you like to see your name in *Who's Who in America?* Silly question! There is hardly a man or woman who wouldn't appreciate that kind of recognition. It is quite an achievement.

In fact, most people would be happy to be in a *Who's Who* of their hometown, even if the town is Tree-in-the-Middle-of-the-Road, Texas.

A recent *Who's Who in America* contained short biographies of over 20,000 Americans. The international *Who's Who* has over 150,000 listings. But that obviously leaves hundreds of millions of people unrecognized.

There are localized social registers published in major cities of the country such as Boston, New York, Philadelphia, Washington, and Los Angeles. Some are called *The Social Register of X Town.* Others use more discreet titles, like *The Blue Book* in Los Angeles, which has over 500 pages of listings.

The local versions list only the most socially prominent people, including politicians and industry leaders. The majority of successful businessmen, executives, ecclesiastics, civic leaders, etc., are left out. The Los Angeles Blue Book, for example, lists only 7,000 people living within 100 miles of Los Angeles. The population of the area is approximately 12 million.

SO WHERE'S THE PROFIT?

At this point you are probably wondering how one makes money in this business. Well, ask yourself this: If you were listed in *Who's Who,* wouldn't you want a copy? And your parents would want a copy—and probably your grandparents too. Even if the publisher charged $35 or more per copy, you wouldn't give it a second thought.

Who's Who in America is published in two 1,800-page volumes to accommodate all the listings. The price is $89 for the set. Local versions usually sell for less, but some publishers charge as much as

$50 a copy. Experience has shown that sales can be as much as 80 percent of the people listed. For 10,000 people listed, it's possible that 8,000 copies will be sold. At a price of $35 a copy, this is a gross of $280,000. Net before taxes will be almost 50 percent.

PROFIT MARGIN ASTOUNDING!

In addition, the higher the volume or number of listings, the lower your cost. With 50,000 listings, net profit may reach 70 percent of the gross.

It is a simple business to start and operate. All your biographies are written by those listed (they fill out a form) and collected by mail. After your book is printed, all sales are made by mail. All you need is a few form letters and a mailing list.

To start, check with your local library or the editor of your newspaper to see if any book is being published or has been published in your city recently. If there is a book listing only upper-crust social names, go ahead. You are interested in the masses.

TRADEMARK INFRINGEMENT

We received two opinions from attorneys whom we consulted on this problem. We feel that if there is any question of being sued, don't use the words "Who's Who" in your title.

Not using them won't affect your success. The only advantage in using the words is that they describe the contents of the book in a few words.

The Blue Book of Grover County will provide as much class as *Who's Who in Grover County.* And since the words "who is who" are conversational, and outside trademark protection, you can use the words descriptively in your letters soliciting biographies.

WHO TO LIST?

You'll need mailing lists of everyone you wish to list in your book. There are mailing-list brokers and compilers in practically every city. If you don't have one in your area, go to the nearest big city. The brokers there will have a list for your town or county.

You may have to rent several lists to get all the names you want. The easiest list to obtain is that of all business owners. These people will comprise the majority of your listings.

Doctors, lawyers, and other professionals will be listed in the telephone directories. We doubt that you will be able to find a list of religious leaders, but phone calls to all the churches will do the trick.

If there is a military base in the area, you will want to include the brass. You will probably have to make a trip to see the commanding officer. Before you go, decide how far down the ranks you want to list.

A list of top executives of companies may be harder to acquire, though it is readily available in many cities.

Most politicians have business interests on the side, so you will get them in the business owners' list. The city and county offices can provide a list of their appointed and elected officials to use as a cross-reference. Don't leave any out. These are your community leaders.

Federal, state, and local civil service executives should also be included; a list of these people may be obtained from their respective offices.

Many mailing-list houses will be glad to compile original lists for you. They charge $25 to $50 per 1,000 names, which will usually come to you on computer-printed address labels.

Start-up Manual #26 is available on this business. See page 379.

RENTAL LIST PUBLISHING

High net profit B/T:	$90,000
Average net profit B/T:	28,000
Minimum investment:	900
Average investment:	6,000

Almost one-third of the people who live in rental units—apartments or homes—will move in the coming year. These millions of tenants can provide a lucrative market for an apartment- and home-finding service.

You might think: "Don't I need to be a real estate broker?" In most states, the answer is no. Better yet, you will probably make much more than the average real estate salesman. No schooling or special license is needed in any city (although you will have to undertake a roundabout procedure in some states).

If a landlord lists his rental unit with a real estate broker, he pays anywhere from $50 to one month's rent as the fee when the broker brings a tenant to him. With the service we will outline, the landlord doesn't pay a cent.

This service is ideal for the prospective tenant who is lazy, who is looking for something special or unusual, who has a problem because of his circumstances—or who just doesn't want to waste time.

How does it work? Let's assume that someone is looking for new lodgings in your area. He needs an apartment with two bedrooms and two baths, since he has a 10-year-old son. In addition, he'd like a garage. And since both he and his wife are professionals with large wardrobes, lots of closet space is essential.

Immediately he has two problems. Even though his son is a quiet boy, many places post a straight-out no-children edict. Also—depending on the area in which he is looking—garages may be scarce.

As a result, locating an apartment promises to be a tedious chore, requiring many hours of telephoning and driving around.

But suppose he can sit down and scan a list which shows every apartment and house available for rent in the area? A list which not only gives him the location, but every detail he'd want to know about the apartment, without his having to take a look at the place. Such a list would save him a lot of time and effort—as well as gas and phone calls.

Most rental advertisements leave out a lot of important details, requirements, and restrictions, because the landlords are trying to save a little money on their advertising costs. They want people to take a look at their units, in the hopes of renting them.

Often landlords and brokers will have many units for rent but advertise only a few. Other landlords are difficult to reach.

These are the limitations of run-of-the-mill "For Rent" ads. Your service, however, is designed to provide a compilation on every apartment and home available for rent on any given day, a listing which includes every detail about the rental unit. The apartment seeker pays you $25 to $35, once, for the opportunity to come by your office every day for up to two years and pick up your updated daily listing bulletin. (Most services do not give listing information over the phone.)

HOW TO OBTAIN LISTINGS

Most of your listings can be obtained simply by calling each new advertiser every day—apartment managers, private landlords and real estate agents. To start, this means a couple of days of steady calling to build up your list. But after this original telephone bout, daily updating will be easy.

Every real estate broker in your town should be contacted. Many don't advertise rental listings, relying instead on signs and their office location to draw prospective tenants. But once the broker realizes you will be advertising his listings free, he will be eager to cooperate with you. This is true of landlords as well.

Next, if the landlord or broker has a vacancy, ask all of the questions on your listing form. Since you guarantee up-to-the-minute information to prospective tenants, you will have to call periodically to check on whether the unit is still available. Once a unit is rented, you need to be called so you can remove it from your listing.

LOW INVESTMENT—HIGH RETURN

Let's turn to the profit picture. In a city of 100,000 people we found not one but three of these services operating successfully, with annual grosses of $42,814 to $90,682. The one with the lowest gross still netted the absentee owner $12,140 last year. The highest-grossing operation netted the owner over $46,000 in this city. He is doing equally well in three other cities.

The service is currently available in many cities, but we feel it could stand some more competition. We suggest covering an area of at least 10,000 rental units per rental service. The chamber of commerce in your city will supply the statistics you need. Just ask them how many rental units there are in the city. A quick scan of the classified ads will let you know how many rental services are operating.

The most appealing part of this business is the ease with which you can set up the operation. Your total cash outlay can be as little as $900.

Start-up Manual #23 is available on this business. See page 379.

_____ **New Idea** _____

THE NOVEL ABOUT YOU

Most of us would love to be a James Bond or a Valentino or a Marilyn Monroe. Now two Toronto brothers are giving people just that chance, and they're pulling in big bucks in the process.

For $12.95 Bob and Tom Beckerman will design, print, and deliver a personalized book that chronicles the buyer's life as an adventurer, hero, or lover. Starting with $30,000, the brothers developed a word processor that enables them to personalize a book with an individual's name, life, and background.

Once a customer's name, sex, and other vital statistics are punched into the computer it takes 12 minutes for the standard plot line to be printed incorporating the customer into it. Then it's just a short trip to the plant for binding.

We've seen companies that offer this type of service with short children's books, using the child's name and background. But this is the first time we've seen the idea applied to full-length novels.

The idea is sure to appeal to almost anyone's ego. Who among us wouldn't want to be immortalized in novel form? This is a great mail-order product.

To get into this business you need to have some computer background or know someone who does. Initial expense is high, but the profits from runaway bestsellers could make you a literary lion.

Collect old paperback books for the plot line. Contact the publishers about buying reprint rights. Make sure you tell them about the alterations you plan to make.

FREE CLASSIFIED NEWSPAPER PUBLISHING

High net profit B/T:	$235,000
Average net profit B/T:	75,000
Minimum investment:	19,000
Average investment:	54,000

Millions of homes across the country have garages and attics full of stuff that's been accumulating for years. Drive through almost any residential neighborhood and you'll find at least one family holding a garage sale, attracting bargain hunters by selling baby furniture, clothing, a dining-room set, or perhaps several boxes of "antiques."

Organized flea markets are popular as one-stop places to bring these buyers and sellers together. But you can capitalize on the trend in another way, and expand the market at the same time, by offering a service to those who don't want the inconvenience of a garage sale, the trouble and expense of flea market booth space, or the cost of classified advertising in the daily papers.

SELL FREE ADS!

What you do is publish a newspaper, or "trader," that runs classified advertising listings only, FREE—unless the ad sells! Four to six short exclusive listings in consecutive issues are given to each individual who has something for sale. This has tremendous appeal from the "something for nothing" and convenience angles, and it works out better than the alternatives for the seller.

When the item sells, you collect a commission based on the advertised price of the item—not the selling price, which is often bartered lower. The commission is payable if an individual decides not to sell and cancels the ad early; it is also collected if a person moves or disconnects the phone. An "exclusive" means that if the item is sold or traded in any other way, even through another paper, you still collect.

Papers that operate this way carry from 3,000 to 10,000 listings an issue. Commissions charged are typically 10 percent of the first $100, 5 percent of the second $100, and 1 percent of anything over $200. Often there's a minimum charge of $1 to $2. A minority of publishers have a maximum commission limit of $25 to $30.

Many listings are for inexpensive items, but there are also many ads for big-ticket articles, from high-priced camera and stereo gear to cars, recreation vehicles, boats, and mobile homes. Prices may be as high as $10,000.

A UNIQUE APPROACH

The trader approach is entirely different than that used by weekly or monthly throwaways or "shoppers," which are free papers that rely on hard-to-get retail display advertising for profit, and are heavily distributed in limited target areas, usually by bulk mail or delivery people.

Shoppers have been around since the '20s, and under ideal marketing conditions can compete successfully on a price basis with other media—and other shoppers—due to lower operating over-heads. But stiff competition means that the failure rate is very high.

As the publisher of a trader, you should arrange for a local newspaper distributor to distribute your newspaper. Large-circulation dailies often franchise distribution rights to such companies, which handle all the work involved for a commission on each copy sold. Even if you pay half the newsstand sales volume to such a company it may be worth it in the long run.

PROFIT FANTASTIC!

We found one classified-only trader in Virginia who grosses nearly $1 million a year and nets an almost unbelievable $235,000 per year! That's a margin of 24 percent—which is remarkable for a publishing operation, where 10 to 15 percent margins are more common.

The Virginia operation is a 28-page weekly crammed with over 10,000 listings. Its circulation is 20,000 in a market area—Norfolk and vicinity—of about 1.5 million people.

Your operation can produce the same kind of margin after a year or two of operation—depending on market area, frequency of issue (weekly or biweekly), production costs, and other variables.

The average item for sale lists for $300. Of course, there are many low-priced articles, but the average price goes up when you factor in big-ticket items. An average commission of $16 per sale is realistic.

Our research indicates that 26 percent of the items listed in a trader are sold through the paper. This is a higher batting average than that of a typical newspaper classified section, because more of your readers are looking for a specific item or bargain.

A salable item is likely to sell in the first three weeks. About 30 percent of the listings are replaced weekly. So in a given month revenue will come from a combination of current and prior listings. It works out to about $43,000 a month, assuming commissions are collected from 80 percent of the sellers.

SOME ADS ARE PREPAID

Some categories of advertising are not feasible on a commission basis: business investments, business property or houses for sale or for rent, help or work wanted, swaps, general notices, and the like. People will phone in with requests to run ads like these, especially as the popularity of your publication builds. Accept the ads and run them on a prepaid basis, charging $1 per column line (minimum four lines).

Prepaid advertising lineage can generate over 10 percent of net income. The Virginia operation brings in $24,000 to $26,000 per year from prepaid advertising.

ANOTHER REVENUE SOURCE

Newsstand sales of each issue are a secondary source of revenue. Price per copy is set according to the market, the competition, and the distribution costs. The Virginia paper costs 50 cents an issue on the newsstand; but it has been in existence for ten years and is quite popular. Most sell out within a short time after they hit the streets. The price for a smaller paper, especially a new one, might be 35 cents.

Most publishers price issues to cover a good part of the production costs. The best you can expect is a break-even situation. A weekly with a circulation of 20,000, priced at 45 cents an issue, would generate $421,000 a year—slightly less than printing cost—assuming only 10 percent return unsold from the news racks.

Start-up Manual #110 is available on this business. See page 379.

NEWSLETTER PUBLISHING

High net profit B/T:	Unlimited
Average net profit B/T:	$35,000
Minimum investment:	2,200
Average investment:	14,000

In 1974 there were over 1,300 newsletters being published. Today there are 6,000, and new ones are popping up every day. Many of the original ones, however, have died a quiet death. The newsletter and magazine publishing field is a very dangerous business; the mortality rate is among the highest of all fields.

Expertise in the areas of advertising and promotion will determine the percentage of profit for any publication. Some make a bundle, netting over 30 percent before taxes—however, most don't.

The business magazine *Entrepreneur* (in which all these excerpts originally appeared) was originally a newsletter which grossed $500,000 a year on subscription revenues. The net profit from circulation was 13.4 percent before income taxes. That's not very high. Our book reprint sales and advertising revenue added another $500,000 to the till, giving a more practical total profit margin of 26.6 percent.

HOW IT ALL STARTED

The publisher and author of this book was a management consultant with a marketing and business investigation service. By having started 18 diverse small businesses of his own, he had accumulated a wealth of experience plus extensive files, information sources, and contacts during 20 years. All of this made it possible for him to answer almost any question a client might have without having to leave his office.

In time, an idea occurred to him. Why not offer this information to the public at large, rather than to a small group of wealthy clients? He realized that there were hundreds of thousands of people eager to start their own businesses, but who lacked the essential knowledge of how to choose a business and go about starting up.

On that premise he spent one day writing a solicitation letter and designed a few small classified ads to test the potential appeal of such a service. An ad was placed in the *Wall Street Journal* classified business opportunities column.

The response was good, and 22 percent of the inquirers sent money to buy a subscription to *Insider's Report,* the first issue of which had not even been written! He spent a hurried week writing the first report, and the newsletter was established as a monthly.

ONLY $5,000 INVESTED

The kernel of a staff was hired or borrowed from his existing operation, and $5,000 was deposited to support the fledgling efforts, with plans to contribute more as needed. Additional capital was never required, though, as the profits generated from each issue supplied the needed growth capital.

NO PROFIT—THE REASON AND THE WISDOM

He realized from the start that he had originated a product that had never been marketed before for a group of people who had never been reached in mass. Research proved that point and pointed out a serious problem. With no precedents to go by, all forms of advertising and promotion would have to be tested slowly and analyzed carefully.

Of course, $50,000 to $100,000 could have been invested at the onset—but this could have led to carelessness with the advertising budget. It was decided to take a safe approach: the ad budget would be increased each month relative to the success of the previous month, which would ensure profitable growth. Only the percentage of budget increase each month would be allowed for gambling on new promotions or media.

He watched hundreds of well-financed organizations blow large sums on new ideas by rushing into them before the staff had gained a proper understanding of the situation. He was determined that this would not happen to *Insider's Report*—and it didn't.

As a consequence, all the profits were plowed back into more advertising, which postponed income taxes until a plateau was reached—which took three years.

Many newsletters and magazines originate as new ideas trying to reach new markets. The author of this book recommends that potential publishers imitate his slow, deliberate pace. Unfortunately, most business investors don't like to look down the road three years for their first profits.

HIDDEN ADVANTAGE WORTH $1 MILLION

The big hidden advantage to a magazine is that there is a healthy market for selling the business later. While a retail store that grosses $150,000 and nets $30,000 per year may be worth only $50,000 to $65,000 (plus assets) if sold, a magazine grossing $1 million is worth that amount if it shows a fair net profit. (However, a newsletter generally won't have the same advantage.)

WHAT IT TAKES TO START YOUR OWN PUBLICATION

Publishing is an information-selling business. You must have some hard-to-get information which is wanted and needed by a particular group of people if you hope to become successful.

Some time ago we discovered that there are many beer-can collectors in this country. They try to collect a can of every brand of beer now made or that has ever been made in any size, anywhere in the world. There was no publication serving this group. Before we could muster our own forces, though, someone got the jump on us with a newsletter serving the beer-can collectors. Of course we could have gone into competition—but such a market was too small for two.

This is the kind of situation you must watch for and be ready to exploit. Collectors are an ideal market for a newsletter. People following new trends or interests are another. For example, hang gliding caught the public's attention several years ago.

MORE IDEAS

Keep your eye out for odd stories in newspapers and newsmagazines. Trends develop slowly; then suddenly the whole nation is fired up. *Mother Earth News* started during the hippie era in the '60s, when health foods and the return-to-nature movement was young. Most of the hippies of those days have returned to the mainstream of society, but the impact of their ideas has affected millions, and lingers on within a solid, dedicated group that began then. *Mother Earth News* is now a phenomenally successful publication serving this group.

GO AFTER ESTABLISHED GROUPS

A hybrid magazine like *Entrepreneur* is directed toward an established group of people who have always been around—people who would like to gain independence by owning their own business. Our research, proved by test advertising, has shown that while perhaps the majority of people are interested in this option, few are willing to do anything about it. *Entrepreneur* serves the small group that is willing to take action.

Look at other large groups. Can you find a smaller subgroup of people who are in some way distinct from the rest, and can you offer them something they are not getting now?

WHAT WILL BE THE TREND OF TOMORROW?

Many special interest groups are not being served. For example, the hundreds of thousands of amateur inventors in this country don't have a publication of their own.

Millions of people are interested in mail order, yet there are only a few newsletters being offered that specialize in this field. You can probably think of similar situations.

Will the antique, health-food, bicycle, blue-jeans, plant, chess, jogging, candlemaking, skiing, and tennis interests of today be replaced in the '80s by hang-gliding, jojoba, aerobics, raw-fish, soccer, wood-burning stove, solar energy, home computer, video recorders, and hot-air ballooning?

Start-up Manual #67 is available on this business. See page 379.

FRANCHISES

FRANCHISING: READY FOR THE '80S

The next time you open your wallet, remember that one of every three dollars you are carrying is likely to be spent on products or services of a franchised company. There are over 400,000 of them in the United States, and they account for nearly one-third of all retail sales.

Some are old-line companies like General Motors and Standard Oil; among the oldest franchisors are automakers and oil companies. But it is possible to spend money in a franchise in almost any sector of the economy, from fast foods and artificial suntans to rental cars, computer dating, and home furnishings.

The impact of franchising on the economy has become pervasive since the early '50s when Ray Kroc drove past a tiny hamburger stand in San Bernardino, California, called McDonald's, and "felt like some latter-day Newton who'd just had an Idaho potato caromed off his skull."

In the past two decades we have seen franchising grow into a proved method of marketing branded products and services. We have seen franchising weather the go-go days of the early '60s, when franchise companies were the darlings of Wall Street—and promoters of untested schemes threatened to destroy what legitimate companies had wrought. Franchise income tripled during the '70s.

It is generally accepted that franchising has matured over the years, led by business format franchisors: McDonald's, Kentucky Fried Chicken, and other giants who have become household words in the process. Unlike GM and other manufacturers, these package franchisors go well beyond authorizing distribution of their products. They provide complete systems for conducting business, keeping the books, and turnkey operations.

WHERE IS THE NEXT McDONALD'S?

No other force in the marketplace has done more to popularize the idea of "going into business for yourself" than franchising. A large percentage of McDonald's franchisees have become millionaires over the years.

But what will be the McDonald's of the '80s? How can a would-be franchisee plug into the system that has the best chance of succeeding in the future? Have changes occurred in technology, buying habits, and consumer attitudes that have an impact on this?

To seek the answers to these and other questions, we have polled thousands of presidents and chief executive officers of franchise companies all over the country.

We conducted in-depth interviews with industry leaders from the fast food, recreation, service, and business sectors of the economy. Educators had their say, as did psychologists and sociologists. Of course, we drew upon our own expertise at "picking the winners."

"FAST AND EASY"

Robert Feinstein, chairman of the board of United Rent-All, a major equipment rental franchise, tells of a time when he was lunching at a McDonald's outlet and overheard two women. "They said they'd eaten dinner there the night before, and had breakfast there earlier in the day. I asked why they came back so often. 'Because it's fast and easy!' "

Convenience and saving time are so essential to the average consumer that he or she is often willing to pay extra for it. Witness the growth of the convenience food store franchises like 7-Eleven.

In the '50s supermarkets virtually wiped out "mom and pop" grocery stores because the big chains could sell at lower prices. People were more concerned then with saving money; now they want to save time. As consumers, we will spend 50 cents more for a product to save five minutes standing in a supermarket line.

Similar examples abound in other sectors of franchising. Years ago the corner garage mechanic was king. Now there are instant tune-up shops, drive-through ten-minute oil change outfits, and so on. Saving time is a key factor in the success of these businesses.

Our researchers have uncovered drive-through liquor stores and even a drive-through mortuary! The franchise concept that can capture the fancy of the public in the next decade should focus on the convenience angle.

One of the hottest new entries in the race for consumers' dollars is artificial suntanning parlors—a classic example of finding new ways to save time. While the jury is still out on the long-term viability of the suntanning parlor concept, there's no question that growth has been dramatic.

In the past year, nine new franchises selling parlor packages have sprung up, capitalizing on the idea that sun worshipers would rather spend three minutes in a tanning booth under ultraviolet lamps than three hours on the beach.

SPECIALIZATION ESSENTIAL

The consumer wants "total flexibility," according to Ralph Weiger, chairman of Authentic Homes Corporation and past president of the International Franchise Association. "He wants to be able to pick the specialist he wants or needs, and not pay for other services he doesn't need."

We see the automotive aftermarket as an example of what is to come in the years ahead for other fields. There are radiator shops, brake shops, front-end shops, tire shops, and rustproofers. As consumers, we like that idea. The man who does the same thing all day long is elevated in status to "specialist" in our minds. In fact, he has to be, simply to keep up with the state of the art. The jack-of-all-trades cannot survive anymore. Consumers would question his ability to be all things to all people.

As Weiger says, referring to his earlier tour of duty with Midas Muffler Shops, "I couldn't believe that you could really make a living just selling mufflers and exhaust systems for cars. Now that level of specialization has become not only a way of life for the consumer, but far more profitable for the marketer."

Several other examples point in the direction of increased specialization as one of the keys to success in the '80s, for franchisor and franchisee alike. Limited-menu "theme" restaurants are performing better than ever in the marketplace, while traditional full-menu restaurants are faltering in many areas.

Fast-food restaurants are the most visible specialty food places, but even here we have seen notable examples of specialization at work. Salad-only restaurants are flourishing, for example. These are serve-yourself setups offering nutritious meals to weight- and budget-conscious consumers looking for a lunchtime alternative to traditional fast foods. A variation is soup kitchen restaurants serving varieties of soup, sometimes with a side of salad or a half sandwich.

On the other hand the hamburger chains, most notably McDonald's, have moved away from specialization. Years ago all you could get was a hamburger, cheeseburger, fries, and soft drink. According to *Restaurant Business* magazine's Peter Berlinski, the change is attributed primarily to "loss of business due to the intense competition from other hamburger chains for the same consumer dollar. If they can't bring the people in for the burgers, they'll try something else." Some experts say that a burger operation that tried to specialize totally today—without breakfast items or other types of food—would falter.

Overcrowding and saturation may exist in the hamburger business, but there are many other areas of food service that are largely untapped. One is the snack food area. We have seen tremendous growth in limited-item snack shops such as chocolate chip cookie stores and old-fashioned ice-cream bar chains.

Ten years ago a single-item outfit like this would have had great difficulty surviving. Now every time you turn around, there's another quick snack operation. Cookie Coach in New York City is

offering turn-of-the-century bakery wagons
and you can see them parked around M
cookies at 50 cents apiece.

Another one to keep an eye on is the ch
springing up on the West Coast, selling deep-
snack food for up to 75 cents apiece. With a
cents, margins in this business are quite attra
franchising is just around the corner.

MEXICAN FOOD HOTTEST

The brightest star in the fast-food heaven is Mexican food. The fastest-growing segment of the restaurant business, Mexican food has moved from being a regional, ethnic favorite to national acceptance. Mario Dovalina, general manager of Pepe's Incorporated, a regional fanchise headquartered in Chicago, cites a desire "for the unusual at low cost" as the reason for burgeoning sales of Mexican food outlets. "Americans are looking for new tastes and nutrition at the same time. That's why Mexcan food is taking off; also, lower pricing compared to other types of fast food."

Other ethnic foods are expected to move quickly through the marketplace in the '80s. Chinese and Japanese foods lend themselves to franchising because many are simple to prepare in quantity with low-cost ingredients. Several major Japanese corporations are testing sushi and teriyaki beef, for example, in fast-food formats. In such unlikely locations as Denver, Colorado, there are 10 Beef Bowl outlets—unlikely until you learn that Denver has a high concentration of Orientals who settled in the area after building the transcontinental railroad.

Beef Bowl, whose outlets vend teriyaki beef on a bed of rice with a side of sour cabbage, does more business in Tokyo than many national chains do here in a year. Last year they averaged 3.5 million bowls a week at the equivalent of 79 cents apiece!

According to Nancy Rathbun of the International Franchise Association, "Chinese food has greater market acceptance here than Japanese at present, but this is expected to change. Both are well worth keeping an eye on in the near future."

RAPID TECHNOLOGICAL CHANGE
CREATES OPPORTUNITIES

Convenience and specialization trends did not happen overnight, but they are expected to increase in importance with the rate of technological change—an important related trend.

Our technological society is moving so fast that it is increasingly difficult to keep up. When run-of-the-mill Detroit automobiles have on-board computers to monitor things like fuel flow, it makes con-

inadequate. In response we seek specialists. Our sphere
edge has become increasingly narrow, focused on the things
ust keep up on.

The $400 hobby computer is an example of where technology
is leading us. Computer stores staffed by specialists are blossoming
all over the country to capitalize on this trend. As this technology
becomes more and more readily available to the mass market, consumer acceptance will increase dramatically.

Inexpensive home computers, likely to be tied to the telephone
and television set in an information/entertainment complex, should
be common by the end of the decade, according to our analysis. And
if you think that's farfetched, consider this:

In 1968 Dr. Alvin Toffler predicted that information needs
would be so great that a "second-level" service industry would be
needed just to explain how to get information and cut through red
tape. Now red-tape services are thriving—though none is franchised
yet.

Similarly, in *Future Shock* he predicted that alienation and con-
fusion would lead to telephones hooked up to automatic answering
equipment to provide counseling. Now we have Dial-a-Prayer,
Dial-a-Joke, Dial-a-Friend, and even Dial-an-Insult!

Advances in infrared technology have allowed huge sensing
devices to be miniaturized so they can be handheld. This has
spawned a new business that's easily franchisable—energy-loss prevention. A serviceman can point the device at your house or industrial building to pinpoint areas of heat loss in seconds.

Similar breakthroughs in inventory control allow automatic inventory of entire warehouses by one man walking down the aisles
with a handheld device and a battery pack. Sensors simply pick up
impulses from tagged items. The implications are enormous in marketing and business during the next decade.

"A NATION OF PRIMA DONNAS"

Related forces are at work in the consumer's mind that lead us in
the direction of "a nation of prima donnas," according to one futurist
we interviewed. We are surrounded by more and more machines
that do our work for us. We are focused on our own narrow fields of
interest in the workplace. Thus it becomes beneath us to mow our
own lawn.

Personal service businesses are well positioned to capitalize on
this trend. Mobile maid services are operating all over the country to
free workingwomen from household chores.

Several franchises offer to set you up in this business with teams
of maids who zip through a home with drill-team precision. Sys-

tematizing the work is the secret here, with one person handling kitchen and bath cleanup while others dust and vacuum.

A few to watch carefully during the next decade are in-home bookkeeping services and lawn and garden care. We spotted one operation in bookkeeping that has tremendous potential. Focused on the affluent professional or two-income family, this service provides a mobile office that comes to your door once or twice a month to handle bill-paying and record-keeping chores. Busy people often allow family finances to fall into disarray—sometimes because they are too busy making money to pay attention to the home front. The real attraction of this is tie-ins such as financial planning and tax preparation.

A high-margin business that has existed for some time in "mom and pop" fashion is lawn and garden care. Once again, we have less time as consumers to spend on menial chores. Already several franchises exist, providing these services in a systematic and professional way. Look for others to come along in this underrated but fertile field.

BUSINESS SERVICES TO MUSHROOM

The service industry in general has never dropped below the inflation rate in terms of growth. In most years it grows at between three and five times the inflation rate, and according to our studies, has reached as high as 15 times the rate of inflationary growth.

Somebody has to take care of all the machines, and the business services field will grow as we become more industrialized. What's more, of all the businesses we've discussed so far, the service industries are the most recession-proof! People don't buy new equipment during recessionary times; they repair what they have.

But business services don't stop with repairing machinery or hardware. A broad spectrum of opportunities are expected to present themselves during the '80s, most related to the everyday use of computers by large and small businesses.

In 1963 *Business Week* conducted a study showing that the average businessman spent about three hours a month keeping up with what was going on in his industry. This has now risen to four hours a week; in some high-tech industries, closer to eight hours a week.

Economic forces at work in the marketplace make it imperative for every business to maintain itself in fighting trim. As J. Paul Langton of Kwik-Kopy Corporation, an instant-print franchisor, put it, "We are facing some volatile crunches in the '80s: credit, energy, inflation, and taxation are sure to bring discontinuity. The affluence of the past 30 years is gone, along with cheap money, cheap energy and a comparatively low cost of living."

For survival in the marketplace, businesses need to respond quickly to these problems. But the opposite side of the coin is that opportunities abound for the would-be franchisor or entrepreneur who can make it easier to conduct business successfully.

Temporary help and employment agencies should benefit from this trend. There are many regional and national franchisors of instant printing services that fall into the same category. We will see them expanding their line of services to include far more than simple printing and copying.

Such service operations succeed partly because it is often more cost-effective to rent desired services on an as-needed basis. As Feinstein of United Rent-All puts it, "Years ago ownership was prized and valued. Now the consumers we deal with in our equipment rental business are looking solely for utility value to solve an immediate problem!"

General Business Services is a franchise that provides a broad range of consulting services to the smaller businessman, as a means of helping the little guy cope with what is going on around him. Some predict that franchising will make inroads into other traditionally sacrosanct areas—such as accounting and the legal field. A harbinger of this is the recent advertising and marketing of services by attorneys.

WHAT ABOUT FREE TIME?

We expect recreation and leisure time activities to be a fertile area for franchising in the '80s. Recreation grows as the economy becomes more industrialized and automated. In the past most people derived pleasure directly from doing work. But something has happened to warp that old Protestant work ethic. Work isn't as hard to do anymore what with automation taking over. In fact, it is often downright boring.

Psychologists tell us that is the reason behind what appears to be a frenetic search for more stimulation outside the work place. The average person derives "psychic income" from this.

That's why the fastest-growing sports in terms of popularity are the riskier ones where limb and even life are threatened. Even in the realm of spectator sports, the more violent ones are becoming increasingly popular. Remember when baseball was the national pastime? Now it's football. By 1990 it is likely to be soccer. Hockey has gained more notoriety recently from the fighting of competing teams than from skating and goal scoring. Boxing is coming off the canvas after a long count.

The hottest consumer recreation today is roller skating, as we predicted years ago. There are tremendous opportunities here over the short term. Roller skating should operate in the marketplace the same way bicycling or skateboarding has. Sports usually have short cycles, but it is not farfetched to expect indoor/outdoor disco roller rinks to spread across the country.

According to Charles Chuinard, president of Leisure Systems, we can look for an increase in neighborhood recreation activities of all sorts during the '80s, due to the energy situation. He's particularly excited about the potential for his company's Yogi Bear miniature golf course operations because "they can operate quite well using fringe land and return 25 percent or more net."

"Campgrounds, especially those that are a place to go rather than the roadside stopover variety, should be very strong in the '80s. Faced with energy, inflation, and recession, people will look for less expensive ways to go get away from it all," Chuinard said.

VIDEO EXPLOSION

Closer to home—in fact right inside it—the video explosion ties together virtually every major consumer trend we've discussed. Convenience, technology, the need to know, and the need for more stimulus come neatly packaged in your TV set. We've reported on the incredible potential of video stores.

Koichi Tsunoda, visionary president of Sony Video Products, explains what he sees ahead. "The computer revolution took place in 20 years, the word processing revolution took 10 years, and the home entertainment revolution is happening right now. The next 5 years (will be) the crucial time period.

"To offer a prediction for the future, it is not unlikely that the simple function of traveling to a place of business will become outmoded. With computer and video links between home and office, and data transferring between any equipped point in a corporate network, a person need not travel any further than his own home communications center. The savings in transit costs, cost of time, and human wear and tear make this a target to strive for."

THE SHAPE OF FRANCHISES TO COME

Many industry insiders we interviewed believe that the future lies with those who can find a way to duplicate the overnight success of many major real estate franchisors such as Century 21 and Red Carpet, two giants in the field.

Real estate operations lend themselves easily to franchising for a number of reasons. The way these franchisors have grown is to capitalize on strengths the right way. For many years, there have been local mom and pop real estate operations, maybe tied in to a local Multiple Listing Service to get leads.

What Century 21 and others have done is to bring existing well-established local operations together under one banner. They offer strong incentives with advertising, training, and other benefits unavailable or too costly for the little guy.

Because these operations are for the most part already up and running with local identity and established clientele, the franchisor avoids the long period of time typically required when starting from scratch, as well as a lot of heavy front-end costs.

We see this happening in other industries currently dominated by independents, yet not franchised. Mortuaries are high-margin operations that could franchise with a tasteful ad campaign stressing the consumer angle. Baby-sitting and child-care services is another where the timing is right, considering the tremendous influx of working mothers and single-parent families in our society. Competent child care is hard to find, and there is a clear need to solve this problem. Strong advertising, training, and easy access are the main ingredients for a franchisable concept that could easily be a winner in the marketplace.

Another field that has historically been dominated by independents is TV repair. But with the video explosion referred to earlier, this field could be ripe for franchising. Why not pull together independents under a bright advertising banner and provide maintenance contracts or guarantees like Midas Muffler?

Think of current hassles involved in finding a service person you can trust. Most people rely on a friend's recommendation or thumb through the Yellow Pages looking for the biggest ad or the closest shop. Imagine what a strong local TV ad campaign could do—perhaps tied to a fixed pricing system similar to those used by the instant tune places.

Virtually the only way a small repair shop can plug into TV advertising, or stay on top of technology, is with the support services and help a national franchisor can provide. Millions can be made in video repair with this concept over the next decade or two by someone with the vision to see the opportunity.

READY FOR THE '80S

With all its pluses and minuses, the franchise marketing system remains one of the most dynamic and vibrant examples of free enterprise at work in the marketplace. Tremendous potential exists in the future for franchisor and franchisee to share in the rich rewards that come from intelligent risk taking.

Hundreds of new franchises will come into being during the next few years. More and more are being formed each day. Some will flourish, others will fade away. We believe those who are keyed into the major market trends we've forecasted here stand the best chance of success.

As Ray Kroc said, "Achievement must be made against the risk of defeat. It is no achievement to walk a tightrope laid flat against the floor. Where there is no risk, there can be no pride of achievement and, consequently, no happiness. We must take risks."

THE PROS AND CONS OF BUYING A FRANCHISE

Everyone has heard tales of franchising being the key to instant riches or instant doom. In fact, there are advantages and disadvantages in franchising that the sharp investor must know.

Statistics show that the success rate for new franchises is higher than the success rate for new small businesses. Of the 9.1 million small businesses in this country, more than 500,000 are franchise operations.

Department of Commerce statistics show that $299 billion—or one out of every three retail sales dollars in 1979—came through a franchise unit. That was more than double the 1970 figure, which shows that franchise sales are booming in all categories.

ADVANTAGE 1: PROVED SYSTEMS

An old business adage is "Why reinvent the wheel?" Perhaps the biggest advantage of a franchise is that the franchisor has already established a successful, well-known product or service.

In addition, existing systems serve to maximize efficiency and returns on investment while minimizing problems. It is simply a matter of passing on experience, which is the best teacher.

Most people, whether they admit it or not, like having their hands held once in a while. During crises, the franchisor is there to help the franchisee over the bumps. There is often truth in the belief that there's safety in numbers.

In any new business a lot of time and money is consumed during the trial-and error period. For example, Pizza Hut spent more than three years developing a popular, well-rounded menu. A good franchise eliminates the majority of bad start-up moves through an intensive training program and through constant counseling and assistance.

AAMCO automobile transmission service conducts a six-week intensive training program, while McDonald's has an intensive 11-day "Hamburger University." Every reputable franchisor has similar intensive programs to make sure that when you open your doors, you know how to solve all the potential problems.

ADVANTAGE 2: LESS CASH NEEDED

Often the franchising company, because of its financial size, credit line, and contractual agreements, can arrange better financing than could be obtained by you individually. Financial leverage is an important consideration in any investment situation, and when you're borrowing money to become part of a winning team, you inherit that leverage.

Also, you won't need to slot so much cash toward grand opening and advertising start-ups, since you will become known immediately in your market area. Someone setting up a McDonald's or a 7-Eleven is almost guaranteed customers the minute the concrete is dry, unlike the independent who often must build an image over a longer period of time.

This ownership of a nationally or regionally known product or service gives you a leg up on the local market, especially when newcomers hit town. You have a built-in consumer acceptance that local merchants don't have.

ADVANTAGE 3: NATIONAL ADVERTISING SUPPORT

Professional advertising and promotion is another important plus. Most small independent businessmen don't, won't, or can't spend sufficient money on advertising. Often their efforts are poorly conceived and inconsistent. What's worse, in large metropolitan areas, they can't use the most effective media because the cost is prohibitive to the one-shop owner.

A good franchise usually has a professional team or contracts an agency to present a consistent, traffic-building campaign with the most effective media. Consequently, the cost per shop is much lower than most independent businesses.

For example, a chain of franchised motels contracted with an advertising agency to sponsor a series of 260 90-second radio spots during the Bicentennial. The total cost of the shows, time lead-ins, and promotion for 300 major markets was just over $400,000. For the same exposure, each motel owner would have had to spend from $60,000 to $150,000. As it turned out, the coverage only cost each owner under $10,000 for a full year of radio advertising! Just as there's safety in numbers, there's also clout.

ADVANTAGE 4: A STAFF OF EXPERTS

Franchisees immediately acquire a staff of experts that offers assistance no independent could afford. Legal advice is often available. The most efficient accounting systems, perfect for the particular business, have been designed by experts in the field.

Some franchisors like Southland Corporation offer computer analysis of all records, and through comparison with other 7-Eleven stores can pinpoint areas of inefficiency or loss as well as profitable aspects of the business that are being neglected. For instance, Pizza

Hut claims that 90 percent of their marketing innovations come from suggestions submitted by franchisees, traceable through computer accounting.

Experts in site selection and marketing choose locations using all the scientific tools available rather than the "hunch and guess" method employed by most independents. Professionals negotiate and arrange leases and contracts to the best advantage, again using the power of a large organization to influence landlords and other important civic figures.

The chain's tremendous buying power and special buying techniques can bring products, equipment, and outside services to the franchisee at a cost much lower than an independent could ever achieve. For example, franchised operators of name-brand gas stations can purchase many repair parts such as spark plugs, tires, and batteries at 15 to 30 percent of what the independent garage must pay.

ADVANTAGE 5: A CAPITAL GAINS PLUS

Finally, because of the nationally or regionally known name, a franchisee usually has an easier time selling his business when the time comes, and frequently at a higher price than an independent could obtain for a similar business.

When a franchised business is built up and is offered for resale, it often sells for twice its earning capabilities. The earnings are figured thus: If the franchisee's salary is $1,500 a month and his profit is $2,500 per month, then his yearly take from the business is $48,000. So at the time of resale his business is priced at $96,000, plus the equity in the business.

Many franchisees discovered this formula for buying franchises at the beginning of the program, selling at the multiple figure and reinvesting their profits in two or three more franchise units. The American Entrepreneurs Association has on file records of one 7-Eleven franchisee who has bought and sold five franchises in five years, and is currently on his sixth. In less than ten years he has developed a seven-figure net worth.

WHAT KIND OF PERSONALITY DOES IT TAKE?

Applicants for an AAMCO franchise must submit to extensive personality testing before they are accepted as franchisees. Last year over 37,000 people inquired about McDonald's franchises and 500 submitted formal applications, but only 64 were accepted. That's less than one-fifth of 1 percent. Personality and character are often the final factors in the selection process.

The advantages of franchising are not universal: they apply only to certain individuals. A maverick, for example, may not be happy with the restrictions that the franchisee must abide by.

Standardization is very important in the success of a franchise chain. The outlet's visual impact, quality, and efficiency of service and operation must be identical in every store. Some businesspeople don't like to maintain the quality of product and service demanded by a franchisor. But remember, one bad hamburger at a McDonald's hurts the reputation of the entire chain.

Perhaps franchising sounds like the perfect system—the ideal way to go into business. In many cases it is. Keep in mind that the franchisor originally developed a very profitable business. By franchising, he chose to give the lion's share of the profits to the franchisee, taking only a small slice for himself. When you look at it that way, the franchise fee and royalties seem only fair for what you receive in benefits outside your profits.

But every coin has two sides, and so you also must look at the disadvantages before making an informed decision.

DISADVANTAGES OF OWNING A FRANCHISE

Most companies franchise because it is a quick way to expand without the need for large amounts of additional capital. But in this very quickness lies several inherent problems. First, to franchise quickly, a company will have to adopt strong standardizations. We already discussed how this can affect a maverick, but what about the average person who has his own definite ideas, concepts, and beliefs?

Some franchisors require and enforce rigid operational procedures. Even if you have an idea that is better than their procedures, many will not allow you to use it.

We've studied some operating manuals that specify the exact spot where a napkin holder and salt shaker should be placed on a table in a restaurant, or exactly where hair-care products are to be placed on a shelf. If you are unable to live with such regimentation, then franchising might not be for you.

DISADVANTAGE 2: TOTAL RELIANCE ON THEIR EXPERTS

As a businessperson, there are three critical areas which determine success or failure: site selection, lease/contract negotiation, and advertising. Yet often in a franchise you have no control over these three areas.

Your most vulnerable area is choosing a location. The majority of franchises are consumer-oriented retail operations that rely on good location, visibility, and easy access to the establishment. To translate this into gross income, we studied some Kentucky Fried Chicken outlets in a major metropolitan area. Some netted as little as $15,000 a year, while others were approaching the $100,000 mark. The reason for the disparity was location.

Most franchisees casually accept the location chosen for them—don't! Look it over thoroughly yourself; you can even hire an outside marketing consultant to evaluate and possibly argue about their choice. It can mean literally millions of dollars' difference in profit over 20 years.

Lease/contract negotiation can mean higher operating expenses if handled the wrong way. Sometimes the size of a franchise operation is a mixed blessing. It can negotiate from a position of power, but often pays higher lease fees for land and buildings than an independent contractor would.

DISADVANTAGE 3: HIDDEN START-UP COSTS

Your first major capitalization is a franchise fee, which ranges from $4,000 to $100,000 or more. This is a one-time fee that the franchisor charges for the privilege of using his concept, attending his training program, and learning the business.

On top of this franchisee fee, you may have to buy land or a building instead of renting it. If you rent a building you face leasehold improvements; you'll have to convert the empty space into a commercial outlet within the guidelines of the franchisor.

In some cases, the owner of properties will provide these improvements and factor it into your monthly rent at $50 or $100 a month. More often you will have to come up with the money yourself, up front, to pay for the conversion. Leasehold improvements can cost $5,000 to $30,000. Most franchisors will give you an estimate of the typical improvements, but then you're faced with buying equipment.

DISADVANTAGE 4: HIDDEN EQUIPMENT COSTS

The most successful business people are those who can shave costs as low as possible and still produce and deliver a quality product. This concept applies to all your start-up expenses, including buying equipment.

Likewise, franchising companies must keep their costs in line. They can't afford to have a man spend a week wandering around a city looking for bargains in equipment. They must have a prearranged source to eliminate expense in this area. To maintain the standardization and quality control mentioned throughout this article, franchisors will often insist that you buy your equipment through their sources.

Suppose, for example, that you start a restaurant franchise, buy the new equipment, and in less than a year go bankrupt. Even though you used the equipment a short time, you will have to resell it used for 50 percent. When you are considering $25,000 worth of equipment, 50 percent can add up to a lot less cash out of your pocket.

DISADVANTAGE 5: ROYALTIES

One major disadvantage to being a franchisee is the royalty which you will pay the franchisor. This fee is generally based on your gross sales, and we found it ranging from 1 to 10 percent depending on the business.

This fee goes to help the franchisor operate a support program, a training program, and most important, make a profit. Most franchisees, when they first start out, don't think much about the royalty fee until they start making a good profit. One we spoke with, however, had his mind changed when his sales hit the $1 million gross mark. He was locked into a 10 percent royalty fee, which meant that he had to turn over $100,000 to the parent company. He is currently negotiating to get a lower fee that would improve his profit position considerably.

In addition to the standard royalty fee, you may be asked to kick in an advertising co-op fee. For example, McDonald's has an advertising fund approaching $100 million that calls for a high payment from each franchisee.

The advertising expenditure generally pays off in more customers and better visibility for the franchise, although the fee may be larger than you had planned on for your own individual advertising—which you also have to keep up. So you will be looking at two ad budgets—one to keep your own business in front of the consumer's eye, and one budget that you have to kick back to headquarters.

DISADVANTAGE 6: LONG-TERM LIABILITIES

To buy your franchise you have committed to a strong "contingent liability." This means you're going to owe money which you don't have to pay back short-term, but that you are liable for long-term. This can be for equipment, land, buildings, mortgages, and sometimes even the franchise fees.

Not only is this a financial liability, it's a personal one. Most franchise agreements favor the franchisor, and are for relatively long periods of time. If you've been on the firing lines a couple months or even a year or two, and you relize that this business isn't your key to instant riches, you may find yourself locked into a very long-term commitment.

There are even disadvantages to short-term agreements. You may find that after you've worked hard building up the business in the area, your franchise agreement has expired, putting you in the position of losing the use of the concept and name, and not being able to continue in that business.

To avoid these difficulties, have legal counsel carefully look over all the details of the franchise agreement, making sure that the cards are stacked as much as possible in your favor.

DISADVANTAGE 7: YOU MAY NOT OWN ANYTHING

Aside from inventories, many franchises do not have anything in their name but a franchising contract. The franchisor owns the property, the building, the fixtures, and the signs, and you will be paying high rent. In others, they own the building and you own the fixtures, signs, and inventory.

This can be a problem if you wish to sell out. Many of the contracts offered by franchisors are not transferable. Even if they are, they often have a "right of first refusal" clause which means that you must first offer the business to the franchisor, and you can't sell to anyone else at a higher price.

Beware of cancellation clauses in franchise agreements. You can build up a healthy business, deviate slightly from the rules, and end up with a cancellation notice and forced sale of your business with no compensation to you. It has happened!

DISADVANTAGE 8: IF THEY GO BROKE

Another pitfall is the possibility of the franchisor overextending itself and going bankrupt. This can affect you even if you are going strong, because your property contracts will either be financed by others or even sold off to pay creditors.

Finally, there is the problem of suppliers. Many franchisors make extra profits supplying the products you sell. Occasionally you can make better deals around them, but this is often in violation of your agreement. Even if you try it, it's pretty hard to hide the transaction on your books, which are always open to them.

Don't forget that franchisors often designate your suppliers. What recourse do you have if service becomes bad or if product quality is inconsistent? Generally a complaint will cause an investigation and maybe a short-term correction, but you are often left out in the cold. It's illegal for a franchisor to take a kickback from a designated supplier, but it sometimes happens, and when it does it's hard to get supply problems corrected.

DISADVANTAGE 9: THE WORK LOAD

One of the biggest complaints of surveyed franchisees is that they have to put in 60 to 70 hours per week. Many claim that the extensive bookkeeping and bushels of forms that must be completed daily, weekly, and monthly, and sent to the franchisor waste a great deal of time.

Check the bookkeeping requirements and the various forms

required by your franchisor. Find out if it has to be done by a book-keeper or if it's the owner/manager's responsibility. Every minute spent filling out forms is a minute when you could be selling.

Most franchising companies won't even consider selling a franchise to someone who wants to be an absentee owner. Many have such tight demands that it is almost impossible for the owner to take a vacation or a long weekend.

IT'S UP TO YOU

Remember, you often can't change methods or try new ideas, and are vulnerable to franchisors' actions. You are totally dependent upon their expertise, efficiency, and integrity.

We hope that full disclosure laws will soon be in effect in every state, because franchising is a good way to get into business if the agreement is designed and administered properly.

Just remember to consider the pros and cons very carefully, since they will influence your success or failure.

WHERE TO FIND THE MONEY FOR YOUR FRANCHISE

"How can I get my hands on $25,000?" That's the question most entrepreneurs ask when considering franchise offerings. Everything else about the opportunity seems sound—good product, steady market, excellent franchisor support. Then comes the one phrase, "capital required," and the dream evaporates—needlessly.

The fact is that anyone with good credit and a sound business head can get the capital he or she needs. You just have to know where to look and what rules to follow.

There are many sources of investment capital—loans, mort-gages, equity conversions, venture capitalists, and even franchisors. Of over 800 franchisors we investigated for this special report, nearly half offered financial assistance to franchisees.

Basically, before you approach any lending source, you must have a firm fix on three major items: your personal net worth, your credit rating, and your business plan.

Going after money is one of the most important things you will ever do in your business career, and it takes a lot of preparation. The first step is determining your net worth.

HOW MUCH ARE YOU WORTH?

Before applying for any kind of financial aid, you must find your net worth by using a balance sheet like the one on page 336. All balance sheets are divided into two sections: assets (what you own) and liabilities (what you owe).

Under assets, list all your holdings—cash on hand, checking accounts, savings accounts, real estate (current market value), automobiles (whether paid off or not), bonds, securities, insurance cash values, and other assets—then total them up. In the example provided, we see $150,000 in total assets.

The second part of the balance sheet is liabilities, and you follow the same steps. List your current bills, all your charges, your home mortgage, auto loans, finance company loans, etc. In the sample provided, these total $90,000.

Subtract your liabilities from your assets. In the sample you see a net worth of $60,000. Once you have worked up this sheet, which is a valuable tool in your campaign for money, then you have to take a good look at your credit rating.

ARE YOU A GOOD CREDIT RISK?

There are three ingredients that all lenders look for in a credit rating: stability, income, and track record.

Most lenders are interested in how long you've been on a certain job and lived in the same location, and whether you have a record of finishing what you start. If your past record doesn't show a history of stability, then be prepared with good explanations.

Not only is the amount of income you earn important, but your ability to live within that income. Some people earn $100,000 a year and still can't pay their debts, while others budget nicely on $20,000 a year.

Most lending institutions look at your income and the way you live within that income for one very good reason. If you can't manage personal finances, the odds of your managing business finances are slim.

The third element lenders look for is your track record—how successful you've been in paying off past obligations. If you have a record of delinquent payments, repossessions, and so on, then you should get these squared away before asking for a loan. Incidentally, cleaning up these obligations is good training for running your own business, since it takes discipline to be successful.

Most lenders will contact a credit bureau to look at your credit file. We suggest that you do the same thing *before* you try to borrow. Under the law, credit bureaus are required to give all the information they have on file about your credit history. Once you have this tool, you should correct any wrong information, or at least make sure your side of the story is on record. For instance, a 90-day delinquency looks bad. But if that 90-day delinquency was caused by being laid off or because of illness, then that is taken into consideration.

After you've determined your net worth and your credit rating, the final step to take before approaching lenders is your business plan.

THE ELEMENTS OF A GOOD BUSINESS PLAN

If you think a business plan isn't worth the time, then consider the case of Ted Nicholas, successful publisher and author. When he was 21, he wanted to borrow $5,000 to start a business, and was turned down cold by four of the five banks in his own hometown. He went to work and put his plan in writing. The last bank he approached gave him the loan, and even convinced him it should be $7,500!

A well-thought-out business plan will make the difference between having your loan application accepted or rejected. A complete business plan should always include an intimate, technical knowledge of this business; accurate pro formas, projections, and cost analyses; estimates of working capital; an indication of your "people skills," and a suitable marketing plan.

It should include certified statements of your net worth and several credit references. One rule of thumb is that the more sophisticated the people you're borrowing from, the more detailed your plan should be. Some pros even believe that the plan should have one page for every $1,000 you are seeking.

To help construct your own business plan, we'll detail each of the five elements of a good proposal.

FIRST, KNOW YOUR BUSINESS

Lenders want you to have in-depth technical knowledge about your business.

By giving lenders a detailed presentation covering all the technical aspects of your business, you will convince them that you know what you're talking about.

Include an analysis of your main competition in the marketplace, and the size of the market itself. If you are going to sell widgets, and you have figures that show the widget market has experienced a steady 22 percent growth for the last five years, and has gross sales of $4 billion, you give the lender a better picture of the overall market.

This has to be followed by the unique position you plan on carving out for yourself in the entire industry. If there are 200 companies doing exactly the same thing, your chances of getting the loan are slim unless you can prove you are going to do something better—deliver a better widget, package it a new way, offer a different pricing structure.

SECOND, WORK OUT THE NUMBERS

There are standard, ritualized documents that people dealing in finance look for. And unless you know the language, it's like visiting a foreign country. If you don't have a solid accounting background, hire a CPA or other accountant to help prepare your plan in language acceptable to lenders.

The basic documents your plan should include are a start-up projection, a pro forma, a fixed/variable cost analysis, and your own documents of net worth, credit status, and so on.

We provide samples of these documents on pages 331—336 as well as an explanation of how each works. Use these as samples in preparing your own business plan.

You need these documents because lenders want a chance to review and analyze them. They will cross-check your projections, study your analyses, and determine if your profit projections are reasonable based on other similar businesses.

One important point! Don't make the numbers too glossy and too dreamy. Anyone involved in finance knows pretty much what is realistic and what isn't. If anything, understate your case and show a conservative projection. You will be able to get many of these figures from the franchise offering, but check them out!

Federal franchise law and internal regulation have put strong guidelines for the amount of "pie in the sky" promises that a franchisor can make. A general guideline is that if anyone promises you overnight fame and fortune, take a walk.

MONTHLY OPERATING STATEMENT
(Typical pro forma for hot tub operation.)**

Income	Range		
Hourly Rentals @ $8/person*	$15,086	to	$25,144
Refreshments.........................	1,500	to	2,500
Other (T-shirts, robes, etc.)	754	to	1,257
Total Income	$17,340	to	$28,901
Cost of Sales	(1,127)	to	(1,878)
Gross Profit	$16,213	to	$27,023

Expenses			
Owner/Operator Salary	$1,250	to	$1,500
Payroll (3 to 5 full time)	3,600	to	4,500
Rent	800	to	1,200
Utilities	1,000	to	1,600
Chemicals	350	to	600
Maintenance/Repairs	500	to	850
Laundry	625	to	1,000
Supplies/Printing.....................	500	to	800
Accounting/Legal	200	to	300
Insurance	350	to	700
Advertising and Promotion	1,100	to	2,000
Miscellaneous	100	to	200
Total Expenses	$10,375	to	$15,250
Net Profit B/T	**$ 5,838**	to	**$11,773**
Percentage of Sales	33.7	to	40.7

**Assumes 40 percent average annual use rate; 10 percent multiple, 85 percent couples, 5 percent singles.
*Sample

START-UP EXPENSES
(Typical hot tub operation.)*

Item	Range		
Rent (first and last months)	$ 1,600	to	$ 2,000
Equipment	33,205	to	50,815
Utility and Phone Deposits	50	to	200
Permits and Licenses	100	to	2,000
Construction Utilities	500	to	1,000
Grading and Land Preparation	1,000	to	5,000
Temp. Fencing Site	500	to	1,000
Cleaning and Landscaping	2,000	to	10,000
Utility Hookups	3,000	to	5,000
Deck, Fencing and Partitions	10,000	to	30,000
Building Preparation	5,000	to	20,000
Decor	2,000	to	10,000
Insurance	700	to	1,400
Legal and Accounting	500	to	2,000
Advertising (Preopening)	3,000	to	5,000
Manager Salary (Preopening)	1,000	to	1,200
Total	**$64,155**	**to**	**$146,615**
Suggested Operating Capital	$30,325	to	$44,550

*Sample

SAMPLE PROJECTED SALES—

Months (of Fiscal Year)	1	2	3	4	5
Sales	5,000	7,000	8,000	9,000	10,000
Cost of Sales	3,000	4,000	4,700	5,000	5,700
Gross Profit	2,000	3,000	3,300	4,000	4,300
Variable Expenses:					
Salaries	1,500	1,500	1,500	1,500	1,500
Payroll Taxes	150	150	150	150	150
Advertising	200	200	200	200	200
Automobile	100	100	100	100	100
Dues and Subscriptions	10	10	10	10	10
Accounting and Legal	100	100	100	100	100
Supplies	25	25	25	25	25
Telephone	50	50	50	50	50
Utilities	50	50	50	50	50
Miscellaneous	50	50	50	50	50
Total Variable Expense	2,235	2,235	2,235	2,235	2,235
Fixed Expenses:					
Depreciation	450	450	450	450	450
Insurance	100	100	100	100	100
Rent	300	300	300	300	300
Taxes and Licenses	25	25	25	25	25
Interest Only	150	150	150	150	150
Total Fixed Expenses	1,125	1,125	1,125	1,125	1,125
Total Expenses	**3,360**	**3,360**	**3,360**	**3,360**	**3,360**
NET PROFIT (LOSS) B/T	**(1,360)**	**(360)**	**(60)**	**640**	**940**

EXPENSE AND PROFITS

6	7	8	9	10	11	12	Total
10,000	10,000	10,000	12,000	13,000	15,000	17,000	126,000
5,700	5,700	5,700	7,000	7,500	8,000	9,500	71,500
4,300	4,300	4,300	5,000	5,500	7,000	7,500	54,500
1,500	1,500	1,500	1,700	1,700	2,000	2,200	
150	150	150	170	170	200	200	
200	200	200	200	200	300	300	
100	100	100	100	100	100	100	
10	10	10	10	10	10	10	
100	100	100	100	100	100	200	
25	25	25	25	25	50	50	
50	50	50	50	70	70	70	
50	50	50	50	50	60	60	
50	50	50	50	50	70	70	
2,235	2,235	2,235	2,455	2,475	2,960	3,160	28,930
450	450	450	450	450	450	450	
100	100	100	100	100	100	100	
300	300	300	300	300	300	300	
25	25	25	25	25	25	25	
150	150	150	150	150	150	150	
1,125	1,125	1,125	1,125	1,125	1,125	1,125	13,000
3,360	3,360	3,360	3,580	3,600	4,085	4,285	42,430
940	940	940	1,420	1,900	2,915	3,215	12,070

GAS-PUMPING CAR WASH UNIT*
CASH FLOW ANALYSIS

Cars Per Month .	6,000	8,000	10,000	12,000
Income**				
Wash	$ 8,500 $	10,000 $	12,500 $	15,000
Gas	53,375	73,500	91,875	110,250
Total Income ...	$ 61,875 $	83,500 $	101,895 $	125,250
Expenses***				
Cost of Gas	$ 44,000 $	56,700 $	64,800 $	85,050
Cost of Wash ..	1,200	1,600	2,000	2,400
Land: Rent and				
Taxes	2,000	2,000	2,000	2,000
Labor	3,000	3,400	4,000	4,600
Maintenance ...	200	300	400	450
Insurance	850	850	850	850
Advertising	1,000	1,500	1,500	2,000
Miscellaneous ..	500	500	500	500
Total Expense ..	$ 52,750 $	66,850 $	76,050 $	97,850
Monthly				
Cash Flow ..	$ 9,125 $	16,650 $	25,845 $	27,400
Annual				
Summary				
Income	$742,500	$1,002,000	$1,222,740	$1,503,000
Expenses	633,000	802,200	912,600	1,174,200
Cash Flow	109,500	199,800	310,140	328,800

**Assumes that of the total number of cars passing through each month, 25 percent will purchase no gas and pay full price of $2 per wash; 25 percent will purchase five gallons of gas and pay $1.50 for wash; 25 percent will purchase 10 gallons of gas and pay $1.25 for wash; 25 percent will purchase 15 gallons of gas and pay 75 cents for the wash.

***Assumes the average cost of gas at $1.11 per gallon, yielding 16 cents per gallon gross profit.

*Sample

TOTAL MONEY NEEDED TO GET STARTED
(Use this form as a worksheet.)

A. **Living Expenses** (from your balance sheet) . . . . .   _____
    x 3 months   _____

B. **Franchise Fee(s)** . . . .   _____

C. **Start-Up Expenses** (include all not
    included in franchise fee)
    Rent (first and last months) . . . .   _____
    Equipment . . . .   _____
    Utility and Phone Deposits . . . .   _____
    Permits and Licenses . . . .   _____
    Building Preparation . . . .   _____
    Decor . . . .   _____
    Insurance . . . .   _____
    Payroll . . . .   _____
    Owner/Operator's Salary . . . .   _____
    Accounting and Legal . . . .   _____
    Advertising (preopening) . . . .   _____
    Miscellaneous . . . .   _____

D. **Working Capital** (one-third of C) . . . .   _____

E. **Total Money Needed** (A + B +C+ D) . . . .   _____

BALANCE SHEET*
(Use this to determine your net worth.)

Assets

Cash and Checking Account	$ 1,000
Savings Account	3,800
Real Estate	100,000
Automobiles.	6,000
Bonds	6,000
Securities	2,700
Insurance Cash Values	25,000
Other: Coin/Stamp Collection/Antiques	5,500
Total Assets . . . . **A**	$150.000

Liabilities

Current Monthly Bills	$ 4,000
Credit Card/Charge Account Bills	3,000
Mortgage	60,000
Auto Loans	3,000
Bank Loans	3,000
Finance Company Loans	3,000
Personal Debts	6,000
Other: Pay back investors	8,000
Total Liabilities . . . . **B**	$ 90,000

Net Worth (A − B = C)

Total Assets	$150,000
Total Liabilities	(90,000)
Total Net Worth . . . . **C**	**$ 60,000**

*Sample

It's also a good idea to get a list of local franchisees in your state, and visit them to hear the other side of the picture. As a final check, contact an attorney to get a legal opinion on the franchise offering, to make sure that you understand exactly what your limitations and your freedoms are.

THIRD, ESTIMATE YOUR WORKING-CAPITAL NEEDS

Most franchises require some or all of the following: an initial franchise or license fee; training cost; an on-site start-up and promotional costs; periodic royalties (weekly or monthly); charges for premises, equipment, inventory, supplies; and, occasionally, bookkeeping charges.

Terms like "initial cost," "capital required," "initial fee," "total cost," "down payment," and "equity investment," are always used in franchise offerings, yet many mean different things from business to business.

Along with the franchise costs, you should plan on working capital for at least three months, and preferably more. You can determine working-capital needs by a simple formula: living expenses times three plus total franchise costs.

FOURTH, INDICATE YOUR "PEOPLE SKILLS"

Basically, this element of your business plan lets the lender know how skillful you are in managing people and yourself. This is a tricky area to get down in writing since it deals with abstract concepts, but there are several tips we can provide.

First, think of your past work experience in terms of your interpersonal relationships—how many people you had to manage, how many customers you had to deal with on a day-to-day basis, the special assignments you performed for your employer.

Then think of what groups you belong to. Put down any position you've held in these clubs that shows you know how to work with people. If you're married and have a family, put that down.

In other words, think of everything about your life that shows you know how to get along with people, and, more importantly, how to motivate them. Lenders want to know this personal side of you because they know from experience that running a business is a demanding, often frustrating job that can put a strain on the wrong kind of person.

FIFTH, SPELL OUT YOUR MARKETING STRATEGY

This will emphasize the existing competition in the field you're entering, and will detail your marketing steps in carving out your share of the market.

Specify whether your main advertising will be done through newspapers, magazines, direct mail, radio or TV. Include what kind of co-op advertising is available through your franchisor or your suppliers.

If there are seasonal markets to your business, be sure to specify the peak seasons, and what you plan to do during the off-months to keep a consistent profit picture.

A well-thought-out marketing plan is simply a blueprint; it is almost always changed once you get on the firing line. So you should emphasize that this is the goal you want to accomplish, and not that the marketing projection will be followed to the letter. Lenders are more concerned with knowing that you know what a marketing plan is, and its importance, rather than with analyzing the reliability of your plan.

With a determination of your net worth, your credit rating, and a business plan that includes all the elements we've just discussed, you're ready to approach lenders.

START WITH THE FRANCHISORS

In 1978 Bob Jones approached an Atlanta-based hamburger franchise. He didn't have the $20,000 franchise fee or the collateral to borrow against. The franchisor believed in him and gave him the franchise for a $5,000 down payment, and helped him set up a loan package. In less than a year, he was grossing more than $1,100 a day (Don't expect this from every franchisor!)

Almost half the franchisors we investigated offer financial help either in the form of time payment loans, or help in setting up loan packages.

When you're borrowing money, there are two types of loans available to you: *debt* and *equity*. Debt loans simply mean that you pay the loan back over an agreed period of time, while equity loans mean that you're giving up a piece of your ownership instead of paying back the loan. The best advice we uncovered from the smart operators in this field is "Don't get an equity loan! You're giving up a certain amount of proprietorship by running a franchise, so why give up more?"

Almost all franchisors in the country provide debt financing only. Some carry the entire loan or a fraction thereof through their own finance company. We found fractions of 15 percent, 20 percent, 25 percent, all the way up to 75 percent of total debt burden. The franchisors we talked to emphasized that these figures are guidelines and not hard-and-fast rules.

Keep in mind that a business is franchising for two basic reasons: to expand and to raise capital. So if you have a reasonably good credit record and pass all the financial requirements, most franchisors will bend over backward to get you on their team.

The help that franchisors provide usually includes assistance with business plans, application help, introduction to lending sources, and in many cases serving as guarantor of the loan.

After you have determined the extent of financing available from the franchisor, make a working list of all available sources of capital. Most astute operators use the following sequence of contacts: friends and relatives, home mortgages, veteran loans, bank loans, Small Business Administration loans, public contact, and finance companies.

FRIENDS AND RELATIVES

Many business people have little money when they start out, and even less credit. That's why many of the country's largest businesses would not have started without loans from friends or relatives: people who believed in their ideas and backed them. Ford, Cessna Aircraft, and Bank of America are three companies that started on a shoestring.

When family and friends finance, they often want equity loans. Try to keep all your transactions on a debt basis so you simply pay the loan back with interest. This keeps financial obligations among relatives on an "arm's length" basis.

Another method of getting capital from friends and relatives is repayment in kind. Approach about ten people and ask for a no-risk loan of $1,000. Promise them that there will be no risk involved, and that you will pay them back in ten years.

Then take that money and buy U.S. Savings Bonds in the lenders' names. A $1,000 bond costs $750, which leaves you with $250 working capital. Twenty lenders gives you $20,000 with $5,000 to keep, and you won't have to worry about your source of repayment—nor will your investors.

Of course, to raise more money you can buy bigger bonds or two or three bonds in each investor's name.

MAKE THEM LIMITED PARTNERS

Often you can turn friends and relatives into limited partners. In an ordinary general partnership, 2 or even 100 persons band together and put up capital jointly to form a company they think is going to be a big success. In this case, each person is a general partner, so each is able to share in all the profits.

And also in all the debts. If a company goes belly up, then each partner is responsible for debts, sometimes even for more than his initial investment.

In a limited partnership, each person's loss is limited to the amount of money invested.

What happens is you become the general partner—you'll do all the work—and your investors become limited partners. If the business goes, they make money. If it doesn't, they lose their initial investment and no more.

PUT YOUR HOME EQUITY TO WORK

Home equity is the cash difference between what you owe on your present home and its current market value, regardless of what you paid for it. If you owe $20,000 on a home you bought for $40,000 but is now valued at $120,000, you have $100,000 equity.

You can either borrow against that equity using your home as collateral, or you can do like many people and sell the home outright. This means looking for new living accommodations and lowering your standard of living for a while, but one of the basics of going into business is making sacrifices.

This major step should not be taken without a thorough investigation of the franchise.

Remember that when you are buying a franchise, you are actually buying three incomes. First, you are seeking a salary from the business. Second, you are looking for a good return on your investment, one which is better than your returns on your other investments. Third, your profit potential if and when you sell the business must bring at least three times the earning factor.

If the opportunity looks sound and you are willing to mortgage your home, your capital search can stop there. If you don't take that big risk, there are still many available sources.

TRY VETERANS LOANS

Vietnam veterans may already qualify for Economic Opportunity loans of up to $50,000 with repayments for as long as 15 years. The major qualification is that you must have been on full-time active duty on or after August 5, 1964. You don't have to have been in Vietnam, but you must have an honorable or general discharge.

The steps in getting an Economic Opportunity loan are simpler than other forms of government borrowing. The Vietnam veteran loan program works in conjunction with SBA loan programs, specifically on training in business knowledge and providing in-depth assistance in preparing your loan applications.

Contact any Economic Opportunity office or SBA outlet in your vicinity to obtain details on getting this special assistance.

APPROACHING BANKS

This is a little more difficult, since you will be dealing toe-to-toe with professional finance people whose only business is making the best possible loans for their investors.

For openers you will need personal financial statements, personal references, a complete business plan, and profit projections for how the loan is to be used. So you see how important getting your house in order is.

When you approach the bank, be positive. Go in with the attitude that they should loan you the money. You can analyze all the pro formas, statements, and references you want, but a large part of the banker's decisions will be based on his or her opinion of your dedication and conviction. Every banker we investigated admitted that when all the analyzing is finished, the gut feeling is what determines the loan.

A large part of this gut feeling is based on personal appearance. You wouldn't call on a client with a rumpled suit, dirty fingernails, unkempt hair, and a hangdog expression. You can have the fanciest written presentation in the world, but if your personal appearance is messy, your chances of getting the loan are not very good.

If you don't get the loan and you've followed all the above steps, then ask why. You want to find out if there's something wrong with your presentation, if your figures are wrong or your projections are screwy. Find out all you can about why you were turned down so you can correct it before visiting the next bank.

If they are rejected for a loan, astute operators realize that this is just one more stepping-stone to the SBA. One of the SBA's criteria before you qualify for a loan is that you must be turned down by three banks. They won't even talk to you until you've been turned down by a bank.

NOW YOU GO TO THE SBA

Small Business Administration loans are shrouded in myth. A recent survey showed the following erroneous reactions to the lending program: "Only minorities get SBA money." "It's impossible. No one ever gets one of those loans." "The SBA takes forever. I need the money now!" These are the myths; now for the facts.

The SBA has very little capital for direct loans, with the majority going for disaster relief. However, the SBA recently guaranteed $2.1 billion in small business loans. Does it really make a difference if the SBA gives you the money directly or arranges for a bank to give you the money?

As far as paperwork goes, the demands of the SBA are similar to any commercial loan company. However, a poorly prepared SBA application will be kicked back to the applicant until it is completed correctly. It doesn't take forever; a properly prepared application is processed in three to six weeks with the applicant receiving money one week after a bank is found.

Of course, during times of heavy loan demand, finding a bank to participate in a loan program may be difficult. You can find out all the application details from any SBA office.

PUBLIC CONTACT

An often overlooked source of capital is your local newspaper. Ads appear in many papers that let you know of individuals or groups of people with capital to invest. A one-day screening of 80 daily newspapers from across the country revealed more than 500 ads similar to this: "I have $30,000 to invest in an ongoing business. Write Box 843." Etc.

Answer all these ads, generally found under the "Business Opportunities" section of the classifieds. If you don't get answers to your response, then write some ads of your own. Here are some samples you can follow:

> Capital sought for promising new franchise outlet. Willing to pay 10 percent on small loan for short period. Sound collateral. Name and phone number to Box 12.

> WANTED: MAN WITH VISION. I need $5,000 operating capital to open local outlet of national franchise chain doing $1.4 billion annually. Will give 9 percent interest. Write Box 123.

Note that both of these ads call for pure *debt financing.*

Other avenues of public contact are government and private industry grants, colleges, and endowment programs.

FINANCE COMPANIES AND OTHER COMMERCIAL LENDERS

We have left finance companies last for a simple reason—the high interest rates. For example, in one state simple interest is 30 percent per year on the first $225, 24 percent per annum on the part of the loan from $225 to $625, 18 percent on amounts from $625 to $1,650, and 12 percent on amounts over $1,650.

On the other hand, commercial finance companies tend to give longer repayment terms, and will accept as collateral items that most banks would shun, such as inventories and receivables. In short, commercial finance companies are more flexible than banks, but you pay for this flexibility.

Life-insurance companies, pension funds, commercial paper houses, and foundations offer money to businesses for real estate, equipment leasing, and sometimes working capital in amounts that are usually higher than bank loans. Generally, their interest rates are only 1 or 2 percentage points above banks. The disadvantages of going to these sources is that they usually only make large loans (in excess of $500,000) and require that the companies applying be financially strong and established.

INNOVATIVE APPROACHES TO FUNDING

One approach that has become popular is the formation of absentee-investor groups. These groups, generally high-income professionals like doctors and lawyers, pool their resources and invest in several franchises at once. They hire on-site management to handle day-to-day chores.

Recently franchisors report being approached by financial brokers—historically more interested in big deals—to put together large pools of money using SBA and private funds. These funds would be available to franchisees through the franchisors, like a trust fund. Groups of smaller banks with funds to invest would contribute to the fund from all over the country.

Several colleges and universities have begun making part of their endowment funds available to would-be franchisees. One large midwestern university that asked not to be identified has made over $700,000 in small business loans. While the program is experimental, the college feels potential returns on investment will be far greater than others in their overall portfolio.

THE BOTTOM LINE

There are many sources of financing available to help you launch the franchise of your dreams. However, operating a franchise with no reserves and blinding yourself to unexpected financial business reverses—which do happen—can be shocking.

A good rule to remember: Never invest more than 75 percent of your cash reserves. If you have $10,000, invest $7,500. If you have $25,000, invest $18,750.

Most important, remember that the price of a franchise does not always reflect the actual cost of the business. Additional costs can include down payments on the land, building, equipment, fixtures, and signs, and can cover inventory, leasehold improvements, training, opening promotional costs, administrative costs, and even sales commissions.

Be sure you understand the requirements of your cash investment. You will need a pillow of working capital to properly guide the business through the ups and downs of activity.

If you do your homework thoroughly, and remember that financing a business is the most important sale you will ever make, then you will be head and shoulders above the competition.

THE UNUSUAL

IMPORT AND EXPORT

(The potential profits in this business are unlimited; average profit is unknown. The investment can range from very little to very great. Since it is not a conventional operation in the manufacturing, retail or wholesale sense, it does not lend itself to our standard report format.)

The potential business in import and export is in the billions of dollars, because there is no country in the world that does not export some products and import others.

Every manufacturer of goods and products in the United States not already exporting is a potential business account for you. Furthermore, the rest of the countries of the world are overflowing with businessmen who want distribution contracts in the rich United States market. In import-export, if it's handled right, you can translate the old proverb "The world is my oyster" into reality.

This is not the usual type of business: you will be dealing with intangibles such as your services as intermediary, your knowledge of markets and banking and shipping, and your ability to match producers with purchasers. While this may seem complex, our start-up manual explains it in such a way, and provides lists of enough reliable sources and references, to make it understandable. Remember, success will be directly proportional to your skill as a salesman and perseverance in initiating contacts.

WHAT IS THE IMPORT-EXPORT BUSINESS?

If you have a men's clothing store and you purchase some of your stock in suits from Korea, you may be importing, but you are not in the import business—you are in the retail men's clothing business and just happen to be purchasing some foreign goods.

Likewise, if you manufacture ladies' earrings and count among your customers a department store in Bonn, West Germany, you are not in the export business—you are in the earring-manufacturing business with one customer who happens to be in Europe.

The business of import and export consists of matching the need to buy a product by a firm somewhere in the world with the desire of another company somewhere else in the world to sell that product. It should be emphasized that the export function, particularly from the U.S. which has so many products for sale, is usually more profitable than importing, has less capital investment and risk problems, and requires less selling by the businessman.

DEVALUATION OF DOLLAR

The old days of purchasing an item for 25 cents in some under-developed country and selling it here for $2 are long gone. This is a direct result of the devaluation of the American dollar and the result-ing worldwide realignment of monetary values. The devaluation of our money was a result of government policy in order to make our exports more competitive overseas while reducing imports. Export sales are thriving in some areas of our economy due to the advan-tageous exchange rate of European and Far Eastern currency against the U.S. dollar.

Today the best entry to international trading is through export-ing. After you've set up your export contacts you'll find it easier to get into importing if you want to work both sides of the business.

You've probably noticed dozens of publications advertised that for $5 to $500 (including seminars) promise to tell you how the authors made fortunes in this field and how you can too. We don't deny it is possible that some of these people did make big money working import and export, but generally speaking, our feeling is that their money comes from selling books. We put them in the same class as the worm-farm promotion which promised a lot but mostly produced revenues for the companies selling the "business opportu-nity."

We do not uncritically recommend the import-and-export busi-ness to our readers. We do believe that it can be a success, but it will take a lot of dedication, considerable time, and expert selling. Until an adequate and sophisticated network of worldwide agents is de-veloped (those with the *right* contacts), it's tough to break through. Our manual explains the basics and tells you which legitimate sources for further information are available to you.

EVERYBODY WANTS TO HELP YOU

The export business is unique in that you have access to so much free expert advice and assistance. Three groups are able and anxious to help you. Their motivations are healthily selfish, but that's all to your good.

The U.S. and every other government wants to increase ex-ports; the banks look upon importer/exporters as businessmen who can be potentially big accounts (if things develop well); and the freight forwarders and custom brokers hope to secure clients who will generate continuing and growing shipping needs (which is where their profits lie).

The 1980 White House Conference on Small Business provided new impetus for government programs designed to encourage smaller firms to start exporting. New proposals include recommenda-tions for more tax deferrals for exporters, the establishment of new funding programs for small businesses, and the creation of a network of "information centers" which will include the services of all federal agencies.

The Small Business Administration has just launched a new funding program in cooperation with the Export-Import Bank. Small exporters can obtain up to $500,000 (at relatively low interest) to cover costs of supplies and inventories, and to use as working capital to develop manufacturing of products for sale overseas. The U.S. government is making the future look rosy for the small exporter.

THERE'S MONEY TO BE MADE

While importing is no longer the quick and easy, high-profit business it was before the world monetary market was redesigned by our devaluation of the dollar, there still are some good opportunities if you can put the right components together.

The most knowledgeable field officers we interviewed estimated that smaller exporters and importers were netting $40,000 and up per year after they'd become established. A handful of top-notch dealers were netting medium six-figure incomes.

So there is the chance for big money in this business with a relatively small investment. Your big investment will be in time, effort, and a good grasp of the techniques of international trading.

Start-up Manual #92 is available on this business. See page 379.

JOJOBA PLANTATION

High net profit B/T (projected, tenth year):	$444,000
Average net profit B/T:	62,800
Minimum investment:	28,000
Average investment:	120,000

Here's how you can turn a 45-ton sperm whale and an evergreen desert shrub called jojoba (pronounced ho-HO-ba) into a dynamic long-range business opportunity. There's big absentee ownership potential as well, combining agribusiness, cosmetics, pharmaceuticals—even energy!

Jojoba was recently selling for $6 to $8 per pound. That makes jojoba oil the highest-priced agricultural product in the world, with the exceptions of opium and marijuana.

Jojoba and the sperm whale produce highly prized unsaturated oils, which have a multitude of industrial and consumer uses. But because the sperm whale is an endangered species, its oil cannot be imported into the United States. This is where the profit picture for jojoba becomes exciting.

PROFITS LIKE LIQUID GOLD

An acre of jojoba can replace the oil taken from 30 sperm whales, and is better in quality for product uses. The ecological bonus is that it's a replaceable natural resource and in no danger of disappearing from the earth.

Total production from the most recent wild harvests of jojoba was 200,000 pounds of oil—nowhere near enough to meet demand from cosmetics firms, small oil companies, and larger corporations doing industrial research and production.

Intense demand has pushed the price for jojoba oil as high as $65 per gallon; 55-gallon drums have sold for over $3,000. Since few buyers take that much at one time, jojoba oil prices are quoted by the pound. There are 7.2 pounds of oil to the gallon, which means that jojoba sells for over $9 per pound.

SUPERHIGH YIELD APPROACH IN YOUR PLANTATION

In 1974 Apaches on southwestern reservations planted the first commercial jojoba crops and have been experimenting with farming methods that may triple annual yields. The secret: planting 1,500 or more female jojobas per acre.

This daring technique is called interplanting, with seed in rows five feet apart. After five years the odd-numbered rows are taken out, and after another five years, the even-numbered rows.

As cuttings are cloned onto each other, each time increasing the strength of the remaining shrubs, yields are maximized and production of oil is a known quantity. Existing analysis figures show 89 percent accuracy in producing maximum consistent commercial yields.

After 8 years a single plant will yield up to 6 pounds of seed. After 13 years the yield jumps to as much as 25 pounds. The key factor is ongoing care in an orchard environment. Amateurs, beware—jojoba is not a low-maintenance crop that can be planted anywhere and forgotten.

SURROUND THE PLANTATION WITH EXPERTISE

The jojoba planter has to keep in mind the vital need for expertise in agribusiness, although get-rich-quick artists sound their siren song and claim that jojoba is a fast-buck proposition.

The watchword is careful planning and ongoing management. With care a jojoba plantation can turn an absentee owner into a unique kind of oil tycoon who capitalizes on a renewable resource instead of drilling holes in the ground or destroying majestic sea creatures.

SITE SELECTION IS ALL-IMPORTANT

Jojoba is basically a desert shrub, although plantation prospects look equally good at sea level or in mile-high arid climates. The Israeli government takes jojoba seriously enough to have invested $4 million in a project in the Negev desert.

With frost the major pitfall, research into climate conditions is important. It's possible to take advantage of technical difficulties by classing a plantation as an agricultural research project. After clearing the government red tape, a smart planter can generate heavy tax write-offs until the first commercial crop is in.

LONG-TERM PROFITABILITY

One acre of plantation jojoba can produce up to 3,750 pounds of seed when plants are mature, based on scientists' best estimates. Thus, if a planter has only one acre producing only 3,000 pounds, it can eventually gross nearly $10,000 at the low end, and as much as $20,000 at the high end (1980 dollars—keep inflation in mind when you consider a long-term investment). No wonder growers are excited about profits.

The market for jojoba is expanding every day as more uses for jojoba oil are discovered. Experts predict that as early as 1983 there will be 500,000 pounds of jojoba oil produced annually; by 1990, 4 million pounds.

Taking into account an initial cash investment for land acreage in 1980 dollars, plus investment for machinery, irrigation, and other start-up expenses, the return on a 1980 investment for a fully mature crop in 1990 looks staggering!

Start-up Manual #166 is available on this business. See page 379.

New Idea

RENT A PICKET

The news media give disproportionate publicity to anyone who parades around with a picket sign. With enough pickets, a three-man group of malcontents can look like a whole revolution on TV!

A Culver City, California man came up with the idea of renting pickets, complete with placards, to people who have a gripe. Any gripe. The cost is $8 per hour per picket, with a minimum of three hours "on the line." Rent-a-Picket pays part-time college students minimum wages, keeping the rest of the money.

Rent-a-Picket's first customer was a man who was unhappy with an auto repair shop. Two pickets carried less-than-complimentary signs back and forth in front of the shop for a whole day.

The possibilities are endless. It's a nice, clean way to air gripes about auto dealers, politicians, unpopular laws, uncooperative spouses, or even your neighbor's blaring rock music.

A picket rental service is unique, easy to set up, and requires practically no investment. You can obtain all the protest-for-pay picketers you need at local schools, and have an art student make the signs. By using replaceable messages, or a wipe-clean surface on the boards, signs become a one-time cost.

Advertising and plenty of free publicity will build the business. Just be sure that pickets keep moving, do not obstruct pedestrians, and obey lawful orders of peace officers. Your right to picket is protected by the freedom of speech guaranteed by the First Amendment to the Constitution!

_____ New Idea _____

BOOK YOUR VALUABLES

On assuming a different look, sometimes a product that originally failed can be successfully resurrected. During the hippie days stash boxes were popular items. One such box was a hollowed-out book where, presumably, illicit drugs could be stored without detection. Because of the limited market, the item wasn't exactly a runaway seller.

But we think a little marketing sense could make this into a winner. Security is the name of the game nowadays. A hollowed-out book is an ideal spot to hide jewels, cash, or other valuables that are kept at home. Once such a book is placed on a bookshelf, it will elude most burglars who are interested in getting in and out as quickly as they can.

Making a book-safe is easy. Old books can be acquired for pennies a pound. A few hours with a jigsaw will produce hundreds of book-safes. In its heyday, this cache sold for $10 a crack!

Notions departments of large stores and gift shops would like this novel idea. The book-safe would make an unusual and thoughtful gift for a housewarming. Mail order would be a good route, too.

PAPER RECYCLING

High net profit B/T:	$125,000
Average net profit B/T:	30,000
Minimum investment:	1,100
Average investment:	4,500

Don't feel sorry for the next guy you see rummaging through a trash can looking for cardboard boxes until you investigate a little further. It just could be he's part of the newest business, which combines a thrifty use of natural resources with unbelievable profit margins. What is it? Paper recycling!

On a hunch, our investigators followed one such entrepreneur around as he dug through piles of discarded waste at various industrial and business locations. What we discovered astounded us! He was making a fortune off what the rest of us were throwing away. By gathering certain grades of wastepaper and cardboard, he could sell it by the ton to recycling plants.

He grossed over $120,000 last year. Another paper recycler we found quit his job as a produce clerk, began a collection route, and grossed $65,000 his first year, with a net after tax of $20,000. Both started with no more than an old pickup truck (cost, $250) and some inside knowledge about the market and supply sources.

PAPER IS EVERYWHERE

The bureaucratic and manufacturing explosions of the 20th century, along with the increasing scarcity of natural resources, have created the perfect conditions for this business. The prices paid for reusable paper has risen tremendously during the past few years: used newsprint goes for $50 a ton; cardboard, $75 a ton; and high-grade office paper, $110 a ton.

There is no doubt that we live in a paper world. In 1979 we used more than 74 million tons of paper for everything from books to cardboard boxes, and from manufacturing to clothing. We threw away more than 40 million tons of paper and cardboard products that could have been recycled. Over $2.4 billion worth of paper that could have been sold to recyclers went up in smoke!

THE MARKET IS WAITING

The age-old, relatively simply process of paper manufacturing is capital- and labor-intensive, and each step of the manufacturing process adds to the cost. This process goes like this: Trees are cut down and mashed to pulp. The pulp is put into gigantic blenders with water and other chemicals and beaten to a gooey dough. The dough is spread out on gigantic screens to dry, and the result is paper.

The only way to get cheaper paper is to cut back somewhere along the way—and that's where recycling comes in. A paper mill using recycled paper eliminates the capital costs of felling and replanting trees, pulverizing trees into pulp, and shipping pulp to the mills. By using recycled paper waste a manufacturer can cut the cost of a ream of standard 20-pound bond paper as much as 45 percent.

You can make big money helping others solve their waste disposal problem. It's estimated that municipal governments spend more than $1 billion annually collecting and disposing of 40 million tons of discarded paper.

Retail stores spend about $800 million a year hauling away paper trash. A savvy paper recycler can set up accounts with local businesses and government agencies to haul away paper trash for a percentage of the take.

For example, a 110-store chain in the Northeast threw out 250 tons of corrugated containers each week. It cost $2 million a year to dispose of it until a paper recycler offered to take it away, splitting the gross 60-40. The management of the chain store quickly saw the advantage: it earned $390,000 from their paper refuse, while the knowledgeable recycler pocketed a gross of $585,000 from this account alone!

PROMOTION COMES NATURALLY!

Obtaining free publicity is a snap in this business. Radio and television stations are required by law to devote a certain amount of air time to public service. Recycling is an ideal topic for editors looking for "meaty" stories. Remember, recycling is not only the business of the future, it's a community service. You're saving trees. You're helping to fight inflation. You're helping to keep the environment clean. You're putting money not just in the taxpayer's pocket, but in your own at the same time!

Start-up Manual #183 is available on this business. See page 379.

YOUR OWN STOCK MARKET

You can make a success of companies that failed years ago by capitalizing on a new craze that is sweeping Europe and growing in the United States. Stock and bond certificates from defunct corporations and governments are bringing big bucks to those who can find them and sell them to collectors.

Some stock certificates are going for more money now than they did when the companies were operating. For example, two years ago a Florida banker paid $20 each for stock certificates from the Pierce-Arrow Motor Car Company, an outfit that went broke in the late '30s. Today they bring $100 each. A part-time dealer in certificates from Fort Wayne, Indiana, reported profits of $25,000 in 1978. Not bad for certificates that can never be redeemed.

The newfound value in these old certificates and bonds derives from their nostalgia and history. They often have high-quality printing, engraving, and color that's unmatched by modern offerings. This makes them interesting, and consequently valuable to collectors. Many stock collectors are former coin and stamp enthusiasts who turned to certificates and bonds because the cost of coins is skyrocketing, and stock engravings are larger and more colorful than engraved stamps.

Europe is an even larger market than the United States. Most dealers report that half their business is with connections overseas. The hobby is sufficiently popular that a London newspaper ran a contest to find a word to describe this kind of collecting and settled on "scripophily." If you can pronounce it, you probably have the brains to locate old certificates and become a dealer.

Attics are the first place to look. Contact relatives and friends and see if they have any defunct bonds or stock stashed away. Perhaps contacting residents of retirement communities will provide sources of certificates. Place ads offering to buy and sell in newspapers, where there is often a section devoted to collectors of antiques and other objects. Try antique and collectors' publications as well as free classified ad publications and swap-meet journals.

Locate dealers through the same sources to determine the criteria for valuing the certificates and establishing further connections. Not every certificate will be worth $100, but the boom is coming, and this could be your chance to get in on it early.

SWAP-MEET PROMOTING

High net profit B/T:	$1,500,000
Average net profit B/T:	45,000
Minimum investment:	500
Average investment:	17,000

It's 4:00 a.m., and one of our researchers was returning with an out-of-town guest from an unusually late Saturday night party. As they passed a drive-in movie, the guest popped up with the exclamation: "What the devil is going on there at this time in the morning?"

They estimated that over one hundred cars, station wagons, panel vans, and pickup and larger trucks were lined up at the entrance to the drive-in.

Swap meets (or flea markets) are gatherings of small-time merchants and amateur sellers—no professionals or big operators. Depending on the meet, 20 to 30 percent of the sellers are people who have decided to empty their garage, basement, or attic of items which they no longer use, but which are still usable. How about an old-fashioned toaster in working order for $1? Items like this are common.

The rest of the sellers are either part-time merchants who buy seconds or closeout, distressed, auctioned, or surplus merchandise—or people who are marketing their own handicrafts. The swap-meet selection is so endless and varied that many people attend for sheer entertainment—not that they don't wind up bringing home their share of the booty.

You can see bargains at a swap meet that you won't find anywhere else. Some of the merchants buy regular products at normal wholesale price; because they have practically no overhead, their markup is low. We found one dealer retailing a $1.25 can of spray paint for 50 cents—and he was making 20 cents!

$1.5 MILLION PROFIT

The most successful operator we found was grossing over $1.4 million per year on space rentals and admissions fees. He was grossing another $850,000 on food and snack-shop sales. After all wages and state and federal taxes on them were paid the gross profit on space and admissions came to an excess of $1,270,000. The gross profit after product cost and wages on food sales topped $630,000 per year. There are few businesses that can show gross profits of 83 percent like this! And such profits are not unusual. Expenses you must subtract to ascertain the net profit before taxes include insurance, maintenance products and labor, phone, utilities, office supplies, printing, legal, accounting, advertising, and depreciation.

In this swap meet, the hidden expenses add up to a scant $50,000 a year. After subtracting 100 percent of the absentee ownership management salaries, the net profit before taxes is still over $1.5 million a year.

These figures were verified by a thorough investigation of the Paramount swap meet in Paramount, California, one of the most successful in the state. It has been operating for a number of years.

THE STORY BEHIND THE NAME

The phrase "swap meet" was originally chosen to ward off business license inspectors and sales-tax collectors. After a while, many cities decided that strict enforcement of license laws would close any swap meet and decided instead to extract a large license fee from the promoters, to cover all merchants participating. The policy varies, however, from city to city; some cities don't bother to ask for additional fees.

HISTORY

The first swap meet was in Los Angeles in 1955, and they spread statewide in the early '60s. The trend has been slow to spread across the nation, but today there are over 200 swap meets in California. Most of them operate on weekends only, although some are open six days a week.

YOU CAN START A SWAP MEET

We found one small operator who held his meet each Sunday in a small parking lot (100 by 120 feet) of a manufacturer next to a main thoroughfare. His only advertising was 10,000 handbills he distributed on cars and tacked to poles in the area. The first few weeks he barely broke even, but after three months he was operating on Saturday and Sunday, with 60 spaces rented at $4 each—and was netting $365 from rentals and over $100 from the sale of cold drinks, a one-worker operation.

His start-up expenses were rent, $35 per day; insurance for three months, $125; initial printing of handbills, $135; cloth banner signs, $38; cleanup brooms, $12; and chalk marker for spaces, $8. After the first week he cut his handbill distribution to 5,000 pieces, which reduced his weekly operating expenses to $105. (Cold-drink stand setup costs are not included.) Since he operated outside the city limits, he didn't need a business license.

BIG MONEY POSSIBILITIES—AND YOU DON'T NEED TO OWN A DRIVE-IN THEATER

Your key arguments when negotiating for drive-in space are that a hefty portion of a drive-in's profit comes from snack-shop sales (the profit margin will be almost as high as that obtained while showing a film), and that a drive-in stands useless during the daylight hours, drawing no income. This should make any owner open to suggestions for making daytime profits from his property.

Of course, the drive-in owner could promote his/her own swap meet, but most are reluctant, feeling it will require a substantial investment to get a swap meet rolling in a new area. If you agree to finance, organize, and promote the operation, he has nothing to lose and everything to gain. You can offer to split all the profits from food sales, rentals, and admissions. All he has to do is make the property available. Or you can take all the income from rentals and admissions while he takes all the income from food sales—each of you handling expenses related to his division. You provide the promotion and he the property.

You should get a lawyer to draw up a solid contract to protect your long-range investment, because less promotion will be needed after the meet is established.

LOCATION

Lower-income areas full of bargain-hungry people are a good choice; however, this is not a strict rule. The Rose Bowl Swap Meet is held in the parking lot of the famous Rose Bowl in Pasadena, surrounded by many stately homes. It is the biggest meet in the state, drawing 1,200 sellers and 20,000 to 40,000 customers every weekend. It is held only one Sunday each month, with space rentals ranging from $30 to $50 per space, and an admission fee of $1. The gross is in excess of $40,000 for one day, including 15 percent of the food sales, which are handled by a concessionaire. So you are not bound to stick to a low-income neighborhood.

We wouldn't advise you to start in a city of less than 250,000 population. Also, the bigger the lot you use, the better. As the idea catches on, you can rent out more spaces and draw a bigger crowd. Paramount uses a double drive-in with 1,600 parking spaces. Each seller gets two spaces so he can park his vehicle and display his merchandise.

When the meet first started, sellers' spaces were grouped near the concession stand and the remainder of the theater was used for consumer parking. Fortunately, there was considerable vacant land around the drive-in which could be obtained for parking as the crowd grew, because all the inside spaces were soon taken by sellers. Future growth must therefore be considered in your choice of a lot.

Start-up Manual #20 is available on this business. See page 379.

See page 379.

New Idea

ANTLER RECOVERY

There are over 8,000 elk on the 24,000-acre Jackson Game Refuge in Jackson, Wyoming. The animals shed over 9,000 pounds of antlers each year. The Jackson Boy Scouts make a sweep of the refuge and auction off the antlers. This year's take was $50,000!

The antlers have to be removed from the refuge because they pose a hazard to fish and game department trucks when they haul in feed for the winter. The antlers puncture tires.

Who buys elk antlers? If you said hunters who want a wall trophy, you'd be wrong. The biggest buyers are oriental businessmen! They're willing to pay up to $5 a pound for the horns.

Seems elk and deer antlers are considered to be something of a magic potion in the Far East. Asians powder the elk horns and then mix them with tea. It's believed that the brew will increase metabolism, improve circulation, and help with the healing of ulcers and wounds.

Whatever the reason, the important thing is that red deer antlers are going for up to $180 a pair in Hong Kong. Buyers wouldn't even tell us what they're getting for elk antlers.

If you've got a game and wildlife preserve near you, get in touch with them and try to make arrangements to harvest the horns of plenty once they're shed.

BONSAI COLLECTING

High net profit B/T:	variable
Average net profit B/T:	variable
Minimum investment:	60
Average investment	450

A tree measuring only 29 inches from the bottom of the pot to the top branch was sold recently for $3,500. Yes, $3,500 for one small tree.

The price was high, but some bonsai trees have brought as much as $15,000. Prices of $500 to $2,000 are not uncommon. Many florists, even those not specializing in bonsai, sell small ornamental trees for $50 to $250 apiece.

A bonsai is a dwarfed tree growing in a tray or pot. The art of dwarfing trees and plants dates back over 4,000 years.

Until recently, only a scattering of people in the United States have pursued bonsai culture. The recent booming interest in indoor green plants, however, has generated tremendous new activity.

MISCONCEPTIONS—WHAT IS A BONSAI?

Many Americans confuse bonsai with ming trees. A ming tree is usually a piece of driftwood to which preserved or plastic pine boughs have been attached to create the appearance of an aged tree.

Another misconception is that bonsai are only pines. A bonsai can be any plant or tree that has been dwarfed, either by human art or by nature. Only rarely are bonsai over four feet tall.

WHAT DETERMINES THE VALUE?

Many people feel that the value of a bonsai is dictated solely by its age. Some bonsai are over 500 years old, but this doesn't mean that they are the most valuable. A 15-year-old tree may be worth more than a 100-year-old specimen.

The price of a bonsai is based on shape, style, grace, trunk, and container. The trunk must be thick and clean, the container must complement the shape of the tree, and the tree itself must be shaped in a graceful, flowing style to resemble a mature, full-blown tree.

THE ANGLE FOR MAKING MONEY

Bonsai may be grown from seeds, from cuttings, from nursery stock, or—most importantly—found naturally dwarfed by nature. This is the angle!

When you grow dwarf trees from seeds, cuttings, or nursery stock it can take 1 to 20 years, depending on the variety, to create a salable bonsai. But we picked up 14 dwarf trees in just two weekends out in the forest; they can reach a value of over $2,000 within one year—or as soon as they graduate from training trays. The trees ranged in age from 8 years to over a century old.

FANTASTIC POTENTIAL

The two best trees will be worth over $500 each, after only a minimum amount of training. Potential acquisitions in one year, at the rate of $1,000 per weekend, would be about $32,000. (The trees can be removed only eight months of the year; they will die if removed during June, July, August, or September.)

All you need is a big backyard or porch that can be shielded from wind and direct sunlight. The only heavy cash outlay comes after one year, when you are ready to place the trees in special bonsai containers.

The tools necessary to remove the trees from the forest are a shovel, pruning shears, knife, ax, saw, and some burlap or plastic trash bags.

WHERE TO FIND BONSAI

Anywhere trees grow wild you'll find some which are naturally dwarfed. Search forests, fields, pastures, hills, mountains, and along the roadside where highways have been cut through hilly areas.

Near ravines, gullies, rocky hills, wind-swept oceansides, beside rivers and creeks, in heavily forested areas—you will find natural bonsai practically anywhere.

Of course, it has probably occurred to you that these trees are growing on someone's property. So before you remove any, ask the owner for permission. Explain that you collect trees that have been dwarfed by nature to less than three feet high. If the owner hesitates, offer to show him or her the trees in question and pay a dollar or two apiece for them. We found no resistance because (at this point) most people don't know the value of bonsai.

WHERE TO SELL YOUR BONSAI

Wholesaling bonsai to florists and nurseries is easy. At one time the few bonsai growers in the U.S. wholesaled their trees to florists and nurseries. Now, since the demand has climbed so high, most growers have stopped wholesaling because they can make much more money retailing.

The only trees we found in florist shops were some varieties of junipers which can be bonsaied in less than a year from nursery stock. In fact, some nursery junipers can be potted, pruned, and wired for only a month and sold at from seven to ten times their cost.

ART SHOWS TO FLEA MARKETS

We found one collector who grossed from $200 to $800 a weekend selling at art shows, flea markets, swap meets, and antique shows.

At the art shows and flea markets he sold most of his trees for less than $50, mostly in the $15-to-$25 range. These were all junipers that he had picked up as nursery stock and trained only a month or so.

At antique shows he was very successful selling higher-priced trees of different varieties—obtaining as much as $500 per bonsai.

Start-up Manual #57 is available on this business. See page 379.

CARDBOARD CASKETS

A Vancouver, British Columbia, funeral director is doing his part to lower the high cost of dying by selling cardboard caskets. Corrugated paper for the trip to the happy hunting grounds is an alternative to the stupendous funeral costs that have caused many people as much pain as the death itself.

Ken Timlick buys the cardboard boxes for $3; his wife sews a pillow and blanket from fake satin fabric for another $3. The result is the "world's first $6 coffin." To keep up appearances, Timlick will rent the use of an ornate catafalque with a hollow bottom that conceals the cardboard. The total cost is $150, a reasonable alternative to the thousand or more most caskets cost. Evidently Timlick hopes to make up in volume the cash he's losing by not charging outlandish prices.

Many funeral directors may not be happy with the concept, since it cuts into their high prices, but it should go over well with consumers. Some cemeteries do not permit the use of cardboard caskets. You can avoid the problem by simply supplying the boxes to funeral homes.

Locate a cardboard box manufacturer who will supply boxes with lids in appropriate sizes. Find a seamstress and a wholesale outlet for polyester fabrics. The rest is up to your sales ability.

Contact funeral directors at traditional homes as well as crematories. Don't forget about the boom in pet cemeteries, where owners may want miniboxes for their services. You can keep this as a part-time business or, once volume builds, go full-time. It requires minimal effort on your part and, considering the clientele, who's going to complain if the boxes get wet?

CONTEST PROMOTING

High net profit B/T:	$500,000
Average net profit B/T:	variable
Minimum investment:	$9,000
Average investment:	$18,000

Do you enter contests? You probably don't read ladies' and mens' pulp magazines such as *True Story, True Confession, Intimate Secrets,* and *Real Life,* but one contest ad appeared in 24 such publications and drew over 375,000 contestants.

The contest promoter showed a profit, before overhead, depreciation, executive salaries, and income taxes, of approximately $115,525. Not bad for one ad running for 60 days before the contest closed.

IS IT LEGAL?

No doubt several questions come to mind immediately. First: "Is it legal?" Yes! This company runs its contests honestly and totally within the framework of the law—and has been in business for almost ten years.

All mention of money is missing in this ad—you can enter the contest free of charge. So, your next question is: "Where do contest promoters make their money?"

They do not request any entry fee for this contest (they do in others), but the contestants are eventually induced to spend $4 to $8 to qualify for larger prizes after they have won the first tie-breaking contest.

In order to give you a better picture of how well the people respond and the cash flows, we will quote some figures from this contest.

Of the 375,000-plus contestants who entered the contest, 94 percent were notified that they were winners and were sent the tie-breaker puzzle. Twenty-eight percent of these people entered the tie-breaker contest. Thirty-six percent chose not to try for the higher prizes and forwarded no money. Forty-one percent sent $4, 16 percent sent $6; and 7 percent sent $8. The promoters of the contest took in $331,004 in cash.

Thirty-five percent of the remaining entrants had the correct answer to the tie-breaking puzzle and were sent another puzzle. Five percent of these people arrived at the correct solution of this puzzle and went on to the final tie-breaker. Prizes totaling $17,000 were awarded the winners.

During the last two tie-breaking puzzles, the entrants paid another $46,408 to qualify for higher prizes. That brings the gross to $377,412.

MONTHLY CONTESTS FOR ALL ENTRANTS

A promotion such as this is done three times each year by this company. This is not the end of their activities. All the entrants paying the additional fee to qualify for the increased prize money are automatically put on a regular mailing list. Each month a puzzle for a new contest is mailed to them. An entry fee of $1, $2, or $3 is required of each contestant upon entering these contests.

From the three annual promotions, the company accumulates a list of nearly 200,000 paying contestants. These contestants will pay over $500,000 in entry fees in the coming year in order to participate in the monthly contests.

Of this group, 18 percent will be hard-core contest enthusiasts, and will be kept on the list until participation ceases.

SMALL-SCALE APPROACH

This company has developed a proved formula that is easily duplicated and can be done on a smaller scale to start. There are a few companies competing with them on an even smaller scale.

Start-up Manual #30 is available on this business. See page 379.

ART-SHOW PROMOTING

High net profit B/T:	Very high
Average net profit B/T:	Unknown
Minimum investment:	$ 450
Average investment:	1,650

You don't have to know the difference between a Renoir and a Picasso. In fact, you don't need to know about art at all to put on an art show. And one fact stands out: it pays much better to be a promoter than an artist. To show this is true, we have only to look at an example in Los Angeles.

For six years Joe Oakes held art shows every Saturday and Sunday in a parking lot on La Cienega Boulevard between Hollywood and Beverly Hills. Joe netted over $30,000 a year, from his two-day-a-week enterprise, and his cash outlay at any one time never exceeded $500.

His expenses included rent for his location (the parking lot of a fancy dinner restaurant next door), at $100 per weekend, liability insurance to protect him and the lot owner, and a very small amount of promotional printing.

Mr. Oakes attracted an average of 54 artists every day and has had as many as 100 on hand to display their wares. Each craftsman paid him $4 per day for a display area about the size of one parking space, 10 by 20 feet. In addition, they agreed to pay him 10 percent of the price of any art object or painting they sold that day. Art galleries, by the way, charge a minimum commission of 20 percent, and often as high as 50 percent.

On the average day, sales totaled $2,000; they reached $5,000 a few times. Mr. Oakes's average weekly gross was about $732, with a net of $600 after expenses.

Subsequently a bank bought the parking lot Mr. Oakes was using. Joe was forced to move to a smaller parking lot across the street; this move reduced the number of artists' displays that he could accommodate. Nevertheless, Joe's lot continued to fill up each weekend.

SECOND CASE HISTORY

Mr. Oakes's story is not unique in Los Angeles. In a pleasure boat harbor 15 minutes' drive from Beverly Hills and Hollywood, another promoter has been operating with comparable success. The area, Marina del Ray, is an exclusive high-rent district catering to the wealthy and the young jet-set crowd. It is also something of a tourist attraction, with many unusual restaurants and a beautiful harbor afloat with yachts and sailboats. It is an ideal area to sell art.

This promoter sets up his show in the parking lot of a medical center which is not used on weekends. He averages 26 artists per day, and total art sales are about $2,000 a day. His weekly gross on commissions is $556. His rent for the parking lot is only $100 per week, which means he maintains a healthy net.

EXPENSES NEGLIGIBLE!

Most property owners will request that you take out insurance on the property you will be using. The liability insurance costs for this type of operation may be $150 to $385 per year. Besides a month's rent in advance, some incidental printing costs, and a business license, this is your only expense.

Many promoters don't allow manufactured craft or art to be sold—only genuine handmade art is permitted. The higher the quality of art displayed, the higher the gross sales are.

Start-up Manual #21 is available on this business. See page 379.

FLEA MARKETS—FINDING PRODUCTS

High net profit B/T:	$35,000
Average net profit B/T:	10,000
Minimum investment:	65
Average investment:	325

The flea market has firmly planted itself on American soil as a new "industry." Almost 2,000 markets are held regularly across the nation. Most are weekend affairs, but some are open seven days a week.

The concept took off in California in the early '60s, with "swap meets." Today there are more than 200 swap meets in California.

One of the biggest flea markets in the country is the monthly Rose Bowl Swap Meet in Pasadena, California, on the grounds of the famous Rose Bowl. On the second Sunday of each month 40,000 to 50,000 people may attend this meet, where 1,500 dealers hawk their wares.

Sellers are so successful at this swap meet that there is a two-year waiting list for the most expensive spaces—the blue and pink inner circle, at $50 per day. Prices of other spaces begin at $30 per day.

Almost any item you can imagine is on sale at this flea market. After many interviews with sellers in flea markets across the nation, we've concluded that the average regular seller nets $100 per day for his trouble.

ANTIQUES ARE BIG MONEY

There are many, however, who earn $300 to $500 per day. They specialize in antiques and memorabilia, selling at flea markets two days a week and spending the rest of their time collecting and buying items to sell.

CLOTHING—NEXT MOST PROFITABLE

Jeans, dresses, blouses, and shirts are second highest in the profit category. Most vendors claimed daily profits in the $100 to $300 range.

We staked out several sellers, investigating their sources of supply, and verified that they were making their stated profits. It didn't amaze us that a few exaggerated. However, most sellers, wisely fearing to encourage competition, tend to understate their profits.

JEWELRY SELLERS NEXT IN LINE!

This was the most closemouthed group we interviewed, and it was difficult to verify the figures we received. After our investigators counted sales and estimated costs during several periods in many FMs, we concluded that average net profits are $100 to $200 per day for those selling costume jewelry—cheap rings, earrings, and necklaces. Those handling slightly more expensive watches and rings didn't fare as well—except the ones with handcrafted silver and high prices.

Those selling new furniture were on about the same level as the jewelers. Yes, new—obviously manufacturing the upholstered pieces themselves. Auto parts sellers and produce salesmen were in much the same profit category—$100 to $150, with a few doing phenomenal business and earning much higher profits.

$30,000 ANNUALLY WORKING FOUR DAYS PER WEEK!

Those selling cast-off and collected items were usually more amateurish in their display and sales efforts. They weren't making as much money. Nevertheless, we found an occasional hustler who was pulling steady high profits on junk items.

One engineer who had been laid off claimed he had found a new niche and would never return to engineering. He told us he was making $600 per week in less than four days—a lot better than he had done in the office.

Anyone can make money at flea markets, provided she or he has the right items at the right prices.

Stay away from used electrically powered items such as radios, phonographs, irons, and toasters. They don't sell well, and you'll have to demonstrate that they are in working order, which takes too much time. Besides, unless you get them for nothing, you won't make much money per piece. The exception is items that are very old or antique-looking. You can pick them up for next to nothing and make a nice profit.

If you buy anything new or as a closeout, try to get it at 75 to 90 percent off regular or current lowest retail price. Remember, you must sell the item for at least 20 percent below the lowest retail price to have a fast turnover.

YOUR PRODUCTS MUST BE CHEAP OR UNUSUAL

Most regular flea market customers are price-conscious bargain hunters. The rest are looking for something special or unique. Therefore, you must offer easily recognized cheap prices or you must stock unusual items.

USE YOUR IMAGINATION

We saw many far-out things sold during our investigation. One young person was selling old engraved printing plates to be used as wall hangings. They were going like hotcakes, at good prices. Letterpress printers either throw the plates away or save up a large enough quantity to be melted down for scrap value in copper or zinc.

In another FM we found someone selling globs of clear plexiglas which had apparently been miscast in a plastic factory. Each time we checked, a crowd was examining and buying these defective scraps of plastic.

So use your imagination to determine other uses for items you see—especially odd-appearing items. Everyone wants something different. Who knows—you may discover another "pet rock."

Start-up Manual #69 is available on this business. See page 379.

New Idea
MAKING CLASS REUNIONS PAY

Most large graduating classes try to have a ten-year reunion. The problem is in tracking down 400 to 500 classmates. Florida entrepreneur Jeffrey Kaplan has come up with the solution with his company, Re-Unite.

Local distributors for Re-Unite pay a $150 distributorship fee and visit high schools, colleges, and universities before graduation when the feeling of camaraderie is at its highest.

For a $6 per student fee, Re-Unite keeps track of each member of the class for the next ten years. Distributors sell the concept by pointing out that when a typical class wants a reunion, it can only find about one-fourth of the alumni because most have moved or have gotten married and changed their names.

By using their communications system and tracking facilities, Re-Unite keeps tab on the students. In the tenth year, Re-Unite mails a computer printout of names and addresses to the class president.

To sweeten the deal, two out of every six dollars paid for the service are placed in an account for the reunion party. Two dollars goes to the company, and the distributor keeps the rest.

With many graduating classes numbering close to 500, a distributor can snare a $1,000 profit from just one sale! The beautiful part is that you've got fresh clients with each new graduation.

Re-Unite handles all the tracking work, so the distributor has virtually no overhead. The idea works best in a major urban area with many high schools, colleges, and universities.

MAIL-ORDER BUSINESS

High net profit B/T:	Unknown
Average net profit B/T:	Unknown
Minimum investment:	$1,000
Average investment:	x,xxx

Profits can be high, but depend on product, cost and pricing, advertising media, and expenditures.

Who is making a bundle in the mail-order business? The truth is, and this isn't a joke, it's the people who sell courses, books, and instructions—*about* the mail-order *business!*

There are dozens of companies selling mail-order instruction of various types. Together, they spend millions of dollars annually on advertising. In addition, innumerable small operators sell the same things. So, using a rule of thumb for projecting ad returns, probably 8 million people respond each year to ads on how to start their own mail-order businesses. Industry estimates reveal that consumers spend in excess of $7 million annually for mail-order instruction and associated gimmicks.

Many people come and go each year in the mail-order business. Since few ever obtain business licenses or register with any government agency, accurate statistics on their failure and success are not available. But it has come to be an accepted fact that this business has the highest mortality rate of any business around.

THE MOST COMPETITIVE BUSINESS AROUND

Most professionals in this business who observe thousands of amateurs enter the mail-order arena guess that fewer than one out of a hundred stick and make a small profit. Yet, of all the different businesses in this country, more people attempt to start a mail-order business than any other. One Commerce Department statistician in Washington estimates that the ratio is 165 to 1 to the next-most-popular business.

YOU MUST BE AN ADVERTISING PROFESSIONAL

Why? The lure is easy money! The dream is of going to the mailbox each day and finding it loaded with envelopes full of money. The people who are attracted to this impossible dream don't want to deal with the public; they are afraid to hire people to make money for them. They feel they can make a lot of money on a small investment. They think they won't need any special talent to be successful in this business. And, obviously, most of them don't have any business education or experience, much less an education in advertising. And advertising is the heart of the mail-order business.

The truth is that none of the foregoing desires and assumptions has any place in the mail-order business.

SUPERSALESMAN, THE BEST MAIL-ORDER MAN

First, and ironically, psychologists say that the majority of people who are attracted to this business are trying to avoid dealing directly with the public. In other words, they don't like face-to-face selling or negotiations of any type. Yet, of all the amateurs who enter the business, the supersalesman type is best equipped to become a success. The salesman knows what people want and need and what makes them buy.

The companies selling mail-order business gimmicks concentrate the full force of their advertising appeal toward this personality profile.

Success in the mail-order business requires a very high degree of professionalism and technical sophistication. You must know and believe in advertising theories, and most of all you must know what people want and how to motivate them to buy it.

TAKES TREMENDOUS CAPITAL

The other assumption, that this is the way to make a lot of money on a small investment, is even more of a fallacy than the others. Actually, the less talent you have in advertising, the more money you had better have. Here's a typical amateur's assumption: He puts a $50 ad in a magazine with a circulation of 1 million, and he says to himself, "If only 1 percent (that's not asking much) respond to this ad—that is 1,000 people—and the product or whatever sells for $5, the gross sales will be $5,000." How disappointed he will be!

Professionals predict what their responses to an ad will be according to the number of dollars spent. The average gross sales for $50 spent in advertising will be between $100 and $150. Over $150 is exceptional. And it doesn't seem to matter much how great your product or service is. What does matter is how you present it in your ad and brochures.

There have been literally hundreds of books written on the subject of mail order—and practically all from the positive viewpoint with very little emphasis on the pitfalls. And of all businesses, no other has as many pitfalls as the mail-order business.

We have tried our best in the foregoing paragraphs to scare you away from this business. There are hundreds of other businesses that are many times as secure, and equally if not more profitable. If you have survived our honest reporting and still want to try the business, though, there are ways to ensure success, which we outline in our mail-order manual complete with tested and proved products and advertising campaigns. Also, we disclose a trick for finding more products—with success almost ensured.

Start-up Manual #15 is available on this business. See page 379.

New Idea

OFF TO THE HUNT

Each year millions of Americans make their annual pilgrimage to the wilds in search of deer, duck, and other legal game. These hunting trips take anywhere from a weekend to a full week. Savvy landowners are beginning to realize that game hunters represent a multimillion-dollar market.

There are two ways you can get into this business. If you own some land, consider turning it into hunting territory during season. If you don't own the land, you may be in an even better position. Approach someone who does own land—a farmer or real estate investor—and tell him your idea. You'll handle the promotion and he'll provide the land.

The best land, of course, is rural, hilly, and crisscrossed with game runs. Real estate agents can help direct you to people who own this kind of territory.

Advertise your hunting territory in the sports sections of newspapers. Contact gun-shop owners and get mailing lists of people who have purchased hunting rifles. The feds may give a helping hand too, since managing herd size is part of their job.

You might consider building a small cabin or two on the land so hunters will have someplace to stay on weekend trips. This gives you a bigger income, since you charge for the lodgings. From there anything can happen: you can provide meals or sell equipment and ammunition. You can even develop a full-fledged hunting lodge.

One good thing about this business is that it'll really get word-of-mouth advertising. Hunters love to tell their friends about new hunting grounds.

You shouldn't have any trouble getting landowners to cooperate, since the land is just sitting there unused in the first place. Good hunting!

CANDID KEYCHAIN PHOTOS

High net profit B/T:	$50,000
Average net profit B/T:	20,000
Minimum investment:	266
Average investment:	700

Remember the old street corner photographer who would snap candids of passersby, mail them proofs of the photos, and hope they'd send in an order? We've found a super update on this old idea that eliminates all the drawbacks and guessing.

Anyone with a basic knowledge of photography can parlay an investment of as little as $266 into a dynamic business that can generate as much as $50,000 in net profit the first year.

What you do is take color action photographs of golfers, tennis players, and others engaging in their favorite pastime and sell them keychain slide viewers with their own picture inside, on the spot, after they've finished the tournament or match, or whatever. The viewers sell like wildfire!

WE'VE SEEN IT WORK!

One of our investigators played in a golf tournament this fall held at a semiprivate course on the outskirts of Chicago. On the way to the "19th hole" his foursome was approached by a clean-cut young man. He said, "Here's your picture," while handing each person a small keychain slide viewer.

As the players were looking at pictures of themselves and passing viewers around, the young man said, "If you want to keep it, the cost is $2.50." Everyone bought!

Later on, in the clubhouse, and at the awards dinner that evening, our reporter noted that at every table viewers were being passed around while everyone admired everyone else's picture—amid plenty of good-natured ribbing.

A survey of the 130 players showed that about 75 percent (or 97.5 of them) had bought a viewer. At $2.50 apiece, the young man had grossed $225 in a single day!

PICTURE THIS OPERATION

We learned later that this young man sets up near the first tee at local golf tournaments, or courtside at a tennis match. He has a

35-mm camera loaded with color film, and a tripod. As play progresses, he takes pictures of all the participants, using a telephoto lens to get close-ups. Well out of the playing area, he's unseen by players and doesn't interfere with the progress of the game.

After taking the photos, he heads for a mobile "darkroom" in the back of a secondhand van, where he develops the slides in less than a half-hour, trims them to size, and inserts them in the keychain viewers. After the game he approaches the players, shows them their pictures, and while they're admiring their form, sells them the keychains for $2 to $3 apiece! He makes change out of a simple carpenter's apron.

MARKET UNLIMITED

Golf tournaments and tennis matches are only two of the places we've seen this in action. There are hundreds of other places where you could do this: all of them are money-makers, and the market is untouched!

What proud parent can resist an action shot of his kid playing little-league baseball? Or "Pop Warner" football? You shoot photos of the little guy or gal from the sidelines or stands during the game—most leagues require that everyone play at least a little while—and catch the parents after the game, using a simple booth or sandwich board sign that gets their attention. Crowds are small, so you'll be seen easily.

This is a dynamite money-maker at nearly any action event that has a lot of participants. Semiprivate golf courses, crowded indoor tennis courts, high school events, city league softball games, bowling alleys, county fairs, and church picnics—all are ideal opportunities for you. All that's required is that you have enough time to develop the film and make the keychains while the event is in progress.

On a semiprivate golf course foursomes tee off every 15 minutes or so, and several hundred players go through in a day's time. Tennis courts are crowded night and day. "Pop Warner" football teams often have 33 players on a side, and up to three games are played on one field in an afternoon.

SNAPPY PROFIT!

Plenty of people will buy a picture of themselves or a loved one presented this unique way—as a keepsake, as a gift, or just for fun! For every 100 sales, at $2.50 apiece, you gross $250. Your materials cost per keychain—25 to 35 cents. Your gross profit on 100 sales—up to $225. That's a markup of a whopping 900 percent. In some situations, such as municipal golf courses or bowling alleys, you may have to price your keychains lower because of the less affluent clientele.

Of course, some won't buy. But losses are minimal, because all that's wasted is 15 to 20 cents per turndown, representing the cost of one frame of film and developer. The keychain viewer can be used again after you remove the unsold photo.

Worked full time, this business can generate unbelievable profits. Working weekends and three days during the week, and selling an average of 90 keychains a day, you can gross $1,000 a week and net up to $1,000!

Start-up Manual #116 is available on this business. See page 379.

New Idea

HOLD FASHIONABLE PARTIES

Tupperware-style parties are a tried-and-true method of selling. A pair of innovative Canadians have taken the concept one step further. C. E. C. Girling and Bonnie Bickle have combined high-fashion clothing with a party atmosphere and come up with sales that are something to celebrate!

The pair contacted manufacturers and bought closeout merchandise at below wholesale prices. They notified all their friends, business associates, and workers that they were giving a fashion party. Word of mouth did the rest.

Because they didn't have to pay rent and had bought below wholesale, the entrepreneurs were able to sell at 30 to 50 percent below retail. Five of the people attending the party asked if they could become representatives and give parties in their homes.

These two entrepreneurs grossed $125,000 in their first year. Last year they pulled in $250,000 with their fashion extravaganzas.

The concept is easy to duplicate, especially if you work in a large office or company. Friends will spread the word, and you'll soon find people wanting to give their own parties. They'll represent you because you've got the merchandise sources. *Keep them confidential.*

Getting merchandise should be no problem. Visit a local clothing mart if there is one in your city. Talk to manufacturers and tell them of your plan.

If there aren't any clothing marts in your city, contact the manufacturers' offices and ask them to have local representatives visit you. Most clothing manufacturers maintain offices in New York.

ROBOTS ARE A REALITY

Long limited to movies like *Forbidden Planet* and *Star Wars*, robots have finally become real. They're even pulling their own weight in the business world!

A Toronto entrepreneur, Brian Mathews, has gone into production on functional robots that are a smash hit at conventions and promotional affairs. Mathews, 19, got started in his senior year at high school when he invented a replica of R2D2 of *Star Wars* fame. The robot's movements were controlled by a seven-channel remote control radio, and Mathews was soon swamped by more than a hundred calls from firms that wanted to hire his robot.

Because R2D2 was protected under 20th Century-Fox copyrights, Mathews had to invent another robot—Q6. This new robot was an improvement in that it could raise its arms and say "I love you." Robolabs, Mathews' company, was inundated with orders. Last month his young company notched up $10,000 in rental and sales.

Robolabs' teams travel throughout the United States to major trade shows. Companies they appear for include Sperry-Univac Computers, Eastman Kodak, plus several television shows and a commercial for a Japanese car company.

Mathews recently sold one of the robots to an Australian insurance company for $13,300. Any of our electrical-minded readers who might be able to tinker up something should take their cue from this recent high-school graduate.

GOLD PROSPECTING AND THE GOLD-PROSPECTING STORE

High net profit B/T:	$100,000+
Average net profit B/T:	50,000
Minimum investment:	1,100
Average investment:	3,300

As stories of gold fever and the escalating price of gold continue to run in newspapers and magazines, and on TV, more and more people are turning to prospecting. Gold fever? In the 20th century? That's right—the rush is on. The great gold rush of the '80s has just begun, and smart entrepreneurs are cashing in on it in two ways— prospecting for gold, and selling equipment to prospectors hot on the trail of instant riches.

For many years gold was regulated; its price was set at $35 per troy ounce, and no one could own more than 200 ounces, so many mines that weren't profitable closed operations. Today the sky's the limit. Gold has zoomed to more than $500 per ounce, and people can own as much as they want.

HOW MUCH GOLD IS LEFT?

If you're worried about being left behind in this mad migration to the hills, don't be! There's plenty of gold just waiting to be discovered by some lucky prospector. The United States Geological Survey has determined that only 10 percent of the world's gold has been found.

All the experts agree that there are millions of ounces of gold left for prospectors to dig up. The chances of finding a mother lode like the big finds of 1849 in California are slim, but armed with today's technology, modern-day sourdoughs are netting up to $100,000 a year mining local waterways on weekends.

Imagine stumbling across a 28-ounce gold nugget worth more than $14,000! Or dredging up 12 ounces of gold from the bottom of a stream and earning more than $6,000 for an afternoon's work! These are just two of many tales we heard from new prospectors.

START-UP IS SIMPLE

Instead of a jenny mule, sourdough biscuits, and a shotgun, today's '49er is more likely to use a jeep, freeze-dried foods, and scientific tools. Oddly enough, all the trappings of the modern prospector are variations of tools and equipment used hundreds of years ago. And these tools can be bought for $1,100 by the beginning gold seeker. Armed with a few simple pieces of equipment and the knowledge of where to look for gold, it's possible to turn this relatively small investment into a gold mine!

Gold has been discovered in at least 35 of the 50 states. Interestingly enough, it was first found in North Carolina, Georgia, Massachusetts, Vermont, and Pennsylvania. Other areas rich in American history are also rich with this yellow metal.

If you mine at least $100 worth of gold on a parcel of Uncle Sam's property each year, you can stake a claim to 20 acres and gain an exceptional vacation site at the same time you're looking for gold.

THERE'S GOLD IN SELLING SUPPLIES, TOO

If you're not interested in trudging through the woods in search of gold, there's a lot of money to be made selling equipment to those who are. It's estimated that there are close to 500,000 amateur prospectors right now, and the number is increasing rapidly each year. Retail sales in this area are starting to take off.

We found small shops of only 600 square feet doing more than $100,000 in sales a year and mammoth stores of 6,000 square feet with annual sales of $500,000 to $1 million. Start-up costs for a prospector's store can be as low as $20,000.

The successful stores we investigated carried more than gold-mining equipment: their inventory ranged from backpacks and camping gear to books, maps, and precious-stone displays. Gold prospecting is an addictive hobby; dealers have told us how customers keep returning and upgrading their inventory.

The average first sale is between $100 and $150, including a gold pan, a pick, and some camping gear. Customers return to buy a sluice box and a dredge. As soon as they find a little gold, they move up the scale, buying bigger and better equipment. One weekend prospector purchased more than $10,000 worth of supplies in 1979, and referred seven friends to the store. Total sales to this group topped the $75,000 mark, according to the retailer we interviewed.

You don't need to locate in the Sierra Madre, either! One of the most successful stores we found was in Houston, 50 miles from the nearest gold-bearing creek. As long as you're near a neighborhood of upscale individuals and families with about 300,000 inhabitants, you'll meet your location requirements.

So there's gold in them there hills, and streams, and rivers—and there's gold in selling supplies to people who want to find it. The rush is on—again!

Start-up Manual #184 is available on this business. See page 379.

Start-Up Manuals Are Available
On Every Business Described
In This Book

From American Entrepreneurs Association

Each Manual Contains Everything You Need To Know
To Start And Successfully Run A Specific Business:

The pitfalls—how to avoid them.

Profit—how much to expect.

Exact Costs—of everything to set up, open and operate.

Equipment—what to buy and where to find it. Ways to save money on equipment, fixtures, etc.

Rent—how much to pay.

Location—how to choose the best.

Leases—how to negotiate important points.

Licenses & Permits—what to expect and how to get them.

Signs—how much, how big, where, and what to say.

Employees—whom to hire, where, and what to pay.

Advertising—how, where, when, and how much.

Promotion—best gimmicks completely detailed.

Insurance—what you need and how much.

Knowledge—where to find it, buy it, or rent it.

Financing—how to finance your opening costs. How to finance your sales to customers.

Customers—how to bring them in and keep them.

Pricing—what price to sell your products or services.

Merchandise—what to buy, how to buy, where to buy.

If Retail—how to lay out your store and display your wares. Quick, cheap and impressive decorating ideas.

Order By No. & Title • Use Special Order Form in This Book Only

SERVICES

Manual No.	Non-member/member
X1012. Window Washing Service	34.50/29.50
X1013. Instant Print Shop	45.00/39.50
X1028. Tool & Equipment Rental	45.00/39.50
X1031. Parking Lot Striping	34.50/29.50
X1033. Pet Hotel & Grooming	45.00/39.50
X1034. Janitorial Service	49.50/45.00
X1037. Dry Cleaning Shop	45.00/39.50
X1038. Copy Shop	45.00/39.50
X1049. Rent-A-Plant	45.00/39.50
X1051. Employment Agency	45.00/39.50
X1052. Furniture Stripping	39.50/34.50
X1053. Carpet Cleaning	39.50/34.50
X1095. Digital Watch Repairing	45.00/39.50
X1105. Kitchen Cabinet Facelifting	45.00/39.50
X1112. Energy Loss Prevention	45.00/39.50
X1130. Roommate Finding Service	45.00/39.50
X1136. Secretarial Service	49.50/44.50
X1145. Insulation Contracting	45.00/39.50
X1148. Telephone Answering Service	45.00/39.50
X1150. Exterior Surfacing Cleaning	45.00/39.50
X1151. Consulting Service	49.50/44.50
X1153. Flat Fee Real Estate	45.00/39.50
X1154. Travel Agency	49.50/44.50
X1155. Chimney Sweep Service	34.50/29.50
X1159. Security Patrol Service	45.00/39.50
X1160. Maid Service	45.00/39.50
X1162. Coin Laundry	45.00/39.50
X1170. Family Hair Salon	45.00/39.50
X1175. Pay-T.V. Service	75.00/67.50
X1176. Rent-A-Soak	45.00/39.50
X1178. Suntanning Center	45.00/39.50
X1189. Temporary Help	45.00/39.50
X1962. Financial Broker Manual	75.00/65.50

RETAIL

Manual No.	Non-member/member
X1002. Plant Shop	34.50/29.50
X1007. Pet Shop	39.50/34.50
X1011. Furniture Shop	45.00/39.50
X1014. Adult Bookstore	45.00/39.50
X1022. Bicycle Shop	45.00/39.50
X1024. Liquor Store	45.00/39.50
X1032. Antique Store	39.50/34.50
X1043. T-Shirt Store	45.00/39.50
X1058. Day Care Center	49.50/44.50
X1060. Costume Jewelry & Earring Shop	34.50/29.50
X1065. Sunglass Shop	29.50/24.50
X1072. Mattress Shop	45.00/39.50
X1106. Gift Shop/Boutique	39.50/34.50
X1107. Women's Apparel Shop	34.50/29.50
X1117. Used Book Store	45.00/39.50
X1129. Pipe Shop	45.00/39.50
X1133. Discount Fabric Shop	39.50/34.50
X1134. Paint & Wallcovering	45.00/39.50
X1135. Do-It-Yourself Cosmetic	39.50/34.50
X1140. Christmas Tree Lot & Ornament Shop	45.00/39.50
X1141. Aquarium & Fish Store	45.00/39.50
X1142. Gourmet Cookware	45.00/39.50
X1143. Flower Shop	39.50/34.50
X1152. Intimate Apparel Store	45.00/39.50
X1161. Children's Apparel Shop	45.00/39.50
X1163. Shell Store	45.00/39.50
X1167. Video Store	45.00/39.50
X1169. Vitamin-Nutrition Store	45.00/39.50
X1171. Phone Store	45.00/39.50
X1173. Convenience Food Store	45.00/39.50
X1174. Oriental Rug Store & Auction	45.00/39.50
X1179. Moped Shop	45.00/39.50
X1180. Waterbed Store	45.00/39.50
X1182. Wedding Shop	45.00/39.50
X1190. Candy & Chocolate Shop	45.00/39.50
X1191. One-Stop Energy Store	45.00/39.50

MANUFACTURING

Manual No.	Non-member/member
X1029. Ghost Dog Mfg.	29.50/24.50
X1061. Stainless-Glass Window Mfg.	34.50/29.50
X1066. Custom Rug Making	34.50/29.50
X1075. Hot Tub Mfg. & Sales	45.00/39.50
X1091. Burglar Alarm Sales	45.00/39.50
X1093. Burlwood Table Mfg. & Ret.	34.50/29.50
X1120. Sculptured Candle Making	29.50/24.50
X1177. Handicraft Mfg.	34.50/29.50

FOOD

Manual No.	Non-member/member
X1006. Pizzeria	49.50/44.50
X1019. Gourmet Cheese & Wine	45.00/39.50
X1025. Popcorn Vending	24.50/19.50
X1036. Old-Fashioned Ice Cream Bar	39.50/34.50
X1055. Fried Chicken Takeout Restaurant	45.00/39.50
X1056. Mobile Restaurant/Sandwich Truck	34.50/29.50
X1059. Coffee Shop	45.00/39.50
X1062. Lo-Cal Baked Goods Shop	39.50/34.50
X1070. Homemade Candy Shop	34.50/29.50
X1073. Hot Dog/Hamburger Stand	45.00/39.50
X1079. Frozen Yogurt Shop	45.00/39.50
X1083. Chocolate-Chip Cookie Shop	45.00/39.50
X1094. Homemade-Cake Shop	34.50/29.50
X1119. Salad-Only Restaurant	45.00/39.50
X1124. No-Alcohol Bar	45.00/39.50
X1125. Health Food Store	39.50/34.50
X1126. Donut Shop	45.00/39.50
X1127. Shrimp Peddling	39.50/34.50
X1128. Soup Kitchen Restaurant	45.00/39.50
X1156. Sandwich (Cold) Shop	45.00/39.50
X1158. Specialty Bread Shop	39.50/34.50
X1164. Frystick (Churro) Shop	45.00/39.50
X1181. Stuffed-Potato Restaurant	45.00/39.50
X1187. Old-Fashioned Ice Cream Parlor	45.00/39.50

TOURIST

Manual No.	Non-member/member
X1001. Dive-For-A-Pearl Shop	34.50/29.50
X1003. Balloon Vending	39.50/34.50
X1008. Handwriting By Computer	29.50/24.50
X1010. Flower Vending	29.50/24.50
X1027. Antique Photo Shop	45.00/39.50
X1039. Stuffed Toy Animal Vending	29.50/24.50

PUBLISHING

Manual No.	Non-member/member
X1023. Rental List Publishing	45.00/39.50
X1026. Who's Who Publishing	45.00/39.50
X1067. Newsletter Publishing	45.00/39.50
X1110. Free Classified Newpaper	45.00/39.50

AUTOMOTIVE

Manual No.	Non-member/member
X1009. 30-Minute Tune-Up Shop	45.00/39.50
X1018. Consignment Used Car Lot	45.00/39.50
X1035. Do-It-Yourself Auto Repair	45.00/39.50
X1044. Muffler Shop	45.00/39.50
X1048. Auto Valet Parking	29.50/24.50
X1050. Auto Painting Shop	45.00/39.50
X1054. 10-Minute Oil Change	45.00/39.50
X1068. Self-Service Gas Station	45.00/39.50
X1076. Car Wash	55.00/49.50
X1077. Vinyl Repair Service	39.50/34.50
X1108. Rent-A-Used-Car Agency	45.00/39.50
X1146. Automobile Detailing	34.50/29.50
X1157. Cross-Country Trucking	34.50/29.50

SPORTS/RECREATION

Manual No.	Non-member/member
X1004. Tennis & Racquetball	45.00/39.50
X1005. Athletic Store	45.00/39.50
X1084. Computer Hardware Store	45.00/39.50
X1088. Roller Skate Rental Shop	34.50/29.50
X1090. Roller-Skating Rink & Skateboard Park	45.00/39.50
X1100. Pinball & Electronic Game Arcade	45.00/39.50
X1109. Windsurfing Sales & School	39.50/34.50
X1116. Candid Keychain Photo	34.50/29.50
X1118. Handicrafts Co-Op Gallery	45.00/39.50
X1131. Backpacking Shop	45.00/39.50
X1132. Hobby Shop	45.00/39.50
X1149. Sailboat Time-Sharing Leasing	45.00/39.50
X1172. Physical Fitness Center	45.00/39.50
X1186. Bar/Tavern	45.00/39.50

UNUSUAL

Manual No.	Non-member/member
X1015. Mail Order	74.50/64.50
X1017. Quit-Smoking Clinic	55.00/47.50
X1020. Swap Meet Promoting	45.00/39.50
X1021. Art Show Promoting	34.50/29.50
X1030. Contest Promoting	45.00/39.50
X1040. Adults-Only Motel	24.50/19.50
X1042. Mini-Storage Facility	45.00/39.50
X1046. Self-Improvement Seminars	45.00/39.50
X1047. Bartender/Waitress Trade School	45.00/39.50
X1057. Bonsai Collecting	29.50/24.50
X1063. Voice Stress/Lie-Detection Service	10.00/8.50
X3360. Finding Bargain Products for Flea Markets	24.50/19.50
X1171. Seminar Promoting	49.50/44.50
X1080. Weight Control Clinic	45.00/39.50
X1089. Teacher's Agency	45.00/39.50
X1092. Import/Export	64.50/54.50
X1098. Liquidator—Selling Distressed Merchandise	45.00/39.50
X1121. Coin-Op T.V.	45.00/39.50
X1122. Plastics Recycling Center	45.00/39.50
X1137. Furniture Rental Store	45.00/39.50
X1138. Pet Cemetery	45.00/39.50
X1144. Do-It-Yourself Framing Shop	45.00/39.50
X1147. Private Post Office	49.50/44.50
X1166. Jojoba Plantation	45.00/39.50
X1183. Used Paper Collection & Recycling	34.50/29.50
X1184. Gold Prospecting & Prospectors' Store	45.00/39.50
X1186. Mobile Locksmithing	45.00/39.50

Send Your Order To:

**American Entrepreneurs Association, Suite D-264
2311 Pontius Avenue, Los Angeles, CA 90064**

MONEY-BACK GUARANTEE

After receiving the AEA manuals, if you are not completely satisfied, simply return them undamaged within 1 year for a full refund. No questions asked.

Send the following manuals immediately:

Manual #_____ Title_____ Price_____

Manual #_____ Title_____ Price_____

Manual #_____ Title_____ Price_____

Manual #_____ Title_____ Price_____

Manual #_____ Title_____ Price_____

Manual #_____ Title_____ Price_____

(Use additional sheet of paper for more titles) Manual Total_____

Plus 6.5% Sales Tax (Calif. Residents)_____

Rush orders add $3.00 per manual for Priority Handling_____
(Not to exceed $9.00)
(delivery in 12–16 business days)
3–6 wks delivery

Shipping and Postage_$2.50_

Payment Enclosed $_____

Charge It To My: VISA_____ MasterCard_____ AmEx_____ Total_____

Card No. _____

Exp. Date _____ **(No orders shipped without Card Expiration Date)**

X _____
(SIGNATURE REQUIRED ON CHARGE ORDERS)

NAME _____
(please print)
ADDRESS _____

CITY _____

STATE _____ **ZIP** _____
CODE

D-264

ABOUT THE AUTHOR

CHASE REVEL made his first million at the age of 21 with an investment of $1,000, and he claims to have never invested more than $5,000 in any project. One of his many profitable business ventures is the American Entrepreneurs Association (AEA), which publishes *Entrepreneur* magazine and offers in-depth research information on how to start your own business.